AF662735

Much Ado Over Coffee

'Coffee House was then the common room of Presidency College in the afternoons. The college was by that time already a co-educational institution.... It was around this time that one group of boys regularly used to take part in an *adda* in Coffee House centring one such girl. We, members of *adda* sans women, felt a little jealous. We called this girl "queen bee." One day I caught her in a sketch I made'.
– Debabrata Mukhopadhyay

Some Books from Social Science Press and Aurum Books

Gitanjali Reborn: William Radice's Writings on Rabindranath Tagore
Edited by Martin Kämpchen

Gandhi: Anti-biography of a Great Soul (HB)
Michael De Saint-Cheron

Shades of Difference: Selected Writings of Rabindranath Tagore wth Audio Visual Material, *Tagore and His World* (HB)
Edited by Radha Chakravarty

Calcutta: The Stormy Decades (HB)
Edited by Tanika Sarkar and Sekhar Bandyopadhyay

Dalit Women: Honour and Patriarchy in South India (HB)
Clarinda Still

Tamil Brahmans: The Creation of a Middle-Class Caste (HB)
CJ Fuller and Haripriya Narasimhan

Persistence of Poverty in India (HB)
Edited by Nandini Gooptu and Jonathan Parry

Savage Attack: Tribal Insurgency in India (HB)
Edited by Crispin Bates and Alpa Shah

The Year of Blood: Essays on the Revolt of 1857 (HB)
Rudrangshu Mukherjee

The Autobiography of a Revolutionary in British India (HB)
Kali Ghosh

The Many Worlds of Sarala Devi: A Diary
Translated by Sukhendu Ray and
The Tagores and Sartorial Styles: A Photo Essay (HB)
Malavika Karlekar

Viramma: Life of a Dalit (PB)
Viramma, Josiane Racine, and Jean-Luc Racine

Everyday Nationalism: Women of the Hindu Right (HB)
Kalyani Devaki Menon

Marriage, Love, Caste & Kinship Support (HB)
Lived Experiences of the Urban Poor in India
Shalini Grover

Religious Division and Social Conflict: The Emergence of Hindu Nationalism in Rural India (PB)
Peggy Froerer

Literature and Nationalist Ideology: Writing Histories of Indian Languages (PB)
Hans Harder

The Everyday State and Society in Modern India (PB)
Edited by CJ Fuller and Veronique Benei

Economics and Its Stories (HB)
Amal Sanyal

Telecommunications Industry in India: State Business and Labour in a Global Economy (HB)
Dilip Subramaniam

Cultural History of Modern India (PB)
Edited by Meenakshi Khanna

Income Poverty and Beyond Human Development in India
Edited by Raja J Chelliah and R Sudarshan

The Politics of the Pharmaceutical Industry and Access to Medicines: World Pharmacy and India (HB)
Edited by Hans Logren

SERIES: EVERYDAY LIFE OF POLITICAL STRUGGLES

Windows into a Revolution: Ethnographies of Maoism in India and Nepal (HB)
Edited by Alpa Shah and Judith Pettigrew

Rebels from the Mud Houses: Dalits and the Making of the Maoist Revolution in Bihar (HB)
George Kunnath

Unruly Hills: Nature and Nation in India's North-East (HB)
Bengt G. Karlsson

SERIES: GERMAN WRITINGS ON INDIA AND SOUTH ASIA

'When the war began we heard of several kings': South Asian Prisoners in World War I Germany (HB)
Edited by Fransizka Roy, Heike Liebau and Ravi Ahuja

Cultural Encounters in India
The Local Co-Workers of the Tranquebar Mission, 18th-19th centuries (HB)
Heike Liebau

'Everwhere is Becoming the Same'? Regulating IT-work between India and Germany (HB)
Nicole Mayer-Ahuja

SERIES: FRENCH WRITINGS ON INDIA AND SOUTH ASIA

Scholars and Prophets: Sociology of India from France in the 19th and 20th Centuries (HB)
Roland Lardinois

Tocqueville in India (HB)
Jean Alphonse Bernard

AURUM BOOKS

Sabotage (PB)
Anita Agnihotri
Translated by Arunava Sinha

Opium Poppy (PB)
Hubert Haddad
Translated by Renuka George

Forthcoming SSP

Revolutionary Passions (HB)
Hamit Bozarslan, Gilles Bataillon and Christophe Jaffrelot
Translated by Soma Datta Gupta

Why Me? (HB)
Edited by Dubet Et Al

Much Ado Over Coffee
Indian Coffee House Then and Now

Bhaswati Bhattacharya

SOCIAL
SCIENCE
PRESS

Published by
Esha Béteille
Social Science Press
69 Jor Bagh, New Delhi 110 003

© Social Science Press 2017

Social Science Press gratefully acknowledges the generous grant from Centre for Modern Indian Studies (CeMIS) at Göttingen.

All rights reserved. No part of this publication may be reproduced, stored in a retrieval system, or transmitted, in any form or by any means, without the prior permission in writing of Social Science Press, or as expressly permitted by law, or under terms agreed with the appropriate reprographics rights organization. Enquiries concerning reproduction outside the scope of the above should be sent to Social Science Press, at the address above.

You must not circulate this book in any other binding or cover and you must impose this same condition on any acquirer.

ISBN: 978-93-83166-16-9

Advisory Board
T.N. Madan
Dipankar Gupta
Jonathan Parry
C.J. Fuller
Veena Das
Bibek Debroy
Kaushik Basu
Abusaleh Shariff
Alaka Basu
Pratap Bhanu Mehta
R. Sudarshan

Cover Design
Debashis Deb
SSP is grateful to Debashis Deb for sketching the illustration specially for this book.
SSP Logo Design
Arpan Mukhopadhyay

Set in Sabon LT Std 10/13.1
Typeset by Manmohan Kumar, Delhi 110 035
Printed by Summit Advertising,
2, DLF (Part) Industrial Area, Moti Nagar,
New Delhi 110 015

For my parents,
Renuka and Raghumani Bhattacharya

'Like many European intellectuals visiting Calcutta, Bernard Verlhac (Tignous), the graphic artist of the French weekly *Charlie Hebdo* too visited the ICH on College Street. The person with long nose on this sketch he made was perhaps a reference to Satyajit Ray, and 'Gosh' refers to the graphic novelist Biswadeep Ghosh accompanying Tignous to the ICH. The text says: "No. 1 'Toupee', the head-dress, is a symbol of Indian servitude. 2. Toque de Nehru, the Nehru cap, is a symbol of revolt against the English. Is their co-habitation a coincidence?"'

Contents

Posters put up by the Coffee Consumers' Forum, India Coffee House in Connaught Place, Delhi, in 2009 against the possible hand-over of the place in view of the non-payment of rent by the coffee workers' cooperative. (Source: BBC News, 'In Pictures: Indian Coffee House', http://news.bbc.co.uk/2/hi/8106639.stm)

Acknowledgements

This book has acquired many debts. I am grateful to my colleagues at the Centre for Modern Indian Studies (CeMIS) at Göttingen, especially Ravi Ahuja, for taking interest in this research and supporting it in all its phases. Aditya Sarkar gave valuable comments on the research proposal. The grant of a generous subsidy from CeMIS facilitated the production of the monograph. Members of the administrative staff, especially Ms Iris Karakus have provided all the technical support the project needed.

The grant of a fellowship by Fritz Thyssen Foundation, Cologne made it possible to take up this research. Much of the fieldwork could be carried out due to a parallel grant from the Indian Council of Historical Research (ICHR) in Delhi. The research in Shimla was funded by the Indian Institute of Advanced Studies and I am grateful to Gangeya Mukherji and Ronald Peter D'Souza for making that possible.

In Amsterdam, my former colleagues of the research department of the International Institute of Social History helped developing my interest in coffee as a commodity. Marcel van Linden introduced me to the German historical world. Dick Plukker of the India Institute in Amsterdam, and Theo Damsteegt, formerly of Leiden University gave useful suggestions with regard to Hindi literature.

I have benefitted from communications with Steven Topik and William Gervase Clarence Smith, pioneer researchers on coffee. Both of them have commented on earlier versions of parts of the current monograph.

In Delhi Roma Chatterjee helped my research at the coffee house in Delhi School of Economics. At ICHR Ishrat Alam was of great help bringing me in contact former patrons of the India(n) Coffee House in Delhi. S.P. Dutt, formerly of Air India, took it upon himself to help me find the direction as to the long-extinct Coffee House on Janpath and the precise developments between 1958 and 1964 leading to the PRRM. Krishna Sobti, Uma Vasudev, Neelabh, Pankaj Bisht, Girdhar Rathi and Chander Mahadev have responded to my queries on numerous occasions. Archana Verma and Mangalesh Dabral have helped in clarifying issues related to the Hindi literary world.

The research in Calcutta has benefitted from a constant interaction with my mentor Gautam Bhadra. He not only drew my attention to literature on coffee and coffee house but also took care to make them available for my research. The discussion in the following pages is a testimony to how indispensable his advice to this research was. Ashim Mukhopadhyay of the National Library enriched the research through conversations and by locating rare books. Poet Gautam Chaudhury and Samir Bhattacharya of the Bengali webzine Parabaas were ever ready in helping finding missing links. Rajarshi Ghosh sent useful information on literature on cooperatives.

Manas Mukul Das introduced me to the world of Allahabad and its Coffee House. Much of the information about ICH Allahabad was collected through exchange of e-mails with Neelabh, who grew up almost next door and was a keen observer of the happenings in and around the Coffee House. He also made his published and unpublished work available for my consultation, and put me in touch with sources in Allahabad.

Whoever goes to Allahabad has to visit the 'madhushala', grapevine of Dinesh Chandra Grover, only hinted at in this work. Dinesh ji offered me the rare photographs of the literary meets in Allahabad. Arindam Ghosh of Indian Press has responded to my thousands of queries, always taking care to send additional information. Among those who assisted the research in Allahabad—Amrita Chatterjee and Neelum Saran Gour became friends.

At Bangalore the officials of the Coffee Board of India, especially Finance Officer Mrs Roop Rashi, and Mr Ramesh Rajah, President of Coffee Exporters' Association of India, have afforded all the help I required. V. G. Siddhartha of Coffee Day Global Limited gave an important interview. Sunalini Menon of the Coffeelab and Aparna Dutta, communications consultant of IIMC, Bangalore kindly allowed me a glimpse into the world of coffee marketing.

I thank all workers of the ICWCSL in Allahabad, Bangalore, Calcutta, Delhi, Simla and Trichur for their cooperation. At Trichur the family of N. Parameswaran Pillai, especially Maya Murali and N.P. Gireesan, were helpful. Debashish Deb of ABP and *The Telegraph* has sketched the cover illustration specially for this book for which I am very grateful, and I am grateful to Anindya Banerjee and Rani Ray for putting us in touch with him. Ajit Rao and Pablo Bartholomew allowed me to use the sketch of the Irani Café and the photograph of the members of *Subterranean Sun* respectively. The cartoon of Indian Coffee House on College Street by Bernard Verlhac (Tignous) of *Charlie Hebdo* was published on website of *The Telegraph*. The photo of Amarnatha Jha and others at Allahabad was provided by Tejakar Jha. Amitabh Sengupta kindly gave permission to use the rare photograph of Amartya Sen, Sibnarayan Ray and others in the College Street Coffee House.

Librarians/staff of the following institutions have extended all assistance in making relevant material available: at Göttingen the university library; the library of the International Institute of Social History, Amsterdam; the library of the University of Leiden; the Royal Library in The Hague; British Library and the Library of School of Oriental and African Studies in London; the National Archives of India, the ICHR library, Nehru Memorial Museum and Research Library, Sapru House Library, Central Secretariat Library, and Delhi Public Library; in Calcutta the Bangiya Sahitya Parishat Library, the archives of *Ananda Bazar Patrika*, the National Library including its newspaper section, and the Centre for Social Science Studies; at Trivandrum the CSDS Library, AK Gopalan Library, the University of Trivandrum Library.

I have received wonderful help from Akeel Ahmad and Paridhi Massey, and Rajatkanti Sur and Manab Mitra, Malini Bhattacharya and Rukmini Chakraborty (Calcutta). In Allahabad Vaibhab Maini, Vaidurya Pratap Sahi and Akshat Lal Srivastava have helped with invaluable information and source material. V.S. Lincy of the National Library translated the Malayalam memoir of N.S. Parameswaran Pillai into English.

The findings of this research have been discussed at different forums: the India International Coffee Festival organized in Delhi in 2012, seminars and history research group meetings at CeMIS, research group meeting at the International Institute of Social History in Amsterdam, the University of Konstanz, University of Hamburg, and at French Institute, Chandernagore, India. The peer reviewer of Social Science Press gave valuable comments on the first draft. Douglas Haynes took keen interest in the work, and made time for going through the manuscript which has enormously benefitted from his suggestions. Frank Perlin read the entire manuscript within a very short time. It was he who advised me to put my observations on *adda* at one place; and the title also owes to him.

My publisher, Esha Beteille of Social Science Press has patiently borne with this book with great enthusiasm. Special thanks are due to Radha Beteille, the commissioning editor, and the young editor Ankita Sharma who deserve all the credit for bringing the large unwieldy manuscript in shape.

Didibhai, Akhil-da and Mohor in Calcutta have been great sources of support. It is a pity that Dada and Boudi the late Pralaykanto and Jayanti Bhattacharya could not live to see this monograph. Tinni has always been attentive to all my whims. Tripti Bhattacharya (Chhordi) and Pinaki Bhattacharya have provided me the comfort of home during the stay in Delhi.

I could not have done without the encouragement received from my friends. Upinder Kaur and Rupalee Verma have put me in touch with important sources. Poet and translator Ruma Chakrabarty has translated the Manna Dey song. 'Coffee-houser shei dingulo' particularly for this book the link for this song is given in a footnote on page 340 of this book. Joyce Yarrow has read parts of the manuscript and has enriched me with her views. Sharmistha Chakrabarty provided details on the band 'Moheen's Stallions'. I received encouragement and help from Nandini Dutta, Chilka Ghosh and Shevanti Narayan in different ways.

It needs the patience of Victor van Bijlert to put up with all my idiosyncrasies. Many of the ideas, concepts were clarified through conversations with him. He went through the manuscript and gave his views. In his defiance of humanities, and especially history, my son Pasha has provided many a jolly moment of intriguing discussions at home. During periods of my long absence, both Victor and Pasha have taken on themselves the responsibility to keep up the ambience at home alive. This research would be impossible without the understanding and cooperation on their part. This book is a tribute long overdue to my parents for the inspiration, encouragement, strength and affection I have received from them all along.

Introduction

The idea of this book originated when I was working on a project on global commodities at the International Institute of Social History in Amsterdam during 2007–09. The main project did not focus on coffee, but allowed me the space to find out about the coffee production and consumption in India. I discovered that there was very little historical literature on coffee in India. Outside India, the country was usually associated with tea, and an inquiry in the market showed that apart from a niche market for specialty coffee, roasters in the West imported coffee from India used in the numerous blends consumed by masses unaware of the origin of this coffee. Let alone supermarkets, even specialty coffee and tea-shops in Amsterdam did not sell Indian coffee. This scenario has changed during the last few years, and Monsooned Malabar and Robusta India share the pride of place side by side with Sidamo and Yirgacheffe from Ethiopia and Blue Mountain coffee from Jamaica on the shelves of cafés and tea/coffee stores.

When I began this work, the idea was to look into the public consumption of coffee with focus on the India Coffee House (after 1958 Indian Coffee House, both referred here as ICH or Coffee House), probably the oldest surviving café chain in the world created in urban India in the late 1930s. Yet, apart from a Sarai (CSDS) paper by two students on the Coffee House in Connaught Place (CP, Delhi), no academic work had studied this institution. Inquiry at the Coffee Board (1942) in Bangalore revealed that original records pertaining to the outlets had not been preserved. The different series of publications of the Board, used in this research, were mechanical and did not answer many relevant questions. How did the Coffee Cess Committee (1935) that had no previous experience of marketing, chance upon the strategy of setting up coffee houses the year after? What guided the choice of the urban places where the outlets were begun? Why did the Board go on to set up 40+ outlets before it dawned upon them that the concept was not profitable? What qualified officials in the marketing department to be entrusted with the responsibility of bringing coffee to the people? Without answers to such questions the research would become a mere reproduction of the statistical reports of number of propaganda units, production of coffee and a sum indicating the Board's total annual profit from all the units. Interestingly, these reports counted the number of cups of coffee sold annually. But how much coffee did go into the making of a cup? Was there perhaps a variation among different regional establishments regarding the amount of coffee, liquid and powder, used and sold?

As there was no way to resolve these problems, I decided to explore a living archive—patrons of the space since it was launched. Indian Coffee House is an institution in public memory associated with many individuals and events of national history. Once I began conversing with former and current customers of ICH soon it became clear that there was more than coffee that attracted them to the space; the practice of drinking coffee in this new urban space became synonymous with sociability.

The title indicates that the consumption of coffee in the Coffee House had multiple points of entry discussed here in chapters as described in the content. The said informal gatherings have been referred to throughout this work as *adda,* a much celebrated practice in twentieth century Bengal as discussed in Chapter One.

Both in Bengali and Hindi, adda is a noun and its meaning as a meeting place is one of the many. In Bengal, however, since the very beginning of the twentieth century the word has been used mainly to denote a place where friends meet and converse informally. However, the impassioned eagerness expressed by my interlocutors outside Bengal while talking about the ICH inspired the question if the practice was limited to Bengal alone. What could possibly happen when several Malayali friends met at a Chaya Kada, implying conversations in a tea shop, or a few writers and poets in Allahabad gathered at a friend's home? Even when coffee was available at different indigenous and globalized cafés, why did my interlocutors in Trivandrum regret the loss of the old ICH? Did something comparable to *adda* exist outside Bengal?

As we shall see below, what took place in ICH Allahabad and Delhi was not much different from the classic *adda*s of the Coffee House in Calcutta. There has been a close connection between the literary worlds of Allahabad and Calcutta exemplified by the lives and works of Suryakant Tripathi Nirala (1896-1961) to Alka Saraogi (b. 1960) on the one hand, to Chintamani Ghosh (1854-1928) and Ramananda Chatterjee (1865-1943) on the other. As a part of the anti-colonial movement, the other north Indian counterpart of the Bengali nationalist elite shared the same political space, often creating common civil society platforms. It is possible that the practice of sociability among Bengalis spread through this circulatory, communicatory interaction. However, if Bengali had gained the status of the vernacular in Bengal in the 1830s, the post-1860 period saw the discourse over the status of the official vernacular in north India that have been talked about at length in Chapter One and succeeding chapters of the book. The mobilization of political support for Hindi and Urdu gave a boost to the print culture in both Hindustani and Nagari.[1] But there was a rich culture of public orality in north India and although not as institutionalized as in Bengal, the practice of *adda* in the Hindi-Urdu literary worlds too drew inspiration from the prevailing practices arising from real-life situations. Like in Calcutta, many of the preexisting *adda* groups in Allahabad and Delhi moved to ICH where we see them in a crystallized form as well. As a glimpse of this sociability can be found in Chapters One and Four.

The reference to the middle class in this book is in the singular as an ideological construct. There is a vast literature on the Indian middle class. Beginning with what constituted this class, attempts have been made in recent times at understanding how the members of the class constructed their identity. In Bengal the *bhadralok* customers

[1] Christopher R. King, *One Language, Two Scripts: The Hindi Movement in Nineteenth Century North India*, New Delhi: Oxford University Press, Chapter 3.

of ICH were a broad category including members from landholding families to temporarily or permanently unemployed individuals discussed especially in Chapters Two and Seven of the book.

The focus on the chain, a new phenomenon across the country, required that I compared the practices at different outlets in order to understand their import to urban north India as I have done throughout the book.

Originally my intention was to study the outlets of ICH in Bangalore, Delhi, Calcutta and Trivandrum. After the field work in 2011 and 2012, I decided to leave Bangalore out. Between Koshy's (1940) on St Marks Road at the one end of Mahatma Gandhi Road and Nilgiri's (1905) on Brigade Road at the other, there were many places of varying sizes offering coffee to people across the social hierarchy with different ranges of budget. Still the ICH was popular with journalists working with *The Deccan Herald* next door, and also with personnel of banks and other offices, as with visitors of neighbourhood bookshops.

The field research suggested that in contrast with the outlets in the south, the Coffee House in Calcutta and Delhi—in spite of the local differences—can be put into one category because coffee in north India was not a commonly available beverage. It was at this stage that the decision to include a third city in north India was made. As the ICH in Allahabad was well-known and still operating in the same building since the 1950s, I decided to focus on the three cities in the mainly Bengali, and Hindi-Urdu language zones. While the monograph focuses on these three cities, insights from the field trips to Bangalore, Trivandrum and Trichur have been added when necessary, especially in Chapter Three while discussing the formation of the cooperative, and for the rest, for the sake of comparison.

There was a time when it was common for many artists, writers, journalists, political activists, college and university teachers and students to go to ICH on a regular basis. It has not been possible to name everyone or interview all concerned, but those cited here will suffice to give some idea of both the structure and the agency at ICH.

Since I began my research, one book on ICH has been published. This is a magnificent coffee-table book by the award-winning photographer Stuart Freedman.[2] A collection of more than a hundred photographs, the book is a token of Freedman's attachment to the chain he discovered on his first trip to Delhi in the 1990s. Photographs of coffee-stained mica-topped tables, plastic chairs, faded, torn sofas revealing their spring guts, bare walls with distemper flaking off at places, stand in stark contrast with the overall changes in the cities, and underline the shabby state the outlets are now in.

The current monograph shows that the ICH was far from shabby at the time of its inception. Adherents of Gandhi, Lohia, Nehru and others thronged there precisely because, judged by contemporary standards of the middle class, the 'comfortably' and 'tastefully' furnished outlets offered an experience unknown before, and were considered 'modern' as mentioned in Chapters One and Two. Another work is the Ph. D. research undertaken by Kristin Plys at the Yale University. Plys highlights the nature of the authoritarian state in post-colonial India under Nehru and argues that this inherent authoritarianism manifested itself under Indira Gandhi. These issues are discussed respectively in Chapter 3 and Chapter 5.

The current work follows the many narratives—autobiographies, essays, fiction, interviews, media reports, poetry, reminiscences, and satire—inspired by the place, official publications of the Coffee Board of India, and field research among patrons and workers of the ICH. It focuses on how space was produced and nurtured in the urban settings in late pre-colonial and post-colonial India. Launched in the interest of coffee-capitalists seeking a destination for the export surplus, the outlets of the ICH were soon appropriated by the urban middle class who used the space for leisure as studied in Chapters One, Two and Four. This association came in good stead of the workers when their economic security was threatened following the announcement by the Coffee Board to close down the outlets in 1955 as discussed at length in Chapter Three and subsequently

[2] Stuart Freedman, *The Palaces of Memory: Tales from the Indian Coffee House*, Stockport: Dewi Lewis, 2015.

throughout the book. A consensus between workers and customers, as we shall see in the chapters that follow, has made the space unique and is essential for ICH to survive.

Most customers first went to the Coffee House as students. Instead of providing the age of persons interviewed, I have indicated the period when a person went to the Coffee House and what s/he was studying at that time. I often interviewed students in large groups of twenty and above. Given that the average school leaving age in India is 18+, a high school student would be in the mid or late teens, a Bachelor student in the late teens and early twenties, a Post-Graduate student in the early twenties, and a Ph.D. scholar usually in between 25 and 35 years.

The Coffee House on College Street replaced a heritage institution and has always remained in the same building. In collective memory, the space is synonymous with cultural and intellectual *adda* of the highest order. I am aware that what is cited here is just a snapshot. However, it sufficiently corroborates the claims made in the book.

All translations from Bengali and Hindi, unless mentioned otherwise, are by me. I have retained the old place names because during most of the period covered here, the places were known by those names.

The currency used in this monograph is the Indian Rupee (INR/Re/Rs) which in 1947 was tied to the GBP at Re 1 = 1 s, 6 d, rate of 28 October 1945. In 1971 INR was pegged to gold and dollar. Over the decades, the ratio between INR and USD has been 1=4.77 (1960), 1=7.56 (1970), 1=7.89 (1780), 1=17.49 (1990), 1=45 (2000), and 1=45.75 (2010). The enthusiasm of (ex-) connoisseurs of the place provided an enormous stimulus to this work. It happened more than once that elderly ex-patrons wanted to narrate their experience, but their memory failed them. A silence usually followed, but the expression on their face conveyed that they were back in that lost world. The interviews also convinced me that everyone had his/her own image of the Coffee House. The narrative in the following pages may not conform to any of those; but at least it will demonstrate how not to approach the Coffee House.

CHAPTER
one

Adda and Public Spaces of Sociability before the ICH

> To enjoy something properly, one has to surround it with a fence of leisure; it has to be unfolded at great length and spread out on all sides. Only then is it possible to grasp it in its totality.[1]

Beginning with the public baths of Mohenjodaro and much later the Greek and Roman baths, sociability in the public sphere has a long history. The elaborate structure of the Roman bathhouses included perfume-booths, books, gymnasiums, libraries and reading rooms. The corporeal activity of bathing promoted some kind of sociability transforming the functional public baths into meeting places for social interaction.[2] Turkish bath or *hamam* that spread to different parts of the Middle East during the Ottoman Empire was a Roman legacy and was much sought after for the convivial atmosphere encouraging sociability. For men in Cairo going to a *hamam* is as important as going to meet his friends in a café.[3] The first coffee houses that came up in Mecca and Cairo in the early sixteenth century were tavern like places where in addition to swallowing of

[1] Rabindranath Tagore, *Chhinnaptrabali* [Collected Letters], Kolkata: Visva Bharati Granthan Bibhag, 1961, letter 101.

[2] Garret G. Fagan, *Bathing in Public in the Roman World,* Michigan: University of Michigan Press, 2002 1, 4, 10–39, 75.

[3] May Telmissany, 'Shared Experiences', in Pascal Meunier (ed.), *The Last Hammams of Cairo: A Disappearing Bathhouse Culture*, Photographs by Pascal Meunier and Text by May Temissany and Eve Gandossi, Cairo: American University, 1999, 30.

the 'intoxicant' coffee, 'a variety of forbidden things' took place.[4] It is from there that the institution later spread throughout the Ottoman Empire, and from Turkey to Western Europe. Coffee houses were the most important place for public socialization in Ottoman Istanbul, and in order to understand what was happening in society in general, one could focus on the coffee houses.[5] Similarly, in other societies, the need for the public to interact socially has seen the emergence of other, similar places where the public came together. In China for example, the tea house formed the microcosm of the larger urban history.[6]

The emergence of coffee houses in the seventeenth and eighteenth century Europe, especially England was, however noted as having considerably transformed the structure of the public sphere.[7] Coffee houses provided a neutral social space between the public and the private realms, where discussions on new socio-political issues of 'common concern' were taken out of the domains of the elite to create the emerging 'bourgeois public sphere'. It was coffee, or rather its most active ingredient caffeine that stimulated the intellectual discourse during the Age of Enlightenment causing fear among the authorities that coffee houses were potential hotbeds for political agitation. The presence of a literary, informed public was a

[4] R.S. Hattox, *Coffee and Coffeehouses*, Seattle: University of Washington Press, 1986, 30–45.

[5] Chengiz Kırlı, 'The Struggle over Space: Coffee-Houses of Ottoman Istanbul, 1780–1845', Unpublished Ph. D. thesis submitted to Binghampton University, 2000.

[6] Di Wang, *The Teahouse: Small Business, Everyday Culture and Public Politics in Chengdu, 1900–1950*, Stanford: Stanford University Press, 2008; also Qin Shao, 'Tempest over Teapots: The Vilification of Teahouses in Early Republican China', *Journal of Asian Studies*, 57.4, 1988, 1009–41.

[7] Coffee houses in the Ottoman Empire were different from their counterparts in Vienna or Paris where alcohol was served. For socialization among the working class of Paris see W. Scott Haine, *The World of the Paris Café: Sociability Among the French Working Class, 1789–1914*, Baltimore: Johns Hopkins Press, 1998; for the Ottoman Empire see Kırlı, *Struggle;* for alcoholic drinks in coffee houses in England, Brian Cowan, *The Social Life of Coffee: The Emergence of the British Coffee House*, New Haven: Yale University Press, 2005; Ellis Markman, *The Eighteenth Century Coffee House Culture*, London: Pickering and Chatto, 2006.

pre-condition for the formation of public opinion in the public sphere Habermas described.[8]

Turning our attention to the India, it is known that there was a strong tradition of association of individuals engaged in critical debate over public matters encompassing the elite and popular political culture, although not always on equal terms, comparable to the public sphere in Europe described by Habermas. With corporate institutions, it was a vibrant, contested domain in which both the elite and the subordinate groups functioning within a shared framework of norms and values jostled over space.[9] In a large part of North India and Pakistan the institution of *chaupal*, functioning somewhat like an informal club, formed the centre of the village in rural India. It was an exclusively male domain and a good part of the lives of the male whether at the level of individual, small group or the total community, was spent at, and revolved around the *chaupal*. Also used for community purposes, the building was constructed separately and distinguished from private houses, usually under a banyan or *pipal* tree at the intersection of the two main streets. The *chaupal* was where the *panchayat* was held, marriages of village girls took place, wandering religious groups and other visitors to the village

[8] Jürgen Habermas, *The Structural Transformation of the Public Sphere: An Inquiry into a Category of Bourgeois Society*, tr. T. Burger with the assistance of F. Lawrence, Cambridge, MS: MIT Press, 1991 (henceforth, Habermas, *Structural Transformation*); also his 'The public sphere', in Chandra Mukherji and Michael Schudson (eds.), *Rethinking Popular Culture: Contemporary Perspectives in Cultural Studies*, Berkeley: University of California Press, 1991, 398–404 according to Habermas popular individual opinions did not have the potential of 'rational discussion' and were to be considered as 'a kind of sediment of history'. See Chapter Five for more on this question.

[9] See Chris Bayly, *Rulers, Townsmen and Bazaars: North Indian Society in the Age of British Expansion, 1770–1880*, Cambridge: Cambridge University Press, 1983 and *Empire and Information: Intelligence Gathering and Social Communication, 1780–1870*, Cambridge: Cambridge University Press, 1996; Vivek Bhandari, 'Civil Society and the Predicaments of Multiple Publics', *Contemporary Studies of South Asia, Africa and the Middle East,* 26.1 (2006), 36–50; Farhat Hasan, 'Forms of Civility and Publicness in Pre-British India', in Rajeev Bhargava and Helmut Reifeld (eds.), *Civil Society, Public Sphere and Citizenship*, Delhi: Sage, 2005, 84–105.

were received, and village politics was delineated. This was where the men also gathered, smoked, played cards, and did all kinds of things. 'Gossip goes on endlessly at the *chaupal* and all sorts of discussions take place here.'[10]

The public orality of *chaupals* had its counterpart in the *chandimandap* in Bengal that went far beyond what the name suggests, a space for the worship of the goddess *Chandi* or *Durga*. Usually constructed by the village landlord, *chandimandaps* were where the elders in the village met, smoked, problems of the village were discussed and cultural programmes like *jatra*, open air folk theatre and *kathakata*, devotional story-telling took place.[11]

A public discourse based on impersonal principles of justice also made its beginning in the colonial period through the mediation of liberal thinkers, albeit in a limited sense.[12] Literary and political activism coupled with institution building marked the late colonial phase of Indian history when communication through associational practice had become the order of the day.[13] Yet, scholars have focused on the differences between the Habermasian public sphere and the one emerging in colonial India. Sudipta Kaviraj has argued that the public sphere in colonial Bengal for example was not equally accessible to all as the public were divided according to caste, education, religion and the like. Access to public spaces were strictly restricted and granted to

[10] There were two types of *chaupals* in jat villages—one serving as dormitory for bachelors and for people visiting the village, the other serving the purpose of a meeting point for the males, S.K. Chandhoke, *Nature and Structure of Rural Habitations*, New Delhi: Concept Publishing Company, 206–16, and passim. *Kuan* or the well, formed the community centre for women; since the 1970s women were seen at the *chaupal*, 212–13.

[11] For *chandimandap* see, 'Adda: A History of Sociability', in Dipesh Chakrabarty, *Provincializing Europe: Post-Colonial Thought and Difference*, Princeton: Princeton University Press, 2000, 184–213; for *kathakata* see Swati Chattopadhyay, *Representing Calcutta: Modernity, Nationalism and the Colonial Uncanny*, Abingdon, Oxon: Routledge, 2006, 189, 191.

[12] Douglas Haynes, *Rhetoric and Ritual in Colonial India: The Shaping of a Public Culture in Surat City, 1852–1928*, Berkeley: University of California Press, 1991.

[13] Francesca Orsini, *The Hindi Public Sphere, 1920–1940: Language and Literature in the Age of Nationalism*, New Delhi: OUP, 2002.

a select few on special occasions. While the *bhadralok* embraced the Western concept of public and private, upper caste dictums considered the public sphere impure enough to be neglected.[14] Writing on the nationalist discourse in Bengal, Partha Chatterjee noted that sovereignty in the cultural domain of language, speech and religion empowered the Bengali elite to demarcate the public or 'material' domain of the state comprising administration, economy, law, and statecraft in which the colonized demanded equality with the colonizer.[15] The spread of English education with an emphasis on English literature accompanied by the increasing number of printing presses and the growth of a genre of Bengali plays in the late nineteenth century saw the emergence of an autonomous public sphere outside European domain. Left outside the political domain controlled by the colonial power, and inspired by European theatre, the Bengali educated literati created the modern Bengali drama. The direct dialogues in this new genre for example between the colonizer and the colonized in pidgin English and 'foul-mouth denunciations' of the former in common Bengali derived their strength from the rhetorical power of speech. Bengali public theatre, while augmenting the power of eloquence and performance, was immensely successful in drawing a popular audience.[16]

While the *chaupal* or the *chandimandap* was often *the* centre of community interaction in rural India, the chain of the India Coffee House (ICH) was created in the late 1930s with the idea to introduce the urban population to coffee, a beverage that was new to a large section of the population in north India. Soon after their creation, the outlets of the chain were seen however, as facilitataing the practice of orality in a convivial ambience with the effect, that this public space soon became a part of urban experience and a landmark in the city where it was located. In order to understand the context in which

[14] Sudipta Kaviraj, 'Filth and the Public Sphere: Concepts and Practices About Space in Calcutta', *Public Culture*, Vol.10.1, 83–113.

[15] Partha Chatterjee, *The Nation and Its Fragments: Colonial and Postcolonial Histories*, Princeton Studies in Culture/Power/History, Princeton: Princeton University Press, 1993, 22-26.

[16] Ibid., 55–58.

the Coffee House functioned, we shall briefly examine the tradition of *adda*, or informal, agendaless social gathering.

ADDA: A UNIVERSAL SOCIAL PRACTICE?

Although *adda*, as we shall see below, is a familiar form of socialization, it is mostly seen as an indispensable part of Bengali culture. *Adda* has been described as a 'long talking session, commonly of a recurrent sort among friends or co-activists. It is not simply conversation, or discussion, or debate, or gossip; and yet it is all these'.[17] In the words of the littérateur Buddhadev Basu, who 'could not live without *adda*', the practice was pan-Indian. He could not find its equivalent in English clubs and French salons, but the 'moisture in the air of Bengal was the reason why it attained its full blossom' there. The soft climate, the seasons in Bengal, were favourable to creative poetic emotions, to the density of...trees...and of *adda*. Its 'clothing is clean, but not too clean, much more than fitting, rather loose, soft-to-touch, not starch-hardened, allows stretching, and if one so wishes, even lying down. Yet, it is not dirty, does not bear any stain of fish curry or betel-juice...is comfortable, but does not bear the mark of carelessness; for comfort does not mean rhythmlessness'.[18] *Adda* is, according to him, like home, an escape from work, a space where everyone irrespective of differences in practical life, receives an equal treatment. In spite of this difference, there has to be an inner similarity among the members. The membership should be limited to those who like each other, and feel attracted to each other by a feeling of kinship.

As mentioned above, Dipesh Chakrabarty has dwelt at length upon the claim of many twentieth century Bengali intellectuals that with its agendaless, free-flowing conversations, *adda*—often reflecting the participants' sense of humour, stock of information and wit, is a quintessentially Bengali form of recreation, representing the 'creative' side of Bengali patriarchy. Indulging in *adda* in Chakrabarty's view

[17] Samarendranath Das (ed.), *Kolkatar Adda*, Kolkata: Gangchil, 2010; Debi Roy, 'Coffee kimba Sidhupaner Adda', in *Kolkatar Adda*, 2009.

[18] Buddhadev Basu, 'Adda', in Biswajit Ghosh (ed.), *Shrestha Probondho* (Choicest Essays), Kolkata: Barnayan, 2009, 98–101.

provided the Bengali elite with a 'comfort zone to cope with the ever-changing forces of capitalist modernity'.[19] Detailing on an array of spaces including bookshops, high schools, *baithak-khana* or parlours of rich persons, hostels, messes (boarding houses), literary clubs and parks that facilitated the practice of *adda* among the Bengali male elite, he states that it is not his aim to 'defend the Bengali metaphysical claim that the practice of *adda* is anything peculiarly Bengali' but concludes the essay with the statement that in spite of the problems of domination and exclusion characterizing the structure of *adda*, 'the institution played enough of a role in Bengali modernity for it to be tagged 'Bengali'.

Writing about late nineteenth century Calcutta, Swati Chattopadhyay has recently argued that *adda* was a critique of a more rational form of getting together, for example in associations and committees (*sabha* and *samiti)*. Further, she claims that in the instance of *adda*, the home and the state—both colonial and post-colonial—'are not in opposition but connected....in a world where home and colonial service lie in a continuum of bondage [responsibilities, obligations at home, and the pursuit of a salaried job, and consequently] *adda* is a space that seeks to escape both home and salaried service'... From the late nineteenth century to the early twentieth century, women/and women's question surfaced in the public space/sphere on numerous occasions and in multifarious ways, but the world of *adda* remained male-centred throughout.[20]

The current research, like that of Chakrabarty and Chatterjee, deals with a context that is urban, and coffee-tea house socialization is often associated only with the educated middle class. But the reference to the *chandimandap* and *chaupal* that also served as the location of informal gatherings of the village male, indicates that *adda* is a practice not limited to the urban, or the Western educated middle class alone.[21]

[19] Chakrabarty, 'Adda', 180–82, 212.

[20] Swati Chattopadhyay, *Representing Calcutta: Modernity, Nationalism and the Colonial Uncanny*, Abingdon, Oxon: Routledge, 2006, 182–85.

[21] A brief account of village *addas* in Bengal can be found in Lokeshchandra Biswas, 'Gramjibaner Bahumukhi Adda' (Multi-faceted *addas* of rural life), in Leena Chaki (ed.), *Bangalir Adda* (henceforth *Bangalir Adda*), Calcutta: Gangchil, 2009, 263–69.

Paan or betel leaf shops and barbershops in rural and urban India are also places where men get together and socialize.[22] As a major form of recreation and pursuit of leisure, *adda* is equally popular among the haves and havenots, irrespective of locale, age and sex. Even the nineteenth century *baithak-khana* gatherings associated with the *bhadralok* may not have been limited to indoors. I shall discuss the public-private relationship in detail later. Here it is suffice to say that by the late 1940s onwards women would gradually assert themselves in the *addas* of the Coffee House.[23]

Although Chattopadhyay rightly critiques the apologetic nature of Chakrabarty's presentation of male-centred *adda*, her delineation of the site of *adda*—as providing an escape route from home and salaried employment—is not far from that offered by Chakrabarty. The condition she describes resulted necessarily from the capitalist modernity to what the latter refers, but does not go into details. Moreover, *adda* was never a preserve of the salaried middle-class; for those getting together for an *adda* in a park, on the ro'ak, or in the hostel mess, mess were often students. Even if not unemployed, connoisseurs of *adda* are required to have an abundance of time to be spent as leisure.[24] Additionally, the informal does not necessarily have to be seen as a critique of the formal. Apart from the fact that the participants of the two kinds of meetings were often the same persons, the idea of a formal meeting could originate in and end with an informal *adda*.

Based on information on *adda* from accounts, memoirs and from personal interviews, the concept of *adda* in this book has been developed

---

Tulika Majumdar, 'Gramin Mahilader Adda', ibid., 216–29, is about women's *adda* in Bengal villages where feudal relationships still hold sway.

[22] Neelabh, interview, 17 October 2012; Mangalesh Dabral, private communication; Neerja Sahasrabudhe, 'Through the Cinema Lens: Understanding the Politics of Space in India', 15 March 2013, http://aainanagar.com/2014/03/15/through-the-cinema-lens-understanding-the-politics-of-space-in-india/.

[23] See Chapter Six for a detailed discussion on the relationship between the public and the private in the ICH.

[24] For example the four admirers crowding around the famous fictional, middle aged, tall tale teller Ghana-*da* alias Ghanashyambabu in the room of his mess—Gaur, Shibu, Shishir and Sudhir, creations of the fiction writer Premendra Mitra—are all young.

by using the perspectives of social practice. These perspectives, although much used in sociology, are not a unified theory.[25] Pierre Bourdieu, Anthony Giddens and Michel Foucault among others have used this concept as an analytical tool in their understanding of society.

Adda, a major form of recreation in South Asia is the most common form of social connection between two or more unrelated humans and is very much an integrated social practice.[26] The epitaph to this chapter suggests that in order to enjoy something, it has to be given some space, to be stretched on all sides, to be unfolded to be appreciated properly. For the connoisseurs, the practice of *adda* gives them the space to cherish the leisure time to its fullest, to extract the maximum pleasure out of it. Although there may be a disagreement as to what it may contain, *adda* conveys an intelligible meaning in that it is a spatially dispersed social practice involving two or more individuals getting together and conversing in an informal setting. As the act of conversation, involving more than one agent, is the sine qua non of an *adda*, participation in an *adda* requires a certain time of day to be reserved for this action when other participating agents are likely to have some time to spare. Consequently, *adda* is time-bound. This is a site where practices of sociability, conversation and public orality, practices of the production and reproduction of culture may come together.

The concept of *adda* is not fixed and is based on personal experience/opinion. The practice is of course connected with a site. According to Basu, whose house had an *adda* of its own,wrote in the mid 1940s that *adda*'s success depended on the choice of its site. One most favourable place, to be replaced from time to time by a

[25] For an idea of the precepts of the theories of practice in anthropology and sociology see for example J. Postill, 'Introduction', in B. Bräuchler and J. Postill (eds.), *Theorising Media and Practice*, Oxford: Berghahn, 2010; Andreas Reckwitz, 'Towards a Theory of Social Practices: A Development in Culturallist Theorizing', *European Journal of Social Theory*, 5.2, 2002, 243–63; Alan Warde, 'Consumption and Theories of Practice', *Journal of Consumer Culture*, 5.2, 2005, 131–53.

[26] *Adda* is not an institution like marriage governed by the rule of law. Nor is it a custom. Further, just as no one is obliged to take part in an *adda*, not everyone is able to appreciate this form of sociability.

couple of subsidiary places, could be ideal for *adda*. That he did not have any public place in mind becomes clear, when we read that in addition to comfortable furniture, drinking water and 'golden and fragrant' tea, some edibles in clean crockery, 'served preferably by the mistress of the house herself' were important indicators of the quality of an *adda*. Further, the numbers of members of a perfect *adda* group varied between three and twelve. Less than three made the conversation private; and more than twelve 'transformed the *adda* into Albert Hall'.[27] Even when Basu was penning these lines, 'Albert Hall' *addas* had become the new social site in the city. What is also important here is to note that the practice of combining consumption of food with that of *adda* seemed normal to him. This combination of the intake of food during *adda* has been looked down upon by later generations. Also, *adda* groups could be large, but all members need not be present all the time. As an informal practice, *adda* does not have fixed guidelines, rules or procedures. But each *adda* may be governed by its own norms and implicit understandings. Moreover, as an almost routinized practice, *adda* affects the schedule of everyday life.

It was not easy to practise *adda*, and even more difficult to keep the practice alive. Basu noted that a silent creativity of one person was essential for an *adda* to come to life. In the words of Nripendrakrishna Chattopadhyay, an eminent Bengali in the early 1960s:[28]

> Most *addas* have a central figure, the *addadhari*, nurturing it... Not everyone is suitable for this role. In addition to orality, many other ingredients are essential for keeping an *adda* alive. One person has to sacrifice a lot silently for the survival of an *adda*...
>
> Planting a crop alone does not yield the harvest. Each crop has a special enemy, and it is necessary to be ever alert in order to save the crop from its grip. *Adda* too has enemies of various kinds. They are the white ants of *adda*; once they enter it, they will leave only holes behind.
>
> For this reason, participating in an *adda* is not as easy as it appears to be...

[27] Basu, '*Adda*'.

[28] Nripendrakrishna Chattopadhyay, *Nana Katha* (Miscellenous Topics), Kolkata: Deb Sahitya Kutir, 1964, 13. In two chapters of this book titled 'Adda', and 'Aro Adda' Chattopadhyay presents his understandings of the homosocial world of men.

That it was not easy to participate in any *adda*, we shall see in the succeeding pages.[29] As it is a social practice, it is governed by the hierarchical rules embedded in social relations. Moreover, any *adda* has to stick to the conditions and norms associated with the space where it occurs. *Adda* in the average tea-shops predating the ICH was a homo-social world of the urban male. Similarly, women visiting the ICH in Allahabad continue to sit in the isolated section meant for women and families. Once these practices, embedded in the social are accepted as the norm, they become part of the practice and influence its structure. For a group of adolescent/young adult school students the purpose behind the practice of *adda* in the neighbouring Coffee House was to experience the thrill of being in a world of adults where they could smoke. But when a few members of one particular profession practice orality in a group or in parallel groups sharing the same space, it may have some utilitarian purpose in the long run, in addition to the immediate recreational purpose of the engagement. The rewards from the practice may also vary. While for a large group it may denote only an ephemeral pleasure, a break from the everyday, for a section of the participating agents, the effects of the practice of *adda* may be several, with larger consequences for the connected practices concerned. Although the event of *adda* is without a *telos*, when an aspiring poet goes to the ICH in order to gain access to the literary world and reads out his poetry to his peer group that consequently discusses it, *adda* becomes instructive. Similarly, when an editor of a magazine participates in an *adda* with poets and others in the social space, s/he might be considering the publication of their work. *Telos* can be injected by an individual in the course of a conversation.[30]

The diverse interests of the members of the group also result in that the *adda* wanders from subject to subject. A specific unit of film-makers seriously discussing the script or technique of a film or of revolutionaries discussing 'the next phase of struggle' would not be *adda*, but simply a classic meeting. Students adhering to different

[29] See especially Chapter Two, Four and Five.

[30] This aspect of *adda* can be best understood in the context of its relationship with literary practices covered in Chapter Four.

political ideologies came together in a public place for an *adda* to discuss and debate the different positions on an issue. But when members of one particular party wanted to chalk out a plan of action, that would not be in a public place, the event would be more formal, with an agenda including a list of speakers.[31]

That *adda* as a loose and flowing flood of undirected talk functions as a social cement is why, although it is not a club with a fixed membership, it is difficult for an 'outsider' to join or to take part in it. And also why invitation, or some kind of bonding was essential: a recognition by the circle that the person concerned matched the standard of the existing group. Serious subject matters were, as we shall see, very much a part of an *adda* as long as the ambience did not replicate that of a formal lecture hall.

The intimate sphere of *adda* is however not entirely free from competition which results in a tension often visible in the tendency to be abreast of the latest in the field of art, film, literature etc. However, members of a group may very well discuss Dostoyevski in the course of their conversation, but coming to a public place with a novel of Dostoyevski must not invoke the impression that it is an attempt to show off. Any pretension, intellectual or otherwise had to be presented in such a manner that was accepted and impressed upon the rest of the members; otherwise it might run amok.

How then does one enter such an intimate sphere where there is no fixed rule or requirement?

The consequence is that adoption into an *adda* circle of a 'stranger' (even a relative or a colleague), is difficult; because one does not know in advance about the person's suitability for such intimacy. Fore-knowledge is essential in order to ensure that he or she would be apt for imbibing the liquid of such intimate conversation, often lacking a pre-defined subject matter.[32]

As indicated in the essay by Chakrabarty, Bengalis have a metaphysical claim to *adda* and from Satyajit Ray, the literatteurs

[31] See the response of the Naxalite student leaders of the 1960s in Chapter Five.

[32] Narratives of *adda* at the ICH are testimony to this tension. See spatial practices in the place in Chapter Two.

Syed Mujtaba Ali and Buddhadev Basu—all great connoisseurs of *adda*—to bloggers, *adda* is a favourite subject with Bengalis.[33] Any attempt at disparaging this tradition, so dear to Bengalis, specially by a non-Bengali was sure to receive severe disapproval. However, it became evident during the field research carried out in connection with the current book that not only are people from different linguistic groups and distant locations from Delhi and Simla to Bangalore and Trivandrum familiar with the concept of *adda* as it is understood in Bengal, but the practice is also common in many other places. In Gujarat for example, the state where alcohol is banned, the *kitli* (literally kettle), the roadside tea shop, open from early hours of the day till very late at night, is the place for the male to socialize for long hours over milky tea, cigarettes and local snacks. *Kitli*s are extremely popular among students and those with a shoestring budget for tea, snacks at a cheap price, and also for having a good time with the peer group; they are the 'perfect place to catch up and brainstorm'. Using a few of the existing spaces of public socialization as a lens, the rest of this chapter will expand the focus outside Bengal to include the north Indian cities of Allahabad and Delhi where the Coffee House had its outlets.

Although *adda* is synonymous with Bengali culture, as a social practice it is equally enjoyed in other parts of India and in countries outside too. Writing about the past-time of the people in Turkey, it is noted that:[34]

> The prime ingredients of the Turks' idea of fun and amusement seem to be relaxation, imagination, sociability and humor. Sitting is almost,

[33] Andrew Robinson, *Satyajit Ray: The Inner Eye: The Biography of a Master Film-Maker,* London: I.B. Tauris, 2004, 62–64. At least two of Ray's films touched upon the theme of *adda*. While *Mahapurush* (The Great Man, 1965) held the tea and coffee house *addas* of Calcutta to be educative, the *adda* in a Calcutta middle class drawing room in his last film *Agantuk* (The Stranger, 1991) attached greater importance to the normative discourses in the gymnasiums of ancient Greece. We shall return to Ray and *adda* in Chapter Seven.

[34] Conversation in informal ambience is the most common form of pastime not only in India. See for example Bisbee, *The New Turks: Pioneers of the Republic, 1920–1950*, Philadelphia: University of Pennsylvania Press, 1951, 145.

> if not quite, the most popular recreation of all. Turks sit at windows, in gardens, at coffee houses...anywhere and everywhere they can see a pleasing view and relax in conversation.

As a spatially dispersed practice, *adda,* as we have seen above, can take place anywhere as long as the location allows conversation in a relaxed mood. A slightly different description of the same social practice could be found in the tea houses in Chengdu, China:[35]

> Most conversations were spontaneous and without purpose; as a saying put it, 'conversation in the teahouse flows wherever it wishes.' One teahouse near West gate was simply called *geshuo ge* (random talks). Joining the conversation required no preparation or qualifications. Men could express any opinion without being held responsible as long as they did not offend anyone and nobody took what they said seriously. In a teahouse people could join conversations with strangers or simply listen if they preferred.

Syed Mujtaba Ali, the erudite linguist and essayist known for his humour and satire who penned some of the best travel literature in Bengali, was also a great connoisseur of *adda*. In his colourful account of the life of the men in Cairo that revolved round coffee houses, he found their devotion to *adda* to be superior to that of the Bengali male. Save for the six hours from midnight to early morning they reluctantly spent at home, and the time they had to work, men in Cairo happily whiled away their time in social gatherings in cafés. In no time after the author had expressed his desire to have a suit tailored, the locals appointed a Greek tailor and in what followed, the coffee house became the venue for selecting and purchasing the dress material, taking measuremens, and trial for a custom-made suit tailored for the author within a few hours.[36] In *Street Corner Society*, his classic ethnographic study of the Italian-American inhabitants of 'Cornerville', the fictitious name of a slum in North End, Boston, William Foote Whyte left a vivid account of the socialization as the

[35] Wang, *Teahouse*, 121.

[36] 'Adda Passport', in Saiyad Mujtaba Ali, *Rachanabali, Saiyad Mujtaba Ali*, Kolkata: Mitra o Ghosh, 1975, Vol. 3, 404–11.

inhabitants gathered, gossiped, gambled and flirted.[37] Barbershop socializing is common in the poor neighbourhoods of New York like Bronx, Harlem and Brooklyn, and in other US cities like Los Angeles, as places where friends run into one another, spend time together and exchange news and gossips, offering stability to a seemingly chaotic and disorderly life.

ADDA IN THE CURRENT CONTEXT

To understand the *adda* in the ICH, I propose to build on the concept of capitalist modernity by looking deeper into what the urbanites thought about their life in the city they inhabited. Reflecting on their life in the city, thinking persons in places like Allahabad, Calcutta and Delhi, through the 1930s to the 1950s, often referred to it as an alienation. I argue here that the social practice of *adda* was an attempt by the individual to provide a 'critique' of their experience, to rise beyond all the mundane of which the everyday consisted.

Modernization of society is a continuous process leaving its imprint on social life. Prospects of higher education and employment are only two of the factors drawing people from the rural areas in India to the cities. On the one hand young adult males leaving home for the city gradually led to the disintegration of the structure of the family and society in the village, while on the other, the same citizens tried to obtain a foothold in a new place. In Calcutta, for example, most of these men stayed in messes; many celebrities like Nirad C. Chaudhuri began their career in such messes scattered over central and north Calcutta.[38]

[37] William Foote Whyte, *Street Corner Society: The Social Structure of an Italian Slum*, Chicago: University of Chicago Press, 1993.

[38] Nirad C. Chaudhuri stayed in a mess near Surya Sen Street. When he was teaching in Ripon (Surendranath) College during 1936–46. Pramatha Nath Bishi, another well-known littérateur, used to stay in a mess on Sitaram Ghosh Street. As a lecturer of Bengali he used to earn 75 rupees a month (lecturers of other subjects earned 100 rupees a month). He would meet his own costs and send money to his family in Rajshahi (now in Bangladesh), Sabitendranath Roy, *College Street-e Sottor Bochhor* (Seventy Years in College Street), Kolkata: Mitra o Ghosh, 4 vols, 2006–08, vol. 3, 149–50; linguist Suniti Kumar Chatterjee too lived in a hostel.

In cities like Calcutta and Delhi most of the people had left their rural homes for the city either for study or for work. In an attempt to explain what the *adda* in the Coffee House meant to the public in Calcutta, Pabitra Kumar Ghosh, a regular customer of the ICH in the 1950s, tried to understand life in the city from the perspectives of the process of urbanization in Europe in the eighteenth and nineteenth centuries. Familiar with the works of Karl Marx, historian of political thought Peter Laslett, Marxist socialist William Morris, philosopher Jean-Jacques, Rousseau, Russian anti-communist academic-activist Pitirim Sorokin and essayist Henry David Thoreau among others, Ghosh noted that the same anti-humanist civilization that had given birth to new cities in the West, created modern cities in India. It was the fragmented, disfigured humanity that took shelter in the cupboard-like residences in the new urban complexes. There were layers in the city where it was possible to feel the warmth of the earth washed by sunlight; but beneath that thin surface was an extensive layer covered by deep darkness, where people lived in distress, where the difference between life and death was very little.[39]

It is interesting to observe that at a time when Henri Lefebvre was configuring the adverse impact of post-World War II Fordist economy on the development of the human being in Paris,[40] his contemporaries were reflecting on their life in a post-colonial Third World country following a socialist mixed-economy model of governance through license-raj, along strikingly similar lines. For Ghosh, chaos and disaster were metaphors for the modern urban space. Calcutta in his view had reached the point where it subordinated life to organized destruction, and it was necessary therefore to regiment, limit and constrict all exhibitions of real life and culture. Those born, raised or settling in such cold and dark parts of Calcutta soon felt that they had lost the essence of their life. Prevailing over the entertainment and the fun, longings and prospects in the city, was the naked truth that it allotted on an average 30 square feet living

[39] Pabitra Kumar Ghosh, *Coffee-house*, Kolkata: Ranjan Publishing House, 1962, 57–71.

[40] Henri Lefebvre, *Critique of Everyday Life*, 3 vols., London: Verso, 1947, 81.

space per inhabitant.[41] 'The result is manifest in the paralysis of all the higher activities of the society: truth shorn or debased to fit the propaganda: the organs of cooperation stiffened into a reflex system of obedience...it is deeply...antagonistic to every valuable manifestation of life.'

Pabitra Kumar was not the only person troubled about the travails of life in the city. Another thinking person bearing the same family name informs us:

> One-third of the population in Calcutta lives in slums *none* of which is fit for human dwelling....And mind you, the families since recently living at railway stations along the vast stretch spanning from Sealdah to Ranaghat, live much more comfortably than us, tenants. I would advise them never to opt for a rented place or slum. Any railway station is heaven compared to the rented house of that friend of mine, and compared to a slum, his rented house is again a royal palace! Therefore, it is much better to live on the concrete footpath under the balcony of huge mansions, or in the wide, open quarters of the railway station. Then you will not be required to pay an irregular, extra fee (*selami*) to landlord, pay a rent four times higher than it should be, and live under a leaking roof (*gamla, balti pete chhati mathay diye*). With regard to the question of the privacy of your family, you do not have that anyway at the 'collective' tubewell or water-tap [of a rented place].[42]

Thus the alienation in a modern urban situation theorists in the West were writing about, was indeed felt by urbanites in post-colonial Calcutta. It should be noted that those living in the narrow space of a rented house with a leaking ceiling were not necessarily the poor or the downtrodden who lived in the slum or in the wide open space of the railway station; it was a reality for many middle class families in pre and post-Partition Calcutta.[43] A section

[41] Ghosh, *Coffee-house*. In a popular song composed by Kabir Suman in the early 1990s this was reduced to 10 square feet.

[42] Binay Ghosh, *Kalpanchar Naksha* (A Satire), Calcutta: Pathabhavan, 1967/1953, 72–73. The first edition was published in 1951.

[43] Till 1950 most of the migrants from East Bengal were *bhadralok* with financial

of the customers of the Coffee House in College Street lived in such dwellings.[44]

Although Ghosh's description of the city was confined to the urban, the imagination of the first-generation urbanites in Calcutta, especially those who had been forced to leave their ancestral houses without the prospect of going back, was often guided by a comparison of the idyllic village they had left (or had been forced to leave) behind. Ashis Nandy wrote that the urbanites were in the city 'by default and under duress. Home has to have a touch of the pastoral, even when a poisoned village has caused the homelessness'.[45] The poet Sankha Ghosh, whose family left their ancenstral home in East Bengal when he was fifteen, missed the place where he grew up from a young boy to a young adolescent, reflected however, in a number of his works differently:[46]

---

and/or educational resources; it was only after the riots of 1950 that poorer people from lower caste and class background began leaving the country. Anwesha Sengupta, 'Breaking up Bengal: People, Things and Land in Times of Partition', Ph.D. thesis submitted to the Centre for Historical Studies, JNU, 2015, ch. 4; Pranati Chaudhuri, 'Refugees in West Bengal: A Study of the Growth and Distribution of Refugee Settlements within the CMD', Occasional paper no. 55, CSSSC.

[44] Scholars from different disciplines have profusely written on this most tragic event in Indian history. Individual memory and pain however has best been preserved in post-Partition literary fiction. In Bengali see for example Manik Bandyopadhyay, *Sarbojonin* (Public), Kolkata: Universal, 1952; and Jyotirindra Nandi, *Baro Ghar Ek Uthon* (Twelve Homes, Common Courtyard), Kolkata, 1955; Sunil Gangopadhyay, *Ardhek Jiban* (Half a Life—Autobiographical), Kolkata: Ananda, 2002; among Gangopadhyay's other works *Purva-Paschim* (East and West), Kolkata: Ananda, 2012, depicts the situation resulting from forceful occupation of deserted buildings by refugees and the antagonism this influx created among the Calcuttans of West Bengal origin, while his *Arjun* is about the effort of a group of refugees to establish a colony in Dum Dum and then to defend it against the lanlord's *goondas*. Also see Mukul Guha, 'Adda kono din o bandho hobar noy', in Samarendra Das (ed.), *Kolkatar Adda*; Tarun Majumdar, 'Adda! Adda', ibid.

[45] Ashis Nandy, *An Ambiguous Journey to the City*, New Delhi: OUP, 2001, 31; see Chakrabarty, *Provincialzing Europe*, for a discussion of the city vs. country in nationalist imagination.

[46] Excerpt from 'Punarbasan' (Rehabilitation), *Sankha Ghosher Kabita Sangraha* (Collected Poetry), vol. 1, Kolkata: Dey's, 1981, 115–16. Tr. by Bhaswati Bhattacharya and Victor van Bijlert.

Once I was surrounded by
grass and stones
snakes and lizards
a temple in ruins
I was surrounded by
banishment
strings of tales
sunset in solitude
I was surrounded by
destruction
arrows and spears
ancestral home
all at once in a stampede facing westward
memories like jostling crowds on a long journey
broken box left in the shadow of a mango-tree
suddenly, with a new step, everyone's a refugee.
Now I am surrounded by
Sealdah
long afternoons
graffiti
I am surrounded by
blind alleys
slogans
the Monument
I am surrounded by
beds with piercing arrows
lampposts
the red Ganges
all of this envelops me in the darkness of the bone-marrow

Rehabilitation in the long run implies reconciliation with the present, as the rest of the poem shows. Similarly, the difference between the native southern and the northern or European part of Allahabad was such that it made the writer-poet Harivansh Rai Bachchan (1907–2003) feel nostalgic about the ambience of the southern part missing in the newer part of the city. Bachchan was born and grew up as a young man at Chowk Mohalla in the southern part of the city. His family had lived there for seven generations. And family ties among the brothers of his father were close until

Harivansh antagonized his relatives and other members of the Kayasth caste by eating at an ostracized woman's place, resulting in the ostracization of his own family. Chowk was like 'a part of a village in the process of turning into a town, or rather a part of a town thrust forcibly into the midst of a village, fields and barns', and was a mixed neighbourhood. The wrestler-cum-market gardener and his low-caste wife, a woman of the Kacchi caste, the Arya Samaji Babu Mukta Prasad, the Shia steward, shared the neighbourhood together with Gujarati, Bengali and Kayasth professionals. On the north, the Chowk bounded by Mohatsimganj or Mosimganj, while west of the property of the market-gardener were small mud-brick huts of Muslim artisans: barbers, butchers, *hookah*-makers, kite makers, locksmiths, tin-smiths etc. Hindu males in that neighbourhood would join in the ceremonial mournings of Muslims during Muharram. This property was confiscated by the state at the time of the construction of Zero Road when they moved to Katghar, where the much-acclaimed poetical works of Bachchan, *Madhushaala, Madhubala, Madhukalash* and *Nisha nimantran* had seen the light of the day. It was at Katghar that he lost his first wife and his father. Since he commuted back and forth between his home and the university, four kilometres apart, everyday, till he obtained a bicycle, he knew the area like the back of his hand, and was very familiar with the life of the people around his house.[47]

Reflecting on the period he later spent in Naya Katra near the university in the northern part of the city, Bachchan attributed the quality of those earlier poems to the human contacts he had experienced in Chowk and Katghar, the traditional part of the city. The newly-settled area of Naya Katra in contrast was 'like a lodging-house where no complete connection with other migrants could really be achieved'.[48] In Civil Lines, the area where he moved to in the mid-1940s, he felt himself like a 'newly transplanted tree':[49]

[47] Harivansh Rai Bachchan, *In the Afternoon of Time: An Autobiography*, edited and translated from the Hindi by Rupert Snell, New Delhi: Penguin, 1998, ch. 6, 'Chak mohalla'; Kathgar area is described on 262–66.

[48] Ibid., 267.

[49] Ibid., 323–24; emphasis added.

> Civil Lines brought a chance to enjoy privacy and freedom from interference, and for a person like me who had turned away from the conventional path in favour of a life of study and writing, this atmosphere was rather favourable; but it exacted a price for these advantages, for one had to accept self-dependent, self-sufficient and solitude....such a life could neither make Teji [his second wife] happy nor provide Amit [his elder son Amitabh] with a healthy environment in which to grow up.

The city brings freedom from rural bondage; but it is also impersonal. There was a *new* kind of socialilty in Civil Lines that offered a '*formal, politely detached*' contact distinct from the informal bond existing in the traditional part of the town, and although his family would gradually assimilate into that world, the difference between the two worlds had made an impact deep enough on the imagination for Bachchan to recount it decades later.[50]

Although brief, the distinction the poet Bachchan makes between the traditional and modern parts of the city in which he had lived almost echos the sentiment about a modern city the two urbanites from Calcutta expressed. The familiarity, interdependence and ties that were part of the old town with its traditional life is missed in the newly settled modern part where a formal, polite and detached contact stands in the way of having an in-depth relationship.

Considering that Bachchan had moved only from the traditional to the modern part of the same town, it can be assumed that the nostalgia would be much stronger among those migrating from the village or small town reflected in the works of Mangalesh Dabral, Neelabh among many others. Reminiscing about the time when he was a newcomer to Delhi in the mid-1950s, Ajit Kumar writes that like many others, he too took the road from the village to the city via the market town, or *kasba*. He often dreamt of going back to his village, and although he never went back, he vividly remembered the ghats, mangroves and ponds of the village associated with his childhood. Losing his way confused among the radial roads and circular spaces in the Connaught Circus, he penned:

[50] Ibid.; emphasis added.

There was a city called Delhi
hell for some, heaven for none:
we all came here in search of our own world!
what is this attachment?
keep even the wilted flower
close to your bosom, are you crazy?
as the custom of this country goes—
pierce it, scratch it, smell it, crush it and cast it away
why don't you try it as well!
Nayeempur your village
why chant the name like a rosary?[51]

Work took him to the capital, but the village he left behind, did not leave him. As the memory faded with the passage of time, the nostalgia for the village close to the heart became stronger. The busy, chaotic life in the city meant that he needed a space in which to relax, and reflect. The Coffee House provided such a space, helping to come to terms with the chaotic, confusing life in the city. The same idea is evoked by the associations made by the customers of the Tea-cum-Coffee House in Delhi:

> It will not be wrong if I say that the Tea House saved the animal called writer from the chaos and boredom of life in the capital.[52]

The introspective analysis of the modern Indian city by Pabitra Kumar is remarkably similar to the urban experience of his counterparts in Allahabad and Delhi, and sheds new light on the *adda* those urbanites participated in.

The section below will cast a cursory glance at the existing spaces of public consumption facilitating sociability in the three cities studied in this book. Not only that the words '*addebaaj*', '*guppbaaj*' (connoisseur of *adda*) are similar to *addabaaj* and *galpobaaj* in Bengali, '*adda jamana*' (to gather at some place regularly) is a usage common in Hindi. A recent collection of memoirs of poets and writers in Hindi connected with various literary movements in post-Independence India is in fact a testimony to the various literary

[51] Ajit Kumar, 'Ab Dilli Door Nahin', in *DTH*, 1–14.

[52] Dharmendra Gupta, 'Shanibar Ke Sham, Tea House Ke Naam', in *DTH*, 156–63.

addas in Delhi, the main centre being the Tea-cum-Coffee House in Connaught Place.[53] Was this a mid-twentieth century phenomenon, or is there a history of informal public association in Delhi and Allahabad too? Is there is a link between the public culture of the *mushairas* where poets recited their own work, or the cosmopolitan heritage of *majlish* of Hindustani classical music, where gossip with juicy anecdotes was intertwined with the flow of music creating a bond between performers and narrators transcending barriers of language, and comparing with the sociability in the Coffee House?[54] What did the ICH replace, if it replaced anything at all?[55]

DELHI

It has been stated that public spaces in Mughal Delhi were dominated by royalty and religion and that it was the British Government formed in the post-1857 period that created a 'civic' realm. With the rise of Indian nationalism, the newly created 'civic' square provided a space for political meetings and public protests.[56] However, the Perso-Islamic civilization of Mughal India that connected the subcontinent with central and west Asia nurtured a public culture beyond these two domains. The fact that both Hindu and Muslim functionaries of the Mughals used Urdu resulted in Urdu becoming commonly accepted

[53] Vanshi, *DTH*, 17; Leena Chaki, 'Adda-r Agey', in Leena Chaki (ed.), *Bangalir Adda*, Kolkata: Gangchil, 7.

[54] See for example the account of the meeting of the North Indian classical singer Siddheswari Bai and T.R. Mahalingam, the Tamil flautist who communicated with each other through music in Kumarprasad Mukhopaddhyay, *Majlish*, Kolkata: Ananda Publishers, 1997, 38–39.

[55] Hotels serving meals have been left out of this survey as they belong to a different category. For an account of eating out in Bombay during the mid-twentieth century, see Frank Conlon, 'Dining Out in Bombay', in Carol Appadurai Breckenridge (ed.), *Consuming Modernity: Public Culture in a South Asian World*, Minneapolis: University of Minnesota Press, 1995, 90–130.

[56] Jyoti Hosagrahar, *Indigenous Modernities: Negotiating Architecture and Urbanism*, London: Routledge, 2005, 11. For a captivating account of Delhi during and after 1857 see William Dalrymple, *The Last Mughal: The Fall of a Dynasty, Delhi, 1857*, Delhi: Penguin, 2006; also Ralph Russell (ed.), *Ghalib: The Poet and His Age*, London: George Allen & Unwin, 1972.

by both the communities.[57] Mirza Ghalib's famous quote in the face of an inquiry by an English official in the days following the capture of Delhi by the colonial forces that only the half of him that did not consume pork was Muslim, but the other half that drank wine, was in fact a testimony to the secular ideology nurtured by the Mughals, and Bahadur Shah Zafar in particular.[58] Consumption of alcohol and merry-making on festive occasions in defiance of religious prohibition had long been a part of the elite culture in urban Mughal India.[59] The bourgeoisie in the European sense was absent in Delhi, but in the public sphere the nobility, the rich and the poor were equal in the literary public sphere of the *mushairas*.[60] Chandni Chowk, the 'most beautiful and profusely decorated passage' in the city, attracted the high and low as a centre of recreation.[61] The eateries, and the shops selling objets d'art, rare and exotic commodities like spices, birds, camels, firearms, horses, jewelleries, and textiles drew the attention of the locals and foreigners alike. Oral transmission through public performances drew the semi-literate and illiterate rural population to the public sphere.[62] It was at Chandni Chowk that people passed time under the shade of the trees, along the canal in the middle, and where *dastangos* (story tellers) held their sessions,[63] courtesans' salons

[57] Shamsur Rahman Faruqi, *Early Urdu Literary Culture and History*, Delhi: OUP, 2001.

[58] Ghalib, who would drink wine even in Mecca, refers to 'salon' owned by his beloved, Russell, *Ghalib*.

[59] Ishrat Haque, *Glimpses of Mughal Society and Culture: A Study Based on Urdu Literature*, Delhi: Concept Publishing House, 1992, 123–24.

[60] Margit Pernau, 'From a private-public to a public-private sphere: Old Delhi in comparative perspective', in G. Mahajan and H. Reifeld (eds.), *The Public and the Private: Issues of Democratic Citizenship*, New Delhi: Sage, 2003; Farhat Hasan has suggested that the subordinate classes excluded from the elitist *mushairas* created alternate spaces in bazars, fairs, festivals and in the house of the courtesans, Farhat, 'Forms of Civility and Publicness in pre-British India', in Rajeev Bhargava and Helmut Reifeld (eds.), *Civil Society, Public Sphere and Citizenship*, Delhi: Sage, 2005, 84–105.

[61] Pavankumar Varma, *Mansions at Dusk: The Havelis of Old Delhi*, Delhi: Spantech Publishers, 1992, 17.

[62] Sandra B. Freitag, 'Introduction: Aspects of the Public in Colonial South Asia', *South Asia*, 14.1, 1991, 1–14.

[63] Ibid.; Pavankumar Varma, 'Shahjahanabad: The City that Once Was', in

offered an escape from the insecurities of everyday life, while flying kites was an entertainment reveled in by the high and low.[64]

That in addition to becoming a part of hospitality in private and official meetings, coffee was available in public spaces like *qahwakhanas* or coffee houses in Mughal Delhi where the coffee house culture had become popular. This is evident from references to the pastime of visiting *qahwakhanas* scattered here and there in the Chowk, where poets assembled daily in the evening to listen to the recitation of each other's verses, and scholars and others from different strata of the society debated on different public issues outside the realm of religion and state. *Mehfils* of music, dance, poetry and repartee were organized at different venues in the market.[65] In whatever was left of the walled city of Shahjahanabad after 1857, some of this public culture persisted even in the high noon of the colonial empire as the pressure of business and trade ensured that Chandni Chowk would thrive again soon. Though the *dastangos* resumed their trade, the *mushairas* seem to have stopped.[66] Common people gathered at milk and sweet shops where both private and public happenings were discussed.[67]

The secular setting of public life in Mughal cities in the *doab* like Agra, Allahabad, Awadh and Lucknow nourished a composite culture, also a characteristic of Delhi and Lahore. Known in the

---

Stephen P. Blake (ed.), *Shahjahanabad: The Sovereign City in Mughal India, 1639–39*, Cambridge: CUP, 1991, 119.

[64] Narayani Gupta, *Delhi Between Two Empires, 1803–1931: Society, Government and Urban Growth*, Delhi: OUP, 1981, 5–6, 13.

[65] Shama Mitra Chenoy, *Shahjahanabad: A City of Delhi, 1638–1857*, Delhi: Munshiram Manoharlal, 1998, 128; all evening story-telling sessions were held on the steps of the *Jama Masjid* too, Dalrymple, *The Last Mughal*, 107.

[66] See Gupta, *Delhi*, for post mutiny Chandni Chowk, 50–54.

[67] Ahmed Ali, *Twilight in Delhi*, Bombay: OUP, 1966 (1940); a kabab seller, a barber, a carpenter and a merchant gathering at Mirza's—the milk and sweet seller—shop where they discuss the fate of the last Mughal Emperor and debate on the positive and negative aspects of the British rule, 139–41; again during WWI the discussion by the same characters draw on the inflation in Delhi, the misery caused by the rule of King 'Jaraj' (George) and the latest they have gathered about German war techniques, 218–21; for politics being discussed in the gents section of private house, ibid., 145–46.

parlance of northern India as *Ganga-Jamuni tehzeeb*, it was the joint handiwork of Hindus, Muslims and Sikhs. In this tradition of a shared cultural history that resulted in endless fusion of Hindu and Muslim forms of art, achitecture, cookery, literature and music among other things. Hindus patronized poets composing in Persian and Urdu, wrote poems and took part in *mushairas*, owned Urdu press and financed Urdu literary journals. Bookshops owned by Hindus became intellectual marts where prominent figures of all religions met.[68] Just as Hindu and Muslim feudal lords had united hands with Begum Hazrat Mahal of Awadh in her fight against the Company's army in 1857, early twentieth century Hindu elite engaged in writing learned articles on Urdu poetry and organized or attended *mushairas*.[69]

In all cities studied here, as will be evident from the description below, there were enough places where people could meet informally. Even so, a large section of the middle class was unfamiliar with both coffee and the coffee house. The post-Mutiny period saw the gradual development of modern Delhi when many western educated natives left their abode in old Delhi for the modern environment in Civil Lines. There were clubs like Chelmsford Club and Windsor Club and coffee-shops serving the British, and surviving account suggests that the latter were modelled on the classic coffee houses of England.[70] The first South Indian eatery that introduced the common public of Delhi to coffee and South Indian food was Madras Hotel in the outer ring of CP where the entire block is commonly known after the hotel.[71] The first Coffee House opened by the Coffee Board in Delhi, the

[68] See for example Malik Mohammad, *The Foundations of the Composite Culture of India*, New Delhi: Aakar Books, 2007; Naz Ikramullah, *Ganga Jamuni: Silver and Gold, A Forgotten Culture*, Dhaka: Bengal Publications, 2013; for Lahore see K. K. Aziz, *Indian Coffee House*, 1–29.

[69] Qurratulain Hyder, *River of Fire*, New Delhi: Kali for Women, 1998, 131, 157–64, 218; Mrs Sarojini Naidu, the poet governor of U.P. in independent India was holding daily mushairas at Raj Bhavan in Lucknow, 273.

[70] The British Library, *The Delhi Sketch Book*, 8.1, (1858), 10–12. cf; 'The resident of the North-west.... after getting ready every morning dropped in at the coffee-shop in order to shop talk and scandal,' *Calcutta Review*, 1857, 15.

[71] Arjun Dev, retired professor of History, University of Delhi, interview, 6 January 2012.

capital of the British-India since 1912, was in Chandni Chowk that had revived much of the commercial activity since the foundation of the East Indian Railway line[72] and again became the commercial hub in the city in the late 1930s.[73] There were of course many eateries and tea shops in this neighbourhood and the one favoured by a section of the literati was Monica Restaurant. In Old Delhi there was a gathering of new generation Hindi writers like Soumitra Mohan, Yogesh Gupta, Bhushan Banamali, Shaktipal Kewal who used to work as proof-readers in Chawri Bazar and Nayi Sadak, or take dictation of established writers like Jainendra.[74] With its stock of pastries and sandwiches, Carlton Café in Kashmiri Gate was favourite with many university students. In the late 1940s, a high school student with a daily allowance of 50 paise could buy two *puris* and a glass of *lassi* at that place. Daryaganj nurtured another hub of writers and publishers as the Central Directorate of Hindi and several vernacular magazines and publishing houses were located here. The restaurant Moti Mahal in this area was known for its quality tandoori dishes where one could enjoy elaborate dinner in open air over programmes of *qawaali*, *ghazal* and other colourful activities organized by the restaurant. Married into the owner's family, Surendra Prakash used to organize lunch-cum story-reading sessions at this place.[75] Close to Moti Mahal there was a *dhaba* bearing the same name and writers unable to afford the pricey restaurant, would usually take guests from other cities to the *dhaba*.[76]

Connaught Place (CP) was *the* upcoming business centre and shopping mall for the elite of the capital. A green *maidan* covered the

[72] Gupta, *Delhi*, 233.

[73] Gurnam Singh, a loyal visitor of ICH since 1957, he has followed the institution through its changing sites, interview, 7 January 2012; see for the growth and transformation of Mughal Shajahanbad to Imperial Delhi, Gupta, *Delhi*; also R. G. Irving, *Indian Summer: Lutyens, Baker and Imperial Delhi,* New Haven: Yale University Press, 1981; Jyoti Hosagrahar, 'Mansions to Margins'; Suparna Chatterjee and Judith T. Kenny, 'Creating a New Capital: Colonial Discourse and the Decolonization of Delhi', *Historical Geography*, 27, 1999, 73–98.

[74] Ravindra Kalia, *Ghalib Chhuti Sharaab* (Ghalib Giving Up Alcohol; henceforth *Ghalib*), Nayi Dilli: Bhartiya Jnanpith, 2013, 99.

[75] Ibid., 105–9; Inder Sharma (83) of Select Groups, interview, 21 October 2012.

[76] Kalia, *Ghalib*, 105–6.

area between the Queensway (Janpath) and the Parliament (Sansad) Street. During World War II barracks were built in the area for housing American soldiers. Three Indian contractors played a prominent role in the construction of the mall in CP built in phases: Sir Sobha Singh, Sardar Dharam Singh and Rai Bahadur Narain Singh.[77] Block A of CP and the Regal Theatre (currently cinema) Hall were constructed by Sir Sobha Singh, Regal being completed in 1928. Those days the Nirula Brothers, running a photography shop in CP, would have to travel to Chandni Chowk or Kashmiri Gate for a proper meal, which inspired them to open a restaurant, Hotel India, on the first floor of a building in D Block (1934), followed by Nirula's bar and restaurant serving Indian and Continental food in the L Block at the heart of the newly developing city. Spencer's, the famous Swiss confectionary of Kashmiri Gate (1926) had moved to A Block in the early 1930s as had Wenger's, where pastries, tarts, mousses and homemade Swiss chocolates are still sold. With a carpeted staircase leading to the bar and restaurant on the first floor, a spacious dance floor and a live band, Nirula's was a large establishment where meetings and parties were held. In addition, there was Davico's, also European-owned, refurbished and renamed Standard in 1957. The presence of British officers and of a large number of Americans during World War II had paved the way for opening of restaurants with art deco interior, a live band with crooners and a dance floor, serving continental menus where the elite would go for dinner and to dance.[78] Alps on Janpath was an air-conditioned cozy restaurant where those seeking privacy would and spend hours over cups of tea.[79] At places like Alps,

[77] Sir Sobha Singh, a prominent builder in Lutyen's Delhi and the father of the eminent journalist and writer Khushwant Singh was also known for betraying the revolutionaries Bhagat Singh and Batukeswar Dutt.

[78] Ranjana Sengupta, *Delhi Metropolitan: The Making of an Unlikely City*, New Delhi: Penguin, 2007, 223–24.

[79] Couples usually preferred Alps, Gaylord or Standard. Habib Tanvir and Monica Mishra used to visit Alps where their romance developed, Anjum Katyal, *Habib Tanvir: Towards an Inclusive Theatre*, New Delhi: Sage, 2012, 53; also see Sengupta, *Delhi Metropolitan*, for Alps and its connection with the literati. Sengupta however confuses the movement of the workers of ICH (see Chapter Three) as that of the workers of Alps, 223–24.

Laguna, Volga and York, the culture of live music and dance would be inherited by the socialites in post-colonial Delhi. Equally plush was the ambience in Gaylord in the Regal Building, a symbol of wealth and aristocracy, where the menu included Chinese food as well as Western delicacies like chocolate, ice cream, and soufflé. Coffee was served here too.[80] Hemchandra Jain of Ferozepur, Punjab, opened Shanghai Bar in 1935 targetting the American and British soldiers in the cantonment. After 1947, Jain turned it into Respo Milk Bar and a pure vegetarian eatery that changed its *avatar* once again in the early 1950s to become Madras Coffee House.[81] Next to Wenger's, Keventer's Milk Bar was another early establishment here. Madan Lamba, who had left his restaurant Volga behind in Lahore, launched Volga and Kwality in CP.[82] With a doorman opening the door, Volga with its lush carpet, stylish furniture, starched white linens, milk white shades mellowing the light and smart bearers greeted the customer.[83] G.K. Ghai and N. Malhotra, who used to run a restaurant business in pre-Partition Karachi, started Embassy in summer 1948, serving Indian and Continental food to an elite clientele including the political high brass and film stars like Manmohan Desai, Raj Kapoor, Jay Parvesh Chandra, the ex-chief executive councillor of Delhi, Rajiv Gandhi, L.K. Advani, Arun Jaitley and Madan Lal Khurana, government and business houses and embassies. Nirula's replaced the earlier restaurant in 1950 with a large cafeteria, a brasserie and the Chinese Room, introducing espresso coffee in India. As live bands became more and more expensive and gradually faded out, Nirula's closed the cafeteria and the brasserie and opened two specialty restaurants without live music in 1960, the Gufa serving Indian food and the trendy La Bohéme, an Austro-Hungarian specialty restaurant

[80] Krishna Sobti, 'Marfat Dilli' (C/O Delhi), in *DTH*, 98–119; for regular coffee-meetings at Gaylord see *Outlook*, vol. 43, nos. 26–29, 30.

[81] Jain, who hailed from a family of zamindars and cotton merchants going bankrupt, passed away in 1977 and the place, in its last legs, is now run by his son-in-law Gauri Shankar Nanda. See Shreya Roy Chowdhury, '75 Years Behind It: Madras Coffee House Guards Legacy Fiercely', *TNN*, 14 March 2014.

[82] Sengupta, *Delhi Metropolitan*, 88. Volga closed down in 2010.

[83] Sobti, 'Marfat Dilli', 100.

serving continental food.[84] Although these places initially catered only to the Western and indigenous elite, by the mid-1930s one could buy a cup of tea for two *anna*s in the CP area.

As Delhi's administrative and commercial importance grew, since the transfer of the capital, so did the city's population. Once it became the national capital in 1947, Delhi saw the influx of refugees resulting in a ninety per cent growth in its population between 1941 and 1951.[85] New Delhi was new, but in the pre-Partition days it was a cultural desert. Many of the migrants were from the culturally rich Lahore—'Paris of the Punjab'—a city where the 'high society' had been 'higher' than that in Allahabad or Lucknow, and was much larger than Delhi.[86] There were also Bengalis from East Pakistan, including government employees, fleeing to Delhi.[87] The establishments of the new Central Government and parliamentary and judiciary institutions needed professionals and a supporting bureaucracy that attracted fortune seekers from far and wide to the metropolis. The University of Delhi

[84] This 'espresso', as we shall see later, was different from the variety known as such. Volga and La Bohéme were the most sought after places for coffee and snacks in CP in the 1950s and 1960s, see Amitabh Bachchan's official blog, http://srbachchan.tumblr.com/post/32472706591, 28 September 2012.

[85] Out of the approximately 4.75 million displaced migrating from the North-West Frontier Province and West Punjab to India, nearly 500,000 went to Delhi, V. N. Datta, 'Panjabi Refugees and the Urban Development of Greater Delhi', in R. E. Frykenberg (ed.), *Delhi Through the Ages: Selected Essays in Urban History, Culture and Society*, Delhi: OUP, 287–305; also, Véronique Dupont, 'Spatial and Demographic Growth of Delhi Since 1947 and the Main Migration Flows', in Véronique Dupont, Emma Tarlo and Denis Vidal (eds.), *Delhi: Urban Space and Human Destinies*, New Delhi: Manohar, 2000, 229–39.

[86] Prakashvati Pal, *Lahore Se Lucknow Tak* (From Lahore to Lucknow), Allahabad: Lokbharti, 2009, 135. People in Lahore spoke better English and were better dressed, Sajjad Zaheer, *The Light: A History of the Movement for Progressive Literature in the Indo-Pakistan Subcontinent*, A translation of *Roshnai* in Urdu by Amina Azfar, Lahore: OUP, 2006, 21.

[87] These refugees were housed in two-storied barrack-like buildings built during WWII called 'chummeries' housing families sharing a common kitchen and bathroom on each floor. For a brief sketch of the life of a young girl of such a displaced family, see Rekha Karmakar, 'Memories of Delhi', 7 August 2012, http://www.finelychopped.net/2012/08/memories-of-delhi-by-rekha-karmakar.html.

became a centre for the cultivation of Hindi literature. The foundation of the Sahitya Akademi in 1954, launching of *Vividh Bharati* (a variety programme in Hindi) in 1956, and the creation of the *Kendriya Hindi Sansthan* in 1962 drew the Hindi and Urdu literati scattered from Lahore, Jullunder (especially after Partition), Jaipur, Indore, to Lucknow, Benares, Patna, Kolkata and other places to Delhi.[88]

Initially cars were the only mode of transport for access to the centre, and before local bus service was begun by DTC (1948) the place was not easily accessible by public transport; most people visiting CP were commuting by cycle, *tonga*, a horse-drawn carriage, or on foot. After Independence the old Harley-Davidsons and Indian motorbikes were used to build an ingenious vehicle which could seat two people facing the front and two people facing the back. This was a new mode of transportation, called *phutphut* or *phatphatiya* because of the sound it produced, was cheaper than a taxi and faster than a *tonga*. To start with, it linked Odeon Cinema in CP with Ajmeri Gate in Old Delhi, but later on they were plying all over the city.[89]

It took quite some time before all shops in the CP began operating. Interspersed with these more expensive eateries, there were affordable tea-shops and *dhaba*s where the ordinary middle class could go for a quick sip and bite.[90] After Partition, CP like the rest of Delhi gave refuge to many fleeing erstwhile West Punjab, and more and more kiosks and shops cropped up in the area. Refugees initially opening stalls (*khokhenuma dukanon*) near the Hanuman Temple in CP

[88] Baldev Vanshi, *DTH*, ix; cf. Delhi, although not the only cultural centre of Hindi, has the largest concentration of writers, publishers, academies etc.; Rashmi Sadana, *English Heart, Hindi Heartland: The Political Life of Literature in India*, Oakland: University of California Press, 2012, 25–26.

[89] Presumably this refers to the Indian Motorcycle Company of the US. I owe this information to Inder Sharma, e-mail, 16 July 2013; the writer Jainendra Kumar would take a *phutphut* to reach CP and then walk to Tea House of ICH, also see Jesse Kochar, 'Promoting Phut-phutys', *The Hindu*, 10 September 2011, http://www.thehindu.com/opinion/open-page/promoting-phutphutys/article2442482.ece.

[90] Many of the Tea House goers would also go to have meals in the *dhaba* in the lane next to Regal, where one would have to take tea standing. *DTH*, 152; there was another shop in the lane across the street from Rivoli selling North Indian food and tea, ibid., 429.

would later shift to Mohan Singh Place and Shankar Market.[91] The *dhaba* began as a shack serving customers sitting on benches on the pavement. It became very popular in the 1950s as *Kake da Hotel* in the municipal market, CP by Amolak Ram Chopra migrating from Lahore where he used to run an eatery since 1931.

Among many private gatherings, Yusuf Dehlvi, the editor and publisher of the Urdu literary and film magazine *Shama*, used to host *mushairas*, *qawwalis*, dance, and music *mehfils* at Shama Kothi, his residence in the Diplomatic Enclave in New Delhi.[92] Similarly, most Punjabi writers, since the Partition mainly Delhi-based, used to meet at Pritam Singh's (of *Navyug*) residence where actors, artists, bureaucrats, journalists, novelists, poets and politicians among others used to meet.[93]

Thus when the Coffee Board decided to shift the location of ICH to Queensway (Janpath), in the heart of the capital in 1940, it did so in order to benefit from the increasing footfall in this still growing business hub. And also because it had to compete with the existing spaces of consumption. The property at 66 Janpath belonged to Jamunadas Puri who had purchased it in the 1930s.[94] In keeping with the other structures then coming up in CP, this building with high ceiling and thick walls was built for office purpose and fitted with modern amenities but had to be transformed in order to turn it into a space of consumption. The menu of the ICH initially did not differ much from that of Alps, Standard or Wenger's. In addition to hot and cold coffee, also served with cream, the menu included coffee ice-cream, omelette, scrambled egg on toast, cucumber/egg/chicken/mutton sandwich, apple/plum/tea-cake, fruit salad and soup.

[91] Baldev Vanshi, 'Sahityik Halchal Dilli Ki', *DTH*, 208–27 (220), 2009; Mohan Singh Place was opened in 1968.

[92] Sadia Dehlvi, 'Dilli Ka Dastarkhwan' (The Great Dining Spread of Delhi), in Khushwant Singh (ed.), *City Improbable*: *An Anthology of Writings on Delhi* (henceforth Singh ed., *City Improbable*), New Delhi: Penguin, 2001, 160–67; see Pranab Bardhan, *Smriti Kanduyan* (Memory Scratching), Kolkata: Ananda Publishers, 2013, for an *adda* of Delhi University teachers and other elites living near the campus.

[93] Renuka Singh, 'A World of Words', in Singh (ed.) *City Improbable*, 102–8.

[94] Rajeev Puri (grandson of Jamunadas) and his wife Nita Puri, interview, 21 October 2012.

If you purchased a cup of coffee here, you were served a plate of cashewnuts on the house.

The India Coffee House had several branches in Delhi: two in the Delhi University (DU) campus,[95] one in Kamla Nagar behind Kirori Mal College and three in Badarpur.[96] The outlets on the campus were extremely popular among students across departments, but if the one near the Dean's office discussed 'Bob Dylan, Bishan Bedi and Jayaprakash Narayan', The Delhi School of Economics (DSE) outlet seems to have concentrated on more serious subjects like the Nobel Prize winning economists Robert Solow and Simon Kuznets and French social scientists like Levi Strauss and Pierre Bourdieu.[97] The DSE outlet continued even after the other outlet near the Dean's Office in the campus and the one in Kamla Nagar closed down, the former in 1973. Arjun Dev recalled that both students and teachers used to go to the outlets, and in the entire campus, the Coffee House was the only place where male and female students could meet and sit at leisure till this too shut down in 1996.[98] In and around the DU campus were (and still are) a variety of places where one could have tea and snacks. Jai Prakash (popularly known as JP) continues to run his tea stall just outside the DSE coffee house with its masala tea, lemon tea, half tea still in high demand among the students. Both ICH and JP's used to attract a lot of students from other colleges on the campus and outside. Residents of that neighbourhood not connected with the university also used to come to ICH through this gate. That flow is now restricted since the gate at the back was closed a few years ago for the sake of security.[99] The teachers now have

[95] The first outlet in DU campus was opened soon after the one at CP. The outlet in DSE, announced in 1964, was opened sometime in 1965; 'Janpath Price Resisters Remain Divided', *The Statesman*, 10 November 1964.

[96] The Badarpur outlets were canteen run on franchise basis.

[97] Ramchandra Guha, 'A Salute to the Coffee House', *The Telegraph*, 29 September 2007.

[98] There was one outlet in the Jawaharlal Nehru University campus during 1975–78. In 2015 the Coffee Board opened an outlet in Aravalli International Guest House in the campus. Since 1996 the DSE outlet runs as a privately owned coffee house. For more on this Coffee House see Chapter Six.

[99] Sujit Thomas, P.G. student sociology, DU, interview, 28 February 2012.

air-conditioned rooms, so they do not go to ICH as often, instead get beverages and snacks delivered to their office.[100] There is also 'Nandu ki chai', a stall bearing the name of its founder, now owned by Bunni Lal outside the Law Faculty. These places successfully compete with 'Dada's coffee house'.[101]

After the Coffee Board decided to close down most of the outlets of ICH in 1955, the establishment on Janpath was sold to the descendants of Jamunadas who had passed away a couple of years prior to that. From 1957 till at least 1964 ICH Janpath was run privately by KARVISKA, a partnership formed by the four daughters-in-law of Jamunadas. In its checkered life in a fast-developing Delhi, ICH had to change its location several times. Moving from place to place each time, it lost groups of customers who, cherished the memory of their time at the previous location and unable to adapt to the new situation moved away to alternate, smaller places. The outlet at CP lost many of its clients after a movement that saw a new branch of the ICH opening in CP.[102]

Beginning with the *dastangos*, *mehfils*, *mushairas* Delhi in the late nineteenth and early twentieth century had a rich culture of public sociability. The first three were performance-oriented where the public were the audience. There were an array of eateries and restaurants where consumption of food was compulsory. *Qahwakhanas* were replaced by roadside tea-shops and by the time the ICH was set up, the memory of the Mughal coffee houses had faded. The tremendous popularity of coffee and ICH can be gauged from the fact that many public and private enterprises soon hurried to imitate the concept. The *cona* (filter) coffee-tea-snack shop begun by Hansraj Kalra in the E Block of the CP in 1942 came to be known as the United Coffee House which only developed into a full-fledged restaurant-cum-dining

[100] Ambarnath Gupta, interview, 28 February 2012.

[101] Hemani Bhandari, 'Delhi University: Few Seats but Food Aplenty', *TOI*, 1 July 2012.

[102] This movement is analysed in Chapter Five. Many of the people who used to visit this place found refuge in the Tea House, Ramkishor Dwivedi, 'Ek Tha Tea House,' in *DTH*, 359.

place in the 1950s.[103] Some time in the early 1950s, Daljit Singh, the younger brother of Khushwant Singh, a regular at ICH Janpath, opened a Tea House at the CP end of the Sansad Marg near the Regal Building. While ICH was a favourite with journalists, businessmen, lawyers, politicians, writers, insurance agents and small traders, the Tea House provided the space for *adda* to the Hindi, Punjabi and Urdu literati during the 1950s through to the 1970s, although, many of them were regulars at ICH too. This Tea House, more often referred to as coffee house, forms part of the current attempt at understanding the coffee-scenario in Delhi.

We shall turn to the role of coffee in this public sociability in Delhi in the following chapter.

ALLAHABAD

From the time that Akbar built his fort at the confluence of the Ganga and Yamuna, Prayag, as Illahabas or Allahabad, nourished a cosmopolitan culture sustaining both Hindus and Muslims among other ethnic groups. Prayag is also synonymous with the Kumbh Mela, the largest religious fair in the world and a place of pilgrimage for Hindus from ancient times. As a centre for distribution of trade between upper India and eastern India, and then as the capital of the Agra Province (1836–38), of the North Western Provinces (1858–77) and the United Provinces (1877–1920), the city of Allahabad continued to draw families of Bengalis, Gujarati Nagars, Kashmiri Pandits, Parsi and Punjabi Khatri entrepreneurs migrating from different parts of the country. The process was accelerated since, after the ruthless suppression of the local uprisings as part of the Rebellion of 1857, Allahabad became the capital. The northern part of the city, built on the razed ground once housing native villages got a total

[103] Initially it was a place to have coffee and the price difference between ICH and UCH was not much, and for many visitors to ICH, the question was, 'will it be ICH or UCH?' Keshav Malik, art critic and poet; editor of the now defunct weekly literary magazine *Thought* and of *Indian Literature*, a bi-monthly magazine published by the Sahitya Akademi, interview, 23 November 2012; Reginald Massey, e-mail, 16 July 2013.

makeover. Since the 1860s the city grew exponentially as a service centre. It attracted building contractors, hoteliers, house agents, general merchants and printers settling down and large numbers of Europeans and Eurasians occupying lower ranks in post and telegraph, press, railway and other departments of the government services.[104] The construction of the railway bridge over the Yamuna opened in 1865, connecting Allahabad to the right bank of the Hoogly in Calcutta with the left bank of the Yamuna to Delhi.[105]

The railroad running horizontally through the city divided it into two parts: the old traditional southern part and the new central and northern parts. The Grand Trunk Road which ran through the older traditional part of the city consisted of the middle class residential quarters of Lukarganj, Mirganj, Shahganj, Muthiganj and Kydganj with only a smattering of roadside shops. The newer parts of city including Civil Lines (Canning Town or Cannington), Cantonment, Police Lines, Colonelganj, Allenganj, Mumfordganj were the seats of the British Government and the modern institutions accompanying it.[106] The imposing buildings of the High Court (1866), Muir Central College (1872), Allahabad University (the Muir Central College and Kayastha Pathshala merged with it, 1887), All Saints Cathedral and other government and service buildings fixed the colonial seal on the face of the city.[107] The difference between the two parts of the

[104] For a thumb-nail but reliable account of the anti-British political activism in Allahabad in the wake of the Rebellion of 1857 see Badri Narayan Tiwari and Neelum Saran Gour, 'Vande Bharatam', in Neelum Saran Gour (ed.), *Allahabad: Where the Rivers Meet*, Marg, 2009, (henceforth, *Allahabad*); A. K. Mehrotra, 'The Descendants: An Introduction', in A. K. Mehrotra (ed.), *The Last Bungalow: Writings on Allahabad*, New Delhi: Penguin, 2007, 1–31.

[105] Daniel Headrick, *The Tentacles of Progress: Technology Transfer in the Age of High Imperialism, 1850–1940*, New York: OUP, 1988, 65–66.

[106] For a brief but captivating account of Allahabad in the 1950s and 1960s see the reminicences of Gyanranjan writer and editor of *Pahal*, 'Taramandal Ke Niche ek Awaragard', http://www.tadbhav.com/site/tadbhav_issue_25/taramandal_ke_nichea_ek_awaragard.pdf; see also his *Kabadkhana*, Nayi Dilli: Rajkamal, 2002 and Neelum Saran Gour, *Speaking of 62*, New Delhi: Penguin, 1995.

[107] Rajeswar Dayal, *A Life of Our Times*, Hyderabad: Orient Longman, 1998, 13–14.

city has been described as the different colours of the Ganga and the Yamuna. There was a concentration of the labouring classes in the southern part of the city while the professional classes began settling down north of the railway lines.[108] Since the early 1880s, the ward structure of the till then predominatly White Civil Lines was gradually changing, matched by an increase in the Indian electorate side by side with the inclusion of Indian professionals in the municipal electorate.[109] The first quarter of the twentieth century represented a change in the structure of power holding at the local level: professional men and publicists replaced old influential wealthy families as local leaders and intermediaries during communal tensions. While the first decade merchants and owners of real estate dominated the municipal board, during 1912–17 professional classes outnumbered them.[110] Till the 1950s, many Anglo-Indians serving the railways lived in the city and those who could prove their British ancestry could reside at the Bundhwah Club Trust property on Thornhill Road, and in the Railway Colony in the western part of the city.[111] If the university symbolized one pillar of modernization, the other pillars supporting the cause were the High Court and the English and vernacular publishing industry. Just like the European university teachers, Indian professionals in these sectors, often instructed in the West, were harbingers of modern European lifestyle in the town. University teachers and lawyers, Indian in increasing number, and migrating indigenous entrepreneurs began inhabiting the Civil Lines from the early twentieth century.[112] With important English language

[108] The unique comparison is provided by Gyanranjan in 'Taramandal'; for the distribution of the population see C.A. Bayly, *The Local Roots of Indian Politics: The Chris Bayly Omnibus*, New Delhi: OUP, 2011, esp., 39–43.

[109] Bayly, *The Local Roots*, 305.

[110] C.A. Bayly, '*Local Control* in Indian Towns: The Case of Allahabad 1880–1920', *Modern Asian Studies*, 5.4 (1971): 289–311, 'Local control'.

[111] Esther Mary Lyons, *Bitter Sweet Truth: An Autobiography*, NSW: Parker Pattison Publishing, 2000, 130–31; also see Saeed Jaffrey, *Saeed: An Actor's Journey*, London: Constable, 1998, 39–41, 45–48, for an impression of the life of the Anglo-Indian community in the city.

[112] It was in the Civil Lines that in 1900 Motilal Nehru built his residence Anand Bhavan. Sir Tej Bahadur Sapru and other lawyers practicing before the High Court began

dailies like *The Leader* and *The Pioneer* and publishing houses, like the Indian Press, the print media had a firm footing in the city.[113]

To what extent did the increasing popularity of the city among the indigenous elite using these institutions as stepping stones to a glamourous career in the civil service or law affect public culture? According to Bayly, the secular and the inclusive culture of Allahabad owed to the shared Indo-Persian cultural traditions of the old provincial communities settling in the town.[114] As we have seen above, this composite culture was prevalent in other cities of northern India and had been fostered by the coexisting multiple ethnic and religious groups. The tradition of Persian and Urdu poetry writing in Allahabad can be traced back at least to the eighteenth century. By the 1830s, the place boasted one hundred full-time poets; Urdu poets from other places attended *mushairas* organized by poets residing here.[115] In the early twentieth century there were at least seven Urdu newspapers which, together with existing and upcoming literary magazines, promoted new writing. The opening of the Urdu department at the University and the setting up of the Hindustani Academy, both in the 1920s, were aimed at furthering the cause of Urdu.[116] The Muslim Boarding House used to organize an annual *mushaira* drawing poets

---

living in this part of the city. Anand Bhavan became the locus of many important political meetings, see Bachchan, *Afternoon* 323; Neelam Saran Gour, e-mail, 24 May 2013. Publishers like Chintamani Ghosh of Indian Press and A.K. Banerjee of Wheelers & Co., Shiv Buksh Raye of B.N. Rama fame are just a few names having their establishment in Civil Lines. Bengali migrant professionals set up colonies in Allenganj, Georgetown, Mumfordganj and Tagore Town, Arindam Roy, interview, 14 September 2013. Many Bengali families were to be found in Lukerganj as well, see Ballabh Dobhal, 'Ekhane Shesh: Ekhane Ontim', in *Kaise Kaise Log*, New Delhi: Maneesha Prakashan, 2009, 10–13; Sanjay Joshi, documentary maker, interview, 2 October 2013.

[113] See Chapter Four for more on the publishing industry in Allahabad but note that working for *The Pioneer*, Rudyard Kipling lived in Allahabad during 1887–89.

[114] C. A. Bayly, *The Local Roots*, 119.

[115] Shamsur Rahman Faruqi, 'Urdu and Persian literature in Allahabad', September 2007, http://www.columbia.edu/itc/mealac/pritchett/00fwp/srf/txt_allahabad.html, 147–55.

[116] The purpose behind creating the Academy was to bridge the gulf between Hindi and Urdu. *Hindustani*, journal published by the Hindustani Academy was in Urdu script, Mehr Afshan Farooqi, (n.d.) 'Glimpses of Literary Allahabad' (unpublished paper).

from all over India.[117] The heritage of Urdu writing in the town was carried forward through the writings of Akbar Ilahabadi, Munshi Premchand, Ahmed Ali, Muhammad Hasan Askari, Raghupati Sahay (1896–1982) writing under his nom de plume Firaq Gorakhpuri and Upendranath Ashk among others.

The diversified population of the city had various spaces for leisurely interaction. The Allahabad Club, Cosmopolitan Club, Gymkhana Club and the likes, initially a monopoly of Europeans, later allowed access to a select few natives, while the United Club opened its doors to Anglo-Indians. By the middle of the twentieth century, the Railway Coral Club and Thornhill Club were popular joints for the latter community.[118] In the early 1930s, Tej Pratap Singh, landholder of Kothi, began the Adelphi Club for the indigenous elite including members of the princely families and landowners. With its tennis courts, rooms for rummy and bridge, bar and residential accommodation for well-to-do visitors, the club was a hive of activity for some time.[119]

Adda was part of Allahabad's culture. There were places at diverse locations in the city from at least the colonial times for informal gatherings. One of such old-time hangouts was at Lokenath Market in Chowk, a place known for traditional food and drinks like *ramdane ki laddu*, *lassi*, *aphim ke laddu*, *dahi kachori*, etc. The entire stretch of Lokenath Gali, the erstwhile Sarai Meer Khan, was dotted with shops selling varieties of *chaat*, *dahi-jalebi*, *kulfi-falooda*, and for the connoisseur *bhang-kulfi*, *bhang lassi* and *bhang-thandai*.[120] It was here that Mitthulal, a bankrupt money-lender from Agra, familiar with Motilal Nehru, set up in the early years of the twentieth century his *Hari ki namkeen*, a shop famous for its *masala samosas* in which the usual potato-stuffing was replaced by a mixture of spices. This

[117] Ibid.

[118] Lyons, *Bitter Sweet,* 108; John Harrison, 'For Company and Queen', in *Allahabad*, 73–85; Hill, 'The Young Kipling' provide an attractive survey of the European world at the place.

[119] The club however was not a commercial success and was temporarily transformed into a students' hostel; see Bachchan, *Afternoon*, 328–30.

[120] Gyanranjan seems to have preferred this bhang lassi to alcohol, see Kalia, *Ghalib*, 153.

lane with its attractions was a gathering point for high and low in the town including administrators, Congress leaders, luminaries of Hindi and Urdu literature like Raghupati Sahay, lawyers and others. There was a very popular *adda* at this market especially for the artisan and working class, connected, for example, with boat-making. Khatris (mostly Arya Samajis) from the Punjab who had settled down in the quarters near Lokenath Market, patronized these outlets.[121] The sweet shops in this locality were popular with song writers and performers who gathered there. From the 1940s through to the 1970s there was an *adda* there attracting literati like Gopi Krishna Gopesh.[122] The office of the magazine *Chand* at Lokenath crossing was known for its revolutionary connection. Not only did the magazine publish news on nationalist activities, but writers and distributors of nationalist pamphlets also used to visit this place and other Daraganj shops like Qadir ka Restaurant.[123] Daraganj was an area in pre-colonial Allahabad with a literary public sphere. Alongside the tradition of story-telling in small gatherings, the area also had small printing presses. Qadir ka Restaurant attracted large crowds for its milk, *bhang-lassi*, *kachori* and sweets. Sumitranandan Pant had a huge following at this restaurant where he used to consume on credit.[124] In another literary circle the *Rasik Mandal,* Ramaprasad Tripathi, Ramshankar Shukla 'Rasal' who worked for *The Pioneer*, and Ramnarayan Chaturvedi used to meet near the Chowk where they discussed *Braja Bhasha* poetry.[125] Writing in the late 1930s, Srivastava noted that while the Hindi Lekhak Sangh had been launched in 1935 for the progress of contemporary Hindi literature, *mushairas* had often been held during the preceding one and half decades and *kavi*

[121] Lalit Joshi, professor, Department of History, Allahabad University, interview, 23 October 2012.

[122] Sriprakash Mishra, retired police officer and writer in Hindi, interview, 26 October 2012.

[123] Ibid.

[124] Gyanranjan, 'Taramandal'.

[125] Saligram Srivastava, *Prayag Pradeep*, Illahabad: Hindustani Academy, 1937, 168; I am grateful to Lalit Joshi, for drawing my attention to this publication; Orsini, *Hindi Public Sphere*.

sammelans or poets' conferences were also organized regularly there since the middle of that decade.[126]

With the sprouting of places of informal congregation like Jagati's and the India Coffee House in the northern part of the city where the literati met, the geographical division of Allahabad seems to have blurred to some extent. Most of the writers in Hindi visiting the ICH lived in Lukerganj. Civil Lines, where India Coffee House was launched, was part of the colonial town planned along the usual checkerboard or grid pattern with radial roads punctuated by squares and circles common to urban planning in the West. This part had mainly bungalows or single storeyed, buildings with red tile roofs occupying the central area on spacious plots, demarcated by hedges or boundary walls separating them from the sidewalks of the wide avenues.[127] The University became a residential educational institution in 1922. During his long tenure at the university, Pandit Amarnatha Jha, the reputed scholar of English, both as professor of English at Muir Central College and as the vice chancellor of the University (for three terms during 1938–46), patronized the cause of the intellectual and literary environment of the town. With polyglot members like Jha, P. Dastoor, Harivansh Rai Bachchan and Raghupati Sahay who wrote under the pen mane Firaq Gorakhpuri, Jha invited Sahay, a Persian and Urdu poet, to join the university in Allahabad.[128] The University's English department went a long way to nurture the multi-lingual literary milieu of Allahabad. Like the elitaire Friday Club launched by Amarnatha Jha for those interested in English literature,[129] its vernacular counterpart Thursday Club set up by Ajaz Husain, the Hindi Parishad, Oriental Society and the Urdu

[126] Srivastava, *Prayag*, 168.

[127] Ujagir Singh, *Allahabad: A Study in Urban Geography*, Varanasi: Banaras Hindu University, 1966, 51–52.

[128] Hakumat Sarin, 'Firaq Gorakhpuri: A Documentary', Films Division, GOI, 16 December 2012, https://www.youtube.com/watch?v=4z32SDnb_3g.

[129] The actor Saeed Jaffrey had been a member of this club, Jaffrey, *Saeed*, 39; however although Pandit Jha patronized Bachchan in his career, the latter never made part of this august gathering, and had no clue to the essence of this exclusivity, Bachchan, *Afternoon*, 351–52.

Association with their office inside the University campus, and the Hindi Sahitya Sammelan that had its office in Allahabad since 1911, nourished the atmosphere for creative writing in Hindi and Urdu by encouraging interaction among teachers and students.[130]

Jagati's Restaurant, a tea shop near the university campus on the University Road, was a popular space for informal interaction in the northern part of the town. Jagati was an entrepreneur from Kumaon (currently in Uttarakhand) who went to Allahabad at the end of the nineteenth century in search of fortune. In course of time, he became the city's busiest caterer serving all the important families there.[131] Jagati's illustrious cleintele comprised literary figures and university teachers, including Harivansh Rai Bachchan, Dr Dustoor, Vijaydev Narayan Sahi, Firaq Gorakhpuri from the Department of English and writers like Sumitranandan Pant, Dharamvir Bharati (1926–97), Bhagwati Charan Verma who were regular customers of the tea shop.[132] Bhagwati Charan was familiar with the place as a student of the University in the early 1920s,[133] and the presence of Verma and other writers attracted later day students to the place where tea was served in a pot containing about two cups of tea.[134] This shop, active till about 1975 was at the height of its popularity when the Coffee Board opened an outlet of the ICH in Allahabad. Although the geographical and social divide between the University and Civil Lines

[130] Singh, *Prayag*, 131, 168; Keshav Chandra Varma, *Parimal*: *Smritiyan Aur Dastabez* (Parimal: Memories and Documents), Allahabad: Pradeep Prakashan, 2003, 35–36; Farooqi, 'Glimpses'.

[131] He was the caterer at the wedding of Motilal Nehru; interview, Lalit Joshi, 23 October 2012. For a nice anecdote involving the place see, V.S. Datta, 'Allahabad University Completes 125 Years: A Big Salute to our Masters', 24 September 2012, http://activeindiatv.com/editorials/476-allahabad-university-completes-125–years--a-big-salute-to-our-masters?tmpl=component&type=raw.

[132] As a student Bhagwati Charan Verma used to go there with his friends, Naresh Mehta, *Pradakshina: Apne Samay Ki* (Circumumbulations of My Times), Illahabad: Illahabad Sangrahalay, 2001, 155.

[133] Bhagwati Charan Verma's novel *Teen Varsh* was dedicated to Manohar Lal Sah Jagati, the proprietor of the shop. The novel begins with the description of the place seen through the eyes of a student coming from Jhansi, to study at the University.

[134] A gratis refill of hot water would ensure the supply of two more cups of tea, albeit weaker; Hemendra Shankar Saxena, 'In Eastmancolor', in *Allahabad*, 107–13.

on one side and the Town and Daraganj on the other described by Orsini in the high noon of the Empire was further smudged especially in the post-Independence period, the accompanying division in the literary sphere between English and Hindi was kept alive.

The question becomes more complicated around the issue who is a proper Allahabadi. An example would help us understand the nature of this divide. In the course of my field research in Allahabad I heard one of my interlocutors dismissing *The Last Bungalow* edited by A.K. Mehrotra on the ground that none of the contributors to the volume was from Allahabad. A week later, another person considering himself an authority on, and insider of the town, communicated to me dismissing the book in the same vein. When I began reading the book later, I was reminded of the comments, and dismayed, I asked the latter if he had seen the said book before commenting on it. He replied in the negative. While Mehrotra writes profusely on Allahabad and the world outside associates him with the place, his disenchantment with post-colonial Allahabad and its vernacular littérateurs has earned him the status of non-Allahabadi. The divide between the two literary spheres has a long history according to one teacher of English at St Mary's College; another teacher of English at the University suggested that some writers in Hindi 'carry a chip on their shoulder', (conversations 11 and 12 September 2013 respectively). I have record of all the communications; but since this is a sensitive issue, shall not disclose the identity of the persons. Consider that Upendranath Ashk who migrated to the city from Julunder in the late 1940s felt the hostility of the local writers towards him, a Punjabi writer writing in Hindi. (Daisy Rockwell, *Upendranath Ashk: A Critical Biography,* New Delhi: Katha, 2004, 5 and chapter 2). Allahabadi writers used to call Ravindra Kalia and Satish Jamali as 'disease from outside' (*agantuk vyadhian*), Neelabh, *Gyanranjan ke bahane* (A Memoir), Nayi Dilli: Nayi Kitab, 2012.

Launched in 1937 by Kishori Mohan De from Krishnagar in West Bengal, Lucky Sweet Mart known especially for its varieties of Bengali sweets was another place that attracted a medley of personalities from a cross-section of society. It was a favourite haunt of H.N. Bahuguna, the Allahabadi Congress leader, who became the Chief Minister of Uttar Pradesh. Their *samosa* and *pakora* with chutney at 1 anna a piece and 2 annas a plate respectively, made the place affordable for the students flocking here. Presently it is visited by members of all the state's political parties, families and students, however *adda* is no longer allowed here.[135]

In addition to these public spaces of sociability, there were private gatherings.

Amarnatha Jha, a connoisseur of Hindi and Urdu poetry, used to organize tea parties and *mushairas* or literary gatherings in Sanskrit, Persian and Maithili, at his home. Sarojini Naidu, Harivansh Rai Bachchan, Pant, Gangaprasad Pande, Samsher, Narendra Sharma, Ramkumar Varma, Bhagwaticharan Verma and others formed an integral part of these gatherings due to their appreciation for such critical literary discussions (image *mushaira* organized by Jha).

Sridhar Pathak, Sumitranandan Pant and others used to meet on a regular basis at Pant's residence. It is said that Pathak, who lived in Lukerganj, would send his horse-driven carriage to fetch Pant from his residence. They would spend a couple of hours conversing before Pant went back on the same carriage.[136] After he joined the university, Bachchan used to organize a poetry reading event called 'Nishant', or 'night's ending', at his place on the last Saturday of every month.[137] During the 1950s and 1960s colourful and 'doctrinal (*matwali*) literary disputes' and 'unconventional liaisons' took place at the 'camp' (*morcha*) of Upendranath Ashk.[138] This tradition of private gatherings of poets and writers in and outside Allahabad continued

[135] S. K. Garg, advocate Allahabad High Court, who went to the university in the late 1960s never went to ICH, but went to Lucky Sweet Mart, interview, 22 October 2012; Md. Naseem (Cong-I) used to go to both India Coffee House and Lucky Sweet Mart, interview, 22 October 2012. The place is now run by the third generation siblings Debashis and Abhishek Dey, interview, 12 September 2013.

[136] Harish Trivedi, 'Prayagvad in Hindi Writing', in *Allahabad*, 138–45,' 139; Sanjay Joshi, interview, 2 October 2013.

[137] The group comprising mostly Bachchan's (ex-) students recited poetry and discussed literary topics till the day-break. This group kept on meeting when he was away in England for two years during 1952–54, Bachchan, *Afternoon*, 340–41.

[138] Gyanranjan, 'Taramandal'.

in the late 1960s and 1970s, often patronized by government officials with a keen interest in literature, like Vibhuti Narain Rai, an IPS officer of the 1975 batch.[139] When Faiz Ahmed Faiz visited Allahabad in 1981, a gathering was organized by poets and writers at Rai's residence in his honour.[140]

The literary movements like Progressive Writers' Association (PWA) and *Parimal* too had their own gatherings and such get-togethers were organized by rotation in the house of one of the members of the core group.[141] Lakshmikant Varma, a member of *Parimal* was the initiator of another circle of *Kayasth* socialists and small writers in a *dhaba* (close to Tara Hotel) near Rambagh railway station where they would meet almost daily to discuss literary, political and other issues; this gathering was active from 1962 up to the Emergency. Another such gathering in the later period was that of *Vaichariki* (1980) initiated by Amar Goswami of Maya Press. Other members of the group included Sriprakash Mishra, Sinheswar Singh, Deviprasad Mishra, Rajendra Kumar and a few others who met fortnightly to discuss new writings including those of its own members. The group still meets, but is not so creative or powerful any more.[142]

Mahatma Gandhi (M.G.) Marg, running parallel to the railway track to its south, is still a major arterial road cutting through different intersections. Civil Lines, with its theatres, especially Palace Theatre and Plaza Talkies, and with shops selling from chewing gum, kites to automobiles, several large and small eateries, was the major area for shopping and social outing.[143] Walking along the wide streets of Civil Lines must have been a pleasing experience till the late 1960s

[139] Kalia, *Ghalib*, passim.

[140] A detailed account of this visit is to be found in Kalia's *Ghalib*, 184–98, see also his 'When Faiz visited Allahabad', *Hindi: Language, Discourse, Learning* (online journal), vol. 6 (2011), Oct-Dec. 58–68, http://hindivishwa.org/pdf/publication/hindi%20oct-dec-11.pdf.

[141] See Chapter Four for more on these two groups.

[142] Interview, Doodhnath Singh and Sriprakash Mishra, 25 and 26 October 2012.

[143] Lyons, *Bitter Sweet*, 98, 130; Saxena, 'In Eastmancolour'. In its previous incarnation, Plaza Talkies was Regent theatre provided with a bar and a dance floor. A property of the descendants of Chintamani Ghosh, the building now houses Rajkiran theatre, interview, Arindam Ghosh, Indian Press, 23 January 2012.

when the number of cars plying the streets of Allahabad was limited to ten or fifteen, and, barring the *ekkas* and *tongas*, the main means of transport was bicycle.[144] Launched in 1945, ICH in Allahabad was initially housed in a spacious bungalow behind the Mercury Range, near the crossing of Clive Road and Canning Road (B.M. Mehta Road and M.G. Marg respectively).[145] With an opening towards M.G. Marg, the bungalow was visible from the road. There was a huge, shady tamarind tree on the sidewalk with a *paan* shop under it. It was a cosy cottage with several rooms and a separate section for family and women as well as a room near the kitchen for students who wanted to study there undisturbed by the brouhaha in the main hall.[146] At least for some time, the ICH seems to have been housed in a building on the other side of the street opposite the Palace Building before it moved again to its current location at Darbari Building.[147]

Built in the late nineteenth century, Darbari Building in the heart of Civil Lines housed different offices and stores at different points of time. One of the few surviving bungalows in the area, is a longish structure with a light pink exterior consisting of two conjoined bungalows. The covered veranda supported by columns and a portico in front of the central part was originally a drive-in provision store styled by Clark & Hathways. This larger bungalow along with a smaller bungalow and precincts at the back, were acquired by Raibahadur R. N. Darbari, a medical doctor by profession, who

[144] Venita Lyall Banerjee, on the forum Allahabad Civil Lines Nostalgic Memories (ACLNM), 9 May 2014; as a result of the encroachment of the side-walks and (where they exist) pavements by unauthorized semi-permanent structures, pedestrians have to share the road with cars, motor bikes, auto-rickshaws, rickshaws and cycles. Almost every middle class family I came across in Allahabad owns at least one car; however, lack of proper public transport within the city makes conveyance from one part of the city to the other cumbersome, see Rachna Singh, 'Those Civil Line Girls', weblog, 4 June 2014, http://rachnaunedited.wordpress.com/2014/06/04/those-civil-lines-girls/. In order to travel from Chatham Lines to Civil Lines, one would still have to take a rickshaw or shared auto rickshaw up to the Hanuman Temple (near the main bus stand). From there you could walk or take a rickshaw to your destination in Civil Lines.

[145] Saxena, 'In Eastmancolor.'

[146] Ibid.

[147] When Grover visited Allahabad in 1951, he went to the coffee house in this building, interview, Dinesh Chandra Grover, 22 October 2012.

changed the building from a store into premises for rent.[148] For some time, an office of the Muir [Cotton] Mills of Kanpur and an agency of the Indian National Airways Co., were established here. The ICH finally moved to the building named after its owner in 1958.[149] The year that ICH shifted to the left wing of this building, Dinesh Chandra Grover, who had joined Rajkamal Prakashan in 1951, set up its Allahabad branch in the hall of the building's other wing. Om Prakash, the owner of Rajkamal also came to live in Allahabad around this time. In December 1960, when the decision was taken to close down the Allahabad branch of Rajkamal, Dinesh took it over and began Lokbharti in 1961, which is still at this location since that time.[150] The portico had been partitioned to house offices including that of Remington Rand (the part currently occupied by Anand Rathi, a share-broking and finance company), and Central Excise and Customs (where now New India Assurance Company has its office). Sometime in 1967–68, the landlord divided the hall housing the insurance company vertically to create another room and a floor above, renting to Dinesh Chandra of Lokbharti, who used the space as godown till he sold the firm to Ashok Maheshwari of Rajkamal Prakashan. Ramesh Chandra Grover, the elder brother of Dinesh Grover, now looks after the branch of Rajkamal upstairs.[151] Next to the insurance company is the office-cum-showroom of Neelabh

[148] Raibahadur Dr RN Darbari who paid Rs 50,000 for the building, continued to practice in Johnstonganj. Neelabh, e-mail, 15 August 2012.

[149] Officially, the transfer took place a year later, Diwakar Pandey, 'Kaffee Ke Chuskiyon Mein Simte Hain Dheron Afsane', *Hindustan Times*, 2007. I am grateful to Vaibhab Maini for drawing my attention to this article. On the day of the inauguration potato wafers were distributed among the visitors, input Sudhir Singhal on the forum ACLNM, 12 May 2014. The ICH pays Rs 22,000 for the wing it occupies and the premises in front to P.K. Darbari, the current owner, interview, P. K. Darbari, October 2012. In view of the pace of development in the area around, but for the aura and memory associated, the Coffee House in Allahabad would have shared the same fate as that of the ICH in Bangalore and the outlet in Anna's Arcade, Trivandrum.

[150] In partnership with Kadam Kumar Jain; interview, Dinesh Chandra Grover, 22 October 2012. The website of the Rajkamal Group of publications however cites 1954 as the year when Lokbharti started.

[151] Ibid., Neelabh, e-mail, 15 August 2012.

Prakashan (1949) that was set up here in October 1959.[152] Taking the bookshops, publishing houses, the Coffee House, eateries and other fancy shops and the theatres together, this area in those days seems to have been epicentre of the town with an ambience similar to Calcutta's College Street and old New Market.

Darbari Building had a very different appearance in the middle of the twentieth century when India Coffee House moved its base there. Right in front across the space of the entire building was a large sprawling lawn with a hedge fencing separating it from the sidewalks of the street. According to Naresh Roy of El Chico, it was perhaps keeping the social norms of the city in view that the 'family section' of ICH was opened on the ground floor of the double-storeyed pink building, built in 1936. During its heyday in the following decades, the smaller lawn in the space between Darbari Building and the 'family section', where the foundation of a hotel was laid in 2012, had also been rented by ICH. And the evening gatherings of visitors—especially during the summer months—took place round the tables laid out in this twin-lawn.[153] Currently, the large concrete building with shops and offices that replaced the open space in the 1990s not only blocks the view of most of the original bungalow in the background, but also affects the business of ICH.

Parallel to the India Coffee House, were private restaurants in Civil Lines retailing liquid coffee. In the 1940s and 1950s, Malani's Café stood facing the Palace Building.[154] Migrating to Allahabad in

[152] Kaushalya Ashk used to run this publishing house owned by her husband Upendranath Ashk. Neelabh, 'Addebaaj Shahar: Illahabad Ka Kaffee House', in Neelabh (ed.), *Hindi Sahitya ka Maukhik Itihaas* (An Oral History of Hindi Literature), 4 volumes, Nayi Dilli: Shilpayan, vol. 2. A small room in front of this defunct shop functions as the office of the secretary of ICH.

[153] Dinesh Chandra Grover, Lokbharti, interview, 23 October 2012. On my visit to the site in October 2012, I found construction work had begun at this site and during my visit in September 2013 the two-storeyed structure allegedly destined to be a hotel was ready.

[154] The first ever literary meet organized by *Parimal* began at 7.00 am on an Autumn Sunday in the paddy-green interior of Malani's Café, preceded by a collective breakfast with tea there, Keshav Chandra Varma, *Parimal: Smritiyan aur Dastabez* (Memories and Documents of Parimal), Allahabad: Pradeep Prakashan, 2003, 25.

the 1850s, Shiv Baksh Raye opened a general merchandise provisions shop styled B.N. Rama & Co. in the Chowk area in 1890. This shop moved to the Civil Lines in 1928 to reopen in a building leased from the Tandons aka Bachchajis. Within a couple of years after the construction of the Lucky Range here in 1940, Rama's Bar and Restaurant was opened by the Roys (Raye) at the crossing of Albert Road and Canning Road.[155] With a shady triangular stretch of lawn in front, B.N. Rama's Café, a space popular for its cold coffee and the juice of *falsa* or *Grewia asiatica* was often visited by littérateurs.[156] While Malani's served the usual coffee and tea, at Rama's one could opt for alcoholic beverages too, and the juke box here added a special attraction.[157] The success of this bar coupled with the popularity of the ICH must have inspired Ganpat and his son Ganesh Roy to launch El Chico (1964), a rather fancy coffee house in the market opposite the Palace Hall.[158] With its 'dimly lit interior, very comfortable sofas [....] and a picturesque [....] false ceiling' El Chico was designed after the likes of La Bohéme in CP in New Delhi and offering varieties of coffee, tea, continental and Indian food, it attracted the Anglophile, status-conscious university students and the cream of the Allahabad society wishing to enjoy the comfort and exclusivity. On his visits to Allahabad, Jawaharlal Nehru could be seen at this place.[159] Kwality

[155] Lala Madhav Prasad and Manmohan Das Tandon, one of the most prominent and richest families of the time purchased this large property comprising a large bungalow and a sprawling garden. Different parts of the building were rented out to the Roy family, Dr R. N. Mullick, Tayeb & Sons, cloth merchants etc. As the business kept growing, in addition to general provisions the business of the Roys extended in scope and magnitude to include the agency for Godrej steel furniture ltd. and typewriters, and later the products of Nestlé, e-mail, Naresh Roy, 28 May 2014.

[156] When he moved to Allahabad in the mid 1950s, Naresh Mehta used to go to BN Rama's café to meet others and it was there that he met Dharamvir Bharti for the first time, Mehta, *Pradakshina,* 160.

[157] Neelabh, *Gyanranjan*, 2.

[158] The beautification drive prior to the Purna Kumbh in 2013 saw this market gone and a splinter new double storeyed classy restaurant added to the original café of El Chico is an indication of the popularity and reputation of the place now run by the four brothers Ganesh, Ramesh, Naresh and Rakesh Roy.

[159] Foreign dignitaries as well as the Indian elite are at home at El Chico. Whenever Rahul Gandhi is in the town, he goes to El Chico. Amitabh Bachchan

Restaurant known for its classy atmosphere and upmarket quality food and ice-cream, Naug Bar, Peshawari, Nankin Bar and Restaurant were other places for family eat outs. Ravindra Kalia reminisced in his memoir that rising poets in the late fifties and early sixties used to meet at Murari's Sweets on the ground floor of the building that housed Saraswati Press, with the office of the magazine *Kahani* above it at the crossing of Civil Lines.

In spite of the existence of various types of spaces for public sociability, the ICH became very popular in Allahabad as well. Naresh Roy recalled that after El Chico was launched, although it offered *cona* coffee at Rs 5 per head, it had to compete with the ICH by offering coffee at 23 paise a cup.[160] El Chico's posh, yet quiet ambience attracted the Anglicized elite quite unlike the ICH with its noisy clientele. Subaltern competitors such as roadside stalls were a more serious threat to the ICH than El Chico. Located en route to the ICH, Amber Coffee House (1971) and New South Indian Coffee House (1980) 'misled' tourists looking for the Indian Coffee House to stop for a cup of coffee there.[161]

CALCUTTA

Compared to Delhi and Allahabad, Calcutta is younger and if the familiarity with coffee for places like Delhi and Lucknow can be dated back to the Mughals, Calcutta, will in all likelihood, associate it with the Europeans.[162] As the seat of the East India Company's government, and then as the second capital of the British Empire, and again as the most important port in British India, this 'City of Palaces' was at the height of its glory in the early twentieth century.

held his press conferences at this place. Interview, Ramesh Chandra Grover, 24 January 2012; also Arindam Roy, 'El Chico: A Way of Life with City Elite', *TOI* (Allahabad), 31 March 2000.

[160] A.K. Mehrotra refers to this place without naming it in his poem on the owner's family, 'The Roys', in his *The Last Bungalow*, 266–69.

[161] See Chapter Six on this.

[162] I am yet to find a reference to coffee in India prior to the advent of the East India Companies though.

For social get-togethers there were many clubs, but these typical institutions of the Raj were exclusively meant for Europeans. The Bengal Club opened its doors to Indians only after 1947. The constitution of the Saturday Club opened in 1875 barred the entry of 'Orientals of Asiatic Origin'.[163] The non-racial Calcutta Club was opened in 1907 to accommodate natives. Women were not allowed to be members of the Tollygunge Club (1895) till as late as 1970. Benjamin Cohen's research on British Indian ladies' clubs operating in India since the late nineteenth century began admitting men as guests only in the late 1930s.[164] However, like the men's clubs, the women's clubs also drew women from distinguished and 'more advanced' families.[165]

Serving the expatriates, were the upmarket restaurants like Federico Peliti's Bakery and Confectionery (1870) Chung Wah (1881), Firpo's (1925), Flury's (1927), and Magnolia and hotels like Grand and Great Eastern. These clubs and hotels naturally offered their customers coffee. Besides, there were many tea shops selling 'one cup of tea, 2 slices of toast and a "mamlet" of two eggs, all for 2 annas' for people with a small purse.[166]

With the Calcutta University, Medical College, Presidency College and Hindu School located on College Street, the entire area was an important hub in Central Calcutta in the late nineteenth century. Mahabodhi Society was located at the other end of College Square; not very far in Bidhan Sarani was the office of the Sadharan Brahma

[163] Chanchal Sarkar recalled an anecdote related to this rule, 'One day my friend whose father was a doctor and a friend of the German doctor (of Jewish origin, fleeing to India during World War II), found him sobbing uncontrollably in his father's consulting room. Apparently the doctor had been called for an interview to the Club and then told he did not qualify because of his Asiatic origin. See 'Why Meddle Around with History so Ham-Handedly?', *The Sunday Tribune*, 17 June 2001, http://www.tribuneindia.com/2001/20010617/spectrum/speaking.htm.

[164] Benjamin Cohen, 'Networks of Sociability: Women's Club in Colonial and Postcolonial India', in *Frontiers: A Journal of Women's Studies*, Special Issue: Women's Clubs at Home and in the World, vol. 30, (2009), no. 3, 169–195.

[165] Ibid.

[166] Radha Prasad Gupta, 'Amader Jubakaler *Adda*: Jhakidarshan', in Das, *Kolkatar Adda,* 39–56, 'A Glimpse of the Adda of Our Youth'; (henceforth Gupta, 'Amader Jubakaler Adda').

Samaj. Albert Hall, on No. 15 Bankim Chatterjee Street, was at the first crossing on the left upon entering the street from the north. It had been a public hall since 1876 and since the late 1940s, the Radical Humanist Association had its office there on the second floor.[167] In and around College Street were schools, and colleges affiliated to the university. A thriving publishing industry developed there catering to a large clientele including these institutions, which made College Street indispensible to university teachers, law-makers, medical practitioners, students, book-binders, writers and others professionally connected with the area.

Even in 1943, the year the notorious Famine crippled the economy of Bengal, Chowringhee, the heart of colonial Calcutta, was a 'boom town'. While dying people lay in front of Firpo's and the price of rice, the staple, sky-rocketed, the price of the three-course lunch at that elite place remained the same and spaces and opportunities were galore where soldiers of diverse ethnic origin could spend the liquid cash they earned during the War on prostitutes, food, alcohol, and merrymaking.[168]

Although outside Bengal, Bengalis are synonymous with *roshogolla*, cottage cheese balls cooked in light syrup, the numerous varieties of savoury snacks—the non-vegetarian varieties often a combination of European and indigenous kitchen—speak a legion about their taste.[169] Catering to the taste of the natives, many eateries and tea stalls sprang up in north and central Calcutta from the late nineteenth century onwards. As some of these places still exist, it is possible to compare the infrastructure of such places with that of the India Coffee House. The oldest surviving one close to College Street is Putiram's Sweets on Mirzapur (Surya Sen) Street. Opened by Putiram Modak in 1889, the

[167] Sibnarayan Ray, 'Ponchasher Doshoke Paikpara-r Adda' (Adda at Paikpara in the 1950s), in *Bangalir Adda*, 13–32 (14).

[168] Tapan Ray Chaudhuri, *Bangalnama* (Autobiography), Kolkata: Ananda, 2007, 127.

[169] Best examples are chop and cutlet (finely chopped or a thin piece respectively of meat, fish or vegetables coated with breadcrumbs going into a batter before it is deep fried). Devilled Egg is a version of Mughlai Nargisi kofta. In the Bengali variety the yolk of the hard-boiled egg is taken out and put back after it is mixed with spices. The whole egg gets a coating of mashed potato and deep fried after it is battered. For details on cosmopolitan food consumption practices in colonial Bengal, see Ray, *Culinary Culture*.

place is now in the hands of the fifth generation. Selling traditional sweets and snacks at a reasonable price, the approximately 20-square metre floor space between the counter and the sitting space with four marble-top four-seater tables, draws a continuous flow of customers, including students. No hot beverage was ever served here with the food, only water was.[170] Basanta Cabin had three outlets, one opposite the Medical College on College Street, the second inside the College Street Market and the third on Bidhan Sarani. The YMCA restaurant at the corner of Bhavani Dutta Lane that also housed Public Restaurant and Gyan Babu's tea shop at the crossing of Harrison (Mahatma Gandhi) Road and Bidhan Sarani are all history now. These places were a favourite with the students who dropped in for a quick bite and to satiate their thirst for tea. Many recall fondly Gyan Babu's shop for the quality of its tea. 'Regulars' at the Coffee House would go to one of these places for a cheaper bite consisting mainly of toast, fried egg or omelette—popularly called 'mamlet'—and at times even *handi kabab* before returning to their table at the ICH.[171] One of the early places in this area surviving the test of time is Favourite Cabin in Mirzapur Street. It was begun in 1918 by the ex-Swadeshi activist brothers Nutan Chandra and Gaur Chandra Barua of the Bengali Buddhist community from Bailatali village near the Sankha River in Chittagong, Bangladesh. Selling tea at one anna (1/16th of a rupee) a cup, and toast at 2 paise, this shop soon became the favourite haunt of Biren Majumdar, the Congress leader from Dhaka. Revolutionary leaders like Ambika Chakraborty, Ganesh Ghosh and Surya Sen, and poets and others gathered here for tea, and of course *adda*.[172] The shop's list of patrons includes names of literary giants like Dadathakur (Sarat Pandit), Bibhutibhushan Bandyopadhyay and Kazi Nazrul Islam in the past to that of the social activist Medha Patkar, to name a few. The importance of this shop is testified in the reminiscences of Achintya Kumar Sengupta:[173]

170 Abhijit Modak (owner), interview, 24 July 2011; the original floor space was halved and one half was rented out now housing a different shop.

171 Gyanbabu's shop had been open for about hundred years before it closed down; Gupta, 'Amader'.

172 Staff reporter, 'Favourite Haunt', *The Statesman*, 1 May 1977.

173 Achintya Kumar Sengupta, *Kallol Jug* (The Kallol Era), Calcutta: D.M. Library, 1960 (1366), 64.

The members of the *Kallol* (a post-Tagore literary movement) group used to visit the Favourite Cabin on Mirzapur Street for tea. They would sit in a tight circle round the white marble tables. Natunchandra Barua from Chittagong, the owner of the shop would welcome everyone with a gentlemanly charm (*sujan sulabh snigdhta*). That reception was so generous that it would send no signal that it was over even when the cups were emptied. You could carry on the *adda* as long as you wanted; the curious would come by attracted to the *adda*. Even if there would not be enough tea, there would not be want of space. Favourite Cabin saw the birth of many debates, bragging, vows and plans for future. *Kallol* would have remained incomplete without Favourite Cabin.

Till date the tea shop has a brisk business drawing regular customers ritually visiting the place every day. Operating since 1908, Dilkhusha Cabin near the Mahatma Gandhi Road crossing is still very much present in its 'pomp and glory' (*jank-jamak*). Founded by Chunilal Dey, with a seating capacity of 65 to 70 persons, the place is known for its *kabiraji* cutlet, the Bengali version of batter-coated, deep fried minced meat dumplings.[174] Most visitors in the 1940s and 1950s could not afford to buy anything here beyond a chop or cutlet.[175] The memory of *adda* at Basanta Cabin has been recalled and retold by many.[176] Moving further north, there was Mitra Café opposite Sovabazar metro station begun in 1910 by Ganesh Mitra, another favourite joint for its chicken, fish, mutton chop, cutlet and *kabiraji*. Among the four outlets of this Café, the Shyambazar outlet was yet another hangout for an *adda*.[177] Of all the eateries in the neighbourhood, Allen Kitchen, also in Sovabazar was perhaps the oldest. The late Jibankrishna Saha was an employee in the original

[174] Current owner Utpal Basu who inherited the place from his uncle, interview, 17 July 2011.

[175] Sengupta, *Kallol Jug*, 65.

[176] Syed Mujtaba Ali, *Panchatantra*, 2 vols., Calcutta, 1960; Mujtaba Ali's *adda* at Basanta Cabin with Sajanikanta Das, recollected by the latter, has been fondly recorded by Sabitendranath Roy, *College Street e Sottor Bochchhor* (Seventy Years on College Street), Kolkata: Mitra o Ghosh, 2006–08, vol. 3, 60.

[177] In collective memory this was another coffee house; Somak Das, interview, 22 November 2012; Sabyasachi Bhattacharya, interview, 20 August 2011.

outlet in Allen Market in Chitpur named after its Scottish owner who left the place to Saha in the late 1890s. Prawn cutlet fried in clarified butter, the speciality of this restaurant, stills draws a large clientele.

While the attraction of restaurants like Allen Kitchen, Dilkhusa and Mitra Café lay in the goodies on their menu, in the 1940s Basanta Cabin and Raybabu's Café adjacent to Presidency College, were a couple of other places college students would go to in addition to the ICH. Basanta Cabin was famous for its 'double half' tea, and 'toash'. A cup of tea with the full measure of milk and sugar used to cost 4 paise and half a cup 2 paise; in double half on the other hand, half measure of milk and sugar was added to the full measure of water for one cup of tea. You could choose between two tastes that 'toash' or butter toast came in: sprinkled with sugar, or black pepper. Since it was so cheap, it used to be very crowded; and 'it was *not* a place where you could stretch your legs and have an *adda*'.[178]

Very few of the connoisseurs of Sanguvalley would know that its name is derived from Sankha, the river in Chittagong. Around the time that the Baruah Brothers opened Favourite Cabin, another member of the same community opened the first Sanguvalley Restaurant in Wellington. It soon became a favourite joint selling tea, chop, cutlet and *Mughlai parota* among other items. Many outlets were opened after the Japanese bombardment of Burma ruined the business of the Chaudhuries, an influential landholding family of Chittagong (not from the Sankha Valley) and the displaced workers moved to Calcutta. Another wave followed after the Partition. Although neither the owners nor the forty outlets spread over north and south Calcutta were related to each other, Sanguvalley became a brand name.[179] Perhaps because they themselves were displaced, like the owner of Favourite

[178] Ray Chaudhuri, *Bangalnama*, 115, emphasis added. This choice is still available in canteens, small restaurants and road-side tea shops in Bengal where the fresh and handy small (one portion) loaf is cut into two thick slices and roasted on fire. It is crunchy outside, but soft inside. The butter usually available in the Indian market is salted.

[179] Interview of Prasun Baruah, the owner of the only surviving outlet bearing the name is at 6AB, S.P. Mukherjee Road, 1 February 2012. His father and uncle migrated from Chittagong after the Partition; also interview, Sanjay Baruah, Favourite Cabin, 13 February 2012.

Cabin, the owners of Sanguvalley were also kind and generous to the unemployed youth who spent endless hours at their place: [180]

> The kind young owner of Sanguvally opposite the tram depot in Kalighat, himself from Chittagong, allowed unemployed penniless youth to take part in *adda* in his shop from 9 am to 12 or 1 pm and from 7 pm to 9 pm without bothering them. He would sometimes supply plain tea, double-half tea, toast, 'mamlet', cake, chop, cutlet to them on credit.

Down Bankim Chatterjee Street past Mahabodhi Society was yet another favourite joint from the yesteryear. Niharranjan Majumdar, the founder of the cold beverage shop Paramount (1918), was a freedom fighter. He was inspired by the chemist Acharya Prafulla Chandra Roy to think of a drink that would both be filling and quench one's thirst at the same time, without pinching the students' pocket too much. That saw the birth of the *daab sharbat*, a mixture of coconut water, tender coconut flesh, crushed ice, and sugar. This narrow shop with four benches was a cover for armed revolutionary movement and the space at the back of this dingy shop served as a hideout. Part of the income of the shop was diverted to finance this movement in the 1920s and 1930s. A framed list of names of eminent personalities who had visited the shop in the past and in recent times, includes Subhas Chandra Bose, Nazrul Islam, Satyendranath Bose and Satyajit Ray among many others. It is the shop's prized exhibit that has overwhelmed many a newcomer adding to its popularity, and increasing footfall especially during the summer months.

Just as in the north, there were many tea shops in the southern part of the city. Reminiscing about the 1940s, Mrinal Sen has noted that during this period, he, along with his friends, used to visit a tea shop called the Paradise Café on Hazra Road where they would spend eight to ten hours of the day. Just like Satyajit Ray, Mrinal Sen, a pioneer of Indian parallel cinema was influenced by existentialism and neo-realism. It was those days when he and his friends interested in film-making were in search of an entry point

[180] Gupta, 'Amader Jubakaler Adda'.

to the world of cinema, this café served as the venue where such plans were discussed:[181]

> There was a tea-shop called *Paradise Café* on Hazra Road; it is not there any longer. A few of my friends including myself—those days we were outsiders to the world of film, but were intent on making films—would sit at that place. We were not able to afford the coffee house, hence. Out of twenty-four hours, eight to ten hours were spent there. I cannot imagine it now. Many of the members of this group became famous in their respective field later in life.

Till the 1980s, Adi Sutripti opposite Deshapriya Park (now a hotel), Shobha Restaurant and Amritayan on the east and west of the crossing of Rashbehari Avenue and S.P. Mukherji Road, were places for whiling away some time over tea and snacks. Another popular joint for tea in the neighbourhood was Radhubabu's tea shop on Jatin Das Road (near the Lake Market end). The shop was always crowded and tea there was immensely popular. It was discovered later that the owner laced the tea with cocaine in order to ensure the serpentine queues of tea-drinkers in front of his shop.[182] Another favourite meeting point in South Calcutta was the Banaphul Cabin near Purna Cinema on S.P. Mukherji Road. Till the 1970s there was a thriving *adda* at this place where a few Leftist intellectuals would meet.[183]

It is interesting to note that while writing about the South Indians in Calcutta, P.T. Nair never mentioned coffee at all, perhaps because hailing from Kerala, he himself did not drink coffee.[184] Gupta, the antiquarian of Calcutta recalled that the culture of coffee drinking had been introduced in Calcutta by the South Indians.[185] Many migrants

[181] Mrinal Sen, 'Addamela Hoke' (Let there be an *adda*-fair), in *Bangalir Adda*, 33–40. One member of this group was Ritwik Ghatak, another luminary in the field of parallel cinema. Another person was Tapas Sen who later earned fame in stage lighting.

[182] Anecdote, the late P. K. Bhattacharya (71), interview, 30 August 2011.

[183] Interview, Dr Sudeshna Banerjee, Department of History, J.U., 28 September 2013.

[184] P.T. Nair, *South Indians in Kolkata: History of Kannadigas, Konkanis, Malayalees, Tamilians, Telugus, South Indian Dishes, and Tippoo Sultan's heirs in Calcutta*, Kolkata: Punthi Pustak, 2004.

[185] Gupta, 'Amader Jubakaler Adda'.

from other states were attracted to the city in the first half of the twentieth century. Institutions of higher education and opportunities in the public and private sector attracted the educated middle class, while the jute factories in Bengal worked as a pull factor for the working class from neighbouring states and states like Tamil Nadu and Karnataka till at least the 1960s.[186] Boarding houses and lodges were required for the many migrants coming from different parts of the country. Founded in the mid-1930s by C.V. Iyer, a Palghat Brahmin from Kerala, Komala Vilas on Rashbehari Avenue was one lodge meant especially for the migrants from the South. Initially people used to put up at the place for a week or two; later many of them stayed on. Young male members would come first and rent a room in a house or a mess. Later, after they secured a job, they would go back to their ancestral village to get married and come back with their newly-wed wives. The first South Indian eatery was set up by P.C. Rama Iyer, also from Palghat, in Paddapukur Road around the year 1922. South Indian restaurants were opened in Central Calcutta around the business centres in Dalhousie Square, Esplanade, Chittaranjan Avenue and Burra Bazar. Madras Café on Hastings Street dates back to 1935.[187] Quite a few typical South Indian eateries came up especially in the residential quarters between Hazra and Deshapriya Park/Lake Market in the south where there is a conglomeration of South Indian communities. While a few Calcuttans like Radha Prasad Gupta and Amitabha Sen familiar with coffee went to restaurants like National Lodge and Paniyan, these joints had not quite attracted the *adda* of the tea shops mentioned above, so the 'onus' was left to the ICH to take coffee to the Bengali middle class.[188]

Although outside the focus of this work, one popular public space especially in Bombay but also in Hyderabad and Poona deserves mention here. Set up by Zoroastrians who migrated from Iran in the late nineteenth century, Irani cafés, often located close to an Iranian bakery,

[186] R. Asokan, the chief manager Canara Bank, Chowringhee branch cited in Subhro Saha, 'South to South', *The Telegraph*, 21 July 2006.

[187] Nair, *South Indians*.

[188] Till 1946 coffee was not the on menu at Komala Vilas begun in the early 1940s. Mr Prem Raj, interview, 15 February 2011.

were informal restaurant-cum-tea houses, and were very popular for their freshly prepared snacks and tea.[189] Beginning with Café Leopold in Colaba (1871), Kayani Café in Dhobi Talao (1904) and Britannia in Ballard Estate (1905), there were about 350 Irani cafés in Bombay in the 1950s. Run by independent families, these cafés were famous for their *maska pau* (butter on breadroll), *brun maska* (hard-crusted bun with butter) that could be enjoyed with minced meat, omelet, scrambled egg or just jam, and of course Irani *chai* and *paani kum chai*, thick milky tea, *khade chammach ki chai*, the extra sweet tea with condensed milk and a 'standing spoon', *gaz* (nougat), nan-khatai, Shrewsbury and other types of biscuit, *falooda* (chilled milk served with vermicelli, rose syrup and basil seeds) along with freshly baked cakes from the bakeries nearby. The café area usually had small square white marble-top tables and black chairs against a backdrop of dark brown glass cupboards stacked with groceries and varieties of cookies. Strategically located at junctions and street corners, these cafés offered not only wholesome food at an affordable price, but made it possible for people to linger over cups of tea, thus becoming a meeting point.

CONCLUSION

The survey above is only sketchy at its best. But is sufficient to demonstrate that although there was a break as far as the *qahwakhanas* of Mughal Delhi were concerned, there was a continuation of the thriving tradition of public gatherings in the shape of *mushairas*, and *kavi sammelans,* bringing the Hindi and Urdu literary worlds together in the early decades of the twentieth century. These formal events, however, had to be organized and lacked the spontaneity of the *adda* which I have suggested was an attempt of the urban man to rise above the mundane existence of everyday life. Considering the spaces of public consumption facilitating informal meetings, it can be said that ranging from posh restaurants on the one hand to neighbourhood tea shops on the other, from at least the early twentieth century there was a tradition of informal socialization in urban North India comparable

[189] I am grateful to Devika Shetti for drawing my attention to the Irani cafés in Bombay.

to the *addas* in Bengal. At the one end of the spectrum were European-style restaurants like Firpo's, Flury's, Peliti's in Calcutta, Alps and Volga in Delhi and B.N. Rama's and the late entrant El Chico in Allahabad together with other clubs and hotels offering a luxury beyond the reach of a majority of the middle class; at the other, were the small-scale tea shops, cabins, restaurants, confectionaries and roadside tea shops run by local entrepreneurs selling tea and light snacks. Consumption of food was compulsory in the restaurants, but tea shops usually patronized *adda*. If Paradise Café and Sanguvalley in Calcutta allowed the unemployed youth to use their space for socializing, tea shops like Jagati's, Malani's among other places in Allahabad and Favourite Cabin or Banaphul in Calcutta were venues where the literati met and spent a considerable amount of time in leisurely *adda*. It should be borne in mind that this socialization at tea shops was inexpensive, and continued even after the Coffee House was launched. What is remarkable is that while these spaces were judged by the quality of the gathering they attracted, very little is said about the infrastructure of such establishments conveying that the agency was more important than the structure. The first time that the structure is mentioned is after the launch of the India Coffee House, when a comparison is made between the pre-existing restaurants and the new Coffee House, only then does it become evident that the Coffee House was not just an addition to the existing spaces of *adda*. The middle class, in spite of Gandhi's practice of frugality which he advised the entire nation to follow, was prone to luxury. Instead of inspiring a movement against consumerism, his philosophy of abstinence was translated into a politics of consumerism.[190] Moreover, consumption of new commodities was often projected as an indispensable part of modernity. So, did the cultural elite patronize the tea shops and cabins because there was no affordable alternative available to them? Was it only coffee, largely unknown to the average north Indian that attacted them to the Coffee House, or was there something more to it? The following chapter will shed light on the process of the production of the the India Coffee House.

[190] Lisa Trivedi, *Clothing Gandhi's Nation: Homespun and Modern India*, Bloomington: Indiana University Press, 2007; Tapan Ray Chaudhuri, interview, 14 February 2012.

CHAPTER two

India Coffee House
A New Space in the City

> [...] there used to be so much fun and addiction in the adda at this coffee house [5, Chittaranjan Avenue, Calcutta] that without being there at least once, the day seemed to be spent in vain.[1]
>
> Adda is the addiction, and coffee provides the excuse; the place where you consume both is the coffee-house.[2]
>
> The Coffee House is itself an attraction.... Perhaps deeper than just the coffee.[3]

Writing about the nationalist elite in urban areas under the colonial rule, Partha Chatterjee maintained that since these were not created by the indigenous elite, devoid of control on the process of the development of urban spaces, they adapted in those areas without investing much energy and thought about the future of the city; they were more concerned about the future of rural India.[4] Recent works on the nationalist middle class suggest however that the middle classes in the late colonial period did not simply adapt to the city life without thinking. By participating in the civic and political associations, publishing and arguing for their own ideology vis-à-vis the dominant one, and often by forcing the colonial authorities to rethink decisions and measures, the nationalist elite left their mark in the public sphere, and the making of the city spaces they inhabited.[5]

[1] Radha Prasad Gupta, *Amader Jubakaler Adda,* 53; full entry, ch.1, note 173.

[2] Subho Basu, lecturer Vidyasagar College, interview, 3 February 2011.

[3] Agyeya, *Nadi Ke Dweep*, New Delhi: Rajkamal, 1952.

[4] Partha Chatterjee, *The Politics of the Governed: Reflections on Popular Politics in Most of the World*, New York: Columbia University Press, 2004, 140.

[5] Sanjay Joshi, *Fractured Modernity: Making of a Middle Class in Colonial North India,* New Delhi: OUP, 2001; Prashant Kidambi, *The Making of an Indian*

The previous chapter has shown that many of those who went to the city to pursue higher education and means of livelihood, did not really adapt without thinking. But for a newcomer often arriving alone in the city, it was a daunting task to carve out a for oneself in a place that was so different from the home and neighbourhood left behind. Many of them, even when not uprooted and rendered homeless, found the transtition overwhelming. Those forced to leave, had to find a new home, new friends in a totally new, often unknown environment. One of the ways of making sense of the changes in the personal life dragged into the course of the larger events of the time was through conversations with the peer group. Exploring the spaces facilitating such interaction and participation in the public life became essential part of the everyday. Literature allows only a glimpse of the investment that went into establishing a stable foothold in the new surroundings, and social practices with *adda* as an important element, were a means to rise beyond the everyday that was imminent. The quotations cited above show how important a role *adda* played in the life of its protagonists. Under the circumstances, the emergence of a new space for leisure—spectacular in view of the pre-existing locations—created for the middle classes was going to make a profound impact

It is with this background in mind, that this chapter will review the process that led to the formation of the ICH as it was conceived by the coffee industry, viewed by its contemporaries and absorbed into the everyday life of its customers using Henri Lefebvre's concept of the production of space. This concept has been successfully used for the exploration of different aspects of South Asian history. Manu Goswami examined how the dichotomy between uneven capitalist development under imperial conditions and economic development of India as a colonial space in the post-1857 period, helped the imagination of India as a bounded territorial unit with a distinct culture and economic geography producing the concept of a national space.[6] Janaki Nair

---

Metropolis: Colonial Governance and Public Culture in Bombay, 1890–1920, Aldershot: Ashgate, 2007.

[6] Henri Lefebvre, *The Production of Space*, MA: Blackwell, 2007; Manu Goswami, *Producing India: From Colonial Economy to National Space*, Chicago Studies in Practices of Meaning, Chicago: University of Chicago Press, 2004.

has underlined how the imagination of the development authorities projecting Bangalore as a space for the elite, aspiring in their turn after particular ways of life, are in conflict with the process of an equitable growth of the city.[7] Roads, railways and other forms of infrastrcure of transport are, in the analysis by Ravi Ahuja, materializations of diverse spatial practices of the social groups concerned.[8]

Many of the small, neighbourhood places, especially tea-shops in Calcutta and elsewhere, as pointed outabove, had served as points of congregation and for maintaining informal social network for like-minded citizens. Hence, there were certainly some elements of continuity between the older tea-shops, restaurants and the newly emerging tea/ and coffee-houses on the one hand and the importance of the social space of *adda* as a criticism of the everyday on the other. What should also be emphasized here is that many of the older tea-shops and restaurants to attract people even after the coffee-houses were launched, just as they still do.[9] How did the Coffee Board visualize the space and how was it received by the urban public? What were the attributes of the newly created space and who went there? Did all sections of the educated urban middle class consider it essential to visit these spaces and if not, what deterred them?

Drawing on representation of the coffee-house in literature and in conversations, and examining the everyday practices and interactions taking place in it, we shall try to understand the structure of this new locus of sociability developing in all major cities in late colonial urban India, and the agency that combined with this structure to produce the new urban space.

[7] Janaki Nair, *The Promise of the Metropolis: Bangalore's Twentieth Century*, New Delhi: OUP, 2005.

[8] Ravi Ahuja, *Pathways of Empire: Circulation, 'Public Works' and Social Space in Colonial Orissa (c. 1780–1914)*, New Perspectives of South Asian History, v. 25, Hyderabad: Orient BlackSwan, 2009.

[9] In Calcutta for example, among the places mentioned in chapter one, Favourite Cabin, Paramount, Dilkhusha around College Street are still thriving, Sanguvalley has only one branch left while Sutripti now runs as a hotel. Jagati's in Allahabad was closed down but Hari's Namkeen, Lucky Sweet Mart, El Chico, Heera Halwaai are still there. In Delhi Alps, Standard, just like the Tea House closed their shutters in the late 1970s and 1980s.

THE BIRTH OF THE INDIA COFFEE HOUSE

Representation of space is the conceptualized space, the technically conceived plan guided by the imagination of the relations of individuals to space on behalf of the authorities concerned. In the current context, the planners of the ICH had attributed a functional value to the space being created. Faced with the challenge posed by the collapse of the export market after the Depression of 1929 mentioned above, the coffee sector was required to take steps in order to stabilize the market and control over the production and marketing of coffee. Coffee exports from British India in the fiscal years of 1901, 1914 and 1920 had been (In cartweight or cwt) 276,002, 291,088, and 305,268 respectively. The quantity of Indian coffee produced during the five fiscal years (1929–30 to 1933–34) before the launch of the Coffee Cess Committee (1935) was (in cwt) 351,999, 294,401.49, 300,211.72, 294,973.66 and 308,937 in 1929–30, 1930–31, 1931–32, 1932–33 and 1933–34 respectively; while the quantity exported to foreign countries, mainly England and France, in the corresponding period amounted to (in cwt) 184,220, 172,889, 155,600, 173,177, and 185,905.[10] By launching the coffee houses the Cess Committee aimed at creating a market at home and regulating the market aborad. With no prior experience of sale in the domestic market, the Cess Committee, tagged in the support of the well-known advertising agency John Walter Thompson & Co. of Bombay and entrusted it with the 'control of the publicity campaign for expansion of coffee [consumption]' in the domestic market.[11]

Before the ICH was launched, almost no concerted effort had been made to promote coffee. Rather, coffee was served through local dealers catering to a niche market, and, the domestic market was fragmented. In South India, where it was grown, the beginning of the twentieth century saw coffee making its way into the urban

[10] 1 hundredweight (cwt). 20 cwt = 1 ton. The decennial calculation for the first decades has been provided by William H. Ukers, *All About Coffee*, New York: The Tea and Coffee Trade Journal Company: 1922, 195; for the later years, Department of Commercial Intelligence and Statistics, India: *Indian Coffee Statistics, 1933–34*, 6–7.

[11] Anonymous, 'Indian Coffee House: Propaganda Campaign', *Times of India*, 26 June 1936.

middle class household.[12] In North India, in contrast, coffee was still a rare and exotic commodity and, in comparison with tea, a novelty to the majority of the urban middle class. The Committee decided that the promotional activities would begin in Bombay and then in Hyderabad, and one of the ways of introducing coffee to the potential customers was through a chain of coffee-houses.

Conceived to function in the line of popular restaurants, this chain, would offer coffee at a reduced rate compared to tea and give demonstrations on how to brew a cup of coffee properly. It was assumed that the urban middle class population would visit the space and get used to drinking coffee. The first coffee-house opened in Bombay in 1936, followed soon after by one in Hyderabad.[13] It was thus an alliance between the coffee industry and the colonial state that made this novel experiment possible. One major difference between the other existing spaces of socialization on the one hand and the ICH on the other was that while most of the eateries and tea-shops accessible to the average middle class were small, private local enterprises, working under the Coffee Cess Committee and later the Coffee Board, the ICH was a pan-Indian initiative on behalf of the coffee capitalists directly aided by the state for the public to come together and take to the consumption of coffee.

Coffee was available in upmarket colonial hotels and restaurants in northern cities and some upper class Indians were indeed familiar with the brew while the not so rich might have tasted coffee in the cafés and hotels opened by migrant South Indians. But by making coffee available at a subsidized price, the Coffee Board of India provided for the bulk of the North Indian middle class urbanites with an experience that had so long been a preserve of a few. The drinking of coffee and *adda*, or *addebaji* of young friends or

[12] See for Tamil Nadu for example A.R. Venkatachalapathy, *In Those Days There Was no Coffee*, New Delhi: Yoda Press, 2006.

[13] John Walter Thompson & Co. (Eastern) Ltd. Bombay (henceforth JWT), 'Campaign for Coffee in India, 1938–39', Unpublished Mss. Hartmann Collection, Duke University Library. I am grateful to Douglas Haynes for making a copy of this document available. See Chapter Three for more on this document. After this date, there is no reference to JWT in the publications of the Coffee Board.

like-minded citizens in a friendly warm ambience, became synonymous with the Coffee House.[14]

One of the characteristics of the places I discussed in the previous chapter was that—leaving the sophisticated places aside—they were not capacious enough to accommodate many people at a time and as soon as the customer had finished consuming his food and tea, he was expected to pay up and leave. Without doubting the importance of Favourite Cabin, associated with the literary *addas* of Kallol group, it should be pointed out that while reminiscing about the place,[15] Achintya Kumar Sengupta was perhaps not referring to the geo-physical space of their favourite meeting place, which had remained unchanged—there were only two round (each accommodating six to eight) and two rectangular (accommodating two to four each) marble-top tables. This did not affect the quality of the *adda* of the regulars there; but its crammed setting would have lead to a serious problem even if a sixth of the visitors occupying the ICH turned up at any given moment at this place.

Adda in a bookshop was bound to be limited to the littérateurs and there were different groups of *adda* around different bookshops. Shops like Putiram in Calcutta never served tea, in order to avoid unwanted crowds.[16] At restaurants serving more than just tea and toast, ordering food was necessary; passing time without consumption was out of the question. Begun as a promotional outlet, the Coffee-House was a place where ordering one cup of coffee was sufficient; ordering food was not necessary:[17]

[14] Interview with Keshav Malik; Dr Jitendranath a regular visitor of Allahabad ICH since 1965 when he was a student at the university, 23 October 2012; and Anathbandhu De in Calcutta, just to give a couple of examples.

[15] See Chapter One.

[16] Dipesh Chakrabarty, 'Adda', in *Provincializing Europe: Postcolonial Thought and Historical Difference*, Princeton: Princeton University Press, footnote 11, ch.1. In addition one can argue that *adda* in an open park, had to be season and time bound. In order to be part of an *adda* in the parlour of a private person, it was necessary to be familiar with at least one member of the group.

[17] Sarat Kumar Mukhopadhyay, 'Krittibaser Adda', in *Bangalir Adda*, 104–14. The only surviving Sanguvalley Restaurant (6 AB, S.P. Mukherjee Road) stopped serving tea about 25 years ago in order to avoid unwanted youth from the neighbourhood

> The ICH opens at 9 am and closes at 9 pm and is on the whole thriving during these twelve hours. There you can sit for two hours over a cup of coffee and you get drinking water on demand, which is unthinkable at Basanta Cabin, Putiram, YMCA or Dilkhusha nearby. Coffee House was the ideal place of adda for students and the unemployed.

Much of the enthusiasm of the initial customers of the ICH was about the infrastructure of the ICH. What kind of knowledge informed the creation/transformation of the physical space of the sites selected for the purpose? The conceived plan did not involve any strategy for changing the urban morphology; in none of the places where the ICH was set up, was any new façade created in order to launch the chain. All the buildings, the physical location of the Coffee House had been constructed for different purposes earlier and were purchased on lease by the Coffee Board from private proprietors such as the Puris in Delhi, Dr Darbari in Allahabad and the Mallik family owning both the buildings at 5CA and College Street in Calcutta. These were then converted into the Coffee House. Yet, the amazement and the enthusiasm that went into the describing of the Coffee House also drew on the fact that both in its form and structure, the ICH was distinct from the other places of *adda* reviewed above and the places of *adda* mentioned by Chakrabarty.

Irani cafés were known for their special ambience and interior decoration distinguishing them from small Indian eateries on the one hand and the up-scale European style restaurants on the other. Owned by Irani immigrants in the nineteenth century, these cafés were typically housed in buildings with high ceilings, often allowing the possibility of creating a mezzanine floor seating arrangement. The thick walls and high ceiling ensured relative comfort from the tropical heat outside. The furniture consisted of small Italian marble-top tables or tables covered with table-cloth under a pane of glass (usually for four persons), and bentwood or bentwood-cane chairs. Wall-clocks, frescos, images of Zarathushtra, and in some cases photographs of

sitting over a cup of tea, and serves Nescafé (at Rs 10 a cup) instead; Prasun Barua, second generation owner, interview, 2 January 2012.

nationalist leaders would hang from walls often decorated with wood panels and mirrors. A list of prohibited actions in Indian English like 'no shaving', 'no bargaining', 'no change', 'no food from outside', 'no water to outsiders', underlined the idiosyncrasies of the restaurants. In keeping up with Indian middle class social values of prospective clients, there were 'family rooms' where women accompanying male visitors could feel at ease.[18] These elements, added to the fact that the cafés were often manned by Parsee staff, generated a hybrid ambience in the Irani cafés.

People from all walks of life, irrespective of caste and class went there. The cafés attracted people of modest means because they sold fresh, wholesome food and snacks at a moderate price. As young, aspiring artists M.F. Husain and Tyeb Mehta would visit Irani cafés where tea was available at 2 paise a cup.[19] The informal setting with friendly owners and freshly prepared fast food soon became a favourite with writers, journalists and artists as well as labourers and rickshaw pullers who would stop by for a quick bite.[20]

Many of the features of these Irani cafés were common to the outlets of the ICH. Notably, the first outlets of the Coffee-House in Bombay and Hyderabad were places where the public were already familiar with Irani cafés. In all the cities where the Coffee House was set up, it was at a major thoroughfare visited by the cross-sections of the society for various reasons.[21] The basic criteria guiding the

[18] Frank Conlon, 'Dining Out in Bombay' Ch. 1, footnote 87, in Carol Appadurai Breckenridge (ed.), *Consuming Modernity: Public Culture in a South Asian World*, Minneapolis: University of Minnesota Press, 1995, 90–130'.

[19] As they would not have even that amount, after ordering, one of them would cancel his order, and then they would share one cup between the two of them, *Inheritance: Part-1* (online video), and Gouri R., *Maqbool Fida Husain* (website), www.arvindguptatoys.com/arvindgupta/maqbool.doc.

[20] Sukhada Tatke, 'Another Iconic Irani Joint Bites the Dust in Mumbai,' *The Hindu*, 14 February 2014.

[21] In Turkey too, the two most important places for social gathering—the mosque and the coffee house—are located in the town square, M.J. Gannon, 'The Turkish Coffee House', in Martin J. Gannon (ed.), *Understanding Global Cultures: Metaphorical Journeys Through 23 Nations, Clusters of Nations, Continents, and Diversity*, Thousand Oaks, CA: Sage, 95–112.

selection of the location and the furnishings seem to have been a spacious hall in a strategic location and a comfortable ambience facilitating close individual interaction. To these, the industry naturally added some particularities that became the hallmark of the ICH. Thus the creation of the ICH saw the conversion of existing buildings to be used for a different purpose. A brief review of the structure of the new space and responses of the contemporaries will help us to understand how the transformation of the space with its unique features left the urban population awestruck.

Originally built as a public lecture hall in honour of Albert, the Prince Consort of Queen Victoria, and inaugurated in April 1876 [22], Albert Hall on College Street stands apart. Its rich heritage has humbled many a visitor A marble plaque to the left of the entrance of the hall announces that the Indian Association held its first meeting in this building in 1876. In that incarnation, the auditorium was blessed by the august presence of many nationalist leaders addressing the nation there. The original one-storeyed building in the place had been replaced by the current building sometime around the turn of the century. Among the leading personalities speaking in Albert Hall were Subhash Chandra Bose, Mahatma Gandhi, Sister Nivedita, Keshav Chandra Sen and Rabindranath Tagore. The bromide photograph of Tagore decorating the wall on the north symbolized the cultural and intellectual legacy of the space.[23] In the wake of World War II, the organization of public lectures in the Hall was put to an end in 1941.[24]

Till the early 1920s the main entrance of the building was next to the bookshop of M.C. Sarkar on College Street. One would take the stairs here—facing the entrance of Presidency College—leading to the public hall on the first floor. By the time the Coffee Board leased the place in 1942, the said bookshop had moved to Shyamacharan De Street and the old entrance was closed and replaced by the current entrance housing the staircase on Bankim Chatterjee Street.

[22] Anathbandhu De, 'Bangalir Sanskriti Rupantare Albert Hall Coffee-house' [Albert Hall: Coffee House in the Transformation of Bengali Culture], in *Coffee-Toffee*, 1993, 79–88, (One time magazine ICH forum).

[23] The photograph hanging now on this wall is not the original one.

[24] Gaurisankar Bhattacharya, *Albert Hall*, Kolkata: Chirayata, 1975 (1958), 10.

Ismail's cigarette shop was at the bottom of the stair-well, facing the entrance. In addition to the large hall on the first floor there is sitting arrangement on the second floor on the south extending into a balcony encompassing the entire floor space. While the public sitting in the main hall cannot see the area and the occupants of the upper floor accessible through the stairs outside the hall, standing near the railing of the second floor one can have a view of the space below.[25] The area space of the first floor of the ICH College Street measures 9,239-sq ft and there are 44 tables on the first floor and 36 tables on the second floor, thus eighty tables in total. The 2´x 2´tables are supposed to accommodate four persons each, and normally this outlet can accommodate 320 visitors at a time. It is however not uncommon to have as many as twelve to fifteen persons sitting around particular tables, when additional folding chairs are placed to accommodate 40 to 50 more visitors. In the papers of the Coffee Board the Coffee House was simply referred to as Albert Hall, and popularly called Albert Hall Coffee House.

Although the furnishings in the ICH at 5CA have now been changed,[26] notices like *Please avoid your stay here beyond one hour*, *Outside food strictly not allowed*, *Business activities inside the Coffee-House strictly not allowed*, *Smoking not allowed*, covering three other walls perhaps taken over from the Irani cafés, decorated the walls at 5CA till recently. Babaji Charan Mahala, working with the Coffee Board since 1979 suggested that visitors often ignored the notices.

Similarly, at Queensway (Janpath) in New Delhi the sitting arrangement was spread over two floors. There were two *paan* and

[25] The ICH at Mohan Singh Place with three sections, the large 'L' shaped terrace, the general and family section is the most commodious. The one in Simla had originally three floors. While the top floor is now leased to a bank, the basement remains almost empty. In my opinion it is this branch that still has the décor that all outlets had when they were launched.

[26] The cane-wood chairs and wooden tables have been replaced by ugly high aluminium stools attached to long and narrow high tables. According to Gautam Roy, secretary in charge, this was in order to prevent manhandling of the furniture by the regular customers. A few customers claimed on the other hand that Roy talked rubbish. Restoring the old furniture would have cost more than the new cheap aluminium products.

cigarette sellers sitting on their *chowkis* on pavement on either side of the entrance with large, round shining copper trays full of *paan* and other ingredients. Customers had to push the double doors to enter the large hall lined on the left with cabins meant for families. Along the wall on the right was the cash-counter followed by low sofas with long tables; the horse-shoe shaped sofa-set in the centre of this row was meant for a larger group. The space in between had rows of small square tables for four. It was occupied by two to any number of persons right up to the end of the hall leading to the kitchen. There was a spiral staircase on the right leading to the balcony. The balcony had three tables with four chairs each and another three pairs of sofas that could accommodate six persons per set.[27] On the first floor was the atelier and painting school run by Sarada Ukil, who, together with his brothers ran a school of art in 1926.[28] There was a lot of (free) parking space for cars and scooter/motor cycles and a taxi stand in front.[29] At its current location in Mohan Singh Place, the ICH at CP has two large halls and a huge open L-shaped terrace.[30]

In Allahabad too ICH was a place where, unlike in the sweet shops or tea stalls, one could sit comfortably around small tables for as long as one wanted; all that it cost was a moderately priced cup of coffee. The floor of the building where the ICH was launched in Allahabad had coir matting. An added attraction of the place was its two air coolers that kept the temperature inside under control during hot summer days, and the cool breeze blowing from the twin-rivers could be enjoyed in the extensive lawn in front on summer evenings. The

[27] S. P. Dutt, former Air India executive, e-mail, 13 November 2013.

[28] Keshav Malik, interview, 23 November 2012; Uma Vasudev, interview, 21 October 2012; for more on Sarada Ukil see http://www.chitralekha.org/articles/sarada-ukil/sarada-ukil-profile-pioneer, (Ukil 2001); the school exists as a polytechnic college under the name Sarada Ukil School of Arts.

[29] S.P. Dutt, e-mail, 13 November 2013.

[30] The sofa-sets at both the covered sections have seen better days. Throughout 2012, I was told that the Delhi government had sanctioned a grant for repairing and refurbishing the place. For a recent description of the place see Stuart Freedman, 'The Palace of Monkeys and Memory', blog, 23 October 2010, http://www.stuartfreedman.com/texts/story.php?nodeID=609.

usual fare, known as hot-mix—coffee with milk and sugar—could initially be had for 10 paise, while special coffee, because it contained an extra dose of milk, used to cost 25 paise.[31] For the connoisseur there was cold coffee and coffee ice-cream. Although not used much in the 1950s and 1960s, one speciality of Allahabad was the totally segregated family section housed in a different building.[32]

Connoisseurs of the old Coffee House in Bangalore informed me that the old building on M.G. Road had a Victorian setting, which spread over two floors, and was fitted with large Belgian mirrors, a stand for coats, hats and umbrella. Initially there were cane-wood chairs with metal-edged legs and glass-top tables meant for four.[33] Those who spent a longer time reading books, chatting with friends or having a quiet meeting, preferred the first floor that had a large round table with chairs in the middle and a long stretch of cushioned sofas along three walls with small tables in front. The large French windows in front formed the overlook to the rich, leafy greens on the other side of M.G. Road.[34]

This infrastructural aspect of the Coffee House contained the potential of drawing and accommodating various scattered groups of *adda* under one roof, and making interaction among individuals across all walks of life irrespective of their age, profession and loyalties possible in all cities studied. In the case of the Irani cafés Conlon has observed that they 'embraced Raj and royalty in nomenclature'.[35] In addition to the comfort and relative luxury of the enormous physical space, what made ICH initially attractive was the uniform of the workers. The thrill of being served by liveried workers dressed in white trousers and shirt secured with a *komarbandh* like

[31] Hemendra Shankar Saxena, English Professor, interview, 23 January 2012.

[32] This section came up after the ICH moved to Darbari Building; the general section was not so large that it could accommodate another section there. At Spencer's Plaza in Trivandrum the space of the main hall is divided and one section is meant for family and ladies.

[33] S. Narayanswami a patron since 1948 when he accompanied his father to the place as a child, interview, 2 August 2011.

[34] Gautam Chenoy, a connoisseur since the 1990s, interview, 3 August 2011.

[35] Conlon, 'Dining Out in Bombay'.

belt and a turban-like headgear was an experience still cherished by many. In addition, as coffee was being promoted, it was served with gratis cashewnuts—twelve for one cup to be precise,[36] while donuts, plum cake and other equally exotic edibles could be enjoyed against payment. Comfort and pleasure associated with the Raj, available at a relatively low cost was the reason behind ICH gaining popularity. Coffee was served—like in up-scale hotels and restaurants—in pot with milk and sugar served separately on a tray. In addition to hot and cold coffee, the menu included coffee with ice-cream, omelette, scrambled egg on toast, variations of sandwich and cake, fruit salad and soup—items not readily available at indigenous tea shops or common above-mentioned restaurants accessible to the average middle class, and nowhere else at least against the price charged at ICH.[37] If coffee ice-cream was the specialty of Janpath and College Street, ICH at DU in the 1960s knew neither gratis cashewnuts nor coffee ice-cream, but coffee-jelly was very much in demand in all Delhi outlets during these decades. While most of the regular visitors only had coffee, there were a few who would also eat at different times of the day.

If omelette, popularly called mamlet in Bengal was available in tea-shops and restaurants, the ones in ICH came in varieties: mutton omelette (very popular at the outlet at Anna's Arcade in Trivandrum), cheese omelette, chicken omelette (a specialty at Jadavpur), etc. For a mouth-

[36] Vishwa Bandhu Gupta (85, a former member of the Rajya Sabha, Chairman of the Tej Group of Companies, President of All India Newspapers Editors' Conference and the editor of *Daily Tej* (Urdu) as well as *Sun* Magazine, and a balloonist) recalled that when he visited the ICH on Janpath for the first time with a classmate as a high school student, they did not like the taste of coffee. They ate the cashew nuts and did not bother to pay as they did not like the taste, interview, 20 October 2012.

[37] Nadaykkal Parameswaran Pillai, *Coffee Housinte Katha,* Thrissur: Current books, 1972. See more on Pillai and his memoir; also Suchit Bandyopadhyay, 'Coffee house: Counter-er Opaar Theke' (henceforth Bandyopadhyay, 'Coffee house'), *Ekshan*, vol. 18, 5–6, 1989,77–94. I am grateful to the late Indranath Majumdar for drawing my attention to this article. Currently, the fruit-salad is available only in Trivandrum.

watering scrambled egg on toast one has to go to the Church Street outlet in Bangalore. Gautam Bhadra was fond of the coffee ice-cream in Calcutta. The best coffee ice-cream that Rajeev Puri ever tasted was at ICH, Janpath. In his opinion, the brand that comes closest to that in quality and taste is Mother Dairy's coffee ice-cream; interview Rajeev Puri, 23 October 2012; for coffee-jelly topped with cream interview Alka Raghuvanshi, 25 July 2013 and Dilip Simeon, historian and political activist, 6 Februray 2012.

Commodious space, western snacks and coffee were not the only novelties the ICH introduced the middle class public to. A still prevalent practice in the informal sector of the hospitality business in India is that not only are bearers and other unskilled workers ill-paid, their sense of hygiene is often notoriously conspicuous by its absence and rarely do employers think about the dress of the lowly paid personnel. Dress is dictated by the tropical climate, and while boys of road side tea-shops and small restaurants can be seen in under-shirts and shorts, shirt and trousers are mostly common among the bearers in other places. Customers are usually aware, but rationalize by comparing the quality of the service with how (little) it affects their pocket. Elite hotels, clubs and restaurants naturally have liveried bearers but those places are beyond the reach of the average student or office-bearer. In this respect ICH presented the public something not experienced before by the common man. As in many other institutions from the time of the Raj, the workers of the Coffee House wore a starched white uniform, a belt with the logo of the Coffee Board in the buckle, and a fan-tailed turban. Being served by 'liveried, turbaned bearers bearing the logo [of the Coffee Board]' moving around like 'walking flower vases' in an 'indigenized version of the foreign hotels, bars and pubs' is as gratifying now as it was in the 1940s and 1950s.

Cleanliness outside in the Indian indigenous city, according to Kaviraj, was not amenable to control.[38] The concept of cleanliness

[38] Sudipta Kaviraj, 'Filth and the Public Sphere: Concepts and Practices about Space in Calcutta', *Public Culture*, 10.1 (1997), 83–113.

as part of ritual purity combined with the economics of the cost of proper maintenance of a toilet meant that most of the traditional small eateries and tea-shops in India do not have restrooms. During my field research I asked the lady at the counter of the popular Dilkhusha Cabin on M.G. Road in Calcutta if they had a toilet. She looked dismayed (Victorian taboo does not allow a *bhadramahila*, lady to use a toilet in unfamiliar circumstances, let alone a public toilet) but quickly said I would have to use the public toilet hundred yards away across the street, for they did not have any. While having tea at that place I noticed however that a dark room at the end of the corridor on the right, with 'office' written on the door concealed a toilet used perhaps by the owners. In this respect too the ICH was an exception, although very few of the women I spoke to actually used the restroom.

Another characteristic that set the ICH apart from existing tea-shops was that manned by Christians, Muslims and Hindus, the Coffee-House was meant for those who (at least outside their home) could not be bothered about the religious and social restrictions imposed by the caste system. That freshly purchased ingredients were hygienically prepared and served by the liveried, well-mannered workers, mattered more to this section of the urban middle class.

During its zenith, ICH had its outlets spread from Lahore in the north to Trivandrum in the south which gave it a pan-Indian character and what made the chain unique was that it was perhaps the oldest surviving chain of a coffee-house in the world.[39] Initially all outlets of ICH served the same menu, and of course coffee.

Another important aspect of the hospitality in the Coffee House was that customarily the visitor got a glass of (filtered) water unasked for. At the outlets of the ICH in Calcutta, Delhi and Trivandrum a small table is still placed at a central location with extra glasses of water kept and replenished at regular intervals.[40] In short, ICH introduced the middle class to the hitherto unaffordable experience

[39] There are older stand alone coffee-houses like Le Procope in Paris, but the first known instance of a chain of coffee shop is Duncan Donuts, the largest chain in the US, which began in 1950 (franchizing since 1963) and Jenny's (1951, selling franchise since 1955) had 1600 outlets, Steven Topik, e-mail, 18 June 2014.

of the luxury of spending as much time as they could afford in a comfortable atmosphere at a much lesser cost.

Not only that the accommodation at the older places mentioned above was scarce, these places lacked the ambience of ICH; the nomenclature of the ICH was mesmerizing to a veteran tea-shop goer, a connoisseur of *adda*: [41]

> Within a couple of days after this Coffee House [5CA] was opened, one evening my friend, Dr Gopal Banerjee took me to that place. [...] even at that "old" age [the narrator was in his early twenties] my jaws dropped at the grand scale, the shimmer and the glimmer (*jhakjhake taktake*) of the polished tables, the liveried boys donning a turban and the badge [of the Coffee Board], and the well-dressed customers at the tables in ICH. All this may appear strange to people *now*, but this is a genuine fact. For although we were desperate enough to go once or twice to the ground floor lounge of the Great Eastern Hotel to have a lemonade for six *anna*, the small Sanguvalley with its fungus-covered walls was as far as we could dream of.

The coffee industry gifted the urban middle class a space that had so far been beyond their dream. Obviously there were other choices, but ICH was *the* place to be. An artist and a loyal connoisseur of *adda* who became a regular face at the Coffee House in the afternoons for more than three decades, informs us:[42]

> [...] After the foundation of the College Street Coffee House, I mean, after the historic Albert Hall was transformed into a *coffeekhana*

[40] Drinking water was available outside the tea-house in CP, but that costed 2 paise and it was not possible to sit there, Kalia, *Ghalib*, 68; cf. 'twice the bearer brings twelve glasses of water', Ravindra Kalia, 'Tea House Hamara Dusra Ghar *Tha*' (Tea House Was Our Second Home), in. *DTH*, 333–44 (henceforth Kalia, Tea House).

[41] Gupta, 'Amader Jubakaler Adda', emphasis added; also his 'Albert Hall Coffee House: Sejug Ejug', *Coffee-Toffee*, 34–35; Till 1957 the value of the rupee was 16 *anna* further subdivided into 8 *anna*, 4 *anna*, 2 *anna*, 1 *anna* etc. Rupee was decimalized in 1957 when it was divided into 100 *naya* paise; *naya* was later dropped.

[42] Debabrata Mukhopadhyay, *Coffee-r Cup e Somoyer Chhobi* (Image of Time in the Coffee-cup: A Memoir) (henceforth '*Coffee-r Cup*'), Kolkata: Camp, 1989, 61–62; cf. part of the clientele of Jagati's Restaurant at Allahabad shifted to the ICH when the latter was opened there, Saxena, 'In Eastmancolor', 107–13.

> by the Coffee Board, we wound up our [*adda*] at Sanguvalley's... in Wellington and Favourite Cabin in Mirzapur... and settled ourselves in ICH.

The attraction of the space evoked this memory decades later:[43]

> Unlike now, Albert Hall was not in ruins then. The plaster on the wall had not come off and the adjacent wall did not bear witness to the culture of chewing *paan*. The world inside ICH was different, the atmosphere bright. As soon as we went up the stairs, we would be saturated with the addictive flavour of [roasted] coffee. Four to five green cane chairs around each table....

The memory of 'green' cane chairs and 'green' glass-topped tables at ICH in Lucknow is still fresh in the memory of Vijay Dutt, a journalist who began visiting the place with his cousins in the late 1940s when he was four.[44] A young Bengali beginning his career as an employee in the ICH on 5 Chittaranjan Avenue, Calcutta, commonly known as 5CA, also noted the difference of the ICH from other places:[45]

> The walls were decorated with paintings by Sudhangshu Chaudhuri. A greenish glow shone from inside the glass-top tables. Comfortable tables [? chairs] for sitting, [electric] lights and [ceiling] fans added to the distinction of the place. And then the coffee-cups with the text: <XL's all pick-me-ups> [Altogether] a taste of wonder... What a dynamic appearance of the ICH that was....

[43] Ashok Mitra, *Apila Chapila* (Memoir), Kolkata: Ananda Publishers, 2003, 45; emphasis added. Earlier, there was a coffee roaster on the ground floor of the building and coffee was freshly roasted here. During World War II, when ICH on College Street was closed down for some time, the ground floor was used as a coffee store.

[44] Also a businessman and farmer interviewed at India International Centre, Delhi, 5 October 2013.

[45] Bandyopadhyay, 'Coffee house', emphasis added; cf. 'Ambika begins doubting if this is Albert Hall; it seems somehow he has arrived at some other place. There are numerous images of creepers, animals and birds on the walls', Bhattacharya, *Albert Hall*, 75; cf. Mr Prem Raj (owner Prema Vilas Lake Market), who used to visit ICH as a university student in the early 1970s, was duly impressed by the enormity of its space, the high ceiling, comfortable chairs around small square tables and the fair-priced coffee of good quality served there, interview, 15 February 2011.

An almost similar description is available about the Coffee House in College Street:[46]

> With the Coffee Board renting Albert Hall and having its walls covered with small murals painted by the late Sudhansgshu Chaudhuri, the Coffee House on College Street began operating in full swing. Chaudhuri, who had painted the frescoes on the walls of the India House in London was back in Calcutta and had just finished the murals of the Metro House in Chowringhee. Who will let such a real non-native spot in the backdrop, created by an artist who had conquered an overseas country, go? Naturally, we all were won over by this fragment of a foreign setting. Gradually this Coffee House affected the *cha-khana*s of the neighbourhood. The morning *adda* at Favourite Cabin, Basanta Cabin, Dilkhusha, Chacha'a Hotel continued, but the evening *adda* of these and other places stretching up to Farepukur began to gather at the Coffee House.

If the city dwellers fascinatedly made the utmost of this novelty in the town,it was bound to have an enchanting effect on a newcomer to the city. Animesh, the protagonist of a Bengali novel set in the 1970s, born and reared in the North Bengal town of Jalpaiguri, experiences the Coffee House on his first visit: [47]

> [...] all over tables and chairs spanning the entire space of the huge hall jampacked with human beings. He has never seen such a large restaurant in his life. All present are talking continuously, and the noise of that collective conversation is recreating a strange humming sound revolving round the high ceiling of the hall.

[46] Mukhopadhyay, '*Coffee-r Cup*', 9–10. Neither the ICH at 5CA nor the ICH on College Street has these murals now. The ICH on College Street underwent a makeover a few years back. These murals seem to have disappeared by the late 1950s. A report on the last working day of the ICH under the Coffee Board noted that 'the white flowers, branches of trees and blue peacocks once decorating the walls of the Coffee House are gone now', Sandipan Bandyopadhyay, 'Shesh Diner Coffee House', *Anandabazar Patrika* (henceforth ABP), 5 October 1958.

[47] Samaresh Majumdar, *Kalbela*, Kolkata: Ananda Publishers, 48. As a student, Majumdar, himself from north Bengal, had been a regular customer of the place.

A contemporary satire published in Calcutta in 1951 sheds further light on the differences between the pre-existing restaurants and the Coffee House. Writing on the restaurants, tea-shops and ICH, Binay Ghosh noted that the era, then current, belonged to the Coffee House.[48] The vanity of post-graduate students, Ghosh noted, prohibited them from frequenting the old fashioned cabins and restaurants. The aroma of coffee was essential for the grey matter in the intellectuals' brain to function; and without cups of coffee 'political comrades' would not be able to engage in any serious discourse. In order to see the cream of the youth in the town, a visitor would have to go to the Coffee House. Those sitting in ordinary cabins and restaurants were 'no longer the cream, but had turned into butter-milk'. The ideal cream found on the other hand in the circles of Coffee House was 'still clotted and neither melted due to constant drinking of hot coffee, nor was the consumption of cold coffee able to transform it into solid refrigerated butter'.

The narrator in the satire could not afford to have his regular *adda* in the Coffee House first because he did not have enough money; and then as his father and grandfather had lived a long, healthy life by consuming tea and snacks at neighbourhood cabins and restaurants, he almost inherited the habit of frequenting such places. But when he was pleading with one of his friends, a connoisseur of Eastern and Western music, a member of the balcony at the Coffee House and of many other cultural clubs in the city, for the old fashioned cabins and restaurants, it nearly caused a rupture in their friendship. The reason, the latter kept on comparing the Coffee House with the salons in Paris and he expressed condescension at the mere mention of the small cabins and restaurants, because he thought these places were allegedly frequented by 'lumpens'. The narrator pointed this out to Tarinicharan, the proprietor of Jai Ma Kali Restaurant (a fictitious place mirroring many real ones) in Hazra during an *adda* in his shop over a cup of tea by saying that unlike ICH, Tarini's restaurant was not spacious enough and had no sitting arrangement to attract the

[48] *Kalpyanchar Naksha* (Sketches: A Satire), Kolkata: Pathabhavan, 1967 (1951).

elite, leading to the following conversation between the narrator and Tarinicharan:[49]

> T: Take your Coffee House friend along to this place once, babu; let him have a mutton chop and a cup of tea here; I shall see if he still brags [about ICH] after that!
>
> N: Why should my friend come to your restaurant? He rides a Buick and is always accompanied by a couple of girl friends; where will they sit here? You cannot expect them to sit on these packing box-turned stools! That apart, if a Buick is parked in front of your shop, it will attract a crowd!
>
> T. (Visibly agitated) What did you say? Why will he come? Where will they sit? Tell him babu, this is where Harish Mukherjee who fought against the blue monkeys [indigo planters][50] used to have his tea; a place often frequented by Deshbandhu Chittaranjan Das during the Independence Movement; where the revolutionaries remained under cover for months at a stretch (*boma-r doler babu ra ga dhaka diye thekechhen*) and a place that has seen crowds of thousands gathering in front at least on three hundred occasions in its history of one hundred years. Not a single person would stop to see the Buick in front, and even if *there is no sitting accommodation* inside, he would not feel ashamed to have tea standing on the footpath here.

In comparing the structure of the pre-existing tea-shops to the Coffee House, the former, with its genealogy linked to crucial moments and luminaries of the Freedom Struggle, it was very much possible that Ghosh had 'Favourite Cabin' in mind when he penned these lines. It had an impeccable pedigree, something that ICH lacked. The author noted that 'quite a few of the old, small restaurants and cafes in the city had an adventurous (*romanchokar*) history'. What is important and worth noting here is that Tarini was not ashamed at all that his restaurant did not have the modern, trendy facilities of ICH, but with hurt pride reminded the narrator

[49] Ibid., 76.

[50] Harish Chandra Mukherjee (1824–61) as editor of the *Hindu Patriot* wrote on and drew attention of the British Government to the atrocities committed by indigo merchants and planters against the cultivators.

of the symbolic value of his establishment. The association with the nationalist struggle enhanced the prestige of his shop and separated it from other ordinary tea-shops This association was enough for clients visiting the place—no matter how humble—*vis-a-vis* upstart places like ICH, and attract *all* irrespective of *their* status; awe and respect for the place as part of the struggle for modernity and inherent notion of austerity were more appropriate than the question of mundane physical comfort. In addition, the author informed, 'the owners of such places were imbued with a deep sense of humanity not to be found among the owners of the Casa Nova coffee-house'. Members of the same family were customers for generations (*bangsho poromporay*), and never regretted taking food there.[51] At the same time, the reader notices that by tolerating mixed groups the Coffee House introduced a change in the homo-social space of *adda* of the pre-existing tea-shops and cabins.

Thus from employees, to customers, and observers, the contrast between the bare, unadorned tea-shops associated with modernity and the tastefully decorated, 'modern' Coffee House was too clear not to take notice of. Consequently, although stormy incidents marked the anti-colonial movement in its last phase, the outlets of ICH were fancied by some sections of the urban educated including nationalists making these establishments popular joints in the city housing them. War-time shortage with the rationing of fresh milk and sugar and prohibition on the preparation and sale of bread, cakes and pastries, the notorious Famine of Bengal (1943) affected the operation and sale in all outlets across the country, occasionally leading to the temporary clousre of some outlets. In spite of these exigent circumstances, ICH became increasingly popular among the civilians. At a time when there was a riot in Calcutta, resulting in a curfew, calm was maintained in ICH by both Hindus and Muslims.[52]

To comprehend the enormous impact of the Coffee House in urban North India we shall bring its immediate legacy, the Tea House in CP which was apparently more popular for its coffee and known

[51] *Kalpyanchar Naksha* (Sketches), Kolkata: Pathabhavan, 77.

[52] Bandyopadhyay, 'Coffee house'.

as coffee house, into the orbit of this discussion. The owner Daljit Singh who came up with the idea had spent many hours at Janpath together with his classmates like Vishwabandhu Gupta.

The Tea House was a large restaurant like the ICH (*unlike* other small tea-shops) with three entrances on three sides.[53] There was a magazine stall on the right followed by the cash counter near the entrance. One of the doors led to the vegetarian section, the kitchen and the restrooms.[54] The furnishings included large shiny, comfortable leather sofas and transparent glass-topped tables.[55] It is remarkable that the contributions to an anthology reminiscing the glorious decades of this Tea House are full of coffee. Not only that, while writing about this Tea House some describe it as coffeehouse, others switch from Tea House to coffee house in such a way that it is not clear if the Tea House is at all the point of reference.[56] The current analysis of the Coffee House milieu in Delhi will draw on this Tea House as well, because not only was coffee more popular than tea here,[57] but the place was commonly known as coffee house:

> My reference to coffee-house here is not to the one in Mohan Singh Place [the site of the third ICH in CP since 1968]. I am talking about *that* coffee-house which was once known as the Tea House. This one was located at one corner of the Regal Building in Connaught Place [...][58]

[53] Vishnu Prabhakar, 'Tea House/Coffee House Mera Vishwavidyalay Tha' (Tea house-coffee house was my university), *DTH*, 410; 'coffee available in the Tea House was of top quality', Dronveer Kohli, 'Bedil Dilli: Dilli ke Goshthi Prasang' (Heartless Dilli: On In-groupism) (henceforth Kohli, 'Bedil Dilli'), ibid., 145–55.

[54] 'This door was not visible from the main hall. If someone did not want to pay for the food of others sitting at the same table, he could leave through the main door and take this one to enter the vegetarian section and consume unnoticed by others', Kalia, 'Tea House', 337.

[55] Upadhyay, 'Dilli ka Tea House'.

[56] Hardayal, 'Tea House se Kaffee House Tak', in *DTH*, 504–14.

[57] Upadhyay, 'Dilli ka Tea house'; Kohli, 'Bedil Dilli'.

[58] Shravan Kumar, 'Sahitya Aur bhi Rachte Hain' (Others write literature too), in *DTH*, 439–44 (440).

Or,

> Currently ICH is of course located at the top floor of Mohan Singh Place, but the original coffee-house was at the left corner of the Regal Building on the ground floor.[59]

Unlike the Coffee Board, when the Tea Board entered the domestic market, it addressed the common man and the housewife with the message that making tea was very easy.[60] Many restaurants called as café or its indigenized version, pronounced as 'kef' in Bengali, sold tea, but never sold coffee. Why would then a Tea House serve coffee, and if it served coffee, why was it called Tea House? Can it be possible, as it has been suggested by a connoisseur of the place (and of the ICH as well), that it was perhaps because the owner did not want to risk competing with the extremely popular ICH, that he began a Tea House?[61]

> ...who opens a Tea House instead of a coffee-house in 1960,[62] when coffee drinking is considered to be ultra-modern? [....] It is possible that the threat of commercial competition was behind this decision. Those days there was a Coffee House [ICH] on Janpath which used to be crowded throughout the day [....] How can the Coffee House

[59] Kumar, 'Tea House vanaam Coffee House ki Smritiyan' (Memories), in *DTH* 454–65; thus he wrongly thinks that the Tea house in the Regal Building was the first ever coffee house in the CP area, and after that, one was closed down, the Tent Coffee House was opened. This was followed by the Coffee House in Mohan Singh Place

[60] The Tea Board also validated the consumption of tea through association with specific social and cultural meanings, Gautam Bhadra, 'From an Imperial Product to a National Drink: The Culture of Tea Consumption in Modern India', Catalogue brought out on the Occasion of an Exhibition on Tea, Kolkata: Centre for Social Science Studies, 2005.

[61] Dharmendra Gupta, 'Shanibar ke Sham, Tea House ke Naam' (Saturday Evenings in Tea House), in *DTH*, 156–163, (156–57), emphasis added; cf. 'Drinking coffee was a special thing in North India. A Tea House would not have been enticing here (Calcutta), because tea was prepared at home', Shibaji Bandyopadhyay, CSSSC, interview, 30 January 2012.

[62] Although it is not clear when exactly the Tea House was opened, the author is mistaken about the date as it seems to have been operational since the early 1950s, Parminder Singh of the family of the owner Daljit Singh, 17 October 2012.

> be challenged by a second coffee-house? So there came the Tea House. But very soon however the owner came to realize his mistake. By that time you could get tea of a very good quality for a little money (*kam paison ki barhiya chai*) in the market; who would go to the Tea House for a cup of tea that cost one rupee and twenty-five paise?... so one day a small board was seen in the Tea House, with "Authorized by the Coffee Board of India" written on it. In other words, coffee became available in the Tea House. Initially coffee here was very cheap [30 paise]; but the price kept on rising till one cup of coffee cost 85 paise. This meant that with one rupee in your pocket you could drink coffee in the Tea House and could consider yourself *modern*.

Whatever motive Daljit Singh might have had behind launching a Tea House, the above observation contains some vital information for understanding the import of the ICH to Delhi, and north India in general. Tea was by that time readily available at an easily affordable price and establishing a fashionable Tea House charging a much higher price for tea did not carry much conviction. On the other hand, drinking coffee was considered a *modern* habit and eighty-five paise seemed a just price to pay for being *modern*.[63] Consequently, the concept of the tea-house proved to be a failed project; the owner had to introduce coffee to attract clients, and although there was an outlet of the ICH at Janpath, there was enough demand for coffee to have another establishment serving the same beverage very much within walking distance.[64]

Operating on these principles the outlets of the ICH and like them the Tea House in Delhi soon caught the imagination of the urban middle class.[65] Many of the urbanites, as we have seen above,

[63] Cf. 'Coffee is just a beverage; but people used to think that drinking it (in the ICH Allahabad) was a part of modernity', Professor Alok Rai, Department of English, DU, telephone conversation, 26 February 2012.

[64] After the ICH on Janpath closed its shutters, Arjun Dev along with his friends started visiting the Tea House; interview, 6 January 2012.

[65] The nearly hundred outlets of the ICH in Kerala are a bit different because they are more like restaurants. Almost everyone is familiar with the brand ICH. People get there the food they usually have for breakfast, lunch or supper at home. In Trivandrum for example, beef-*biriyani* at lunch time introduced in the 1980s is very popular. The outlets at Thampanoor, MLA Hostel and Medical College are so crowded around

were new to the city either seeking a new home in a new country, or had internally migrated for higher education and jobs. There were public halls for organized meetings, private places of gathering and small restaurants (eateries) and tea-shops. But there was *not* a single place of the scale and stature of ICH addressing the tastes of the large western educated cultured elite fulfilling their need for public association under one roof all at once. The coffee capitalists wanted a destination for the export surplus in coffee. But the aesthetically pleasing large structures with comfortable furnishings signified a differential socio-economic space mediated in this case, by the Coffee Cess Committee, and later, the Coffee Board. The earlier tea-shops, cabins and restaurants owned by small entrepreneurs operated at the micro-level and at the local, urban scale. As a consequence of the intervention of the state in the space of consumption via the bureaucratic apparatus of the Coffee Board functioning under the government, the ICH operated at the macro-level of the state. The pavemet tea-stall of the fiction, Jagati's in Allahabad or Favourite Cabin in Calcutta, were structurally different considering their geo-spatial scale of operation. The subsidy from the state helped the Board to produce and reproduce the new space in numerous large and small towns of undivided India.[66] What the state and the industry had planned was a future possibility. Whether the plan would work, depended on the occupants of the space. One of the conditions of the production of space is that spaces created for one

this time that the traditional elaborate *thali system* is considered impractical and time consuming. By contrast, one plate of *biriyani* has vegetables, meat, rice, and sometimes an egg, thus all requirements of a proper meal.

[66] There is a fast increasing amount of literature on the social construction of scale as an important part of understanding the implications of global economic and human geography especially since the 1970s. See e.g. D. Harvey, *The Limits To Capital*, Chicago: University of Chicago Press, 1982 and *The Condition of Postmodernity: An Enquiry into the Origins of Cultural Change*, Oxford: Blakwell, 1990; Neil Brenner, 'State Territorial Restructuring and the Production of Spatial Scale: Urban andRegional Planning in the Federal Republic of Germany, 1960–1990', in *Political Geography*, 16.4 (1997), 273–306. For a summary of the most important contributions to this approach see Sallie A. Marston, 'The Social Construction of scale', *Progress in Human Geography*, 24.2 (2000), 219–42.

purpose are often adapted to suit the requirements of the users and may serve an entirely different purpose. The following section will elaborate on the everyday interaction of different social groups that characterized the ICH.

EVERYDAY PRACTICES IN THE NEW URBAN SPACE

The dimensions of space are determined to a large extent by its everyday use by the people inhabiting, occupying the space. The objective nature of the spatial structure and the subjective structures developing partly from the incorporation of the objective structure creates social space.[67] The material use of the created infrastructure signifies that the perceived space is not only related to the realm of idea. Through constructions, improvisations and innovations and otherwise use by the occupants of a space, it accumulates a meaning that speaks of their need and goes beyond the original purpose for which it was created. The multifarious use of the pavements in Indian cities for the purpose of hawking, bathing, begging, dwelling, eating, sleeping, and worshipping among other activities is an example of how spatial practices go far beyond the functional purpose for which they were created. In the current context the spatial structure of the ICH shapes the relationship between the workers and the visitors on the one hand, communications among the visitors themselves on the other, and the combined activities of all occupying the place.

As the name suggests, the ICH was a space where its patrons could consume coffee, allotted at a subsized price to the ICH. Initially, coffee was roasted fresh in the premises of most of the outlets. The brew was prepared in an indigenous two-part coffee filter, a variant of the French coffee press, manufactured for commercial use, a practice that still continues. Coarsely ground coffee powder added to the top part acting as a sieve set atop the bottom container and the powder secured in place through a press. Boiling hot water is poured on the powder

[67] To coin Pierre Bourdieu's phrase, this is habitus, see his *Distinction*, Cambridge: CUP, 1984; Walter Prigge, 'Reading the Urban Rrevolution: Space and Representation', in Kanishka Goonewardena, Stefan Kipfer, et.al., *Space, Difference, Everyday Life: Reading Henri Lefebvre*, New York: Routledge, 2008, 46–61.

and a thick decoction is collected in the bottom container. Tapped periodically in small quantity, this decoction is kept hot in an electric steamer through the bain-marie process, and served with either boiled frothing milk or as infusion, mixed with hot water, with or without sugar as per taste. The decoction prepared from 1 kg of coffee would traditionally yield about 120–140 cups of milk coffee and 50 cups of infusion. As the day passed on, the stock of the decoction was replenished according to the demand on the floor.[68] Earlier all outlets of the ICH had one person who was trained as the coffee-maker and would control the quality of coffee i.e. the ratio of coffee-powder and water and the quality of the milk. During the field research it was found that only a couple of the outlets still employed a coffee-maker.

During the prohibition period, the workers learned the basics of coffee-making which was considered sufficient and the same amount of coffee powder was said to yield 225–250 cups of coffee on an average. Addition of milk diluted with water often produces a brownish liquid often far removed from coffee.Regulars at the ICH, for whom the practice of drinking coffee began in the space, mostly consumed infusion.[69]

The aroma of the freshly roasted coffee set the ICH apart from existing spaces of consumption. Although for many it took some time to get used to the bitter taste of the brew, consuming this beverage in the Coffee House as part of the European lifestyle was considered modern and fashionable.[70] Written and oral testimonies including the epigraphs to this chapter suggest however that like the paisanos of Steinbeck who did not really love wine but wanted it for what it

[68] Babaji Charan Mahala, 5CA, Calcutta, interview, 4 Februray 2011; and V.M. Peter John, ICH Bangalore, interview, 2 August 2011.

[69] The best coffee prepared in the ICH tasted by me was in Bangalore, Simla and Trichur. At all locations, it is desirable that a particular preference (for example very strong; sugar on the side etc.) is specified at the time of placing the order.

[70] Inder Sharma recalled that when he first visited ICH along with a friend as a final year school student in the year 1945, they did not like the bitter taste of the coffee. They ate the cashew nuts served with the coffee, and decided to leave quietly without paying. Later, as a student of the DU, Sharma visited the ICH in the campus in 1949–50. By that time he had gathered that coffee drinking was fashionable, and developed the taste for it, Inder Sharma, interview, 17 October 2012.

did to them, the patrons of the Coffee House consumed coffee for what it brought along: the instant stimulous provided by coffee, the ambience, the association and the endless debates and discussions. It is crucial to understand this aspect of the Coffee House, as it is through these associated practices and performative acts that the users of the space altered and expanded its meaning. it. For them the Coffee House did not remain just a place for drinking coffee; it far exceeded the original intention of the planners.

According to Pabitra Kumar Ghosh, whose concern about life in the modern Indian city has been noted in Chapter One, modern man had two special needs: his hunger for life took him to the street to join the procession, public meetings and political parties; but the Coffee House was the place that satisfied the creative and cultural need of his mind:[71]

> Those who visit the place every day do not go there only for drinking coffee, for consultation or interlocution. They go there in order to think in public. That is why they sit in a circle around a table, ponder while they converse, and contemplate as they weave a tapestry of words. Animated discussions with loud bangs on table do take place here, but less in comparison with tea shops. Discussions here focus more on literature, society and the writings of thinkers of the world than on cheap politics. There is warmth in this discussion, an intention to comprehend and explain, but no attempt to impose one's opinion on others. This is because the Coffee House conversations are not just between any two persons. A few like-minded people familiar

[71] Pabitra Kumar Ghosh, *Coffee House*, Kolkata: Ranjan Publishing House, 70, emphasis added; cf. 'This corner of Hazratganj (in Lucknow) forms the axis around which the urban life here revolves. It is a different issue altogether that the usual actions of livelihood are not performed here; it only offers relaxation from those actions. Yet, this corner forms a natural confluence of those who regulate the life circulations elsewhere in the city. It is for this reason that since he is in Lucknow, Bhuvan (the protagonist, a scientist teaching in the university) has been visiting the Coffee House together with Chandramadhav (a journalist and a regular at the space) without fail at least once, but often two to three times a day. Saturated with the essence, flavours and forms of life, that corner seems to be very much in the centre of life holding the pulse reflecting the vital flow of life which it can stop at any moment by pressing it hard', Agyeya, *Nadi ke Dweep*.

> with each other customarily form the everyday circles of discussion in this place....normally members of a group respect each other's views.... Consequently, although the conversations of the compact groups resound in this space, no one creates a racket or uproar here. Public meetings have lectures accompanied by loud pronouncement of slogans. Coffee House discussions begin with purposeless conversations and end with an analysis of all kinds of slogans.

Like in the satire cited above, here too a distinction is being made between the coffee house and tea-shops—the discussions at the former civil, the bangs on the table less louder in comparison with those at the latter. But the spatial structure of the Coffee House, while remaining a part of everyday life, also separates it from the life outside.[72] This explanation finds resonance with reminiscences of other Coffee House patrons. The uniqueness of the newly conceived space was to a great extent due to its ambience. The novelty it constituted in its spatial particularities, its magnitude, the aroma of roasted coffee tickling the senses, and the sight of a house full of young and old engaged in conversation. But *adda* was the *sine qua non* of the Coffee House and it is through a glimpse of these *adda*s that we can have some idea of the everyday practices in the space. Not only is being widely read and interested in knowledge and discourse essential for such *adda*s, the citations from Pabitra Kumar Ghosh are just the tip of an iceberg. But these citations will familiarize the reader with the intellectual world of the cultured elite which, combined with quick wittedness and sharp sense of humour, took the age-old Indian tradition of orality to its climax in the Coffee House *addas*. In the following passage Krishna Basu shows how beginning with something trivial, the conversation would flow from subject to subject with no one directing its course in particular:[73]

> We were discussing the monsoon in Calcutta at our Coffee House *adda* in College Street. Suddenly the conversation moved to group

[72] Prigge, 'Reading the Urban Revolution'.

[73] Krishna Basu (a poet and a retired university teacher is not to be confused with the politician), 'Adda: Ekti Abikalpo Janala' (Adda, an unparalleled window), in *Kolkatar Adda*, 195–208, 207–8; emphasis added.

> theatre, and having touched *Mrichchhakatik*, *Ranikahini*, *Nathbati anathbat*, *Jokhon eka*, *Football*... *Ghasiram Kotwal* and *Charandas chor*[74] it moved to poetry writing, rhythm and rhyme, surrealism, and then to the problems of communication before turning again to [film-directors like] Utpalendu Chakrabarti, Gautam Ghosh, Buddhadev Dasgupta, Shyam Benegal, Govind Nilhani. There is no certainty which direction the *adda*-river would flow. From time to time this is spiced up with pure and tasteful gossip. Editors of little magazines talk about their financial problem. Some sell their own magazine, express dissatisfaction over the fact of not getting advertisements, while others dismiss the current trends of art and literature in an aggressive manner. There are a few who cannot help expressing personal ill-feelings and hatred, but in spite of all that poison, the nectar is the final word here. The warmth of the friendly company helps us shake off the cold, and we warm up our hands a little; is this bitter-sweet warmth not enough in our life full of monotony?....There is such an ambience created by the combination of this humming noise, the smoke of cigarette, the aroma of coffee, the proud announcement on behalf of the editors of little magazines, confident faces of young male and female writers, that I begin feeling dizzy.

A similar account of the intellectual gatherings of the ICH Lucknow during the 1950s has been provided by another Bengali, Ashok Mitra:[75]

> The glitterati were all there: D.P. Mukerji, the extraordinary scholar was joined by the enlightening Zain Ahmed, the communist trade unionist expert on what distinguished a Marxologist from a Marxist and Narendra Deva, a savant socialist and at the time the university's vice-chancellor. Deva would listen stoically even as Feroze Gandhi kept narrating one naughty political gossip after another. Fariq Malihabad would exchange graceful banter on the asymmetries of Urdu and English prosody with the redoubtable professor of English, N.K. Siddhanta. A batch of young university lecturers usually provoked a

[74] These are well-known stage productions in Bengali and Hindi by celebrity theatre personalities in India.

[75] Ashok Mitra, 'Identity and Inheritance: Talking About Revolution', *The Telegraph*, 30 July 2010.

> visiting Rammanohar Lohia to explain why he thought Nehru's foreign policy was all wet. The range of themes covered was truly astounding, from the sociology of knowledge to Nye Bevan's National Health Service to the on-going campaign against betterment levies in Punjab, and from the historiography of Arnold Toynbee to Edgar Snow's latest book on China to the debate in the pages of the New Statesman on the Two Cultures, and again to Begum Akhtar's recent recital at a private soirée and Maurice Thorez cold-shouldering the French socialists.

Albeit subjective—Ghosh, Basu and Mitra represent an elitist view of the *adda*—this is a close account of what constitutes an intellectual *adda*. This conversation does not limit itself to any singular subject, knowledge of the latest works on economics, politics, sociology, literature and interest in classical music are essential attributes for such an *adda*. Not only that, the conversation flows like a river. It moves smoothly from the past to the present and through the cycle of seasons, from subject to subject to the truth of life here and now: momentary respite from the monotony of the life outside, a state of intimacy *sans* the feeling of concern or responsibility (*dayitvashunya nishchinto antarangata)*.[76] The idea that in this space they could just be themselves among friends or in friendly company, free from the tension of the everyday struggle in the concrete jungle outside was the life essence of the Coffee-Tea House. As evident from the following testimony of a writer migrating from rural Punjab to Delhi, who discovered the village *chaupal* in the Tea House: [77]

> *Chaupal* is a centre of folk-culture in rurban areas, whereas this big *chaupal* [the Tea House] is the centre of culture in this mega city.... The Tea House [serving coffee] was not only a meeting place of the intellectuals. It was an addiction without which you would not know peace of mind.

While the idea of opening a coffee or tea-house was commercial and inspired by the prospect of profit, what attracted the customers

[76] Bhattacharya, *Albert Hall*, 1; for similar comments about the Tea House, see *DTH*, 511.

[77] Bhimsen Tyagi, 'Dilli mein Chaupal', in *DTH*, 260–66, (265); cf. *DTH*, 511.

to the place was the chance of coming across friends, acquaintances and other familiar faces. That possibility was so alluring that visiting the locus became a compulsion to the extent that if for some reason they were unable to visit the Coffee House, they felt that the day had been spent in vain.[78]

People from different walks of life were drawn to the new space. Many of them were familiar with the location that already formed a part of their public life; not only that they did not have to go out of their way to reach the place, the coming up of the Coffee House definitely added a new dimension to their life experiences. Since not everyone came from the same background, we shall now look at the visitors, occupants of the space. Who were the participants of the Coffee House *adda*s? Writing about the Tea House in Delhi one author noted:

> People used to come to the Tea House from different corners of Delhi. Different kinds of animal used to come there.... All had their different points of view, different social norms, their own sufferings and pleasure, own frustration and pride. They all had their separate world; still they were one in the Tea House [...] [79]

Who were these 'animals' going to the tea and coffee house? Did all belonging to the urban middle class become addicted to the new beverage that attracted them to the new space of leisure? Was there a certain kind of people who were attracted to the ICH, and if so, is it possible to categorize such public?

Undoubtedly, not all members of the educated urban middle class became Coffee House addicts. Prominent among them was a section of the intellectual elite drawn broadly from the middle class familiar with the role of the coffee houses, pubs and salons in Europe, with the knowledge of the use of coffee from Western literature and films who were the first to welcome the new institution into the city. Like the extensive quote from Ghosh above shows, the availability of cheap editions of the classics of world literature, sociology and other

[78] Gupta, 'Amader Jubakaler Adda,' 53.

[79] Tyagi, 'Dilli mein Chaupal', 265; for coffee in the Tea House see ibid., 261; also Upadhyay, 'Dilli ka Tea House', 323.

subjects had allowed them to embrace literary cosmopolitanism.[80] Whether in Allahabad, Calcutta, Delhi, Lucknow or any other city, these elite had read about Honoré de Balzac's passion for coffee and the debate of the philosophers in the coffee-houses as well as the artists' gatherings at Montmartre in Paris. They had relished the works of Camus, Gorky, Kafka, Satre, Shaw, Shakespeare, Tolstoy among others either in original or in translation and were acquainted with the Western ritual of after-dinner coffee via films and were perhaps aware of the connection between French café culture, the War of American Independence. Like Ghosh, many of them believed in Leftist ideology—often encountered during their study abroad—and had been inspired by the spirit of the French Revolution and the Russian Revolution:[81]

> There was a sense of '*antlami*' [a Bengali word from French 'intello'] in our decision to... settle down at the Coffee House as the place of our *adda*; we had heard that the intellectuals in France used to keep the pubs in Monmartre shining and thriving through the flow of their works. In those days we were influenced by the French Revolution and inspired by a revolutionary spirit. Naturally, although it was not a pub, following the French example we all gathered at the Coffee House.

This is a testimony to how the new space was perceived by the urbanites. They did not link the Coffee House with the Mughal *qahwakhana*, nor did they celebrate drinking coffee and discussing literature, philosophy, politics, etc. as reviving a forgotten indigenous tradition. The long association with the colonial culture, in some cases through English medium education, had mediated the process of acquisition of the modern 'cultural capital' by the indigenous elite.

[80] Hardayal, 'Tea House', in *DTH*, 514; Gupta, 'Amader Jubakaler Adda'; Mukhopadhyay, *Coffee-r Cup*, passim; cf. Interview H.S. Saxena on the availability of imported books in Allahabad during and after World War II, when a copy of the *Times Literary Supplement* could be purchased for a few *annas*.

[81] Mukhopadhyay, *Coffee-r Cup*, 62; cf. Mukul Guha, 'Adda Konodin o Bondho hobar Noy' (There is no end to *adda*), in *Kolkatar Adda*, 128–34; for Delhi see Kalia, 'Tea House', 334.

The Coffee House was seen as extension of Western modernity. It is not to claim that all who possessed the specific assets of this cultural capital went to the ICH or vice versa. But those among the visitors who had some idea about the potential of the space as facilitator of intellectual discourse and exchange of ideas, accepted the space with open arms, and transformed the commercial outlets of the ICH or for that matter the Tea House into a space of lively, intellectual conversations through long sessions of *adda*. Of course the memory of the European coffee houses was a part of more recent history for a city like Calcutta. But in the same vein, the conversations in the Coffee House of Allahabad and Lucknow reminded Markendey Katju of Dr Johnson, Samuel Boswell, Charles James Fox, and John Wilkes passionately arguing on some issue in the coffee houses and salons of the West. In this sense, the image of the Coffee-House, as it is remembered now, is a creation of a section of the patrons but there were definitely others, as noted in Lucknow for example:[82]

> The Coffee House was an institution in which coffee was the least important. It was a meeting place of nihilists, communists, socialists, journalists, middle-of-the-roaders, intellectuals as well as of non-intellectuals whose ambition was to be mistaken as intellectuals.

The regular customers of the Coffee House at Calcutta in the 1940s to 1960s can be divided roughly in three socio-economic groups on the basis of the bits and pieces of information available with regard to their economic situation. One group was composed of salaried professionals: employees of government or private companies and banks, journalists of the established media, university teachers, doctors, lawyers, etc. A second group consisted of self-employed individuals: brokers, businessmen, gamblers, and not to forget, poets and writers.[83] Reminiscences of *adda* in the space are narcissistic and often do not relate to the presence of brokers, gamblers and traders there. The cultural elite undoubtedly dominated the space but an

[82] Dayaram Varma, 'In memory of Sudarshan Punhani (1933–2009), South Asia Citizens', http://www.sacw.net/article920.html.

[83] It is, however, a common practice to combine it with professions like journalism, publishing or teaching.

observant eye could not overlook other kinds of activities, including business, taking place here: [84]

> At that place someone read poems, some composed lyrics, some hummed a song, some conversed with women, some talked about women and some gossiped about who eloped with whose wife. Everything used to take place there... business was also carried on....

There is a strong feeling in Bengal that the ICH is associated with the practice of liberal arts and is not the place to discuss financial speculation/business matters. There are other places for that. According to this view the presence of brokers and speculators is damaging for the sanctity of the ICH. They believe that the presence of gamblers and share brokers encourages those connected with flesh trade to frequent the space. Consequently, this group is conspicuous by its absence in classic accounts of the ICH projected as a place frequented by artists, intellectuals and litterateurs.[85] However, like many others, share brokers and small traders too discovered the public place soon after it was launched. I came across Ashok Dudhoria in College Street who ran a family business, and was familiar with the ICH since the late 1950s when he was a student. When asked about the kind of business he ran, he avoided the subject. He shared his interest in numismatics, philately and old documents, all of which he

[84] Mrinal Sen, 'Addamela Hoke', 38; cf. Mrinal De, who had a business in spices was in a regular in the ICH was deeply interested in music and literature and the poetry weekly *Kavita Saptahiki* edited by the poet Shakti Chattopadhyay; Parthpratim Kanjilal, interview, 17 August 2011 but corporate houses however were never a part of the Coffee House.

[85] Nirmalya Ghosh, university lecturer in Bengali, a visitor since 2005 when he was a BA student, interview, 16 July, 2011; also Gautam Ray, secretary ICH at 5CA, interview, 18 February 2011. Ray commented that it was impossible to stop them from visiting the place. Nityapriya Ghosh, columnist, *The Statesman,* recalled the presence of brokers in the ICH, but he did not bother about it, interview, 11 February 2012; a group of brokers is to be seen at Jadavpur as well, Abhijit Mukherjee, Head, Department of Engineering, JU, interview, 16 February 2011; the presence of prostitutes in ICH College Street was for a short period and could be stopped due to measures taken among others by the late poet Saibal Mitra, interview, Sabyasachi Bhattacharya and Debatosh Mitra, 20 August 2011.

had collected in the ICH.[86] Being close to Chowringhee, 5CA however had a strong presence of share brokers from the beginning. Subhash Chandra Bose, a professional gambler, frequented the ICH since 1960s and knew others in his profession who visited both the outlets.[87] Gopal Chandra Das, a retired broker was a regular client at the 5CA outlet where he enjoyed a lunchtime *adda* with Dipak Saha, also a broker.[88] There has been no such prejudice against businessmen and traders visiting the ICH in Delhi. Subhash Goyal, a fresh graduate from Sri Ram College of Commerce in 1973 was allowed to use one table at the ICH in Mohan Singh Place (Delhi) to launch his travel agency Students' Travel Information Centre (STIC). At present, the agency has more than forty registered offices and 300 employees all over India. Even now, medical representatives and small agents of companies like Mars, carry on day-long conferences at this very outlet of the ICH.

Some of the other groups of regulars at the Coffee House in Cacutta and Delhi comprised students budding poets and writers, temporarily or permanently unemployed persons. Intermixing with them were persons with ridiculous ideosyncracies—social misfits in various degrees. The formation of such informal groups in the ICH cut across this economic division if it was felt that the economically disadvantaged person shared the same cultural capital, or at least aspirations, as other members of the group.

Since the Coffee House at 5CA was close to the heart of Anglicized Calcutta,visitors to this place in the 1950s and the 1960s included the cream of the Bengali social elite. One of the famous personalities associated with 5CA was Satyajit Ray, especially in the pre-*Pather Panchali* days when he was a commercial artist with Keymer's,

[86] Ashok Dudhoria, interview, 25 February 2012. See more on him in Chapter Five.

[87] Subhash Chandra Bose, interview, 2 February, 2011.

[88] He would often see Hemchandra Barua the MP from Assam, Pratap Chandra Chandra, Madhu Limaye, Dina Pathak and others entering the air-conditioned section of the ICH, Gopal Chandra Das, interview, 18 February 2011; cf. Suresh Ramaswamy, a consulting accountant of Sanjay Modi & Co. who university student in the ealy 1970s was familiar with the Coffee House culture and has been visiting 5CA regularly since 1998, 18 February 2011.

designing covers for books published by Signet Press. He visited the Coffee House regularly during the lunch-break.[89] Ray was usually seen sitting at a corner table, unofficially reserved for a group that included the who's who of the Bengali cultural world: Kumar Prasad Mukhopadhyay, Radha Prasad Gupta, Chidananda Das Gupta, Subhash Ghosal, Kamal Kumar Majumdar, Paritosh Sen (artist), Biren Roy of the family of zamindars in Behala, members of the Dutta family of Hatkhola, others. Ray found the discussions here stimulating and it was to this small group in 5CA that Satyajit presented the script of *Pather Panchali* for the first time.[90] Gupta, a bibliophile, profound scholar, antiquarian of Calcutta, an avid art collector and a great conversationalist, was without employment for a considerable period of time.[91] Mukhopadhyay grew up in Lucknow where he was trained in the Agra *gharana*, a tradition of North Indian classical music, by his father, the musicologist Dhurjati Prasad. An employee of Coal India, he was also interested in cricket and photography. The duo has been celebrated as *adda* greats of all time.[92] Subhash Ghosal, a legend in the world of advertising, used to work with the advertising agency John Walter Thompson. Film-maker Chidananda Das Gupta was the co-founder of Calcutta Film Society that was set up in his house in 1947.[93] They would meet at the 'House of Lords', the popular name of the air-conditioned section of the Coffee-House where there was a butler. During 1945–55 in one section of the ICH, a couple of tables were unofficially reserved for members of this group.[94] Sometimes they would be joined by other dignitaries like journalists of *The*

[89] Andrew Robinson, *Satyajit Ray*, 356–57.

[90] Tapan Raychaudhuri (1926–2014), interview, 14 February 2012.

[91] See Ian Jack, 'The Raconteur of Life's Little Tales', *Outlook*, 2000, for a short biography of Radha Prasad Gupta; for a glimpse of the range of his knowledge see his interview in L. Fruzzetti and Á. Östör (ed.) *Calcutta Conversations*, New Delhi: DC Publishers, 2003, 16–31.

[92] Sajni Mukherji, 'Adda Greats', *The Telegraph*, 14 March 2010.

[93] Kumar Purnendu Narayan (Jute Corporation of India, and founding member of Calcutta Film Society, interview, 22 August 2009.

[94] This part of the building is now sold to a bank. Coffee here used to cost 8 *paise* more than in the other section called the House of Commons.

Statesman, or the ICS Satyen Ray who used to solve crossword puzzles in the Coffee House. When Aneurin Bevan, the British Labour Party politician visited Calcutta, Satyen Ray took him to 5CA to introduce him to his friends.[95]

Brought up in Lucknow, Kumar Prasad must have felt self-conscious in the presence of these Calcutta-bred intelligentsia. He would take out a rupee coin (in those days a lot of money) and roll it on the table in order to impress his elite Lucknow-style upbringing. That one rupee was enough to impress the members of the group, in the cash-starved economy of post-Independence India, and post-famine Bengal in particular, a large section of the cultural elite too faced economic hardship, often lacking even the money to pay for a cup of coffee on a regular basis. Coffee at the Coffee House cost 4 *anna* (six *anna* in the House of Lords) which was quite high in comparison with the purchasing capacity of the average middle class people in Calcutta in the late 1940s. A lunch for Rs 1.50 at Chung Wah was considered expensive, and those who could afford an occasional three-course lunch at Firpo's for Rs 3 were well aware of the fact that it was a luxury.[96] It can be added in this context that even after becoming world famous for his films, Satyajit Ray did not have enough capital to build a house.[97]

There was thus an important section of the customers with cultural capital but lacking in matching economic security. Spending on a cup of coffee cannot be compared with spending on a piece of jewellery or a car but right from the 1940s through to the 1960s there were, (and for that matter even now there are) people who found a cup of coffee even in the Coffee-House expensive and not easily affordable.[98]

[95] Kumar Prasad Mukhopadhyay, *Majlish*, 18; the date was 14 February 1953.

[96] Ibid.; Tapan Raychaudhuri recalled having lunch at Firpo's once in a while, and that only a few went to the brasserie on top of the New Empire Cinema; cf. the first time Sunil Gangopadhyay went to the Grand Hotel, he accompanied a wealthy friend, Sunil Gangopadhya, *Ardhek Jiban*.

[97] Ray's films were seldom box office hits and most of his income came from the science fictions and the detective series he wrote for the youth.

[98] Sunil Munshi, *Thikana Kolkata*, Kolkata: Thema, 2010; Sen, 'Addamela Hoke'; for Ratnabir Guha, a student of Presidency College (PC, 2000–03) this was one of the

Mrinal Sen for instance, could not afford to visit the Coffee-House. When Radha Prasad Gupta was without a job, he would sit on the staircase in front of 5CA, along with another unemployed friend, till someone familiar came along and invited them in.[99] Although Radha Prasad was a part of an economically secure elevated group, Mrinal Sen had to wait. He could visit the ICH only after he earned some money from the films he made. Then he accompanied Renoir to the place.[100] According to Vijay Dutt, in Lucknow there was a numerologist and a poet reciting Urdu poetry who used to subsist on other customers' generosity. As the ICH closed its doors, each of them would get a packet of food courtesy the fellow occupants of the place.[101]

Little is known about the personal life of a small section of visitors who frequented the ICH at all above locations. They drank coffee sitting in a solitary corner, always unaccompanied, apparently without work, and were never in a hurry. They talked to no one, read the newspaper, and silently observed the happenings in the place, while the rest of the crowd had no clue as to the purpose of their visit.[102] I suggest that these individuals were attracted to the ambience of the place and lived vicariously through the enjoyment of others. Their silent presence in the place may be understood by the concept of modern consumption as a system that stimulates the imagination.

---

reasons why he and his friends avoided the ICH and went to the shed on the footpath known as Chini's (now extinct). Ratnabir, coming from a family in South Calcutta did not, however, lack money, cf. Anwesha Sengupta, another student of PC (2006–09), interview, 11 July 2014.

[99] Gupta, 'Amader Jubakaler Adda'.

[100] Sen, 'Addamela Hoke', 38; in order to supplement the insignificant income from tuition fee Radha Prasad (48 kg) appeared in a commercial of Deluxe cigarette in which he defeated his friend Ranen Roy (98 kg) in a mock duel, Mukhopadhyay, *Majlish*, 16.

[101] Vijay Dutt, op.cit.

[102] Shishir Bhattacharya, 'Coffee Houser Shei Lok Ta' (That Man of the Coffee House), in *Coffee Houser Shei Lok Ta*, Kolkata: Anubhab Prakashani, 1967, 4–5; Gautam Bhadra, 'why they came, and why they sat there without talking to anyone, remained an enigma', interview with Sunil Gangopadhyay, 22 February 2011; interview with Anirban Mukhopadhyay, 14 August 2011; Neelabh, e-mail, 12 August, 2012.

This enables the consumer to control passion and construct a mental image, and the imagination in its turn brings the direct pleasure of consumption.[103] It was innocent recreation at hardly any cost, spotting iconic figures like Satyajit Ray or eloquent stage and film personalities like Soumitra Chatterjee or Aparna Sen, a charismatic personality like Firaq Gorakhpuri or Ram Manohar Lohia or even the spiritedly engaged discussions among young students. The aesthetics of the space including its liveried workers and comfortable sitting arrangement, the opportunity to share the same space with an indulging luminary temporarily resolves the contradiction between ambition and frustration and the objective condition of their life becomes irrelevant at least for some time.

High school and university students were one group that discovered ICH soon after it was launched. Distinguished institutions such as Calcutta Medical College, the University of Calcutta, Mahabodhi Society, Presidency College, Sanskrit College, Umesh Chandra College of Commerce, Hindu School, Hare School were all on College Street. One could reach this place within five to fifteen minutes from many other colleges in central-North Calcutta.[104] While most of the postgraduate classes for the humanities section were held in the campus till the 1970s, all teachers and students had to go to the College Street campus for administrative and financial purposes. Earlier many of the student hostels were also located in the same neighbourhood. Consequently, for students and others connected with the University visiting the ICH was easy. High school students in the area were sometimes already acquainted with the place before they joined college. I often came across groups of high school students from the neighbourhood there, and one such group from Hare School put off their cigarette as they did not want to be seen smoking while in school uniform, students were in the early decades of the Coffee

[103] C. Campbell, *The Romantic Ethic and the Spirit of Modern Consumerism*, Macmillan: Oxford, 1987, 69, 77–78. This explains why window-shopping is in itself a satisfying experience (rather than a desire-laden step towards ownership); ibid., 24.

[104] For example Sanskrit College, the branches of City College on Surya Sen Street and Amherst Street, Vidyasagar College, Surendranath College, St. Paul's College and Scottish Church College.

House perennially short of cash. When he was a student of class X in the early 1960s, one afternoon, Dhruba Bhaduri sold his Logic book to one of the secondhand booksellers on College Street to be able to pay for a cup of coffee at the ICH with other absconding school-boys. Bhaduri, grandson of the legendary dramatist Sisir Kumar, had heard about the Coffee-House from his father and his friends. He was a regular visitor of the place till 2004. [105] Students like Nirmal Brahmachari, Ashim Chatterjee and Sudarshan Roy Chaudhuri began a club in the ICH called *sarbavuk* (omnivorous) which was subscription-based. The collections from the subscription enabled them to purchase food which they consumed collectively.[106]

> Soon after the Coffee-House on College Street opened its doors in the morning, local petty traders, shop-keepers, brokers from the neighbourhood came here for their morning cup of coffee. A few elderly bachelors, widowers and a group of students came around the same time for their breakfast. For students living in hostel this is not a new phenomenon. [107]At seven-thirty in the morning we would usually be the first customers (*bouni kora*) ordering coffee, omelette, bread and butter, or plum cake. As the day advanced, we would perhaps have a chop or cutlet in the afternoon. And again some other item to fill the stomach while having coffee in the late afternoon or evening.

At around 10.00 am the place was buzzing with students from the neighbourhood morning colleges. From around mid-day till the evening, there was a continuous flow of pre-university and university students from different schools and colleges near and far, who were joined by local tradesmen taking a break with their second cup of

[105] Dhruba Bhaduri, interview, 21 February 2011; when he was in high school in the early 1960s, Siddhartha Basu had heard from the Headmaster of his school that Satyajiy Ray used to go to the Coffee House. One day Basu skipped his school in order to see Ray. He got hooked on to the Coffee House himself, interview, 16 July 2011. Bodhisattva Kar of Hindu School who had accompanied his parents to the place as a child, began going there with his friends since he was twelve. He used to bring out the magazine *Parthenon*, Bodhisattva Kar, interview, 7 November 2011.

[106] Nirmal Brahmachari, ex-Naxalite, editor of *Purbasha Ekhon*, interview, 17 February 2011.

[107] Bhattacharya, *Albert Hall*.

coffee, and some idlers.[108] Some of the other people who either came to shop at College Street, buy books, or on some other business also went to the Coffee House during these hours. Students usually only ordered coffee because the main purpose of their visit was to pass time and have an extended *adda*. They did not mind if their order took long.[109] A new group comprising bank employees and other office-goers, poets, writers and editors of little magazines, joined by the locals visiting the place for the third time in a day, began pouring in in the evenings. Many of these office-goers ordered some food along with coffee, and because they tipped the workers well, the latter were busier and more alert around this time.[110] The crowd began thinning out gradually from around 8.00 pm. Some continued to talk standing even when the workers begin re-arranging the tables and chairs and cleaning the floor at around 8.45 pm.[111]

Situated in the middle of a colony market near a bus terminus, ICH at Jadavpur, across the street from the Jadavpur University named after the locality was much smaller and did not have the same ambience compared to College Street. Opening at 11.00 am, this outlet first welcomed a few retired persons from the neighbourhood and a couple of persons visiting the area on business. By the time students began crowding the place, followed by a few teachers from the university, the morning guests had already left. From lunch time onwards, it was brisk business till it closed its doors at 8.00 pm. The two air-conditioned restaurants on the way to the ICH on the first

[108] Earlier students, especially female students left the space before it became dark; currently students of both sexes can be seen at the CP outlet in Delhi, and in both the outlets in Calcutta.

[109] Interview with Sankha Ghosh and Sunil Gangopadhyay; Bhattacharya, *Albert Hall*, 115.

[110] Bhattacharya, *Albert Hall*, 116.

[111] Currently at 5CA the first customers are share brokers and traders from the neighbourhood, who often visit the space for business negotiations. They are joined by a few office-goers dropping in for a quick coffee on the way to their work. Journalists from *ABP* or *Statesman* might drop in during the luch time. Since this is located in the business quarters of Esplanade and close to a metro station, occasional visitors outnumber college students at this place.

floor depended on those who preferred to stop here rather than walk up ahead knowing the Coffee House was full.

Visiting the Coffee House was thus something special that made the visitor distinct from others visiting neighbourhood tea-shops and restaurants. Important aspects of this distinction were the rarity of coffee in north India and the unique principle behind the creation of the chain. Also remarkable in this context was that consumption of tea, available everywhere, was not considered modern enough.

Right from its beginning the ICH at Janpath was a place for all kinds of intellectual discussions and political gossip which inspired students and youth leaders to frequent this place. Mir Mustaq Ahmed, the youth leader of Quit India Movement, Daljit Singh, the president of the first Tonga Union in Delhi, Trilokinath Purwar, the freedom fighter from Garhwal,[112] Vishwa Bandhu Gupta, a student revolutionary from Hindu College who together with his father Desh Bandhu Gupta had participated in the Quit India Movement were among the regulars here. Budding political leaders and adherents of the Congress and the Congress Socialist Party engaged in exchanging their views and visions of independent India here. This place not only discussed news and exchanged information, but also functioned as a post-office.[113] After he became an aide to Shyamaprasad Mukherjee of Bharatiya Jana Sangh in 1951, Atal Bihari Vajpayee would be seen there with his adherents, not that high politics was always the topic. Soon it became the point of congregation for the intellectuals and future intellectuals of Delhi—Frank and Veda Thakurdas,[114] Surojeet Sen, Saeed Jaffrey, Reggie Carapiet and Roshan Menon of All India Radio, Charles Fabri,[115] photographer Richard Bartholomew and

[112] Till he died in early 2012, Trilokinath was a connoisseur of the Coffee House.

[113] If it was necessary for example to send any information to revolutionaries in Simla, it would be done through mutual contacts in ICH at Delhi; Vishwa Bandhu Gupta.

[114] The first Indian principal of Miranda House College, DU.

[115] Chales Louis Fabri (1899–1968) was a Hungarian archaeologist, novelist and playwright, editor of the the Annual reports of the Archaeological Survey of India for the years, 1930–34.

his (future) wife Rati Batra,[116] the chief of the Little Theatre Group Michael Overman and his wife, journalist-poets Keshav Malik and Rakshat Puri,[117] the barefoot Maqbool Fida Husain, Satish Gujral among many other aspiring artists and writers.[118] The ICH catered to the parties hosted by Jawaharlal Nehru, celebrating the independence of India.[119] Barring a few days in September 1947 when it was closed due to communal riots, the ICH drew a steady clientele and soon became a hub of the intelligentsia migrating from Pakistan: Inder Kumar Gujral,[120] Satish Gujral, Reginald Massey,[121] Jaipal Nangia, Krishna Sobti, Uma Vasudev, to name a few. On any normal day at around 10.30 am in I.K. Gujral could be seen sitting at the first table in the centre near the hall's entrance, together with Surinder Nihal Singh of *(The Statesman)* and Inder Malhotra *(Times Of India, TOI)*, Ajit Bhattacharya and Rakshat Puri *(Hindustan Times)*, to be joined sometimes by Uma Vasudev and the Congress leader Tarlochan Singh. Girlal Jain, the chief reporter of *TOI*, Kamla Mankekar, the wife of the editor of *TOI*, Krishan Malik, the airport (and later London) correspondent of the *TOI* and other journalists usually sat in the middle seat of the horse-shoe shaped sofa on the right. A group of DU students from Zakir Husain College, Hindu College and Kirorimal College used to share one table near the kitchen at the back of the hall with a few senior working friends. Another group of young clients consisted of S.P. Dutt (known among his friends as Speedy), G.V. Krishnan (HT),

[116] Born during World War II in Burma, Richard Bartholomew was an art critic, photographer, poet and writer; Rati Batra migrated from West Punjab in 1947, journalist and art critique, Reginald Massey, email, 13 August 2013.

[117] Rakshat Puri was a journalist and poet in Hindi and English.

[118] Reginald Massey, e-mail, 16 July 2013.

[119] *8th Annual Report of the Coffee Board*, 1947–48, 18.

[120] Born in Jhelum in pre-Partition west Punjab, Inder Kumar Gujral (1919–2012) a freedom fighter, held different portfolios in the central government since 1967 and was the Prime Minister of India (PM) during 1997–98.

[121] Reginald Massey, *Azaadi!: Stories and Histories of the Indian Subcontinent After Independence*, New Delhi: Abhinav Publications, 2005; Massey used to spend more time at ICH than in St Stephen's where he was enrolled, Massey, e-mail, 16 July 2013.

Sushil Nangia, Irshad Panjatan, R.G. Anand, Balraj Komal among others.[122] Yet another group comprised Satinder Singh, an expert on Akali and Communist politics, 'Professor' Joginder Singh, teaching in private colleges, his brother Hardev Singh and a fourth person popularly called 'Judge Singh'. Satinder was especially known for his short blond beard, argumentative nature and the loudest laugh in the ICH.[123] Few other Congress leaders seen at that place were Ashoka Mehta with his followers and Satyanarayan Sinha. ICH helped displaced members of the newly emerged nation state find a footing in Delhi—a city most of them were not familiar with. At the ICH they met other persons like them.

The Coffee House in Delhi had a few tables earmarked for certain customers where no one else was allowed to sit. During the initial years of the Coffee-House coffee cost two and a half *anna* including sales tax![124] Because ICH offered coffee and snacks at an affordable rate, it also attracted a lot of office-goers in the neighbourhood and workers of moderate means visiting CP on business, including Life Insurance agents formed a major clientele of ICH in the 1950s. The ICH was the only place in this area where ordinary middle class workers like Life Insurance agents on field work could meet their clients and agents.

Unlike in College Street, Calcutta and Delhi where students comprised a bulk of the visitors, the ICH at Allahabad was a bastion of professionals who had their fixed time for visiting the place. In the words of Neelabh, who experienced the place from next door where his parents owned a publishing house named after him, and then as a regular customer:[125]

[122] S. P. Dutt later joined Air India; Irshad Panjatan was a pantomime actor; Balraj Komal was an architect, playwright and dramatist, interview with Irshad Panjatan, 23 July 2012.

[123] Jatinder Sethi, 'Delhi-'o'-Delhi: Memories of Fifties', Academy of the Punjab in North America, web article, http://www.apnaorg.com/articles/sethi-2/.

[124] Vishwa Bandhu Gupta; Inder Sharma; historian Arjun Dev began frequenting ICH in Janpath and DU more regularly since he joined KM College, interview, Dev, 6 January 2012.

[125] Neelabh, 'Addebaaj Shahar'.

> As such, the Coffee-House is not a compartmentalized place that can be divided in blocks like morning, noon and evening. There is a continuous flow of people at that place; and yet it is possible to divide them according to the three meal times because the groups assembling there are opposing in nature and come at their own fixed time.

In addition to medical representatives and idlers, usually sportsmen and some local political leaders could be seen there in the morning. Accompanied by their clients, lawyers from the High Court went to the ICH during lunch hours. A handful of university students, interested in politics, gathered there around the same time. Lawyers often went back for a coffee at the end of the working day. It was then that the literati went to the ICH, and stayed on until after it had closed for the day.

Ex-patriates from the US and Europe stationed in India were attracted to the ICH which had a predominantly Western menu. Initially, when food was served, cutlery and napkins were also provided. The first generation of visitors were conscious of table manners, considered important and meticulously observed those days.[126] Workers too knew the use of cutlery. With the indigenization of the place accompanying the take-over by the workers' cooperatives, the menu changed gradually and service etiquette disappeared.[127] As *adda* became the most important attraction of the place, consuming food was incidental, and no one usually bothered about table manners, or etiquettes. In the informal ambience of the ICH, where a plate of onion fritters or sandwich was very often shared by more than one, cutlery gradually became superfluous.[128] In spite of the distinctive nature of the place with liveried workers donning fan-tailed headgear serving coffee, the 'Spartan ambience' of the ICH was

[126] H.S. Saxena, interview, 22 January 2012.

[127] Currently, Allahabad and Simla are the only places where the napkin is still provided.

[128] For many second-generation visitors ICH was not the place to have food; Gauri Saxena, senior railway officer interview, 22 January 2012; also Bodhisattva Kar. Referring to the 1970s Allahabad, Gauri recalled that in general the practice of eating out was not common. Negotiation of food like Fish Afghani, Chinese noodles or cutlets however makes the use of cutlery necessary.

one characteristic fondly recalled by my interlocutors: 'there was no dress code, no etiquette, no frills, no tensions; what mattered was exchange of ideas and intellectual conversation'.[129]

Yet, the usual social norms, including sense of propriety, respect for the older generation and abstaining from eve-teasing, were usually respected at the place.[130] Asked why he stopped visiting his once favourite place, Sunil Gangopadhyay replied that he thought he would make space for the younger generation. But the ICH was perhaps the first public space in urban India that saw the intermingling of old and the young unrelated members, often sharing the same table, engaging in an informal conversation. Students accompanying teachers could form such groups. As one elderly visitor put it, 'this is a place where the old becomes young and the young becomes old'. The presence of the older generation works as a mechanism that prevents the younger generation from crossing the line of decency. On the other hand, long familiarity and acquaintance encourages the older generation to indulgently overlook the spontaneous outburst of energy of the youth at the threshold of adulthood.

Referring to the custom of 'going Dutch' (implying individual footing of bills) among Bengalis in the *addas* in restaurants and the Coffee-House in Calcutta, Dipesh Chakrabarty noted that the origin of the custom lay perhaps in the fact that they felt embarrassed for not offering the hospitality at home and that the democratic *adda* of the tea and coffee-houses knew no patrons. Narratives of *addas* come across in the course of this research do not confirm this. One, *adda* in the Coffee House was not necessarily democratic or without a patron. Second, emphasis on culture ignores the economic aspect of the issue. Recent research has shown that although championing the use of homespun

[129] Gauri Saxena; Meena Sharma (64) who accompanied her parents Mr and Mrs Kanwarlal Sharma as a kid to ICH in CP, interview, 24 November 2012; Neelum Saran Gour, English Professor, interview, 12 September 2013.

[130] My observation in College Street and Jadavpur outlets in Calcutta and CP in Delhi, is that apart from the regular college students, in groups involving members of the academia, civil society organizations, literary and media circuits, age does not form a barrier.

cloth Gandhi appealed to the sense of frugality. It nevertheless led to the commodification and consumption of *khadi*, and that consumption practice formed part of the discourse of middle class lifestyle, often entering the domestic sphere.[131] I argue here that if the aesthetics of the interior decoration and coffee were the attractions of ICH, the other reason behind its popularity was that the middle class was not necessarily averse to consumption as long as it came at an affordable price. This fact was as true in the 1940s as it in the new millennium; and there are sections of the middle class, then as well as now, for whom even a place like ICH remains expensive. Mrinal Sen's testimony that he stayed away from the ICH or smoked cheap Kingstar cigarettes because he could not afford otherwise, while another celebrity film director Ritwik Ghatak smoked beedi, is just one example. Even the moderately priced coffee in the Coffee House was often shared by two or three. Sen and his friends used to share one cup of tea among four of them. They were worried about their health as they had heard from a doctor friend that cheap cigarettes were bad for health. Ritwik Ghatak, was also a part of this group. Economic hardship was common in many middle class families and we know about Sunil Ganguli or Mrinal Sen because they became famous and wrote about this. Sen, 'Addamela', 35; cf. Sumanta Banerjee, *Thema Book of Naxalite Poetry*, Calcutta: Thema, 26; A considerable section of the visitors in the ICH Queensway and DU seems to have fared better throughout; compare for example Reginald Massey's statement that the dilemma they sometimes faced was 'Will it be ICH or UCH?' United Coffee House was a regular restaurant like Alps and Standard, and more expensive. Dilip Simeon did not believe that Mrinal Sen could have gone through a phase when he was not able to pay for a (shared) cup of coffee available at a price far below the market rate, and informed that he had not seen something similar in the ICH in DU, but see Anita Rakesh, 'Antim basiyat', *DTH*, 15–29 for the penury that induced the writer Mohan Rakesh to take up all kinds of jobs.

[131] Emma Tarlo, *Clothing Matters: Dress and Identity in India*, London: Hurst & Co., 1996; Lisa Trivedi, *Clothing Gandhi's Nation: Homespun and Modern India*, Bloomington: Indiana University Press, 2007; Judith Walsh, *Domesticity in Colonial*

Although he came from a land-holders' family and could occasionally afford a three-course Rs 3 lunch at Firpo's, Tapan Raychaudhuri reminisced about six decades later that in comparison with Basanta Cabin, ICH was more expensive. For four annas, the cost of one cup of coffee, one could travel all the way (by tram) from College Street to the Lake in Dhakuria in south Calcutta and back.[132] It was not uncommon for regular visitors to spend a few hours without consuming anything at all.

According to Neelabh, those in Allahabad usually went 'Dutch', a practice his father Upendranath Ashk did not like at all, and called *baniyagiri*, tradesman like. He was of the opinion that regulars at one table should pay for others by turn. Both Hemendra Shankar Saxena and Manas Mukul Das thought however that 'going Dutch' made ICH sociability easier for rising poets and not established lawyers.

According to one insider of ICH and Tea House in Delhi, the custom of bill payment at the two places was different. At the Tea House the bill was paid by turn, by one person (by implication, those at ICH went 'Dutch'), and there were only a few who would not mind paying. Even established and well to do members like Harishankar Dwivedi and Jainendra in the Tea House in Delhi were not keen on paying the bill. Once when sharing the table with the 'doctor', Surendra Malhotra, Balraj Pandit and Balswaroop Rahi, Jainendra said, 'let me pay the bill today', Rahi is said to have quickly taken the bill from the plate saying, 'let it be; why should you break your tradition?' Many sensed discomfort and embarrassment at the sight of a worker approaching a table with the bill: [133]

India: What Women Learned When Men Gave Them Advice, New York: Rowan and Little, 2004.

[132] Raychaudhuri, *Bangalnama,* 115; for an eyewitness's account and analysis of the Famine see 126–30; the stage personality Rudraprasad Sen Gupta lived under straitened circumstances when his widowed mother had to bring up eight children on her own, interview, 21 August, 2011; cf. 'Around the year 1950, Rs 10,000 was an inconcievable amount of money', Rabindra Kumar Paul, owner, Hindustan Sweets, Jadavpur, Calcutta.

[133] Kalia, 'Tea House', 335; see the poem of Narendra Dheer cited on the same page; also see, 337; those in the Tea House who did not want to pay for others would

> The moment when the bearer in the Tea House crops up like the *Yamaraj* [god of death] with the bill in his hand, is unforgettable. Those who do not want to face this moment, quickly go to the toilet, or to another table. Some begin searching their pockets at the sight of the bearer, and keep on searching till the bill is paid. Some become nervous and focus on lighting their cigarette, while others begin playing with their match box. Yet others in the group look away and just keep mum.

Delhi being the capital and the home of many government and publishing firms patronizing Hindi, there was a constant flow of visitors to the city. Since the Tea and Coffee House were usually the places where everyone could be met, visiting writers too came here. Consequently, the groups could be large with the result that there were occasions when there would be many coffee drinkers but no one to pay the bill. Gradually, there was a consensus that everyone would sit and drink together, but everyone would pay for their own coffee. Vishnu Prabhakar too recollected hilarious situations when it came to the payment of bills for coffee at the Tea/Coffee House. One visitor always carried a hundred rupee note that could not be changed easily in those days when a cup of coffee used to cost 30 paise and commodities were cheap. The writer Devraj Dinesh once stealthily took out a note of 10 rupees from another patron who never paid for coffee.[134] While the practice of payment by turn was common among classmates and close friends, members of a large group usually went Dutch. But the attitude of the middle class toward consumption and expenditure could also have played a role in the case of persons like Jainendra.

DEMOCRACY IN ICH AND THE *BHADRALOK*

The Coffee House is, according to its patrons, a 'totally democratic place'. To what extent is this claim sustainable? Can it be said that

---

disappear from the main hall for some time and enter the vegetarian section through the third entrance at the back, and enjoy a stuffed *parantha* or other snacks there secretly, Upadhyay, 'Dilli ka Tea House', 319–20.

[134] Prabhakar, 'Tea House', 411.

the educated middle class congregating in the Coffee House formed one homogenous group?

When the coffee houses emerged in early modern Europe, one way to attract the public was to draw attention to the novelty, openness of the place where the old gentry and the nouveau riche tradesmen could sit next to each other irrespective of their social hierarchy. It was not necessary to get up and make room for a pre-eminent person in reverence for his distinct social rank; anyone walking in could occupy a seat that was empty. The intention was not to show any disrespect to the high and mighty, but in the cosmopolitan atmosphere of the metropolis, the gentlemen discarded the old provincial customs and the strict formalities of the past and created a genteel ambience where differences were overlooked.[135] It is interesting to note that in the prevalent narrative of the ICH, it is one of those places where, from the very beginning, persons of different social status have been welcome, including the unemployed. Testimonies, written and oral, attempt at underlining the inclusive nature of the place.

In the words of Sarat Kumar Mukhopahyay, an eminent member of the *Krittibas* group, the ICH was *the* ideal place for those on a tight budget to spend a few hours:

> Coffee-House opens at nine [in the morning] and closes at nine [in the evening]. It is more or less busy during these twelve hours. There one can order one cup of coffee and spend a couple of hours at that place at leisure. One gets drinking water on demand, what cannot be expected at Basanta Cabin, Putiram, the YMCA or Dilkhusha in the neighbourhood. Coffee House was the ideal place of *adda* (*addakhana*) for students and unemployed persons.[136]

[135] Aytoun Ellis, *The Penny Universities: A History of the Coffee-Houses*, London: Secker and Warburg, 1956 xv; Richard Sennett, *The Fall of Public Man*, 81–82; Brian Cowan, 'What was Masculine about the Public Sphere? Gender and the Coffee-house Milieu in post-Restoration England', *History Workshop Journal*, 51, 127–57'; Tapan Raychaudhuri recalled, however, that the elite coffee houses in Oxford were not visited by the working class, interview, 14 February 2012.

[136] See *Krittibas*. The reference in this note and in the following one is in connection with the College street outlet; Mukhopadhyay, 'Coffee-r cup', 108. When Amartya Sen was teaching in DSE, students would accompany him to the Coffee House there and he would buy food and coffee for them.

> Everyone is independent (*swatantro*) here; everyone a king; each table is earmarked by freedom, sovereignty and distinction. For Bengali intellectuals of the day, especially the youth, this Coffee House is the mecca.[137]

Reminiscing about the *adda* in Coffee House, Jagannath Chakraborty, another well-known litterateur wrote:[138]

> At the very moment we first entered this place, we left our respective vanity born out of caste, creed and book-centred knowledge outside its door. We did not have to make any special attempt (*kasrat*) to forget the statistics of who possessed how much. How to articulate it in words? Did the Coffee House hypnotize us those days?

A major reason behind this bonhomie was the knowledge that coffee in ICH was cheap and anyone with 25 paise in the 1960s (and between Rs 12 to Rs 18 during 2010–13) could enjoy the hospitality there. In the eyes of its connoisseurs, the Coffee House was such a place where those better off economically took care of the less fortunate. But does it imply that the occupants of the place, in fact temporarily forgot their own social identity and that of others in the place? NGO worker Shoubhik Mukherjee, who had been visiting ICH since the early 1980s recalled a person who was of no material worth and depended on the patronage of others for his visits to the Coffee House:[139]

> A very ordinary person; [you could say a] failure in life. His real name was Siddhartha, an indispensable character of the Coffee House. He wanted to be a writer, but did not succeed in that effort. Then he began a spectacles-shop; but that business did not take off either. He was a failure in every respect but due to his amiability had an easy access to persons like even Ayan Rashid Khan and Aparna Sen. He knew many poems of Shakti Chattopadhyay by heart and the latter

[137] Apurvakumar Saha, *College Street Coffee-House*, Kolkata: Jagori, 1972, 10–11.

[138] Jagannath Chakraborty, 'Choddosho Bongabdo: Amader Coffeehouse', in *Coffee-Toffee*, 1993, 46–51. It is possible that while writing this line Chakraborty was thinking of the personnel of the ICH comprising Christians, Muslims and Hindus; cf. 'People leave their social status behind and meet and share the space as equals', Gupta, 'Amader Jubakaler Add;' similar comments were made by Ram Shastri, columnist and chairman of the Coffee House Consumers' Forum, Delhi, interview, 5 January 2012.

[139] Shoubhik Mukherjee, interview, 1 February 2011.

named him 'Bhetki.' For Shakti Chattopadhyay, Ritwik Ghatak and others who would go for a glass of Bangla liquor after the *adda* in Coffee House, Bhetki was a pleasurable companion.

The mention of Bhetki's presence was supposed to convey the democratic nature of the place. But the moment Bhetki was remembered, his social status was also mentioned in the same breath, which leads one to wonder if it was not an act on the part of the 'patrons', in seemingly enhancing the democratic spirit of the place.[140]

Tapan Raychaudhuri remembered a figure called BNtul, whom he had come across at 5CA. Clad in *dhuti* covering up to his knees and a *banyan*, BNtul did not belong to their social class and would hesitantly share their table, but was welcomed because he brought entertaining, queer types of people along.

One such person looked at the forehead of Satyajit Ray and predicted that he would be world famous, but as that person had no idea about films, he said he saw a white piece of cloth and light falling on it through a funnel. At College Street the same person predicted that Amartya Sen would conquer the world some day (interview with Tapan Raychaudhuri on 14 February 2012).

It should be remembered here that the terms 'poor' and 'poverty' are relative, for there is a difference between the real poor like beggars or factory workers who would never visit the Coffee House and the unemployed university graduate, who earned their pocket money by giving private tuition and later spent it in the Coffee House. However, till the recent revisions of the pay scales, salary in the public sector and especially for teachers in schools and universities was very low, and pension even lower and uncertain, making daily expenditure on coffee a luxury.[141] Consequently, a person with an unshaven face

[140] Ibid.; Sunil Gangopadhyay, interview, 11 February 2011; I personally met a few such persons in College Street Coffee House. They were friendly and greeted me whenever I was there. The members of groups they sat with were aware of their financial situation, but did not manifest any sign of disrespect and shared coffee etc. with them.

[141] The salary of a university lecturer in the 1940s through to the 1960s was about Rs 150–200; best students used to get a monthly scholarship of Rs 40 (for the 1940s

and in ragged clothes sitting next to you could well be a renounced revolutionary or a renown personality in his field. A classic account of such a person sipping his cup of coffee quietly in ICH has been provided by Tapan Raychaudhuri:[142]

> I think when I came to know him, Bhupenbabu [Bhupendranath Datta] had reached the extreme limits of poverty. He used to wear a semi-clean *dhuti* and a *panjabee* made of *matka*. Most probably that was the only *panjabee* he had. He would spend a long time over one cup of coffee in the Coffee-House, and would be very glad if we ordered sandwich or some other refreshments for him.

A noted revolutionary and a socialist, and the younger brother of Swami Vivekananda, Datta (1880–1961) was a member of the radical group in early 20th century known as the *Anushilan Samiti* and editor (1906–7) of the *Jugantar Patrika* brought out by this group. Detained for his revolutionary activities, he escaped British rule in disguise and did his M.A. from Brown University and became a member of the Ghadar Party in California. During World War I he was engaged in revolutionary activities in Germany and during 1916–18 he was the secretary of the Indian Independence Committee in Berlin. In 1921 he went to Moscow to join the Comintern, and handed Lenin a paper on the contemporary political condition in India he had authored. He obtained his Ph.D. degree from the University of Hamburg in 1923 and subsequently returned to India to join the Indian National Congress. During the 1930s he chaired two annual sessions of the Indian Trade Union Congress, but was again arrested. Datta was in his sixties in the mid-1940s when Tapan Raychadhuri saw him in the ICH.

Raychaudhuri, *Bangalnama*, 115; for the 1960s Sumanta Bandyopadhyay, *In the Wake of Naxalbari: Four Decades of a Simmering Revolution*, Kolkata: Sansad 2009: 11); retired persons, if at all, drew a pension on which a large family would be dependent.

[142] Raychaudhuri, *Bangalnama*, 115, 116; *Dhoti* or *dhuti* the long, unstitched usually white piece of cloth and *panjabee*, were the typical lower and upper garment used by the *bhadralok* male; *matka* is a rough handloom silk fabric made from very thick yarns; cf. 'Everyone fell silent after hearing the response of Trilochan Shastri on sonnet; they kept on admiring the knowledge and the genius of the person looking like a simple villager', Sudesh Kumar, 'Tea House', 2002 458–59, emphasis added.

The poverty of many sung and unsung heroes of the Indian freedom movement is a legacy that independent India has lived with indifferently. However, that a large section of the customers of the Coffee House were financially insecure, is more applicable to College Street where university students, unemployed ex-students, (budding) poets and writers, painters, theatre personalities and persons connected with other forms of liberal arts dominated the scene. A brief look at the early career of the late Sunil Gangopadhyay, eminent poet and writer later connected with the *Ananda Bazar* group will help us to understand the potential of the ICH. The oldest child of a family migrating from erstwhile East Bengal lived in a cramped rented dwelling in north Calcutta, which could not offer the space or privacy this young adult needed. Sunil began visiting the Coffee House as a pre-university student of the Calcutta University in 1951. He recalled having paid 25 paise for a cup of coffee, and a cup of infusion—as black coffee is called in the ICH—used to cost three *anna*. He lost his father at the age of twenty-seven when he had to take charge of his mother and siblings. In between private tuitions that he gave, he would find time to visit the ICH, but he could not afford to have mutton omelette, his favourite at the Coffee House without some patronage, because it cost 75 paise.[143]

The examples of Bhupendranath Dutta, (unemployed) Sunil Gangopadhyay, BNtul and Siddhartha alias Bhetki seem to claim that free access and the possibility to communicate with other visitors freely, lent the space a kind of transparency. Although the customers of the Coffee House were aware of the temporary or permanent hardship of persons like Siddhartha, Radha Prasad or Bhupendranath, this fact was ignored in order to create a feeling of *esprit de corps* among the *bhadralok* instilling a spirit of democracy in the space. Not everybody came to the Coffee House, and those who did come, belonged to or aspired to belong to a certain cultural category. This is not to suggest

[143] Interview with Sunil Gangopadhyay; for similar comment on not having enough money to spend cf. Debdulal Bandyopadhyay, 'Addaheen Jeebon Boro Biswad Lage' (Life without adda is rather monotonous), in *Bangalir Adda*, 120; the reminiscences in Chandrima Bhattacharya 'Coffee and Cigarettes', 2009, http://www.telegraphindia.com/1090419/jsp/calcutta/story_10843651.jsp.

that an ex-revolutionary, for that matter Bhupendranath's father who had been an attorney and thus hailed from an affluent family, is being equated here with the unsuccessful Siddhartha. But the civility of the *bhadralok* allows him to gently accept both esteem for the former and patronage of the latter who gracefully and generously found their way into footing the bill on their behalf.

In the discourse on the composition of the *bhadralok* in Bengal, Partha Chatterjee has argued that the literati, intelligentsia and petty bourgeoisie, also described as the middle class of Calcutta were conscious about its middleness. And they used this consciousness to construct a new form of public discourse by setting a 'new criteria of social respectability, ... new aesthetic and moral standards of judgement, and, suffused with its spirit of nationalism, fashioned the new forms of political mobilization' that deeply influenced the political history of Bengal in the twentieth century. The *bhadralok* holding their sway over the cultural, political and social life in the nineteenth century pioneering for the upliftment of their countrymen, were in Chatterjee's study not a class but a social category, a homogenous group.[144] Expanding on the works of Sumit Sarkar, Tithi Bhattacharya has recently drawn our attention to the process during the hundred years beginning from the eighteenth century during which while some old privileged groups disappeared. English education as a ladder to upward social mobility allowed the emergence of other social groups forming a new middle class eligible for salaried jobs under the colonial government. Within this class, groups with access to power and wealth also to better education and the top strata of government jobs. These groups were systematically trying at the same time to exclude those below them from the privileged position they enjoyed.[145] In the individual narratives of the *adda* at the Coffee House, BNtul and Bhetki enjoy as prominent a place as Datta. But the narratives also demonstrate that economically the *bhadralok* in the Coffee House did not comprise one homogenous group but came from varied backgrounds within the middle class. For instance there

[144] Partha Chatterjee, *The Nation*, 35–36.

[145] Tithi Bhattacharya, *The Sentinels of Culture: Class, Education and the Colonial Intellectual in Bengal*, New York: OUP, 2005.

were persons like Tapan Raychaudhuri who came from a family of landholders, Bhupendranath Dutta originally from an upper middle class family but reduced to poverty because of his jobless past, and Sunil Gangopadhyay whose father was a schoolmaster drawing a salary that was hardly sufficient to maintain his extended family. There were many other families migrating from erstwhile East Bengal, like that of Shirshendu Mukhopadhyay who migrated during Partition and whose father had been a railway employee. Hobnobbing with them were persons like Bhetki who were permanently or temporarily unemployed, and BNtul, of whom we know only this much that he had access to the Coffee House. It were the norms of civility and the shared moral standards of judgement that bound them together in the Coffee House.

Could any new visitor join any group or conversation uninvited and express his opinion on topics being discussed in that group? Or, was the notion of equality in the Coffee House a fiction, a myth? How far could this civility, the feeling of equality be stretched?

ADDA: SPACE OF DOMINION AND INVISIBLE HIERARCHY

The *addas* of Monday Club and *Porichay*, among other literary groups studied by Dipesh Chakrabarty were spaces of Bengali intellectual interaction for like-minded people. Set up by Sukumar Ray, the Monday Club was based on a regular subscription of four *annas* a month, and *Porichay* consisted of members of the CPI.[146] As we have seen, the ICH was open to persons who would otherwise never have access to such elite groups. Consequently, narratives of *addas* in this public space allowing visitors irrespective of their social status often reveal a dimension of the participants' character, which will not manifest itself in a group of persons coming from a homogenous socio-economic background or mindset. This is especially true of the outlet at 5CA in Calcutta. Storytelling is an art, and narratives of *adda* present Radha

[146] Chakrabarty, 'Adda'; Hirankumar Sanyal, *Parichayer Kuribochhor O Onyanyo Smritichitro*, [Memories of Parichay] Calcutta: Papyrus 1978; Chinmohan Sehanavis, *46 No: Ekti Sanskriti Andolon Prasange* [No. 46: In the Context of a Cultural Movement], Calcutta: Research India Publications, 1986.

Prasad as a master raconteur.[147] At the same time, the narratives indicate that the site of *adda* is far from egalitarian; and that one had to earn the membership of a group. There were invisible boundaries one needed to cautiously negotiate. The fact that even in the group of like-minded individuals with similar cultural capital, Kumar Prasad felt the need to prove his worth by showing off his one-rupee coin, is symptomatic of the inner tension such a constellation of luminaries could evoke even among its own members, who then had to earn mutual respect by arousing awe among the lesser beings present in the place. The city-bred intellectuals might boast of their literary cosmopolitanism the memoirs of the ICH regulars constantly refer to:[148]

> Far from having an idea about the life in rural areas [of Bengal], those days we did not care much even about the daily life of the common man in Calcutta. We were engrossed in the world of Joyce, Wolff, Huxley, Eliot, Pound, Faulkner and the like. We used to read Russian, Italian, Spanish and German literature in translation. Many of us had not read the works of the great [Bengali] authorities like Bharatchandra, Ishwar Gupta, Bankim, Tekchand, Hutom, Dasharathi Ray, Hemchandra or even Rabindranath and Sarat Chatterjee attentively.

But that variant of culture with its history of only a couple of hundred years was an upstart compared to the the legacy of the indigenous Mughal aristocracy, especially from Lucknow, famous for their patronage of fine arts and their refined lifestyle. Reminding his table-mates of that distinction was a strategy for Kumar Prasad to impress upon them and to draw attention to himself.

Kamal Kumar Majumdar was by far the most colourful personality of the group. He used to visit the outlet in College Street too and irrespective of the location he would dominate the group through his manner of speech, dress and loud guffaws. One of the most influential novelists in post-War Bengali literature, Majumdar was a teacher of

[147] Mukhopadhyay, *Majlish*, 16; also Ian Jack, 'The Raconteur of Life's Little Tales', *Outlook*, 3 April 2000, 243–45.

[148] Gupta, 'Amader Jubakaler Adda'; the reference here is to eminent Bengali writers from the eighteenth to the mid-twentieth century; also on this issue Ranajit Das, 'Coffee Houser Adda', in *Bangalir Adda,* 174.

South Point School and known as a 'Francophile' who used to dress up like a French aristocrat:[149]

> Those days, both in his attire and his attitude (*poshak ashak*), Kamalbabu was like a European of the aristocratic French type. He would wear expensive suits from Herman's or Ranken's, his silk shirt, tie, underwear and handkerchief were purchased from the famous Parisian company called Sulkar. A very exclusive small Chinese shop in Middleton Row had wooden lass of his feet, and he ordered his shoes from there as per requirement [...]

Majumdar was, however, equally adroit in invoking the essence of Bengali culture. When Gupta and others would have a heated discussion on Western forms of art, literature, food, music or Marxism, Majumdar would bring in topics of genuine Bengali food, folk art and indigenous music, thereby surprising and impressing them through his use of vocabulary, typical of the different dialects of Bengali. The following account of an intruder in their group penned by Kumar Prasad is worth noting in the context of the hierarchy in *adda*:[150]

> One man called Debsharan, familiar with Shnatulbabu [Radha Prasad] used to move about our table. [One day] he boxed the ears of Niranjan Majumdar, [....] a noted Anglicist of the time. Although he appeared at the Coffee-House now and then, Majumdar's actual address was *Olympia* [a bar on Park Street]. Niranjan relished the atmosphere of English pubs at that place. He would often be accompanied by Mr. [Lindsay] Emerson of *the Statesman*. All of a sudden this Niranjan received some acclaim for the book *Sheete upekshita* (neglected in winter) he penned in Bengali. He was writing something else as well published serially by a renowned Bengali daily. I can't recall the title exactly now, but illicit love with a friend's wife was the subject of the story. This should not have offended the sense of ethics of Debsharan, and there is no question of any personal objection on his side [....] because he did knew neither Niranjan nor the real life heroine....
>
> ...Coming to the Coffee-House all on a sudden Debsharan grabbed Niranjan by his neck and said, 'mind you sir; it is fine if you wish to go on the spree after a drinking bout; and if you wish to speak

149 Gupta, 'Amader Jubakaler Adda'.

150 Mukhopadhyay, *Majlish*, 23–24.

> English with your affected accent like a snob, that's not a problem either. But writing [such wayward stories] on women of respectable families is not permissible'. Niranjan.... retorted, 'a writer writes on the basis of his own experience. Do you want me to write about the Mars?' At this, while boxing Majumdar in his right ear, Debsharan said, 'I don't care. But if I come across such obscenity in print again, you will meet a sticky end (*jutiye khal khniche debo*)'.

Debsharan was then a familiar face in the Coffee House, known even to Radha Prasad, one of the core members of the most elevated group in the space. That he was seen around their table indicates he had been noticed, perhaps looking for an entry point to the group. Boxing someone in the ears is traditionally a prerogative of a senior person expressing dispproval of some mischief committed by a minor. Although we assume that both of them were adults, we are not informed about the age of either Debsharan or Niranjan. Kamal Kumar was known for using the kind of collouiqual Bengali in which Niranjan swore; but Debsharan did not have the social status of Kamal Kumar. What is important here is that Mukhopadhyay introduces Debsharan as 'a man' (*ekti lok*). This usage is also in order to distinguish himself from a person like Debsharan. In the beginning of the narrative Mukhopadhyay already indicates that members of their group were known to each other, and that it was not unusual to snub an outsider, *bhadralok* or not, for trying to penetrate the invisible walls around the table:[151]

> Sitting in the Coffee House.... Radha Prasad Gupta, nowadays famous in the world of art and culture, was recounting the story of our travel to Puri. Two days prior to that, a gentleman we knew, had flown back from England [*bilet*] to Calcutta by Gypsy moth in a journey that lasted ten to twelve days. He didn't really belong to our table; perhaps he joined us hoping that we would be thrilled to hear the story of this boisterous adventure. Kamal Majumdar silenced him at once by brushing him off: "These days, even housewives and girls of ordinary families are travelling to foreign countries by Kundu Special.[152] *Sarengi-*

[151] ibid., 16; emphasis added.

[152] A domestic tour operating agency.

> players and *tabla*-players too are going abroad. It is far more difficult to travel to Jajpur [a place of pilgrimage in Orissa]. Why don't you rather listen to their story; they have just returned from Puri yesterday".

The message was clear; however commonplace a visit to Puri and Jajpur in Orissa might be, the story was being narrated by the group's own Radha Prasad, the great storyteller. The account of a travel by Gipsy moth looked like a stunt trying to divert attention. Moreover, the attempt to disrupt the flow of storytelling could not be tolerated.

The implicit rules of *adda* of course demanded that outsiders better be careful than to abruptly interrupt the flow of a conversation. But scholars have emphasized the exclusionary politics of the upper echelons of the Bengali *bhadralok* since the nineteenth century.[153] *Adda* seems to have facilitated and reinforced the old practice of groupism and exclusion and it needed someone as persistent as Debsharan to snap at them, to compel them to take off their mask. This is how Mukhopadhyay tells the story of a particular incident:[154]

> Another member at our table in the Coffee House was Pratap Roy, the son of Kumar Rabindranarayan of Santosh [a family of landholders]. With a fair complexion and a thin moustache, he looked quite manly.... In a soft voice he would tell us plenty of fantastic, unbelievable stories, mostly invented, but thoroughly enjoyable. At one time he was associated with Little Theatre [of the film and stage giant Utpal Dutt in Calcutta], and since then they had become friends. It seems, that day Utpal was explaining to Pratap the interpretation of Hamlet by Sir Laurence Olivier.[155] [In Utpal's view] Olivier had brought out the 'Puritanic streak' in Hamlet extremely well. Olivier's close-cropped hair helped him embody this characteristic aspect of Hamlet etc. etc.
>
> Now, due to lack of space, Debsharan was also sitting at our table and having coffee.... he knew neither Utpal nor Pratap personally. Suddenly, after he had finished his coffee and paid his bill, Debsharan spoke up: "[you] dare analyse the character of Hamlet, a character

[153] S. N. Mukherjee, *Calcutta: Myths and History*, Calcutta: Subarnarekha, 1977; and Bhattacharya, *Sentinels*.

[154] Mukhopadhyay, *Majlish*, 24; emphasis added.

[155] The 1948 film adaptation (and direction) by Olivier in which he himself played the role of Hamlet.

> that up till now no one has comprehended fully. None of his parents, or his uncle was able to fathom him; but you guys dare say you have understood him! [pointing to Utpal Dutt and Pratap Roy alternately] Your understanding is as inconsiderable as your knowledge; neither do you know anything, nor are you able to grasp it." He shook his thumb as he said this [a familiar disapproving gesture] and marched out.... We had no idea where this Debsharan came from, and where he went to; and I still do not have a clue. Nothing in the way he talked or did, indicated that he was a regular member of our adda in the Coffee House. He appeared all of a sudden like a comet and disappeared again in the pages of history after being a hero of the said two historic incidents.

It is not that Debsharan did not know the subject being discussed, and evidently he could pay for the cup of coffee he consumed in the House of Lords where coffee was slightly more expensive; yet he did not belong to the group sitting at that table. Was it because he was not formally introduced to the group? (Note that the author writes Debsharan did not know them—so although we are informed above that Debsharan was an acquaintance of Radha Prasad, that was not enough for him to qualify for a membership of the cherished group and he is described as an intruder. Is it because they could not relate to the way he spoke and behaved? Although the refined gentlemen could not imagine Debsharan coming from their own fold yet, similar anecdotes provided by the antiquarian Radha Prasad Gupta suggest that the elite in the Coffee House could be much more malicious than Debsharan.

Reminiscing about the days when he and his bosom friend Ranen Roy had no work and would sit outside 5CA awaiting the arrival of a well-wisher patron, Radha Prasad Gupta wrote:[156]

> One of those days I saw Ranen relishing cake, omelette and cold coffee with cream in the company of Satyen Roy. Taken by surprise, I wondered about the mystery behind this royal treat, revealed to me by

[156] Gupta, 'Amader Jubakaler Adda', 51; Radhaprasad's description of Ranen Sen weighing approximately 16 stone or 200 kg seems to be an exaggeration in a true *adda* fashion. In Kumar Prasad's account he weighed 98 kg, Mukhopadhyay, *Majlis*, 16.

> Ranen later. Sukumar Sen [an ICS, (1899–1961)], a regular member of the group of Satyen Roy had suddenly passed away. Soon after that one person introduced himself as a friend of the late Sen and began sitting at their table. Neither Roy nor anyone else could ask him on his face not to sit at their table; yet his presence hampered their conversation.
>
> Then Satyen Roy used his brain. He had noticed a huge corn on the foot of that man. One day he called the excessively heavy Ranen and told him: 'when that man comes [to share our table tomorrow], sit next to him and step on his corn as hard as you can. It is my deep conviction that if you do that, he will not return to the Coffee House during the rest of his life. But I shall watch for three days. If he continues to be absent, I shall treat you with whatever you wish'. Surprisingly enough, it happened just as he had planned. Consequently, at least for a day Ranen's luck favoured him....

Leg-pulling and outwitting is common at any friendly gathering and the ICH was no exception to these. In Allahabad, for example, one visitor, supposed to be the king of a small principality, was known in the Coffee House as Rajasaheb whose claim to this title was once challenged in the Coffee House. Next day the poor fellow was seen walking in with a huge framed charter in defence of his claim.[157] On another occasion, also at Allahabad, Upendranath Ashk wrote 'purchase books and read them' in the autograph book of a child; writing after him, Dharamvir Bharati wrote 'books are available at 5 Khusro Bag' [the address of Ashk]. [158] No one took offence at such playful innocent banters.

By revealing the politics of *adda* at 5CA the anecdotes suggest that *adda* was a much contested site, and even the most distinguished elite could forget the questions of civility, indulgence and tolerance in underlining the boundaries of their domain. Physical proximity did not remove social distance. Such narratives go a long way to expose the myth of democracy in the social space. In the third incident above, the identity of the stranger could not be verified because he introduced himself as a friend of a person who was dead. It was below the dignity of Satyen Roy, an ICS and a revered member of the elite, to address

[157] Neelabh, 'Kaffee Haus', unpublished manuscript.

[158] Mehta, *Pradakshina*, 204–5.

this person personally. He would rather use Ranen, a familiar face in the Coffee House [Roy perhaps knew that Ranen was unemployed] to humiliate this stranger in such a way as the latter would learn his life's lesson. The appropriated space was the site where the unperceived force of symbolic power manifested itself;[159] and for Ranen it seemed it was an offer he could not refuse. By obliging Satyen Roy—it was a token that Roy accepted him as part of *his* group—he conformed to the practices embedded in social hierarchy; and at least once he had the chance to eat to his heart's content.[160]

From the way the anecdote is presented, it seems, such incidents were commonly accepted in the circles of the Coffee House, especially at 5CA. Radha Prasad Gupta introduces the incident as one of the funny acts (*mojar kando*) of Satyen Roy in the Coffee House, and simply continues to talk about him:

> It was the same Satyen Roy who took Aneurin Bevan, an elocutionist and a key figure of the [British] Labour Party whom Churchill used to hold in high esteem in the [British] Parliament for an *adda* at our table one afternoon. Mr. Bevan was very glad after he talked with us for an hour or so.[161]

It could be thus read as: a person of the stature of Satyen Roy who kept the company of Aneurin Bevan, had the right to keep a stranger in his Coffee House group at bay. This expression of material dominion through non-material ways can be termed as 'symbolic violence'.[162] As a cultural elite, Roy could determine who could share

[159] Walter Prigge, 'Reading the urban Revolution'.

[160] Cf. 'No *adda* can be democratic', Chakrabarty, 'Adda'; my personal observation is that regular visitors usually go there with the assumption/knowledge that they will find someone they know, and that people go in groups, with friends. While any newcomer able to afford a cup of coffee can go in and have that cup, being accepted by one of the groups occupying the space is not easy without any prior acquaintance. If you are lucky, you may bump into someone by chance who will show interest in talking to you. This person can introduce you to others. Patience and time are required for one to get used to the ICH and vice versa.

[161] Gupta, 'Amader Jubakaler Adda'.

[162] L.J.D. Wacquant, 'Durkheim and Bourdieu: The Common Plinth and its Cracks', in B. Fowler (ed.), *Reading Bourdieu on Society and Culture*, Oxford: Blackwell, 2000, 105–20, 14.

the table with him in a public space like the ICH and the members of his group found it normal. The appearance of equality conveyed by the right to share the same space is thus an illusion that conceals invisible boundaries one may not transgress.[163] The in-groupism of the circles though more applicable to 5CA, were present at ICH College Street too. Sabyasachi Bhattacharya, a regular at College Street since his college days in the late 1970s was an accounts officer with a government undertaking in the energy sector. His multiple hobbies like philately, playing sitar, sketching, translating works of his favourite writers from the Coffee House into English and collecting fountain pens, a few always peeping out of his shirt pocket, earned him friends young and old sharing similar interests scattered at different tables. Narrating what attracted him to the ICH, Sabyasachi recalled his meeting with Nirmalya Acharya, the co-editor of the little magazine *Ekshan*. Acharya according to Sabyasachi was a person serious by nature and appearance. Once while waiting for his friends, Sabyasachi asked Acharya if he could share the table with him. 'Not if you wish to talk; not if you are going to waste my time. If you just wish to sit quietly, you may sit.' Sabyasachi did not mind, for it was well-known that Acharya used the place also for the editorial work of *Ekshan*; the ice was broken. On another occasion when Sabyasachi expressed his wish to subscribe to the magazine, Acharya brushed him off by saying, 'we do not allow just any Tom, Dick or Harry to subscribe to the magazine. There are criteria to be met'.[164] Sabyasachi accepted; and did not question why the right to subscribe to an established literary magazine should not be open to everyone. The spatial practice in the ICH had to toe the line with the structure, the social practices outside.[165]

Then there were those like Dharani Ghosh, the erudite columnist of *The Statesman*, famous for his splitting hair analysis of stage productions and also known for giving everyone the cold shoulder

[163] Space evokes the illusion of transparency, Lefebvre, *Production*, 29.

[164] Sabyasachi Bhattacharya, interview, 20 August 2011.

[165] An intruder is usually discouraged to join the same table by statements like, *Ekhon Amra Ekta Alochona Korchhi: Pore Asben* (We are Having a Discussion Now: Come Later). Although the formal 'you' is used, 'please' is left out on such occasions.

while mostly sitting alone and ordering three cups of coffee and three plates of *pakora*.[166]

My interlocutors at Allahabad denied having such invisible places of dominion in the Coffee House. But a rare account may convince us that the place was not entirely free from tension, although the arrogance experienced in Calcutta may not have been entirely emulated there. Before he became a judge at the Allahabad High Court in 1991, Markendey Katju was a regular in the place and noted that:

> There were several tables in the Coffee House, and though theoretically one could sit wherever one wanted, if you sat at the wrong table you were regarded a stranger. Certain tables were 'reserved' for the top intellectuals and professors in the University. So I could not sit at one of these tables, but tried to sit at a table closest to these, so that I could overhear the conversation.

The unwritten demarcation was so evident that it discouraged a practising lawyer from sharing the table with the eminent littérateurs. Regarding the ICH at Delhi, journalist Rajinder Puri noted that the right to entry to the place was not restricted, but to the respective groups was.[167]

The seeming presence of democracy in the Coffee House is however testified by the fact that a person like Debsharan could (and did) enter the Coffee House without being stopped by any one.[168] Similarly, Acharya did oblige Sabyasachi by allowing him to share the same table. The Coffee House brought people from different walks of life, who would have never met outside the place, face-to-face under one roof. But, familiarity was crucial in order to gain access to the *adda* there. Both Bhupendranath, a solitary figure known for his revolutionary past and Bhetki unpretentiously winning sympathy because of his

[166] Sabyasachi Bhattacharya remembers Ghosh rebuffing a university teacher who had humbly questioned the accuracy of the information Ghosh had provided in one of his columns thus, 'Why should I care about what you know?', interview, op. cit.

[167] This was in response to my comment that Embassy and the ICH were not perhaps comparable, the latter was a public space, more accessible than the former, interview, 5 October 2013.

[168] The early coffee houses in the Ottoman Empire had this trait in them in that people from common ranks could sit next to highly placed bureaucrats.

appreciation of modern Bengali poetry, were known figures in the place, whereas the whereabouts of Debsharan were vague. There was a tacit understanding that although ICH was not like the existing tea-shops with a shabby appearance, yet an average middle class person could walk in there, drink a glass of water, use the restroom or drink coffee while reading a book or newspaper or do nothing and leave the place without being accosted by anyone. However, a stranger was required to observe and perceive the mechanisms of the place and allow it the time to accept him; understanding this was absolutely necessary in order to prevent any unpleasant experience at ICH.[169]

SEMIOTICS OF THE COFFEE HOUSE

The same author who commented on the difference between the existing restaurants and the Coffee House also observed a class difference among visitors of the two sections—House of Commons and House of Lords at both 5CA and College Street. At 5CA, the House of Lords had air-conditioning; coffee and other food items here were slightly more expensive than the other section. In College Street, the space on the gallery of second floor with the long balcony on both sides and a long row of single tables were often used for couples who needed some privacy away from the cacophony and crowd of the first floor. Here too prices were more expensive than on the first floor:[170]

> As it is the Coffee House stands for aristocracy; yet by dividing it into floors and rooms, it has been made more sophisticated. Apart from those bohemian vagabonds who, instead of having a piece of butter-toast with tea, like to discuss politics over a cup of coffee on an empty stomach, all clients of the coffee-house have a status. This status is retained intact as it is in the main hall. Still, those who do not wish to face the ragtag, long to spend leisure time together with the person close to their heart, or those who prefer to sit at a cosy

[169] After the first couple of times, for some reason the secretary of the Consumers' Forum in ICH, CP decided to ignore me. At his table he was obviously the deciding figure, so elderly familiar faces otherwise buying coffee for me would not even ask to take a seat when they would sit at his table.

[170] Binay Ghosh, *Kalpanchar naksha*, 74; emphasis added.

> nook to engage into reflexive thought while chewing cashew nuts, or prefer to discuss modern literature, art, music, dance film etc. together with (girl)friends or flatterers in a safe distance from the ordinary crowd, may make use of the special service available almost at a double cost in the section next door [at 5CA] or on the second floor [College Street].

The paragraph cited above presents ICH as a desired destination. The incident with Debsharan demonstrates that sharing the House of Lords with great personalities did not put him at par with the august gathering there. It is not surprising then that members visiting the second floor of ICH, College Street and paying more for the same cup of coffee would want to distinguish themselves from the ragtags on the first floor.

It should be emphasized however that not everyone liked the Coffee House and it was not synonymous with the cream of the intellectual elite. In a Puritan, utilitarian view spending time in *adda* or at leisure not yielding any tangible result is not only morally unacceptable, but condemned.[171] By extension spending time in the Tea/Coffee House is symbolic of the carelessness of the youth coupled with light fun and mischievous pranks often considered a sheer waste of time.[172] Moreover, many were repulsed by the semiotics associated with the place and its users, and Tea/Coffee House visitors were often termed as bohemian. According to this view, while it is not necessary to visit certain places like ICH in order to establish one's intellect, not all visiting it were intellectuals. There were many pseudo-intellectuals who opined that visiting the place and trying to look intellectual was enough to be considered as intellectual. But what was the precise criteria for looking like an intellectual?

[171] The poet Sankha Ghosh recalled that when he had just taken admission into the Presidency College, one elderly member of the extended family asked, 'you have joined the university; hope you have not begun visiting the coffee-house?' (which had a negative connotation), interview, 11 February 2011; cf. 'those with a utilitarian mentality (...) look down upon *adda* and *addebaji* as if *adda* is a bad place and *addebaji* is a bad thing (...)', Upadhyay, 'Dilli Ka Tea House'.

[172] Upadhyay, 'Dilli ka Tea House', *DTH*, in 320; Dwivedi, 'Ek tha Tea House', in *DTH*, 363–64; Krishna Sobti, telephone conversation, 21 June 2012.

Even at a time when there was no satellite television there seems to have been some sort of consensus among the urban youth in India about the appearance of a 'Coffee House intellectual'. The typical image of a Coffee House intellectual in Calcutta was of someone wearing a handloom *panjabee* and *pajama*, the latter often replaced by jeans trousers,[173] unkempt hair, glasses with thick lens, carrying a cloth shoulder-bag, smoking cheap brands of cigarette like Charminar or Panama or *beedi* (unfiltered country cigarette) and Kolhapuri leather sandals. This gave the Coffee House intellectual a distinct semiotics.[174] In Calcutta, Allen Ginsberg and Peter Orlovsky began the trend of wearing this outfit as the 'badge of the intellectual'.[175] Actor-director and politician Bratya Basu, a student of Presidency College during 1987–90 recalled that one day Pradip Das Gupta, one of his friends looked very sad and serious in the Coffee House gathering. On repeatedly being asked if something was wrong, he replied that he had been verbally abused; unknown persons had inscribed 'Pradip Das Gupta is a bohemian' on the doors of his hostel room.[176] In the description of Harishankar Parsai, the Marxist Hindi satirist, the Coffee-House revolutionary was someone with a trimmed beard and a constantly burning cigarette in his hand.[177] Leading a bohemian lifestyle, like visiting the Coffee House, however seems to have been consciously cultivated, and the connotation was not always negative.[178]

[173] In the 1960s Calcutta however, it represented American imperialism.

[174] Sibaji Bandyopadhyay, interview, 30 January 2012; see Sumanta Banerjee describes the Naxalite student Dipen Bandyopadhyay dressing up the same way; but instead of smoking, he used snuff, *In the Wake of Naxalbari: Four Decades of a Simmering Revolution*, Kolkata: Sansad, 2009, 70, 90–91.

[175] Deborah Baker, *A Blue Hand: The Beats in India*, New Delhi: Penguin, 2008, 165, 237–38.

[176] Bratya Basu, interview, 13 February 2011; cf. Anirban Mukhopadhyay, interview, 14 August 2011.

[177] Harishankar Parsai (1924–95) was a regular visitor of the ICH Jabalpur where he lived. See his 'Ati Krantikari'; see also his story 'Krantikari Ki Katha', http://apnikahaani.blogspot.de/2013/06/story-of-revolutionist-by-harishankar.html.

[178] Radha Prasad Gupta was known as a bohemian. Mukul Guha noted that his friend Prasun Mitra, a regular member of the *adda* at Saki mess near Wellington where Guha was staying, was essentially a bohemian one, Guha, 'Adda'; cf. the Naxalite poet Ajay Sen had a typically bohemian nest somewhere in College Street, Das, 'Coffee

That the public in Delhi associated the ICH with similar bohemian lifestyle can be gauged from the following episode of a fiction. Yugmukh, the protagonist of a novel by Rajkumar Saini used to go the ICH in the DU campus where he studied MA and LLB. Even after he had left the university, he continued to visit that outlet for some time. As a government employee, when he began going to the ICH in CP following the 'doctrine of compensation', he took some time to plan his first visit to the new place in order to evoke a dramatic effect: [179]

> He went out of his way (*wakayda*) to purchase Binny's fabric for two *kurtas* (*panjabee* like upper garment) and denim cloth for a pair of trousers, and had them tailored. He also purchased a cloth shoulder bag with Islamic initials, a pair of leather sandals from Kanpur and a pair of sunglasses. With *this appearance of an 'intellectual'* (*'buddhijivi' dikhnewali mudra mein*) he entered a group of writers sitting at one table.

Thus being an intellectual or the possibility of participating in an intellectual conversation in the Coffee House was not enough for Yugmukh to impress upon others. He made a special effort to look like an intellectual and the new outfit together with the accessories were the symbols of an intellectual, and the idea was that the moment he entered the place, his appearance would draw attention of those present, and identify him as an intellectual. While the *kurta*, denim trousers and sandals took care of the casual, indifferent appearance, the Islamic initials underlined his secular credentials; if something was still lacking, that was covered up by the sun glasses. Again, in Allahabad there was Gyanranjan, a fan of poets like Ezra Pound, Arthur Rimbaud and the Urdu fiction writer Asrar Ahmad alias

---

Houser Adda', 172; it is worth noting that the media continuously reiterates the bohemian life-style of the Coffee House regulars; see for example Rakhi Chakrabarty, 'Calcutta Coffee House', http://www.hardnewsmedia.com/2009/10/3272; also the review of the ICH Calcutta in *Lonely Planet* http://www.lonelyplanet.com/india/kolkata-calcutta/restaurants/cafe/indian-coffee-house.

[179] Rajkumar Saini, *Khidki se Jhankta Hai Kaun*, Nayi Dilli: Samayik Prakashan, 2001, 82–83; in its orginal location on Janpath too there were bohemians dressing up in the same casual way, Vijay Dutt.

Ibn-e-Safi, who with several kinds of addiction, was considered to lead a bohemian life, like Baudelaire.[180] Looking closely, one could see the bearded Gyanranjan appearing in his usual attire of *kameez* and *patloon* (same as *panjabee* and *pajama* respectively). Many of the budding poets and writers, contemporaries of the Angry and Beat generation in the West, not only took care to look casual and unconventional by dressing in this fashion, but followed a bohemian lifestyle. Such figures still abound in the place although this is far from universal.

To the chagrin and irritation of other visitors, a few of the Coffee House regulars believed in exhibitionism. In Allahabad, in an obvious attempt to impress upon others, one person was seen carrying a hardbound copy of Dostoyevsky's *Idiot* regularly for some time. One day Tej Narayan Sapru walked up to him and told him quite loudly 'do not carry your biography so openly'.[181] In Calcutta, the poet and writer Buddhadev Bose never went to the Coffee House. There was an *adda* at his house in South Calcutta where his followers, popularly called *Bouddha* (follower of the Buddha, a pun), would gather.[182] Known for his bohemian lifestyle, Shakti Chattopadhyay would get drunk before he went to the ICH where his loud gestures would draw attention. 'This drunken state symbolized his ideal image (*bhaavmoorti*) and he consciously cultivated this image.'[183] The poet Binoy Majumdar, a trained engineer who was a mathematical and a poetic genius who used to live in a mess had made the ICH his second home where he would spend most of his time. He would be seen

[180] Neelabh, *Gyanranjan*, 3, 17; but Neelabh himself leads a bohemian life.

[181] H.S. Saxena, interview, 23 January 2012.

[182] Sanyal, *Parichayer Kuri Bochhor*, 76–78 for the *adda* of *Kavita*. The poet Joy Goswami is known for not going to the ICH. Even if he had to meet someone who was in the Coffee House, he would wait downstairs while his friends went up and fetched that person, Das, 'Coffee Houser Adda', 176.

In Allahabad too there have been persons disapproving of the atmosphere in ICH. Professor S.C. Deb used to compare it with a pub, and never went there (interview, H.S. Saxena); the Parimalian editor of *Kadambini* and *Madhyam* and poet Balakrishna Rao, and the novelist and story writer Amrit Rai never visited the place Neelabh, email, 22 August, 2012.

[183] Das, 'Coffee Houser Adda', 166–67.

writing every day sitting at a table near the windows on the street-side. Only in the evening he would join the table of his friend Ashok Bhattacharya, a Naxalite, who would buy him food.[184] It was the time however when he was losing his mental composure. Sometime in August 1969 after he had been to the restroom, Majumdar appeared in the main sitting area with his trousers unzipped. This was considered unacceptable and he was thrown out of the ICH.[185] Those who criticized the place did not wish to go there because they did not like the idiosyncrasies of the Coffee House intellectuals who, although well off, would appear in tattered clothes. With unkempt appearances and unshaven faces, they would spend hours drinking endless cups of coffee and blowing rings of smoke in the air. Shyamal Guha, the owner of the gallery Boichitro on the second floor of the Coffee House never went to the Coffee House because of the exhibitionism on the part of the occupants of the place:[186]

> [They thought that] showing/telling people that you were going to the Coffee House was already an indication that you were a great intellectual; this was supposed to make a great impression

The exhibitionism of 'pseudo-intellectuals' who pretended that visiting the ICH was a prerequisite for being an intellectual put off a section of the students, who were always encouraged to stay away from the ICH in order to make a statement.[187]

Through the everyday interaction, adaptations, alterations as per the perception of the occupants of the place, however, the conceived

[184] Mukhopdhyay, *Coffee-r Cup*, 85.

[185] Prasun Bandyopadhyay and Gautam Chaudhury, interview.

[186] Shyamal Guha, interview, 15 February 2011; many regular visitors did not like the attitude of some of those 30-plus visitors who, it seemed have just sent off the response to the much awaited letter from Bertrand Russell, Saha, *College Street*, 33.

[187] Nandita Chaudhuri, 'The first interview of the poet Nandita Chaudhuri', *Aspardha*, vol. 7, (2007–08) no. 6, 84–89; Ashim Mukhopadhyay, Assistant Librarian at the National Library in Calcutta and a student in the 1980s informed that some Naxalite students functioning as contact persons would make appointment with *Kaka* only in the ICH and that would then become a point of reference. Like many other members of the Students' Steering Committee Mukhopadhyay himself did not visit the ICH during the five years he was in the university; Mukhopadhyay, interview, 4 September 2013.

Coffee House took its real shape. Continuous production and reproduction of the spatial practices of the visitors of the Coffee House not only attested to the materiality of the planned public space, but transcended the original purpose for which it was created, viz. popularizing coffee, and went into the production of the space associated with the leisure time spent there. The everyday practices reflected how prolonged occupation here over cups of infusion seemingly in a democratic ambience reproduced the established social norms and practices. Yet, the Coffee House secured a distinct identity as an exclusive place in the collective imagination of the urbanites in India. It is ironic that considered to be alienated from the everyday, the practice of frequenting the Coffee House very much became embedded in the everyday.

THE COFFEE HOUSE AND IMAGINATION

The relation between identity and place is not limited to the physical space alone; it is mediated through constant imagination that links the place with certain practices rooted there, reiterating the spatial character of imagination. Meanings and symbolisms working through imagination, guiding the experience of a place, play a significant role in the process of the production of the a place. The many reminiscences of the Coffee House bear a testimony to the fact that in spite of all its peculiarities, the space of the ICH, became a part and parcel of those who discovered the charms of the place.

In many Bengali poems the space has been associated with memory of the past. For Sunil Gangopadhyay it was a part of his youth, when he used to walk from the Coffee House at random without destination, or of his many discussions at the place deconstructing literary and nationalist luminaries, denouncing Naxalite vandalism that left its mark on the place. In the poem 'Yeti' by Gautam Chaudhury the ambience of the place became part of a nostalgic and surreal construction of the past by an elderly person narrating tales of his youth to his grandchildren. The memory of the staircase of the ICH on College Street reminded Samarendra

Sengupta of the significance of the space and the personalities he came across there.[188]

The assemblage of so many groups at one place, the prolonged sessions of *adda,* the animated discussions on literature and heated arguments on politics at different tables, visitors entering and leaving the place, workers moving around busily—altogether created an ambience of a carnival where multifarious activities taking place at the same time. Yet, it was possible to seek a solitary moment in the midst of this crowd and contemplate:[189]

> This apparently busy cacophony of the coffee-house will inevitably work as an illusion to any idle (*kormo-bimukh*) mind. This ever busy atmosphere (*byastotar somaroho*) seems to open up the mind's window. The observer gathers so many ingredients from the floating bits and pieces of the conversations of those sitting at tables nearby, slight gestures and passé which then through wings of conjecture and imagination lead to numerous small variations .... there is no expectation of anything great, nor is there any special urge to solve anything. Day after day has passed on this understanding; there is no indication that there will be a new star on the sky in days yet to come. This precisely is the coffee-house. Its outlook is slowed down by idle, lethargic rumination (*olos monthor romonthone mondakranto er drishti*).

Another testimony of the same idea that the place, in spite of its busy ambience offers solitude, can be found in the following lines of Parsai:[190]

> The Coffee House is not a mere restaurant. It is an institution. It is a different world, encompassing all worlds. The Coffee House is a

[188] Sunil Gangopadhyay, 'Kichhu Paglami' [Bits of Madness], in *Kabita Samagro* [Collected Poems], vol. 2, Kolkata: Ananda, 2013, 166; 'Smritir Shohor-20' [The City in Memory], in *Kabita Samagro*, vol. 3 Kolkata: Ananda, 2013, 34; Gautam Chaudhury, 'Yeti', in *Colombuser Jahaj* [The ship of Columbus], Kolkata: Rabon Prakashani, 2016; Samarendra Sengupta, 'Coffeehouser SNiri', in *Coffeehouser SNiri* [The Staircase of the Coffee House], Kolkata: Dey's, 1994, 12–13.

[189] Bhattacharya, *Albert Hall,* 136.

[190] N.D. Sharma, 'Indian Coffee House Shows the Way', blog, 26 June 2009, http://ndsharma.wordpress.com/2009/06/26/indian-coffee-house-shows-the-way/.

cocktail of different lives. A cross section of society is always found here. The Coffee House is also a place of quietude ... like home....

What the Coffee House signifies to its patrons has thus been expressed in a myriad of ways, considering it as 'a home away from home' is the most common of them. The quality of the time spent there makes the place a second home, and the loss of such a refuge is not momentary but evokes the memory of a national crisis that aggressively stalled the progress of democracy in India and forever left a mark on the country's history: [191]

The Coffee House was demolished in June
a demolition not limited to June but will have an everlasting effect
like the destruction carried out by Indira Gandhi in another June
was not limited to that June alone
all demolitions have enduring consequences,
whether we wanted or not did not matter
what was there in June, ceased to exist in June....
only those who have fought in an encounter
know what war frenzy is,
those who have loved
alone know what pain that is,
only those who have lost a Coffee House,
know what displacement is

Regarding the suitability of place for *adda*, Buddhadev Basu wrote that it should feel like home, where one could return every now and then. In this poem of Rajkumar Kumbhaj, the coffee-house is a home. Like the Emergency proclaimed in June 1975 was not just another measure adopted by the Congress Government under Indira Gandhi, but was a grievous attack on the fundaments of Indian democracy with far-reaching consequences for the future, the taking down of the Coffee House created a vacuum that was as strong as war frenzy, so distressing as losing a loved one, and so deep that the demolition of such a place left one homeless causing anguish long after the

[191] Rajkumar Kumbhaj, 'Yahan Ek Kaafihouse Tha' (There used to be a Coffee House Here); see Chapter Five for more on Emergency; I am grateful to Mr Kumbhaj for making the unpublished poem available for my use.

incident had taken place. This association takes the place out of its materiality—a restaurant—and elevates it to that of a cherished shelter.

CONCLUSION

Exploring the social life of coffee, Brian Cowan observed that it was the cosmopolitan social elite virtuosos who popularized coffee in the coffee-houses in early modern England.[192] Created with similar vision, the ICH launched at the end of the colonial rule was new in the eyes of the educated urban middle class in India. These Indians were more familiar with tea often consumed at home and otherwise ubiquitous by the 1930s.[193] The Coffee House which was set up by the Coffee Cess Committee with the support of the colonial state, was primarily to boost the coffee economy. Modelled on the popular hybrid Irani cafés, this place was conceived to facilitate the consumption of coffee. In this vision commerce and profit were the goals behind the physical production of the place. Visiting ICH and the Tea House in Delhi became a part of the lifestyle of a section of the Western educated middle class in whose imagination the quiddity of both the place and the beverage lay in their association with Western modernity. Moreover, coffee became a signifier of the Coffee House which, in its turn, signified informal social gatherings. By providing a comfortably furnished sitting pace in a decent atmosphere where educated, modern, urban public from different walks of life gathered in order to take part in *adda*, or agenda-less conversation, this institution allowed the free space (*mukto parisar*) needed for the thinking people to come together and exchange ideas on a scale previously unknown. Unlike what was claimed by the Coffee Board, as we shall see in the next chapter, the Coffee House helped popularizing coffee in north India. At the same time, it also became the largest institution for socialization, thus transcending the original idea behind the creation of this place. Comparable to

[192] Brian Cowan, *The Social Life of Coffee: The Emergence of the British Coffeehouse,* New Haven: Yale University Press, 2005.

[193] The consumption of hot beverages, whether coffee or tea, is often associated with the use of other addictives; see Chapters Six and Seven.

the Kizilay Square in Ankara, the Coffee House became the most dynamic space for *adda* generating identities, practices and discourses which influenced the reproduction of practices of future generations occupying the place.[194] Equally important, as I have suggested here, was the differential character of the structure in comparison with the pre-existing places of sociability. While the tea-shops, cabins and restaurants visited by the average middle class were local, urban-level enterprises, the ICH, resulting from intervention of the state in the coffee industry and in the sphere of consumption, was a state-level initiative operating throughout India. However, the new place did not replace the local structures; many of them survived and coexisted together with the ICH.

Attracted to this new structure in the urban space, a section of the modern Western educated middle class made visiting the Coffee House a part of their daily routine. The trauma of Partition and communal riots had left the common man vanquished. Independence did not deliver economic affluence. If the monotony of the quotidian in the city put them in shackles, the Coffee House was a place where they could be free from all tensions. It was the feeling of temporary freedom from all harrowing worldly concerns, the possibility of transcending everyday life outside as soon as one entered the space that made everyone seemingly equal. This sense of equality could however be an illusion. One of the reasons behind the popularity of the new place was that coffee available here was affordable for the distressed urban middle class. The urban public embraced the place and effortlessly established their claim over it through their practice of *adda*. But if the coffee industry created the ICH chain with a view to boost the internal market for coffee, in other words, to facilitate capitalist accumulation, did this silent, sloganless takeover and adaptation of the place to a space for sociability also add to the coffers of the industry? The following chapter will focus on this aspect of the Coffee House and the measures taken by the industry with far reaching consequences on the structure of the institution and its workers.

[194] Bülent Batuman, 'Imagination as Appropriation: Students Riots and the Reclaiming of Public Space', in *Space and Culture*, 6.3, 2003, 261–75.

CHAPTER three

The Workers and the Coffee House

From 'India' to 'Indian'

The novelty associated with the Coffee House and the sociability that it generated concealed the fact that the ICH was conceived in order to aid the process of accumulation. Devoid of its export market in the aftermath of the Great Depression, the coffee industry was facing a crisis and an immediate solution was imminent. The intervention of the state and brainstorming between the members of the Coffee Cess Committee on the one hand and the JWT on the other resulted in the creation of the world's oldest surviving coffee house chain—the India Coffee House. As we have seen above, from the very conception the outlets became a favourite spot in urban India during the 1940s and at least for a section of the middle class a regular visit to the place was an indispensable part of their daily routine. Yet, already by the by the end of that decade the Coffee Board was thinking of closing down many of the outlets,[1] and by 1955 it was officially announced.[2] This chapter will focus on the process that saw the Coffee Board withdrawing from the ICH, ultimately leading to the setting up of the regional Coffee Workers' Cooperatives that took over the management of the outlets. Why did the Board set up over forty outlets for one and a half decades before it decided to withdraw itself from the ICH? To what extent did the measure of opening the Coffee Houses meet the goal of aiding the sick industry and what

[1] The outlet in Jaipur was closed down in February 1950, Coffee Board, *Monthly Bulletin*, March 1950, 56.

[2] K. Srinivasan, Chairman of the Coffee Board defending the decision of the Board in *Deccan Herald*, 13 February 1959.

did the change in the name imply for the institution that continues up till now? Finally, since the chain of the ICH is the world's only example of coffee houses run by the working class, we shall have a close look at the management and functioning of the outlets.

Drawing on the proceedings of the Coffee Board, a rare autobiography of a worker of the Coffee Board supplemented with ethnographic research among the workers of the outlets, I argue here that since promoting coffee in the domestic market became a concern only when export of the commodity showed no prospect, ICH as a part of that promotion, was viewed as a temporary measure. As soon as the export market looked positive again, concern for the domestic market became secondary. At this critical juncture in the life of the Coffee House when its closure threatened the livelihood of its workers, they asserted their agency in the public sphere and began a counter movement against the Board to regain their foothold in the place. These workers, backed by the labour union, went on strike and petitioned the government; and a few among them took the pioneering role to raise awareness among their colleagues regarding the benefit of cooperation. Their community or religious identities did not play any role in the formation of the workers' autonomy and consensus that compelled the Coffee Board to succumb to their demand.

THE COFFEE BOARD, THE INTERNAL MARKET AND THE COFFEE HOUSE[3]

The Cess Committee was replaced by the Coffee Market Expansion Board (1940) enacted by the Coffee Act of 1942 as the Coffee Board of India. Ivor Bull, Chairman of the Consolidated Company, and President of the coffee section of the United Planters' Association of South India (1893) became the Chairman of the Coffee Marketing Expansion Board. It was to the credit of Bull and M.J. Simon, in

[3] This section is a summary of a part of Bhaswati Bhattacharya, 'Kaffeekonsum in Indien: Ein Blick Auf Die Vermarktung Von Kaffee in Indien, 1935–2010', in Christiane Berth, Dorothee Wierling, Volker Wünderich (Hg.), *Kaffee Global, Regional, Lokal. Zur Geschichte Eines Genussmittels im 19. und 20. Jahrhundert*, Göttingen: Vandenhoeck & Ruprecht, 179–200.

charge of coffee marketing since 1935 and Secretary of the Coffee Board, that the ICH spread throughout India. The Board enjoyed a monopoly over the distribution and marketing of all coffee produced in India till the Indian coffee market was deregulated in the wake of the economic liberalization.

As stated in Chapter Two earlier, popularizing coffee as a measure to develop the domestic market was the idea behind the creation of the ICH. It was under Ivor Bull and M.J. Simon that became synonymous with the consumption of coffee in north India. As late as 1954, H. Siddaveerappa, then chairman of the Coffee Board expressed his intention to open more outlets of the ICH in north India 'where now it is almost impossible to get a good cup of coffee'.[4] Yet, when the decision to close down the outlets was made public the following year, it was stated that many private restaurants had taken over the function of the Coffee House. Officially, the Board announced that the decision to close down the outlets was prompted by the facts that: (1) the outlets were not serving the purpose of popularizing coffee; (2) retaining all the outlets was economically unviable; (3) most of the money, energy and time was spent on personnel matters and official routine; (4) increasing wastage, leakage and malpractices stood in the way of proper functioning of the outlets; (5) it was difficult to maintain nearly fifty coffee houses throughout India in top condition from a centrally located office of the Board; (6) there was a deterioration in the quality of salesmanship and the services offered to customers; (7) running coffee houses was primarily the work of private enterprises; (8) increase in the number of good hotels and restaurants serving good coffee made the ICH superfluous.[5]

In 1959, Bimal Bose, Director of Propaganda of the Coffee Board emphasized that the consumption of coffee in India had increased more than four times in between 1940 and 1958, but the increase was not due to ICH, and was only in parts of South India. The sale

[4] 'Coffee Production in India up by 39 p.c.: Board Chief Reviews Condition', *TOI*, 12 June 1954.

[5] K. Srinivasan, Chairman of the Coffee Board of India, *Indian Coffee*, February 1959.

in North India was limited to South Indians living in the North, no market had been created in North India for coffee. For a section of urban intellectuals who went to ICH, the habit of drinking coffee was limited to the walls of the restaurant.[6] In other words, the Board admitted that its experiments with ICH were a failure.

Not all concerned however, were, convinced by the argument that the coffee houses had outlived their purpose. In a press conference, A.K. Gopalan, Vice President of the Coffee Board Labour Union (CBLU), refuted such statements, saying the Board was unable to present any detailed account as to why and how the Coffee Houses had become redundant.[7] Gopalan of course knew what he was talking about.

Beginning with 1939–40, the monthly and annual reports of the Board registered an increase in the sale of liquid coffee, which more than trebled between 1940 and 1944—from 1.1 million to 6.8 million cups, reaching a climax in 1946–47 when more than 9.85 million cups of coffee were sold (See Table on p. 409). The decline immediately after 1947 must be seen in the context of decolonization and mass migration on the part of European, Anglo-Indian, Armenian and other communities consuming coffee. While in 1950–51, 1952–53 and 1953–54 the sales were 7.8 and 7.5 and 7.9 million cups respectively, between 1954–55 and 1956–57 the sales remained steady at above 8 million cups with a climax in 1955–56 when 8.9 million cups were sold. At a time when tea was being projected as a beverage consumed at home, advertising coffee through the coffee houses associated its consumption outside home, as part of the sociability of the Coffee House. The popularity of the ICH and the increased sale of liquid coffee showed that the measure was successful in introducing urban north India to coffee.

The monthly reports of the Coffee Board in its magazine called *Indian Coffee* also gave the impression that the outlets served the purpose of propaganda the way the Board wanted. Reference to visits of national and international dignitaries to different outlets and their comments on the coffee served, often accompanied by photographs,

[6] Bimal Bose, 'Propaganda: New Phase', *Indian Coffee*, April 1959, 162–64.

[7] 'Mr Gopalan's Appeal to Coffee Board', *TOI*, 12 August 1957.

found pride of place in the publications of the Board.[8] Similarly, the revenue from the outlets increased from Rs 159,000 in 1940–41 to more than Rs 8,880,000 in 1950–51. The sale of coffee fell to 6.6 million cups in the tumultuous year of 1957–58, when the protest movement against the closure was on and some of the outlets had been closed. The lion's share in the total turnover of the Propaganda Department came from the sale of the liquid and dry coffee. Most of the liquid coffee was sold in the Coffee Houses, but without any indication of what the target was for individual establishments, what measures were taken to achieve the goal, or any explanation for the fluctuations in the annual turnover on different heads, the documentations appear to be mechanical. The bias against the internal market was loud and clear in the comment of V. Balu, Director of Propaganda Department since 1964, when he said—almost a decade after the closure of the ICH—if the Indian consumer could not pay as much as the foreign customer did, he would have to wait. However, what this had to do if ICH had lost its relevance in popularizing coffee was unclear.[9] In fact the Board contradicted itself again when it decided to set up a coffee house in Patna in 1971, which in addition to 'encouraging the production of coffee, was also part of the Board's responsibility to facilitate the growth of the domestic market for coffee'.[10] As late as the new millennium, the Board had one outlet each at Bangalore, Calcutta, Hyderabad, Patna, Srinagar, Tirumala and coffee rooms in different departments in Delhi.

The inconsistency in the position of the Board can be understood if we remember that the coffee industry had in the past always focused on the export market where the price of coffee was regulated by global demand and supply. When the crisis-ridden coffee sector sought government assistance in order to survive, the government induced the Board to introduce differential pricing that made the price of allotments such that the supply of coffee in the Indian market cheaper than the price of the exportable variety. A small amount of

[8] See the monthly issues of *Indian Coffee* from 1951–71.

[9] V. Balu, 'The Challenge of Coffee Promotion', *Indian Coffee*, April 1966, 7–8.

[10] *Indian Coffee*, June 1971, 9–14.

coffee disbursed through the Propaganda Department of the Board found its way to ICH at a subsidized cost.

In the early phase of commercial advertising, advertisers often initiated a pedagogical project in order to instruct the hesitant consumer to use new commodities.[11] In an attempt to persuade the Indian middle class during the inter-war period, advertisements were used by well-known brands to appeal to notions of conjugality, domesticity, health, male body—concepts critical to the achievement of modernity.[12] During the early decades of the ICH, the middle class homemaker in northern India was seldom addressed. Gautam Bhadra has detailed how the advertisements of tea during this period highlighted the product, gender, private space, traditional domestic practices, issues absent in the advertisements of the Coffee Board welcoming each and all to ICH.[13] Because the consumption of tea was widespread in northern India, the industry projected coffee as a beverage for sociability at urban public places, a fixation that has continued into the age of the globalized coffee culture in India.

The production of exportable coffee in India had increased between 1940–44 and 1946–50 from 3,600 tons to 18,000 tons.[14] And the demand for coffee in the domestic market increased by leaps and bounds, resulting in a shortfall in the exportable surplus.[15] Apart from A.K. Gopalan, sources from the industry acknowledged the contribution of the India Coffee House in popularizing coffee.[16] The steady increase in demand notwithstanding, the internal market had

[11] Arvind Rajagopal, 'Advertisement, Politics and the Sentimental Education of the Indian Consumer', *Visual Anthropology Review*, 14.2, (1998) 14–31.

[12] Douglas Haynes, 'Creating the Consumer? Advertising, Capitalism, and the Middle Class in Urban Western India, 1914–40', in Douglas Haynes, Abigail McGowan, Tirthankar Roy, Haruka Yanagisawa (ed.), *Towards a History of Consumption in South Asia*, New Delhi: OUP, 2010, 185–223.

[13] Gautam Bhadra, 'From an Imperial Product'.

[14] Instituto Inter-Americano de Ciencias Agricolas, *Coffee Industry*, Costa Rica, (N.D.), 65.

[15] Bose, 'Propaganda'.

[16] Anonymous, 'Coffee Marketing Anomalies', *The Economic Weekly*, 18 October 1952.

not however stabilized and when the Board increased the price suddenly in 1952–53, the total turnover of coffee was 7000 lb less than in the previous year. In an address to the Coffee Board T.T. Krishnamachari, the Union Minister for Commerce and Industry reiterated that the consumer was the ultimate master of the grower and the government would not allow any drastic increase in the price of coffee in the internal market.[17] Yet, it is clear that the price differentiation was the problem and the Board was accused of holding back stocks of coffee to create an artificial scarcity leading to an unparalleled increase in the price that encouraged corruption and leakage.[18]

While in 1952–53 the quantity available for home consumption was 45.3 million lb, it was observed that a potential area of the market still remained untouched and that the internal consumption showed a tendency of further increase.[19] Due to a shift in the demand in the export market from dollar to non-dollar in East European countries and the high level of prices in the international market, it was felt that the export market could further be explored. Consequently, there was enough room for substantial increase in the production of coffee. The Board vacillated between the export and the domestic market. Substantial increase in the production of coffee in the post-war period notwithstanding, the unusual increase in domestic demand led to a decrease in the exportable surplus. As foreign exchange earner coffee contributed to the national coffer, and its export was considered important for the best interests of the planters and the national economy.[20] Meanwhile, world coffee exports had increased by more than 25 per cent between 1947 and 1953, and the price of coffee in the US had gone up considerably. The Plantation Enquiry

[17] 'Future of Coffee Industry: Minister's View', *TOI*, 1 January 1953.

[18] Anonymous, 'Coffee Marketing'.

[19] *Coffee in India,* Delhi: Ministry of Food and Agriculture, Government of India, 1952–53, iii-iv; cf. shortage of supply in the market in comparison with the demand for coffee led to the smuggling of coffee from the estates, *Indian Coffee*, May 1966, 8.

[20] Bose, 'Propaganda'; during July 1951–June 1952 the total allotment for the internal market was (in 1000 lbs.) as follows (a)by auction to bona fide dealers registered with the Board 29,935, (b) to cooperative societies retailing coffee 5,011, (c) to the propaganda department 3,799, *Coffee in India, 1952–53,* iii.

Commission appointed in April 1954 to explore the possibility of further development and expansion of the coffee industry in India, recommended advertisement campaigns and propaganda through mobile vans and cinema shows, but was against maintaining permanent coffee houses. Moreover, the industry was advised to further exploit the export market.[21] The potential of external market looked more promising than the economics of providing coffee in the coffee houses at a subsidized cost: [22]

> In the past the policy of the Government was directed towards making larger quantities of coffee available for home consumption. However, in recent years there has been a shift in emphasis from the domestic to the foreign markets.

Following a bumper crop ICH in 1954–55 the planters demanded a relaxation of the rules regarding export.[23] The export of coffee increased from 319,000 tons in 1950–51 to 589,000 tons in 1960–61. The decision to close down the outlets has to be understood in the context of these developments in the overseas market. On 26 June 1955 the Board decided to close down the outlets 'not yielding any profit' and hand over the rest of the outlets to private entrepreneurs. When the dust settled in the late 1950s, the Coffee Board retained only a few outlets under its control, among them was the one adjacent to the headquarters of the Board in Bangalore, and 5CA in Calcutta, still known as India Coffee House. Backed by the CBLU and patrons, manual workers of the ICH formed workers' cooperatives that took over the rest of the branches since known as the Indian Coffee House.[24] The following section will have a look at the organization of the workers under the Coffee Board and the process that led to the formation of the coffee workers' coooperatives. (See illustration on Page 409—Appendix XII [a]).

[21] *Coffee in India, 1953–54*, iii-v; 'Summary of the main conclusions and recommendations of the Plantation Inquiry Commission in respect of the coffee industry', *Coffee in India,* 1955–56FAG, ix.

[22] *Coffee in India,* 1958–59, ix.

[23] 'Coffee Growers Worried Over Stock Positions', *TOI,* 1 May 1954.

[24] Ibid., a few of the outlets, like the one on Janpath, taken over by private entrepreneurs, retained the old name. See Chapter Five for more on that outlet.

THE FORMATION OF THE COFFEE BOARD LABOUR UNION

Unlike in the railway and tea industry where foreign capital played a major role, the coffee plantation sector was predominated by a large number of native smallholders.[25] Although export was controlled mostly by large multinational brands, from plantations on the one hand, to the Coffee House on the other, most of the heavy work was of course done by Indian labour. The twentieth century witnessed the politics of mass mobilization as a part of elite politics, especially after the emergence of Gandhi on the national scene. It was a trend that later gained momentum during the inter-war period when it penetrated the lives of wider social groups leading to the development of the politics of the poor.[26] The foundation of the All India Trade Union Congress (AITUC) in 1920 and the Trade Union Act of 1926 were parts of the new institution offering platforms for collective political action.[27] The growth of shared consciousness among the railway workers played a major role in the development of the Trade Union Movement in India;[28] and this movement became an important part of the struggle for Independence. It is important to remember here that since 1929, the AITUC was controlled by the Communist Party of India. Soon after the launch of the Coffee Board, the necessity of organizing the workers to negotiate with the employers led to the formation of the CBLU.

Most of the workers in the ICH were Malayalis recruited by Mr Simon, who was from Tranquebar (Kerala). That the coffee workers of Kerala took the lead in organzing the workers was also due to the political atmosphere in Malabar in the early 1940s. Malabar

[25] Bhaswati Bhattacharya, 'Local History of a Global Commodity: The Production of Coffee in Mysore and Coorg in the Nineteenth Century', *Indian Historical Review*, 41.1, 2014, 67–86.

[26] Nandini Gooptu, *The Politics of the Urban Poor in EarlyTwentieth-Century India*, Cambridge: Cambridge University Press, 2001, 8.

[27] For link between the workplace politics of Kanpur *bazar* and the nationalist movement ibid., 376–411.

[28] Ian J. Kerr, *Building the Railways of the Raj, 1850–1900*, Delhi: OUP, 1995.

had been a stronghold of the Congress Socialist Party (CSP) since its inception in 1934. Constituted as a cohesive platform, CSP became a dominant party in Kerala. Members of this party were continuously engaged in creating awareness among a growing number of peasants and workers in cottage industries like coir, *beedi*, agriculture, and in coffee and rubber plantations. Nationalists like Sardar Chandroth K. Nair (1900–64), K. Damodaran (1912–76), A.K. Gopalan (1904–77), E.P. Gopalan (1912–2001), K. Madhavan (1915–) not only actively partipated in the movements of the peasants, industrial workers, students and teachers, but inspired them to organize themselves into unions and to go on strike in support of their demands. In the late 1930s *beedi* workers, fishermen, municipal workers, peasants, soap and tile factory workers began to organize themselves into unions in their struggle against unjust retrenchment on the part of their employers.[29] The Commonwealth Tile Factory workers in Calicut struck their work, the unions of the *beedi* workers of Cannanore, Tellichery and neighbouring areas went on a successfully organized strike. In 1938 there was a general strike by the coir workers in Alleppey and Shertalai.[30] Dissatisfaction among the radicals of the CSP with the mild protest of the CSP after the outbreak of the World War II led to the birth of the Kerala Communist Party (KCP) in 1939. Militant activities of the KCP among the poor continued after 1947. Gopalan became a member of KCP in 1946.

An account of the challenges faced by the workers of the Coffee Board to close the outlets of the ICH, was chronicled by a worker from Kerala. The memoir of Nadakkal Parameswaran Pillai (1931–2010), a former manual worker of the Coffee Board, offers us a rare insight into the hardship the workers had to go through under the Board when he, like other class IV workers, was faced the threat of

[29] A.K. Gopalan, *In the Cause of the People: Reminiscences*, Bombay: Orient Longman, 1973, 92–98 and passim.

[30] Manali Desai, 'From Movement to Party to Government: A Comparison of Kerala and West Bengal, India', in Jack Goldstone (ed.), *States, Parties and Social Movements: Pushing the Boundaries of Institutional Change*, Cambridge: Cambridge University Press, 2003.

losing his job following the Board's decision to close down the outlets of the ICH. A native of the Pallippuram village in Alappuzha ditstrict (better known as Alleppey), Pillai had attended primary school up to class four when he had to drop out at the age of ten due to poverty. He worked in a coir factory, in a cashewnut shop, and then as the clerk of an advocate before he found a job as a daily worker at the ICH in Ernakulam in 1944.[31]

Apart from the office bearers—accountant, manager and secretary—the work in ICH involved menial labour. Workers who began their career as dish washers *(masalchi)* and gradually climbed up as they learned other aspects of work on the floor, constituted the life-breath of the outlets. Most of them came from rural background and even if they had had some schooling, they were dropouts who migrated to the city at a tender age in the pursuit of livelihood. As we shall see subsequently, that pattern has not changed.

Life under the Coffee Board was one of exploitation and the workers of the ICH had to toil for 14 to 18 hours a day without any weekly holiday, living on the unsold leftovers. The salary was minimal and they were required to do the domestic work for the office-bearers. In addition, the workers were addressed and referred to by their first name without any courtesy title/surname being added to their name. Any slightest show of protest was likely to be 'rewarded' with dismissal or transfer. While it was normal for the officials at the top level to get promotion and increments, low grade workers were often forgotten.

It was under these circumstances that three workers of the Board viz. M. Chathukutty, K.N. Narayanan and T.P. Raghavan took the

[31] Mrs K. Lalitha, founder member, ICH Cooperative Society, Trichur (widow of N.S. Parameswaran Pillai). Pillai rose to be the State Secretary to the Labour Union of the Coffee Board and later a founder member of the ICWCSL. He wrote *Coffee Housinte Katha*, Thrissur: Current Books, 1972. Unless otherwise mentioned, the following account of the formation of the Coffee Board Labour Union and of the movement leading to the formation of the Coffee Workers' Cooperative is based on this autobiographical work in Malayalam. I am grateful to Ms V.S. Lincy of the National Library, Calcutta for translating Pillai's book for my use.

initiative to form a labour union in 1946. By distributing leaflets with slogans like 'Coffee House employees are also human beings' and 'if you want to live a decent life join the union' they tried to instill a spirit of awareness and unity among the workers of the Coffee Board. These leaflets were circulated among workers in other parts of the country. Secret informal meetings were organized to discuss and make drafts of their demands for better working conditions, that included: (1) the right to create a common platform of workers in the shape of a union; (2) the proposals of the Pay Commission with regard to promotion and increments should take the interests of grade IV workers into consideration; (3) after a probation period of six months, workers would be made permanent; (4) the rules and regulations promulgated by the Board would have to be extended to include the menial workers; (5) workers should get a minimum of two months bonus annually; (6) they should have the right to one month's earned leave and sick leave; (7) transfers would have to be justified; (8) the Board would provide a provident fund for the future security of the workers; (9) free medical treatment for the workers; (10) managers would not have the right to dismiss workers at whim.

At a meeting held in Bangalore on 9 November 1947, the workers formed a Union with T.P. Raghavan elected as its secretary. The Union was officially approved and registered in 1948 as the Coffee Board Labour Union (CBLU), formally affiliated with the AITUC in 1952 when its headquarters was shifted to Delhi. The first success of the Union was booked in 1948 when the workers in the Calcutta outlets observed a strike, demanding a free day during the Easter which was granted. The first official meeting of the Union took place in Calicut in October 1948, which witnessed the participation of 30 members representing 700 members of the Union from different parts of the country. The meeting inaugurated by K.P. Kesava Menon (1886–1978), the founder-editor of *Mathrubhumi* (Malayali mouthpiece of the nationalist struggle) elected the following officiating members of the Union: Kalathil Varghese (President), T.P. Raghavan (General Secretary), P.J. John, P.Z. Thomas, P.V. Sivaraman Nayar and O.V. Sankaran (Assistant Secretaries), and M.S. Pankajakshi Menon

(Treasurer).[32] Between this time and 1957 when the outlets of ICH were closed down, the CBLU was successful in extracting certain benefits for the employees. Whereas the minimum basic pay was fixed at Rs 30, sanction of an annual dearness allowance, the provision for the reimbursement of healthcare costs and reappointment of 100 workers whose jobs had been unjustly terminated were some of the victories booked by the Union. The formation of the CBLU and its struggle against the exploitation of the workers by their employers had thus created a consciousness among the manual workers of the Board about their dignity and rights on the work-floor and this experience stood them in good stead once their existence was threatened.

FROM INDIA TO INDIAN: THE STRUGGLE FOR SURVIVAL

In 1955 the decision to close down 43 outlets of the Coffee House was made public by the Coffee Board. The outlets would be handed over to interested private parties. More than 1000 members of the class IV staff were threatened with permanent lay-offs. The class IV workers of the Board comprised coffee-makers, bearers, pantry-men, cleaners, scullions, darbans, dishwashers, men under training and peons drawing a fixed basic salary of Rs 32 or below per month.[33] In response, the workers went into direct action in order to avoid being 'coolie slaves' of private hoteliers. They announced a relay strike demanding the rehabilitation of the dismissed workers. Since the service in the ICH was not interrupted, it helped in generating public support and sympathy among the patrons in favour of the workers' movement. The other factor that helped the course of the workers' struggle was the second parliamentary elections in 1956 that brought a communist government to power in Kerala. A.K. Gopalan, the

[32] Meeting every alternate year, the succeeding meetings of the Union were held in Bangalore in 1950, in Delhi in 1952, in Mumbai in 1954 and in Bangalore in 1956. As the Union later extended to include employees of the coffee marketing and plantation sectors, its membership increased to 1200 by 1955.

[33] One of the workers losing work in Calcutta was Bishnupada Maiti who later joined the Cooperative, Sukumar Bera, cooperator ICH College Sreet, interview, 28 January 2012.

communist leader who had earlier been familiar with the organization of the *beedi* and other unions of Kerala, then the Vice President of the CBLU became the leader of the Opposition in Parliament. Gopalan played a crucial role in shaping the future of the ICH and its workers.

The Board's decision was followed by a meeting among the members of the CBLU that delegated C. Madhavan Nair, the then General Secretary of the Union to approach K. Srinivasan, the Chairman of the Coffee Board with the request that the decision of the Board be reconsidered. Srinivasan refused to intervene on the ground that the decision had not been taken by him, but by the entire Board.[34] Support for the workers came from the Press and some other quarters but the Board stuck to its decision prompting the workers to boost their strike. The CBLU sought government intervention into the matter and Gopalan mediated by appealing to both sides: together with T.C.M. Menon, he met Mr G.L. Nanda, the Union Labour Minister and other representatives of the Ministries of Labour, Commerce and Industry. It was decided at the meeting that either a national tribunal be set up or some other alternative be sought for an early settlement of disputes. At the same time Gopalan requested the CBLU to put off the decision to go on a hunger strike.[35] As there was no indication that the Board would accede to the demand of the workers, in addition to wearing a black badge on the workfloor, the workers took recourse to relay hunger strike and began organizing meetings in different cities in order to inform the public about the crisis they faced.

Another delegation of the Union under the leadership of Gopalan met Morarji Desai, the Federal Minister of Commerce, Industry and Finance on 25 May 1957. As the Union was still awaiting a response from the Minister, the Coffee Board announced its decision to hand over the coffee houses to private owners. While the future of the workers in the outlets concerned was hanging by a thread, the announcement was followed by the notice of retrenchment to 112 workers working in various outlets from 1 September 1957.

[34] K. Lalitha, widow of N. Parameswaran Pillai, interview in Trichur, 8 December 2011.

[35] 'Plea to Coffee Board Union: Put Off Direct Action', *TOI*, 1 September 1956.

There was no indication of any redress from the Board, or of any intervention on behalf of the Government. Moreover, the movement of the workers was for a while threatened from inside. Going on strike implied sacrificing a part of the salary which was meagre but indispensable for the workers. At a time when it seemed that the movement had come to a standstill with no end of the road in view, it was A.K. Gopalan who came up with a solution. This was the time when the paradigm of development in India was guided by the assumption that the government had to be directly involved as far as the removal of poverty and the economic development of the country were concerned. The recommendations of the All India Rural Credit Survey Committee (1951–54) included active involvement of the government in the cooperative movement. Consequently, private sectors, cooperatives and other initiatives were brought under the umbrella of the government.[36] As Vice President of the CBLU, Gopalan was aware of both the strength and weaknesses of the Board. One month after the Coffee Board had announced its decision, he came out with a revolutionary suggestion. In a meeting of the central executive committee of the CBLU organized at the Cubbon Park, Bangalore on 25 June 1957, Gopalan suggested that the labourers themselves take over the charge of running the outlets of the ICH.[37] In the speech that went a long way in empowering the workrers in their struggle to regain their place, he stated that, 'labourers ought to rule the world; the Coffee House is a small thing [in comparison]; your work experience has put you in a position to manage it in a satisfactory way. Instead of serving the capitalists, take over the Coffee House from them and manage them yourselves. The Coffee House belongs to the workers!'. As to the question of the funds required for the takeover and the running of the Coffee

[36] Government of India, Second Administrative Reforms Commission (henceforth SARC), 9 Report, 'Social Capital: A Shared Destiny', 2009, http://www.darpg.gov.in/sites/default/files/Social_Capital9_0.pdf; A. Virmani, 'A New Development Paradigm: Employment, Eentitlement and Empowerment', *EPW*, 37.2, 1 June 2002, 2145–54.

[37] T. M. Isaac, Richard W. Franke, P. Raghavan, *Democracy at Work in An Indian Industrial Cooperative: The Story of Kerala Dinesh Beedi*, Ithaca: Cornell University Press, 1998, (henceforth *Kerala Dinesh Beedi*), 35–39.

Houses, he assured them that everything would fall in place as soon as they and their supporters were united in action and purpose, by forming cooperatives to enable the takeover. He also announced that the handover would take place on 15 August 1957, the tenth anniversary of Independence Day.

On 11 August, a few days prior to handover, the central executive committee of the CBLU held another meeting in Delhi at which three demands were put before the Coffee Board: (1) All workers threatened with the loss of work would have to be taken back failing which they would proceed to take over the closed outlets. (2) If the Board was unable to stop the retrenchment, the closure of the outlets and the termination of contracts must be postponed by six months in order to assist the process of the formation of the cooperative societies of the workers and the takeover. (3) The central government should actively intervene in solving this problem by either taking over the firms or employing the erstwhile workers of the Coffee Board in railway canteens among other places and by sanctioning subsidy and loan to the worker's cooperative society for making the takeover possible. If these demands were not met, the members of the Union would go on hunger strike for an indefinite period under the leadership of Gopalan. In a press conference held on the same day, Gopalan reiterated the demands by stating that the CBLU would explore all possibilities to stop the retrenchment of the workers. Alternately, employment for the retrenched workers would be sought in canteens under the Government of India. If no solution was found through either of these two means, workers' cooperatives would take over the outlets. But if these attempts to settle the disputes in a peaceful manner ended in a failure due to the unhelpful and adamant attitude of the Coffee Board, the responsibility of driving the workers to starvation and death would have to be borne by the Coffee Board.[38]

Pillai wrote that Gopalan's suggestion about the formation of the workers' cooperatives initially did not receive the approval of the then prime minister, Jawaharlal Nehru, universally known as the

[38] 'Mr Gopalan's Appeal to Coffee Board', *TOI*, 12 August 1957.

father of the mixed economy and patron of ICH.[39] Nehru apparently demanded that the proposed handover of individual outlets was to be decided by the Coffee Board that would first monitor the management of the firms for a year, and that a handover could take place only if the workers could pay half the cost of the outlets to the Board. As it was clearly a demand made by the Board, the workers rejected to acquiesce, and staged a sit-in strike in protest on 15 August 1957.

It was only at this point that for the first time during this tumultuous period of negotiation that the Coffee Board appeared acquiescent and agreed to hand over the furniture, premises and the kitchen equipments of the existing outlets to the workers' cooperatives against a financial compensation. Still the Board maintained that the laid-off workers alone would be permitted to take over some outlets while the Board would allow private entrepreneurs to run the rest of the outlets.[40] The Board also agreed to supply coffee to the Coffee Houses at a subsidized rate. In return, the CBLU agreed not to fight the dismissal of the labourers in the court. Following an agreement between the Coffee Board and the CBLU on 30 August, regional cooperative societies were to be formed with the idea to take over the management of forty-three Coffee Houses throughout the country.

The problems of the workers however did not come to an end even after signing the agreement. The members of the CBLU were now divided internally as one section opined that by agreeing not to fight the Board's decision of retrenchment of the workers the agreement had betrayed their cause; they were in favour of continuing the hunger strike and were opposed to the idea of the formation of a cooperative. The other section did not want to run into any trouble and would rather take the monetary compensation and return to their respective village. The agreement implied that the CBLU would have to report the formation of the cooperative societies within two weeks after it

[39] In addition to the party Nehru hosted celebrating the Independence of India, there were numerous occasions when the ICH catered to parties, seminars organized by various ministries of the Government of India and other organizations with Nehru as the chief guest, *Indian Coffee*, 1952–56, passim.

[40] Interview Govinda Pillai, librarian, AK Gopalan Centre, Trivandrum, 6 December 2011.

had been signed. The outlets not taken over by the CBLU would then be handed over to private entrepreneurs.

There were other problems. At the base of a cooperative is combined investment on behalf of the co-operators, that ensures their own employment and income. Coming from poor families, most of the workers neither possessed much cash nor did they have any savings which could be invested as capital. At the same time, not knowing what the future of such an initiative would have in store for them, many were reluctant to borrow. Out of the Rs 5,000 needed for the Trichur Society, only Rs 2,100 had been collected within the stipulated time: Rs 1,500 donated by workers, 500 raised by their wives who sold their wedding jewellery, and 500 from patrons in Kottayam. Before the agreement was signed, the first regional cooperative society of coffee workers had already been launched in Bangalore in August 1957; but without any experience of management, the members of the Society did not dare take over the ICH. In Jabalpur, the landlord of the building initially refused the idea to rent out the place to a workers' cooperative unsure if they would be able to pay the rent. The workers demanded that the cooperatives be run by the state. To make matters worse, soon after the agreement was signed, Gopalan resigned from the CBLU. The workers felt that their cause was betrayed. The chaotic situation lasted till December when the Secretary General of the CBLU issued a circular and called a meeting.

The meeting was held at Bangalore during 9–12 December 1957 and was attended by representatives from all over India to discuss among other issues the three burning questions: whether (1) to resume strike, (2) to form self-managed cooperatives, (3) to accept the retrenchment notice and the compensation. It was at this meeting that the proposal to form cooperatives as a temporary solution was passed by a vote of 21:9 with the idea to continue the demand for nationalization. It took about 15 months to organize the India Coffee Workers' Cooperative Society Limited (ICWCSL) in different regions of India. Except for Mr Subbaia in Madras, secretaries of all regional societies hailed from Kerala, and all workers including the secretaries had been workers of the Coffee Board.

When declared superfluous, the manual workers in a union with the elite used the new modes and institutions of protest and mobilization available to them to lay their claim on the public space. In post-Indendence India, it was in the interest of the nation to encourage the formation of cooperatives as a measure to alleviate poverty through equitable distribution of resources. In Nehru's vision of India, each village had a panchayat, a school and a cooperative. But Nehru visualized the cooperatives as self-reliant instruments of development, without much intervention from the state.[41] None of the interlocutors including his son cooperator Gireeshan I addressed could provide more information regarding Pillai's claim of the demand for nationalizing the Indian Coffee House. During the annual conference of the CBLU held in Delhi 1952, Gopalan had called for 'immediate nationalisation of coffee estates in India' in view of the enormous discrepancy between the profit from coffee and the daily wage of the workers of the Coffee Board.[42] Gandhi's vision of the economic development of the country laid emphasis on labour intensive agriculture and village level cottage industries. B.R. Ambedkar on the other hand suggested rapid industrialization and large-scale production with the precondition that land, water and key industries would be nationalized and land would be distributed among the landless.[43] But in order to boost the national economy Nehru's policy in the 1950s rested on the Bombay Model recommending industrialization of key industries like chemicals, electric power, life insurance, steel, transport, coal and banking. Coffee, like tea has been an important source of foreign exchange reserves in the Indian economy, and the demand for nationalization of coffee estates has never been strong.

The formation of the ICWCSL was a milestone in the history of the global coffee industry. The regional societies of the coffee workers' cooperatives are to this date, the only instances where coffee houses

[41] Madhavan K. Palat (ed.), *Selected Works of Jawaharlal Nehru*, Second Series, v. 44, 390, http://nehruportal.nic.in/selected-works-jawaharlal-nehru-second-series-volume-44#page/446/mode/2up; SARC, 9th Report.

[42] 'Red MP Advocates Nationalisation', *TOI*, 19 May 1952.

[43] Sukhdeo Thorat, *Ambedkar's Role in Economic Planning, Power and Water Policy*, New Delhi: Shipra Publications, 1998.

are run by workers-cum-owners. Through active intervention of A.K. Gopalan and the support of numerous intellectuals, the workers were able to transform the ICH into self-managed firms and establish their foothold in this urban space.

THE ICWCSL AND THE ICH

Eleven regional societies known as the India Coffee Workers' Cooperative Society Limited (ICWCSL), except for the Trichur Society for Travancore-Cochin area in Kerala where it was called the India Coffee Board Workers' Cooperative Society Limited (ICWCSL), were to take charge of the outlets of the ICH. These coffee workers' cooperatives were set up as non-profit organizations belonging to the category of industrial cooperatives.[44] The first ICH under the workers' cooperative opened its doors in Delhi University in October 1957. While the state governments extended a helping hand, the formation of the ICWCSL at the regional level received patronage and active support from external agencies, mostly from the Leftist intellectuals familiar with the place and the ideology behind cooperation. In Kerala, the land for the Trichur Coffee House was donated by the founder-director of Mangalodayam Printing Press, A.K.T.K.M. Vasudevan Namboodiripad while the state government under E.M.S. Namboodiripad allowed tax concession to it. In Calcutta, the closure of the ICH robbed the connoisseurs of their favourite place for *adda*, and a candlelight procession was taken out by its patrons in order to mourn the death of the institution.[45] Professor Nirmal Bhattacharya of the University of Calcutta, and Kamal Ganguli along with other members of the CPI wrote to the Parliament expressing their concern for the future of the workers. Due to intervention on their part, the government of West Bengal under Dr Bidhan Chandra Roy supported the formation of the cooperative

[44] T.P. Kattukoran, 'India Coffee Board Workers' Co-operative Society Ltd. No. 4227, Thrissur: Challenges Under the Agenda of Economic Reforms', *Indian Coffee House Golden Jubilee Smaranika* (henceforth ICHGJS), Thrissur: ICBWCS 2008, 73–75.

[45] Sunil Gangopadhyay, interview.

by acting as a mediator between the owner of the building and the cooperators, and, each time the workers failed to pay the rent, it was paid by the government.[46] Out of solidarity with the workers, some patrons like the screen and stage personality Utpal Dutt purchased shares of the cooperative in order to help the newborn society. This was of course a token of friendly gesture as Dutt would never claim his share of dividend from this investment. Advocates P. Sadashiva Nair, L.N. Mehrotra in Jabalpur and T.K. Krishnan in Trichur, Congress leader Subhadra Joshi in Delhi were a few among those who extended their help through advice, knowledge and sympathy to the cooperating workers.

The importance of the cooperative sector in eliminating poverty was already recognized in Europe during the late nineteenth century. The colonial government in India formalized its first effort at setting up cooperatives in the early twentieth century through the passing of the Cooperative Credit Societies Act in 1904 followed by the Cooperative Societies Act of 1912. And the latter paved the way for the formation of non-credit societies and federal cooperative organizations. The apex organization of the Indian Cooperative Movement was formed in 1929.[47] Economists and public personalities paid serious attention to issues related to cooperation and its application in India, and took initiatives in forming cooperatives at the primary, secondary and apex levels in different provinces of colonial India.[48]

A recent study of the handloom industry in the Bombay Presidency has analysed the attempts of the government in setting up weavers' cooperatives in the early twentieth century in detail. These cooperatives were supposed to boost the industry by freeing weavers

[46] Again in 1994 when the future of the outlet became uncertain due to the Supreme Court's directions that all buildings acquired on lease for longer than 25 years would have to be returned to the original owner, the state government stepped in and acquired the space of the ICH by purchasing the space from the owner at Rs 2,613,304, Dipankar Dasgupta, Administrative officer, ICH College Street, interview, 25 January 2011.

[47] SARC, 9th Report.

[48] D.R. Gadgil, *Writings and Speeches of Professor D.R. Gadgil on Cooperation*, Pune: Gokhale Institute of Politics and Economics, 1975.

from the bondage of moneylenders (*sahukars*) who advanced them credit at an exorbitant rate and purchased the finished product from them at a fixed rate. Established by government officials and based on pre-existing values of caste and community, the purpose of these cooperatives was to discipline weavers and to contain individual efforts on the part of weavers to maximize profit and minimize loss, and to undercut the techniques of their everyday resistance. While the cooperatives intended to stop the interference of the intermediary between the weaver and the market, weavers often saw the cooperative societies as outside agencies that failed to take over the role of *sahukar,* who traditionally supplied credit to weavers for social purposes, such as weddings.[49]

The cooperative movement in the 1950s was different from the earlier attempts during the colonial regime. While the officials during the colonial period thought of the cooperatives as a means to control the weavers and to discipline them, in the post-Independence period attempts were made by indigenous leaders who were interested in promoting the welfare of the workers. At the time when Gopalan advised the workers of the Coffee Board to organize themselves into cooperative societies, cooperatives formed a part of the national economic strategy adopted by the Jawaharlal Nehru government for ensuring rapid and equitable economic development.[50] The Second Five-Year Plan (1956–1961), underlined the 'building up a cooperative sector as part of a scheme of planned development', as one of the central aims of National Policy. Although Pillai wrote that the workers felt betrayed as the ICH was not nationalized, Pillai and other workers can be seen on the photograph together with Gopalan taken on the occasion of the inauguration of the Trichur Society, of which Pillai became the secretary.

Each regional ICWCSL was to be managed by a board of directors (elected from the rank of the worker-members) consisting of 12 members including three office bearers: secretary, chairman

[49] Douglas Haynes, *Small Town Capitalism in Western India: Artisans, Merchants and the Making of the Informal Economy, 1870–1960*, Cambridge: CUP, 2012, 219–28, and passim.

[50] SARC, 9th Report.

and treasurer elected by the members of the respective society. In their new avatar, the ICH took over the old buildings where the old outlets were located. They also took over the furniture, crockery, cutlery and other kitchenware, and continued to operate on the principle of providing coffee and food at a subsidized price. The legacy of the Coffee Board was also retained in the uniform but the logo of the Coffee Board was replaced by that of the ICWCSL. The All India Coffee Workers' Cooperative Societies Federation (ICWCSF, 1960) became an umbrella organization providing a platform to the different regional cooperative societies.[51] Currently, there are 183 establishments run by 10 coffee workers' cooperative societies all over India employing about 6000 workers.[52]

Owned and controlled by employees themselves, workers' cooperatives have several characteristic features:[53]

(1) They are autonomous organizations not subsidiaries to another firm.
(2) Through nominal holdings of share capital workers become members of these enterprises.
(3) The structure allows its member-workers to participate directly and indirectly in decision-making at all levels.
(4) Worker-members, by virtue of their functional role as workers, share in the profit after the payment of all costs of production.
(5) The cooperative principles of 'one member—one vote' and 'limited return on capital' apply.

The demand to form cooperatives naturally implied that the workers would now believe in the concept of cooperation and take

[51] The ICWCSF meets once a year to discuss their problems but that apart it does not have any influence on the operation of the societies. The Calcutta ICWCS dissociated itself from this umbrella organization some time back.

[52] Many of these establishments are canteens and guest houses of public sector undertakings like the National Thermal Power Corporation (NTPC), National Mineral Development Corporation (NMDC) etc. run on contract basis; the Calcutta Society runs one canteen at the NTPC premises in Farakka and Haldia each; the 'Hotel India' chain in the Madhya Pradesh and Chhatisgarh are under the ICWCS Jabalpur.

[53] Derrick Jones cited in S. Bhowmik and K. Sarkar, 'Worker Cooperatives as Alternative Production Systems: A Study in Kolkata, India', in *Work and Occupations*, 9.4 (2002), 160–82.

upon themselves to make these principles denoting democrary on the workfloor, a reality. The memoir of Pillai mentioned above offers some vital information about the initial response of the workers in the Travancore-Cochin area that constituted the Trichur Cooperative Society. Pillai was twenty-seven when he lost his job, and received Rs 280 as compensation. He took it upon himself to organize the coffee workers in south Kerala forming their cooperative. The would-be owners were asked to purchase shares worth Rs 500 (Rs 10 a share) to become a member of the society. Without any working knowledge of what cooperation entailed and thus uncertain of the future, most of the grade IV employees were reluctant to take the risk of parting with such a large sum of money, which they would have to borrow any way. After travelling continuously for 18 months, a period during which his wife gave birth to a baby boy that unfortunately died in its crib, Pillai was able to collect only Rs 350. Lalitha, his wife, sold off her gold jewellery and donated the money for the cause of the Society, recalled that her husband had not seen the baby. Since they did not have adequate number of members, Lalitha, and the wives of other cooperating male members were made members of the Trichur Society, (ICBWS Limited No. 4227), formed on 10 February 1958 under the Travancore-Cochin Cooperative Societies Act with the advocate T.K. Krishnan as the president and Pillai as the secretary. Up until now Mrs Pillai is the only female member in all ICWCSL throughout India manned by male members; she however does not have any say in the running of the Society. After the initial years of difficulty, things gradually turned for the better. During 1963–65 the Society was able to introduce dearness allowance, bonus, provident fund for pension, medical and other benefits for its members. From this time on the tips given by customers were also collected toward the common fund for pension. Reminiscing about those early days, one former employee noted that the work they had to perform was heavy. For a long time before the connection of cooking gas was readily available in small towns, they had to depend on wood and other traditional fuel. They sometimes had to cater outdoor to courts, secretariats, government offices and other public places and the only mode of transport available to carry everything around was a bicycle.[54]

The same year that Trichur Society was founded, another society was formed in Malabar (northern Kerala) with its centre in Tellicherry under the chairmanship of A.V.K. Nair. Although Pillai, T.K. Krishnan and P.T. Raghavan of the Trichur Society were members of the Board in Tellicherry too, the former did not have any control over the latter which was directly responsible to the Registrar of Cooperatives in Trivandrum. At the time of the formation of this society there were 11 employees and 16 members. The headquarters of this Society was based in Cannanore (Kannur). At the time of entry, members there were required to buy 10 shares of Rs 100 each. Elsewhere too, while the cooperators themselves scrambled to put together the basic capital they needed, visitors of the ICH encouraged them by purchasing a few shares themselves.

Since the beginning, it became customary for potential individuals to deposit an amount at the time of entry toward the share capital. Currently this amounted to Rs 15,000 for a membership of the Trichur Society. The new entrant gets an informal on-the-floor training for six months followed by a probation period of one year after which he is made permanent. There are fifty outlets employing 2,045 member-workers under this Society. The minimum and maximum wage of workers under the Trichur Society currently range from Rs 5000 for a beginner to Rs 20,000–25,000 (with additional benefits in both cases) for a senior member with thirty years of experience.[55]

Unlike in Kerala, where the amount charged as share capital has been revised several times, members of the Calcutta Society (formed on 13 September 1958) still have to deposit Rs 500 at the time of entry. The Society has four outlets employing sixty-five workers.[56]

[54] V.R.V. Nair, 'The Mother Who Rears More Than 2000 Children', in *ICHGJS*, 54.

[55] Venugopal, accountant, ICBWCS Ltd., Trichur, interview, 8 December 2011; the Delhi society has 13 outlets with 350 workers, Susanta Das, secretary, Delhi Cooperative Society, interview, 22 January 2012.

[56] Fifty-eight of them are members while seven are working on probation. Two of the outlets are the Coffee House in College Street and Jadavpur. The branch in the

A new entrant to the society is kept on probation for a period of three years. The initial deposit is returned once a member is made permanent. S.N. Jana, a worker of the Calcutta Society who joined the service in 1993 as *masalchi* (dishwasher) against the monthly wage of Rs 700, was an 'all-rounder' by 2011 working alternately as cook, coffee-maker, counter manager, waiter and boy, earning Rs 5,000 a month.[57] Every year the workers get a raise of Rs 200–300. In addition to a dearness allowance of 35 per cent, they are entitled to the Employees State Insurance (ESI, since 2000) scheme and provident fund.

Almost all workers of the ICWCSL came from a very humble rural background, often the only earning member in the family. Initially the workers of the Coffee Board were recruited, as noted above, by the propaganda officer. The formation of the cooperatives implied a shift in the nature of control of the workspace. Scholars working on labour in India have emphasized the blurred boundaries of formal and informal labour. The labour market for cooperatives in India in general is known to be neither completely formal nor informal and recruitment of personnel on an *ad hoc* basis is a characteristic of these societies.[58] Since the workers became their own employers, recruitment was regulated by them in a way that was helpful to the members of the society. Old members introduced new members who were usually recruited from family and kin, and failing these sources from among acquaintances in their ancestral villages.[59] After the

Medical College premises was closed down recently on the ground of lack of safety in the aftermath of the devastating fire in the AMRI hospital in 2011. This apart the Society runs a canteen at Farakka (1992), DVC (Bokaro, 1993) on a contract basis, Zahir Hussain, interview, 31 July 2011. Under the Delhi Society, where the deposit is Rs 2000, the minimum salary is Rs 7,680. As this society did not opt for the ESI scheme, members get an additional Rs 1000–1500 per month towards medical expenses; interview, Susanta Das, op.cit., 22 January 2012.

[57] S.K. Jana, interview, 14 February 2011; cf. V.M. Peter John, who joined the Bangalore Society at the age of 15 in 1978 against a daily wage of 8 rupees, earned 10,000 a month in 2011, interview, 2 August 2011.

[58] T.J. Thoomkuzy, 'Professionalizaion of Management in Co-Operatives', *The Co-Operator,* vol. 32, 1995, no. 1.

[59] Cf. the dynastic rule in sugar cooperatives of Maharashtra where chairmanship of

retirement of one member, his place was usually taken by his son or nephew. Ramjatan Kahar of Ayodhya, popular as 'Ramuda' in College Street ICH was succeeded in 1985 by his son Mahendrakumar who currently works at the Jadavpur outlet. S.K. Nasiruddin, chairman of the same society and a worker for the last 20 years was brought in by his uncle Saidullah Khan from Puri district in Orissa.[60] Most of the current workers of different societies began their careers by accompanying their fathers or uncles to the coffee house as teenagers and started out as sweepers or kitchen boys. Every new member had to go through this initiation whereafter he rose to become a bearer, kitchen assistant, cook, head cook, counter-manager, accountant and manager. Bijay Kumar Nayek of Jajpur in Orissa, who joined the ICH Calcutta as bearer in 1979, is now the secretary of the board of the Calcutta ICWCSL. Consequently, members of the cooperatives usually have the experience of working in all departments and can in principle perform any work.[61] Initially, they wear just the white trousers and bush shirts unless appointed as sweepers who can be identified by their khaki shorts and bush shirts. Senior members wear a green belt and turban with green piping while senior-most workers wear a red belt and a turban with red piping. When the outlets were under the Coffee Board, the metal buckle of the belt

---

a cooperative was hereditary, B.S. Baviskar, 'Cooperatives in Maharashtra: Challenges Ahead', *EPW*, 42.42, 20 October 2007, 4217–21.

[60] Saidulla Khan had been an employee of ICH since it was under the Coffee Board. Zahir Hussain, a worker for 36 years, was introduced by his late uncle, working in Calcutta since 1960 and still remembered by many ICH regulars, Zahir Hussain, interview, 31 July 2011; Sukumar Bera who has been a cooperator for the last 32 years, took the place of his brother Barendranath Bera who had served at the College Street outlet since 1964, Sukumar Bera, interview, 28 January 2012. Susanta Das, Manager, Delhi Cooperative Society was brought in introduced by his uncle who had been manager of the Allahabad ICH; NP Gireesan of ICH Thrichur 'succeded' his father N S Parameswar Pillai in the Trichur Society; Kalam Singh working under the ICWCS Delhi joined the Society just before his father retired, Kalam Singh, interview, 15 November 2011; Venugopal, accountant of the Thrichur Society, P.D. Pradeep, manager of the Allahabad ICH are no exception to this rule.

[61] Unlike in other cooperatives, in Calcutta there are two non-members—an administrative officer and an accounts officer employed by the members of the society.

bore the logo of the Coffee Board (as is still the case in the ICH at Chittaranjan Avenue, Calcutta and in Bangalore) while at places run by the cooperative it was replaced by that of the ICWCSL.

FUNCTIONING

There are many cooperatives of coffee growers throughout the world, but Indian Coffee House is the only instance where coffee shops are run by the workers themselves. Since control of the cooperatives rests with the members-employees-cum-owners, the members-workers of a given society own and manage it, employ themselves, earn their own livelihood and benefit from the work of their colleagues. As democratic institutions formed by members voluntarily on an equal basis, the importance of the cooperatives as a third alternative next to state-funded enterprises on the one hand and capitalist enterprises on the other in ensuring equitable development and redistribution of resources is well recognized in literature. In the opinion of Drèze and Sen, the current debate on liberalization and ensuing economic growth is too limited in scope because it highlights only the negative roles of the government. Overtly pre-occupied with narrow economic reforms, it neglects the role of cooperative action as an instrument of socio-economic reforms.[62] Joining the cooperatives has allowed the workers, representing socio-economically backward sections of the society, to improve their condition through self-management. Development of the employees toward their self-actualization is one of the major objectives of cooperation.[63]

At the same time, the success of a given cooperative depends on the belief on the cooperational values on behalf of the workers individually and collectively, is matched by behavioural attitude at the organizational, social commitment level on the one hand and

[62] Jean Drèze and Amartya Sen, *Economic Development and Social Opportunity in India: Development and Participation*, New Delhi: OUP, ch. 2.

[63] R. Arvidsson and K.K. Taimni, *A Study of Personnel Management in Selected Co-operative Super Markets in India*, New Delhi: International Co-operative Alliance, 1971.

satisfaction with the facets of employment on the other.[64] The target of a cooperative can be said to have met only when per capita surplus per member exceeds the amount realized by them individually. One of the best examples of the success of the principle of cooperation in alleviating poverty in South Asia is the Grameen Bank, the microfinance institution of Bangladesh that broke up the interlocked capital and labour markets and helped rural women in avoiding the trap of the local financial network.[65] Closer at home there is of course the success story of Amul that formed the genesis of the Gujarat Cooperative Milk Marketing Foundation. Begun in 1946, it is one of the best examples of a successful, vast network of cooperatives producing milk and other dairy products distributed throughout India. The small rural milk producers' cooperative bear a testimony of strong commitment toward the principle of cooperation.[66]

When the workers' cooperatives were set up, the concept of providing food and beverage of good quality at a reasonable cost became extremely popular. And as cooperatives, the ICWCSL, were allowed to function in different ministries of the government of India in places like the secretariat and the legislators' hostel in Trivandrum where private enterprises did not have access.[67] Since the ICWCSL works under hard budget constraints in a competitive market condition, the survival of the cooperatives is a testimony to the hard work on behalf of their members. However, the varied performance of different outlets of the Indian Coffee House suggests that although cooperatives are meant to further the cause of industrial democracy, the success of a cooperative depends on the politico-economic environment in a given state. One of the most successful ICWCSL in

[64] S.N. Biswas and C. Balaji, 1996. 'Belief in Cooperative Values and Employee Attitude', *Indian Journal of Industrial Relations*, 32.1 (July), 21–33.

[65] M. Yunus, *Banker to the Poor: The Autobiography of Muhammad Yunus, Founder of the Grameen Bank*, London: Aurum Press, 1998.

[66] R. Hereida, *The Amul India Story*, Tata McGraw Hill, 1997; Sujata Patel, in Martin Doornbos and K.N. Nair (eds.), *Resources, Institutions and Strategies: Operation Flood and Indian Dairying*, New Delhi: Sage, 1986, 27–56.

[67] Sriram, chief librarian, Centre for Development Studies, Trivandrum, interview, 16 December 2011.

northern India is that of the Jabalpur Coffee Workers' Society. It is a part of the chain undergoing the same fate as other outlets in 1958 of being dumped by the Coffee Board that began with 16 members and a capital of Rs 1,365. Five decades later it amassed a capital of Rs 14.93 crore spreading across over 80 outlets and eight lodges in Chhatisgarh and Madhya Pradesh at the end of the financial year 2008–09. This horizontal expansion is matched by vertical expansion as the society has been entrusted by public undertakings like Bharat Aluninium Company, Bhilai Steel Plant and National Mineral Development Corporation to run their canteens in the two states.[68] The Jabalpur Society is an example where the surplus resulting from collective action has been reinvested in value-adding assets like hotels with an increasing number of agents as stakeholders. While this has increased their mutual dependency, it has worked as an incentive for the workers to increase their productivity. [69]

In the case of Kerala too, where the general political culture fosters the unity among the middle class, working class and farmers, there are other successful examples of industrial cooperation. For instance, the substantial increase in the investment made by members of the cooperatives has led to its expansion over the last fifty years.[70] Here the ICH is part of the popular culture. In 2009–10 the capital of the Cannanore Society amounted to Rs 2,000,000 (in shares) while the turnover during 2008–09 was Rs 183,897,040.60. Recently, the Society

[68] See the retired journalist and an old hand at ICH Bhopal N.D. Sharma's blog 'Indian Coffee House Shows the Way', 26 June 2009, https://ndsharma.wordpress.com/2009/06/26/indian-coffee-house-shows-the-way/.

[69] In addition to a respectable salary drawn by the employees, they enjoy earned leave for 52 days in a year, leave travel allowance, medical allowance, education allowance for their children, house rent allowance, group insurance and two types of pension—one paid by the Society and the other by the Provident Fund Organization. By the time an employee retires at the age of 60 years, it is likely that he will have his own house (with the liberal loan granted by the Society), and have his children educated and well settled. At retirement, an employee gets roughly Rs 15 lakh in cash from his contribution to the provident fund, gratuity and other allowances, Sharma, 'Indian Coffee House'.

[70] See for example the fascinating account of the country cigarette manufacturing industry in *Kerala Dinesh Beedi*.

was reported to have set aside a substantial amount (Rs 1.25 crore) it needed to allow an increase in the wage of its 750 workers.[71] Although there was a problem with the Coffee Houses under the Trichur Society running at loss at the time of the liberalization of the Indian economy, according to Venugopal, the secretary of the Society, the cooperative was running smoothly during my field research in 2011–12. The sale per day at the Thampanoor outlet in Trivandrum housed in the famous piece of architecture created by Laurie Baker amounted to Rs 125,000 yielding the Society a gross profit of Rs 50,000 per day. When the Society was facing a crisis in the mid-1990s in the wake of the economic liberalization of the Indian economy, the members of the Society decided to sacrifice their bonus in order to keep the outlets going. The spirit of cooperation is reflected in the creation of the common pool of tips and all workers work toward the same goal.

The Delhi Society had mixed results with the outlets in Chandigarh yielding a surplus and the outlet in CP, Delhi suffering from a deficit budget, with the result that the Society on the whole functions on a 'no profit, no loss' basis. In the words of Zahir Hussain of the Society in Calcutta, deficit budget was a perennial problem faced by them as well.

The concept behind the Indian Coffee House rests on the ideology of working for the benefit of workers and consumers alike.[72] Usually the outlets of the Indian Coffee House are open for twelve hours a day and the ones in the cities of Bangalore and Trivandrum have a very popular breakfast menu.[73] The chain is extremely popular especially

[71] P. Divakaran, 'Denied Pay-hike Indian Coffee House Workers on Warpath', *The Indian Express*, 3 July 2013.

[72] Dipankar Dasgupta (administrative Officer, College Street Coffee House) in an interview to the BBC journalist Howard Johnson, BBC documentary on the Indian Coffee House by Howard Johnson, 2010; Dasgupta repeated this in his interview to this author.

[73] In Bangalore it is the young employees working in banks and the IT sector while the different outlets in Trivandrum cater to different kinds of customers; at Anna's arcade it is mainly university students who go there for breakfast. The opening time also varies from place to place: in Lucknow it was 8 a.m. to 6 p.m., at Bangalore and Trivandrum it is 8 a.m, at College Street, Calcutta it is 9 a.m. to 9 p.m. (on Sundays 9 a.m.–12 p.m., 5–9 p.m.), at Jadavpur, Calcutta it is 11 a.m. to 8 p.m..

in Kerala where it is a 'brand' trusted by the common people. The food available here is similar to what they have at home (*idli*, *dosa*, *vada*) with no variation in food quality across all the outlets.[74] For those who prefer non-vegetarian food, the outlets have varieties of omelets and *biryani*, the latter added to the menu about fifteen years back. Such items on the ICH menu are usually not available in vegetarian restaurants. The branches at the Medical College and MLA hostel in Trivandrum serve *thali* (meals) at lunch time. The ICH at Allahabad has a breakfast menu and is popular as a family outing. It is important to note in this connection that personal relationship between customers and workers is something both the workers and visitors of the Indian Coffee House value very much. In his work on bazaars, Akos Östör has pointed to the role of the place as productive of social relations. Addressing the stranger using a kinship term like *dada* or *bhai*, brother, or as *chacha*, uncle, reduces the risk in economic transaction.[75] Constant interaction at this site leads to a duality between the outside (public) and the inside (home); although linkages can be established through the medium of communications and exchanges, the elements of characteristic strangeness and risk remain part of it. The Coffee House is an enclosed and regulated place. Here, long-term familiarity with the place and its workers, often over generations, in cases of both workers and consumers in the Coffee House generates social relationship.

In the 1960s and 1970s male students in Calcutta would spend the night in the Coffee House.[76] Even when the place was crowded, regulars could reckon on their favourite worker to find them a place.[77] While the workers would allow students to consume on credit, regular customers would help the workers in different ways. As the workers

[74] In both Bangalore and Trivandrum interlocutors related their fascination as 'children', for the masala dosa and vegetable cutlet of the Indian Coffee House with their 'red' filling because of the beetroot added to the usual potato mixture.

[75] Akos Östör, *Culture and Power: Legend, Ritual, Bazaar and Rebellion in a Bengali Society,* New Delhi: Sage, 1984.

[76] See Chapter Five; cf. in China too, the teahouse often served as home away from home, Wang, *Teahouse*, 19.

[77] Swati Lal, interview, 21 February 2011.

were transferred after some time, a newcomer in a totally unfamiliar place would be pleasantly surprised at the familiar face of a worker greeting him in the Coffee House.

Even now the regular visitors know the workers by their name and the workers on their part know how the former want their coffee, which snacks they like to have and can identify families visiting the place for generations. Workers employed at one place for a long time, have often served two generations and assume a patronizing attitude toward young visitors of the second generation, a gesture fondly reciprocated by visitors. Many regulars in College Street still remember the head bearer Ramjatan Kahar, popularly known as 'Ramuda'.[78] It is not unusual that during busy hours impatient gestures on behalf of customers waiting for the first cup of coffee are returned with an irritated 'do you not see I am busy?' like response. This apparent rudeness however, is supposed to be part of the game and is not meant to humiliate anyone. There seems to be an understanding on both sides and many regular visitors think the workers, overburdened with work, behave like long-time household helps who have almost become part of the family.[79] This makes the ICH a 'second home' for many; those living/working nearby visit the space two to three times a day.

The blurring of the distinction between the private and the public is thus inherent in the structure of ICH. Since the outlets are managed by cooperatives, not only are the workers the major driving force in the space; they consider themselves owners of the place and accordingly extend their hospitality by supplying water free of cost. In other words, the place removes the ambiguity, danger and risk that scholars like Freitag associate with the public space of bazaar, the outside.[80] The social relations at the Coffee House are of

[78] Probal Basak, 'Coffee and Much More', 31 July 2011, http://www.business-standard.com/article/beyond-business/coffee-and-much-more-111073100008_1.html.

[79] Prasun Bhaumik, editor *Bijalpa*; Dipankar Bagchi, Ph.D. student, Jadavpur University and editor *Charbak*, 21 February 2011; cf. Sugandhi Ravindranathan, journalist, *The Hindu* (Bangalore), interview, 30 November 2011, thought the workers were 'grumpy but nice'.

[80] Freitag, *Collective Action and Community*, Berkeley [etc.]: UCP, 1989.

different types. By addressing the workers as *dada* or *chacha*, one immediately establishes a kinship with them. Second, like at many middle class homes, the owners of the cooperative wait on their clientele in the capacity of workers, and carelessness on the part of the workers is usually forgiven by the customers.[81] Third, a feature that is especially applicable to the outlets of ICH in Kerala, food there is best trusted next to the food cooked at home. Indeed, many of the interlocutors see ICH as a second home, a 'day-time home', or as a home outside home.

The spirit of confidence this bond instils is reflected in the attitude of the workers who often put the visitors in their place. Talking about Allahabad in the 1960s one interlocutor narrated an anecdote of a young rising political leader eating a mutton cutlet using only the knife. A conscious visitor pointed out that the knife is usually used to cut the food in small portions which is then put into the mouth with the help of a fork. At this, the would-be politician flared up and said that he was not going to abide by the rules introduced by the colonial rulers; he would eat the way it suited him. One worker who had been watching him went up to him and said politely 'with that knife you will cut your own tongue, not that of an Englishman'. While a roar of laughter ensued, the young man got up and shook hands with the worker.[82]

The bond established in the space is one of the positive aspects of the work especially as far as the workers are concerned. That well-known public figures share the same space, although briefly, seems to elevate the workers' status in the social hierarchy by proxy and is a source of inspiration in the otherwise dull and mechanical life the workers live. And of course if there is an exchange of words, that often becomes a cherished memory for the workers. Many customers visiting the ICH as students become doctor, municipal or government officers, MLAs, engineers in their later life. When the workers of the

[81] As the workers take only mental note of the orders, often, especially during rush hours, orders placed by table A are brought to table B. Similarly, if C orders a Coca Cola which is out of stock, the worker might take the liberty to open a bottle of Fanta and supply it without asking, personal observation during fieldwork.

[82] H.S. Saxena, interview, 22 January 2012.

ICH visit them on business, they are recognized and offered help. This instils in the workers a tremendous sense of job satisfaction.[83] Mani, a young worker from Kerala posted in Allahabad in the 1970s used to feel very homesick especially because he had a rudimentray knowledge of Hindi and was therefore unable to communicate with the customers. He used to paint in his free time. This was conveyed to a visitor by Vijayan, a senior worker, also from Kerala. The son of the customer concerned, seeking admission to the mass media department of Jamia Milia Islamia University, wrote an article which, together with the reproduction of a few of Mani's works, was published on the Allahabad page of the *Hindustan Times*. This made Mani a local celebrity and soon there developed a clientele for his work. After some time Mani left the ICH in order to devote all his time to art.[84] The worker Narayan in ICH College Street too was an artist and received encouragement from customers.[85] Charanmasi in the Tea House in CP attracted the attention of his clients for the poems he used to write.[86]

Most of the visitors interviewed—from Delhi to Calcutta to Trivandrum—had no doubt that 'value for money' was and still is a considerable factor behind the popularity of the Indian Coffee House. In Trivandrum itself two new branches were opened in the last two months of 2011.

In exploring the politics of the poor, the Subaltern Studies school of studies emphasizes that the autonomy of the poorer classes developed

[83] Zahir Hussain, Calcutta, interview, 16 February 2011; cf. Ashok Mitra, writer, economist, politician and poet, was happy to note that when he visited the ICH in Pune on an official trip to the city, one of the workers came up to him and said he knew him from ICH Calcutta where Mitra was a regular as a student, *Apila Chapila*, 45; Ramesh Chandra Grover of Rajkamal in Allahabad who tours all over India on business, met ex-employees of the ICH Allahabad in the ICH Chandigarh. They rushed to greet him, and offered him coffee; interview, 23 January 2012; Sarasija Basu in Calcutta arranged with one of his doctor friends to check the ailing workers and distribute medicine among them free of cost.

[84] I owe this information to Professor Neelum Saran Gour whose son Devangshu had penned the article in *Hindustan Times*.

[85] Bhattacharya, *Albert Hall*, 121–26.

[86] Kalia, 'Tea House'; Upadhyay, 'Dilli Ka Tea House'.

from a subjective culture that stood in the way of their accepting modern institutions and practices of bourgeois politics. Further, it has been suggested that religion played an important part in the formation of identity of the poor workers in factories.[87] A recent study of the urban poor in North India argues, however, that working class politics often borrowed from and appropriated bourgeois institutions, ideals of democracy and citizenship which they moulded for their purpose.[88] Religious identity of the poor is, according to this latter position, important, but needs to be separated because class, occupation and other affiliations play an equally significant role in the politics of the subaltern.[89] The role played by the subaltern workers of the Coffee Board in the formation of the coffee workers' cooperatives confirms this latter view. An ordinary worker like Pillai had no difficulty in comprehending the significance of the principle of cooperation. And in spite of the initial hesitationof the workers, Pillai and others embraced the ideology in their conflict with capital. Moreover, in a country where the elite often indulge in politics along the communal divide, the coffee workers' cooperatives deserve admiration for the non-communal nature of their organization. Since its inititation, Hindus, Muslims and Christians have worked in the ICH together without allowing personal faith to interfere with their work. Keeping the religious sentiment of the Muslim workers and patrons in mind, all meat dishes served in the outlets of the Indian Coffee House are prepared with *halal* meat.

CHALLENGES TO OVERCOME

Being a member of the ICWCSL has definitely improved the lot of the workers and their family. The success of cooperative action depends to a large extent on the opportunities available at the level, from where cooperators are recruited. Marx emphasized the importance of the spontaneous and voluntary nature of workers' cooperatives and

[87] Dipesh Chakrabarty, *Rethinking Working-Class History: Bengal, 1890–1940*, Princeton: Princeton University Press, 213–17.

[88] Gooptu, *The Politics*, 9–10, 22.

[89] Ibid., Chapters Six and Seven.

was cautious about the danger of the imposition of any doctrinary system from above. He also observed that without changes in the general conditions of the society at large, the cooperative system will never transform the capitalist society. Personnel management in the cooperative sector requires a balanced combination of principles of management with those of cooperation.[90] Once it was established and organized, the members of the Grameen Bank could manage the cooperative without outside intervention. In the case of Amul, the cooperative expanded both horizontally by bringing other milk producing villages under the organization, and vertically by producing milk powder, chocolate, ice cream, cold beverages.[91] In the cases where the surplus equation of the Cooperative Society is positive, like in Jabalpur and Cannanore, a brief survey of the assets and liabilities are provided on the web for anyone concerned. That all is not that well with the outlets under the Trichur Society—in spite of the claims made by the secretary—is clear from the fact that they are allegedly burdened with an arrear of over Rs 2.5 million (USD 494, 186) on account of unpaid sales tax.[92] Although the members of the Trichur Society are comparatively better off than their counterparts for example in Calcutta, the general problems facing the cooperatives become clear after a couple of visits to the outlets in Calcutta and Delhi. In the case of India in general, not only does the performance of the cooperatives vary across activities, regions and sectors, it has been noted that government control through the Registrar of the Cooperative Societies exerting control over the institutions has stood in the way of their fully developing into a people's movement. At the same time the cooperative sector has failed to inculcate the

[90] G.S. Kamat, *New Directions of Co-operative Management*, Bombay: Himalaya Publishing House, 1987, 34.

[91] P. Chandra and D. Tirupati, *Successful Business Strategies for Firms in Large Emerging Economies: The Story of Amul*, Ahmedabad: IIM, 2003.

[92] 'The day the state government demands payment of that sum, Coffee Houses here have to close down', Calvin Miranda, employee Brocade Communications and musician, a regular at ICH Anna's arcade, Trivandrum, interview, 21 December 2011; my repeated enquiry with the headquarters of the Society at Trichur on this question went unanswered but it was not denied either.

principle of self-help, the basic formula that is supposed to help the cooperators develop complementary to the mechanism of capital.[93] Both the weaknesses are very much present in the case of the ICH. Since most of the workers of the ICH begin working at an early age, it does not seem to be a conscious, voluntary choice on their part but the only alternative for many of them. The ideology behind cooperation cannot be fully reached unless and until the members are aware of the tenets of the ideology and what it entails upon them as far as the question of input and output is concerned. Since incentive remains low in most cases, direction of the cooperatives along strictly democratic lines and upholding the main objective of self-actualization of the worker becomes a difficult task.

The management of the regional cooperatives often claims that the Coffee Houses do not make enough profit.[94] Customarily, anyone walking into these outlets can occupy a place and get a glass of water and not really have to order any drink or food. Because most of the regular visitors only drink coffee but do not consume food and yet occupy tables for an indefinite period of time, the outlets of the ICH incur losses.[95] Regular patrons have however something different to add. Lack of commitment to the ideal of cooperation and financial irregularities are according to many plaguing the institution. Commenting on the bleak prospects of the cooperative movement in Bengal, a regular visitor to the ICH College Street noted that the Coffee Workers' Cooperative there was in a bad shape because the workers, conscious that they owned the place, were not open to

[93] SARC, 9th Report.

[94] In 2008–09 the total turnover of the Calcutta Society was $450,000 while the turnover at the College Street branch was $210,000; still the Society encountered a loss of $19,000: accounts officer Subhas Ganguli in an interview to the BBC journalist Howard Johnson BBC documentary on the Indian Coffee House by Howard Johnson, 2010.

[95] Janak Raj, Manager, ICH Delhi, interview, 6 January 2012; Subhash Ganguli, accountant ICH Calcutta, interview, 22 July and 24 August 2011; Zahir Hussain, a member of the Calcutta Society since 1976 thinks that a daily sale of Rs 80–90,000 is needed in order to make the College Street branch a viable enterprise. But the actual sale there is between Rs 40,000–50,000. All people do not come here to eat; only 30 per cent of the visitors take food, interview, 16 February 2011.

any advice.[96] This has to be understood in the context of the poor social capital of the co-operators. When the Coffee House in Delhi was about to close down in 2009, a part of the then management had allegedly made a deal with an MNC to vacate the venue for a lump sum.[97] Rumour has it that there was similar hobnobbing on the part of the Coffee House workers in Calcutta who were supposedly willing to dissolve the cooperative against a modest compensation to be paid to individual workers by an estate developer. According to the accounts officer of the Calcutta Society, the board of directors 'does not have a single member who can think properly and take steps for the advancement of the cooperative society. Nor are they open to any advice. Even the secretary is corrupt'.[98]

The availability of adequate working capital is a problem these workers' cooperatives face and the ICWCSL has been more successful in places where the share of the initial investment made by cooperators has been increased. In Calcutta, where the initial payment toward the creation of a share capital has not been reviewed at all, the stake of the members is too low to motivate them to function properly. Vidyadhar Nayek (42; working in the Calcutta Society since he was 18), has to support himself living in the city and his family in Kedrapada, Orissa consisting of his widowed mother and elder sister, wife, two daughters and one son with a paltry sum of Rs 5,200 (wage Rs 4,900 and the rest from tips).[99] Although the pay day is on the 20th of every month, workers begin taking advance by the end of the first week of the

[96] Shyamal Basu, businessman and secretary of the (defunct) Coffee House Consumers' Forum, interview, 4 February 2011.

[97] Ram Shastri, secretary of the Consumers' Forum, ICH, CP, interview, 6 January 2012.

[98] Subhash Ganguli, interview, 13 February 2012. This could be a class bias of the *bhadralok* Ganguli. Because, according to a reliable source the accounts filed by the ICH to the Registrar of Cooperatives, which is Ganguli's responsibility, is again full of inconsistencies; for lack of commitment and problem of discipline in other cooperatives see *Kerala Dinesh Beedi*, 152.

[99] Raghab Bandyopadhyay, interview, 24 August 2011. He pointed out that the capital of a cooperative society can increase when members capable of investing a higher amount of capital are encouraged to invest more than other co-operators, a measure that cannot be put into practice in Bengal.

month. Consequently, at the end of each month there is invariably a deficit of Rs 2,00,000 leading to the non-payment of the sales tax due around the same time. In order to achieve the goal of accumulating resources that could be expanded through re-investment, it is necessary to generate enough profit for improving the bargaining position of the cooperatives vis-à-vis the state and capital. The buildings housing the ICH were taken on lease by the Coffee Board and this remained unchanged when the societies took over the management. Problems arose at the end of the lease period when the property was supposed to be returned to the owner. Both in Bangalore and at Spencer Plaza in Trivandrum the old buildings of the Indian Coffee House were taken back by the original owner of the property due to non-payment of rent. In Trivandrum Anna's Arcade, a multi-storeyed shopping mall came up in its place, and the building on M.G. Road in Bangalore was under construction when I visited the ICH for field research in 2011. In Calcutta, a property developer was interested in buying up the building, but in order to save the Coffee House the customers of the space persuadeed the state government to lease the building. In Delhi, the municipal government stepped in by writing off a substantial part of the rent due from the Society and sanctioning a grant for refurbishing the outlet. It is important to note that the outlets of the ICH cannot survive capitalist onslaught without state intervention.

As a consequence of the problems associated with the socio-economic milieu governing rural India in general, the cooperatives lack qualified and competent personnel and even ICWC Societies recruit personnel from the same pool without exception.[100] Although most regular visitors of the Coffee House are in general satisfied with the service of the workers and the quality of the food, given the fact that the coffee here costs a fraction of what it costs at the Café Coffee Day for example, the service at most of the outlets lack professionalism.[101] Lack of any training in hospitality is clear

[100] Umesh C. Patnaik, *Introduction to Co-operative Management*, New Delhi: Kalyani Publishers, 1988.

[101] Personal observation: students at the ICH in Delhi ordered Fanta, but got Sprite without any explanation. In Calcutta a group of tourists from Korea who had

from their often arrogant attitude leading to loud verbal skirmishes between a worker and a customer.

In the case of the Calcutta Society, there is no age of retirement. So, in order to have some income workers continue to work even after they are over seventy, when they are no longer agile. According to the accounts officer the workers have no idea what is good for the society and are satisfied with the monthly sale and the wage and the overtime they get. The proposal to begin a mobile operation for catering to a broader public by selling food and coffee at different points in the city was not even considered seriously by the members because that would entail too much work. Almost every day the management receives complaints about the service, food and coffee not being up to the mark. It is a common complaint in Calcutta that there is no work discipline. Workers think that they can do whatever they like because they own the place. They do not want to work full-time for the meager wage: they leave the floor after four to five hours, whereas the work-shift is for eight hours. It is not uncommon for workers to ask for one week's leave, only to return after two months.[102]

Both in the public and private sectors in India the trade union movement has a strong presence in securing the position of the worker. The ICWCSL was formed by members of the Labour Union of the Coffee Board. Since they became their own employers, there has been no trade union in the Coffee Workers' Cooperatives. Individual members of the societies have allegiance to different political parties. And the influence of these parties is clearly visible in the Calcutta Society where there are too many workers, and the internal dissention

---

ordered fish Afghani with fried rice had finished the side dish before they received the fried rice. Often the workers came and took away the coffee cup without bothering to take permission. S.K. Nasiruddin of ICH Calcutta thought that there should be a formal training programme for the workers. On 12 February 2011, a worker in ICH College Street affronted a visitor because the latter took photographs at the former's 'home' without permission.

[102] Bijay Nayek, Nasiruddin and Zahir Hussain of ICWCS Calcutta think that there are workers who are indifferent to their duty; interviews, 22 July 2011, 16 February 2011 respectively; cf. Arvidsson and Taimni, *A study*, 114–19 for misconduct among the employees of some cooperative supermarkets in India.

among them (divided along the four political lines of ideology) makes it difficult to reach a decision rendering any restructuring impossible.[103] This selective alliance-making at work stands in the way of common efforts to analyze and redistribute risks and rewards on the basis of a consensus essential for the success of cooperatives. It shows that electing management from the rank of the workers does not ensure absence of conflict.[104] Under the Delhi Society, where employees can be transferred among thirteen places, newcomers can be caught between interference on behalf of the management in Delhi on the one hand and local vested interest on the other, making day-to-day running of an outlet complicated and cumbersome.[105]

As a marginalized institution, the members of the ICWCSL feel threatened and are not open about their problems. Both Calcutta and Delhi outlets have a consumers' forum. Since the forum is not represented in the board of the respective cooperatives, consumers have no say with regard to the day-to-day running of the Coffee House. Among others Shyamal Basu and Sarasija Basu pointed out that earlier there was a complaint book where visitors could make suggestions or lodge complaints if the service of some worker was unsatisfactory. If there were ten to fifteen complaints against one worker, he would be suspended for some time. Of late, the complaint

[103] Interview Shyamal Basu, businessman, secretary of the non-active Indian Coffee House Consumers' Forum, Calcutta, 4 February 2011. The four political parties are CPI (M), CPI (ML), Congress and Trinamul Congress; the administrative officer here boasts of his links with the higher dignitaries of the CPI in the state (according to a few he was hobnobbing with Trinamool Congress after the Party came to power. Bijay Naik, the secretary confessed to me that he believed in the ideology of the CPI M-L. P.D. Pradeep, the assistant manager of the Allahabad outlet recognized the problem and added that the salary scale was too low to change the recruitment system; cf. cooperatives in Tamil Nadu are hot-bed of party politics leading to increased bureaucratization of the people's movement A. Rajagopal, 'Tamil Nadu Co-operative Movement in Peril', *EPW*, 23.44, 29 October 1988, 2258–59.

[104] Cf. B.S. Baviskar and D.W. Atwood (eds.), *Who Shares? Co-operatives and Rural Development*, Delhi: OUP, 1988, 1–18.

[105] An official of the Delhi Society who did not want to be named claimed that although traditionally new recruits had to begin as *masalchi*, superiors often wanted their recruits to work not in the kitchen but in the 'front part' where workers could earn extra as tips.

book has disappeared. One of the preconditions of the proletarian public sphere is that it has to free itself from the inhibiting influence of the bourgeois public sphere.[106] Although the public sphere of the Coffee House has been a zone of conflicts offering the working class a foothold and is much different from its early modern European counterparts, the above factors show that it still has to go a long way before the workers can fully recognize its potential and actualize the dream of equitable development.[107]

CONCLUSION

This chapter discussed the transformation of the ICH from a restaurant under the Coffee Board to that owned by coffee workers' cooperatives. The chain of the India Coffee House was created in order to boost the sick coffee industry. The Coffee Board created the unique medium of Coffee House outlets spread throughout the length and the breadth of British India. This, together with other measures of propaganda were successful in that the consumption of coffee increased remarkably in the domestic market. But at a time when the economy of the country was shaken by Partition and relocation, the industry would have needed more patience for the domestic market to take off. For the coffee industry, oriented to the export market where coffee fetched a higher price, this experiment with the Coffee Houses seems to have been a temporary measure. Moreover, creating and maintaining the infrastructure of the Coffee House at an all India level was an expensive experiment. Consequently, when in the post-WWII period the world coffee market looked positive with Indian coffee finding new destinations in the US and in Eastern Europe, it provided an excuse to the Coffee Board to reorient the industry to the changed circumstances. When the Plantation Enquiry Commission recommended a marketing policy oriented to the export market, it became easier for the Board to withdraw itself from the ICH.

[106] Oskar Negt and Alexander Kluge, *Public Sphere and Experience: Toward an Analysis of the Bourgeois and Proletarian Public*, Theory and History of Literature, vol. 85, tr. by Peter Labanyi et. al, Minneapolis: University of Minnesota Press, 1993.

[107] See Chapter Six and Seven for more on the Coffee House Cooperatives.

This social space that the middle class urbanites cherished constituted, to coin the terms of Oskar Negt and Alexander Kluge the 'block of real life' of unskilled workers serving in the Coffee Houses. The decision of the Coffee Board to withdraw from the forty-three outlets of the ICH and hand them over to private entrepreneurs directly threatened the existence of the workers whose labour, unsuitable for assimilation into the changed policy of the planters and traders in the Coffee Board, suddenly became redundant. According to the theory of space, protest against the conceived plan of space comes from the lived experience of the space.[108] Through the creation of the CBLU, the workers had been able to fight the overexploitation of labour by the officials of the Board and demand dignity that made the menial work acceptable. Threatened with retrenchment, the workers challenged the decision of the Board and with active support from communist leaders like A.K. Gopalan and other customers of the ICH, the agency of the working class altered the structure of its existence from one of subalternity to that with identity.[109] Personal sacrifice, hard work on the the part of the workers found an ally in the state that encouraged cooperation as a means to ameliorate poverty and ensure equitable growth. That these cooperatives took over from the point where the Coffee Board left off, and carved out a niche for themselves where competition and outmanoeuvring increasingly redraw the economic geography of the city, upholds the agency and stake of the workers in the public sphere.

Nehru visualized the cooperatives as instruments of self-help, without the intervention of the state. It has been recognized that the only way to offer long-standing economic redress to the asset-poor and asset-less rural population—the pool from where recruitments for the CWCS are made throughout the country—is to encourage 'genuinely democratic and self-governing cooperatives based on the principles of mutual help and thrift'.[110] Cooperatives as complementary to market

[108] Lefebvre, *Production*.

[109] 'Subalternity is a Position Without Identity', Gayatri Chakravorty Spivak, *An Aesthetic Education in an Era of Globalization*, Cambridge: Harvard University Press, 2012, 431.

[110] Editorial, *EPW* 41.8, 25 February 2006, 668.

mechanism are common in all industries in the developed world and are viewed as resilient, stable employers.[111] In India, with nearly one half of the primary agricultural cooperative societies and a third of the district cooperative banks incurring losses, the weaknesses in the financial structure of the cooperatives in the rural sector have drawn attention. Experts have attributed their failure to the faulty methods of organization, management and supervision. Traditional methods of recruitment, low wages and lack of quality in the resources of the membership however often stand in the way of the cooperatives further fulfilling their economic justification and defeat the cause of cooperation.[112] Moreover, attempts made by political parties at controlling cooperatives as instruments of patronage and political mobilization have led to the politicization of the movement at the cost of the self-actualization of the cooperators.

The economic success of the cooperative societies depends, however, on the general socio-economic and political environment of the state concerned that provides the infrastructure for proper functioning of such initiatives. This is where commitment of the state and the elite at large is necessary for developing more equitable economic institutions, protecting the rural infrastructure by targeting the exploitation of the poor, removing caste inequalities, criminalization of politics, and offering equal opportunity for education.

[111] See e.g. Virginie Pérotin, 'What do we Really Know of Worker Co-operatives?', http://www.uk.coop/sites/default/files/uploads/attachments/worker_co-op_report.pdf.

[112] V.K.R.V. Rao, 'Cooperation, Democratic Socialism and Economic Planning', speech delivered at the meeting of the National Co-operative Study Forum organized by the National Co-operative Union of India, New Delhi, 1 September 1966.

CHAPTER four

The Indian Coffee House and the World of Literature

The Tea and Coffee House, as noted above, were not the *only* places facilitating literary discussions, or *adda* for that matter. Just like the private gatherings at a writer's place, offices of publishing agencies too were meeting places that brought writers and publishers under the same roof. Even now, in public imagination, the Indian Coffee House is most often associated with the presence of stalwarts from the academia, film, literature and theatre, making them 'sites of cultural pilgrimage'. Chapter Two examined both the nature of the *adda* and the space of the ICH that facilitated it. This chapter will explore the integrative nature of the *adda* at the Coffee and Tea House and its connection especially with literary practices influencing production in that field. I argue here that although *adda* without a *telos* as such is a prime medium for multiple free communications, *telos* can be injected into it and the ensuing *adda* can lead to diverse consequences beyond it, leaking into the professional and the social. When a few students in the Coffee House discussed a recently published novella like *Bibar* (Hell, 1965) that created a despondency and uproar for its content and the use of the obscene language, the *adda* covered inter alia social taboos and literary styles which might influence their viewpoint and their own style of writing, if they were to take up that profession later.[1] In a recent work Ulrike Stark

[1] Journalist and writer Shankarlal Bhattacharya writes how he as a student discussed together with his friends the serially published issues of the novella at their *addas* in Jamaida's restaurant, Sanguvally and the ICH, 'Path Poribartan' (Change of reading habits), *ABP*, 25 April 2015.

has underlined the dual nature of the Indian publishing houses as a modern capitalist enterprise and an important site of scholarly pursuits 'turning them into vibrant meeting places for intellectuals and writers'.[2] Through a combination of entrepreneurial and intellectual engagement publishers like Fardunji Sorabji Marzban in Bombay, Munshi Harsukh Rai in Lahore, Maulvi Abdul Rahman Khan in Kanpur and Mustafa Khan and Munshi Naval Kishore in Lucknow contributed to 'Indian modernity through the diffusion of education and knowledge' in the nineteenth century.[3] Publishing houses, as we shall see here, played a crucial role in bringing those connected with the literary and scholarly world. The regular *adda* at a publishing house would still be limited to a number of intellectuals especially in view of the physical space available for the practice of leisure.

In the case of Europe, Jürgen Habermas' analysis of the formation of public opinion in the public sphere of the coffee house hinged on the development of a literary bourgeoisie. The mass-produced newspapers in the eighteenth century read and debated widely in the coffee house comprised the public space of the coffee house. Rational discourse on the theories of art and literature on the one hand, and on the other, practices of the absolutist state among private persons associating in a free manner was the distinctive feature that set the coffee houses apart from the existing clubs and pubs. Coffee houses in London were associated with the city's intellectual culture.[4] One famous friendship that immortalized the close link between literature and the coffee house was that between Samuel Johnson and James Boswell that began in a coffee house and resulted inter alia in the biography of the former written by the latter.[5] With cafés like Griensteidl (1847) a meeting point of young Vienna artists, Café Central frequented by Sigmund Freud, the modernist writer

[2] Ulrike Stark, *An Empire of Books: The Naval Kishore Press and the Diffusion of the World of Print in Colonial India*, Delhi: Permanent Black, 2007.

[3] Ibid.

[4] Habermas, *The Structural Transformation*; Markman Ellis, 'Coffee-House Libraries in Mid Eighteenth-Century London', *The Library*, March 2009, 3–40.

[5] James Boswell, Christopher Hibbert (eds.), *The Life of Samuel Johnson*, New York: Penguin Classics, 1986.

and poet Peter Altenberg, and the dramatist Arthur Schnitzler or Hawelka, the favourite café of Alfred Schmeller, the coffee houses in Vienna were synonymous with Austrian literature and culture. Coffee houses like Le Procope in Paris visited by businessmen, intellectuals and politicians, like their their English counterparts, had a library.[6]

When the urbanites in India got together in the ICH from the 1940s onwards, they were greatly inspired, as seen above, by the imagined practices of conversation among littérateurs, philosophers and politicians among others in the coffee houses in Europe. The third decade of the twentieth century saw the beginnings of Left politics in India. While the communal divide between the Hindus and Muslims assumed more and more importance in the national politics in the 1930s, informed by Marxism, progressivism, social realism and other Leftist ideology, Indian artists, writers and other intellectuals engaged in a discourse on a purposeful form of creative art addressing issues concerning fascism, imperialism, and social inequality. If the Indian Progressive Writers' Association was set up in the 1930s, the 1940s saw the birth of the Indian Peoples Theatre Association. Before the 1980s when the television invaded the drawing room, recreation included reading, listening to the radio, and watching film and stage productions when possible. Whether in Allahabad or Calcutta reading was a passionate pastime and keeping an eye out for the latest arrivals from abroad was part of the practice.[7] As a considerable section of the visitors to the tea and coffee houses consisted of persons involved in the production of creative arts—aspiring artists, littérateurs—poets and writers, film and theatre personalities—interaction among them resulted in the cross-fertilization of ideas and practices. Here I shall focus on the association between *adda* in the coffee and tea house with a special emphasis on the literary movements in Bengali and Hindi and argue that literary practices and practices of publication were intimately connected with the *adda* in the Coffee House at Allahabad, Calcutta and Delhi. Not only did the institution facilitate

[6] For Vienna Harold B. Segel tr. and (ed.), with an Introduction, *The Vienna Coffeehouse Wits, 1890–1938*, Indiana: Purdue University Press, 1993; see M. Ellis, *Coffee House Culture*, 82 and M. Ellis, 'Coffee-House Libraries'.

[7] H.S. Saxena, interview, 22 January; Chattopadhyay, *Nana Katha*.

discussions on literary practices, but publishing houses and ICH/Tea House were also often located within a close distance from each other. While some publishing houses like Lokbharti/Rajkamal functioned as a parallel Coffee House, the latter could draw members of many small gatherings at one place by offering them the opportunity of diversified encounters too.[8] The combination of artists, playwrights, writers, film and stage personalities, university teachers across disciplines prepared the ground for the reciprocation of ideas through conversations affecting the performers and performance of the action concerned.[9]

CALCUTTA: ALL ROADS LED TO THE COFFEE HOUSE?

Right from Buddhadev Basu in the 1930s to the contemporary poet Joy Goswami, one of the finest poets of the post-Jibanananda phase of Bengali poetry, there have been poets and writers who did not attach importance to the conviviality of the coffee house. Similarly, among those who are familiar with the social space, not everyone agrees about the role of the ICH in Bengali cultural production. There are a few who maintain that the Coffee House was nothing more than a conveniently located place where many could sit at one time.[10] Referring to the regular lunch-time visits of Samar Sen, the journalist-poet and editor of the *Frontier* to 5CA in the 1970s, Nityapriya Ghosh suggested that it was the *adda* and friendly conversation that attracted him to the ICH. Friendly conversations.[11] At the same time there are poets like (his elder brother) Sankha Ghosh alias the 'pope of Bengali poetry', Anil Acharya, Anuradha Mahapatra,

[8] The celebrated book shop of Ram Advani in Hazratganj, Lucknow was a similar meeting place for university teachers and students, publishers and writers, who on their way to the Coffee House would visit the shop in search of freshly imported books, Mitra, *Apila Chapila*, 83; Gautam Bhadra, private communication, 24 August 2011.

[9] Ashok Mitra, 'Identity and Inheritance: Talking about Revolution', http://www.sacw.net/article1550.html.

[10] Raghab Bandyopadhyay, the owner of the publishing house *Charchapad*, an ex-student of the PC who took part in the Naxalite Movement, interview, 10 February 2011.

[11] Nityapriya Ghosh, retired bank officer, writer and columnist of *The Statesman*, interview, 26 February 2012.

Gautam Chaudhury, Anirban Mukhopadhyay, stage personalities like Rudraprasad Sengupta, Abhijit Kar Gupta and others who emphasized the contribution of the social space on Bengali literature and creative art. A thoughtful account acquaints the reader with the literary discussions in the ICH in the 1970s and later:[12]

> .... *Adda* means the cultivation of thought, theoretical analysis, debate, leading to the birth of new creative ideas—a combined effort. These characterized the *addas* of *Parichay*....*Krittibas*....*Andhajug* [Blind Age; Parthapratim Kanjilal and Nishith Bhar] and *Punarbasu* [Prasun Bandyopadhyay] among other magazines. Our gatherings at the Coffee House were no exception to that...The proof was in the [quality of] the above and many other short-lived literary magazines edited at different times by our friends... A large part of the planning and materialization of these magazines took place in the Coffee House. This *adda* played *the* major role in our early publications. The details of publications of later generation poets were also discussed there. Parthapratim Kanjilal played a unique role in taking the initiative to publish the works of the youngest poets with an almost religious passion.

It can be assumed that such *addas* included some homework that would enable the participant even if it were only to grasp what was being talked about. Here we shall consider a few of the *adda* groups and the activities flowing from these gatherings.

Serving the need of the academic institutions in and around College Street, there are numerous types of bookshops in the entire neighbourhood. The street is famous for the makeshift bookstalls on pavements casually displaying the works of Marx, Engels, Hitler, Lenin, Rousseau together with fiction of indigenous and foreign origin, reference and textbooks. The book market there has one of the largest collections of second hand, often rare books. Many of the Bengali publishing houses also have their offices and bookshops there that budding and established authors visit. Printers and binders serving these trades are available nearby. At least twenty bookshops use the same address as that of the Coffee House. Sharing the first

[12] Das, 'Coffee-houser Adda', 118; also see Bhattacharya, 'Path Paribartan'.

floor of the building where the Coffee House has its main seating accommodation, there are three bookshops—Rupa, Chakraborty & Chatterjee and Sansad. On the second floor there is the office of the Radical Humanists Association, All Bengal Teachers' Association (1921) and since 1924 the studio of the pioneer photographer Charu Guha, recently turned into an exhibition gallery called Boi-chitra.

Many of the bookshops in the neighbourhood had their own *adda*.[13] College Street was already a very busy area when the Coffee House began its operations there with the schools, colleges, university, book trade and supporting cottage industries. But within a short span ICH became the hub of many of these *adda*s. Conversations revolved around books of different genres among students, aspiring scholars and littérateurs. Amartya Sen, who was taken to the ICH on the first day of his college by the fellow economist Sukhamoy Chakravarty, discovered, among other books the works of the American economist Kenneth Arrow and the British Marxist historian Eric Hobsbawm there.[14] There was an unofficial, yet healthy competition with regard to what had been read, and what was worth reading. Although the enthusiasm regarding reading and discussing occasionally bordered on exhibitionism—like in the case of the *Rajasaheb* who used to carry a copy of *The Idiot* to the Coffee House in Allahabad, in general, it encouraged reading. Those taking part in these discussions, were usually abreast of the latest arrivals on the shelves of the bookshops, had read latest works of colleagues and friends, and this added to the quality of the practice of *adda*. The Bengali weekly *Desh* was a major literary magazine that came out on Saturdays. Coffee House aficionado or not, voracious readers looked forward to each new issue of *Desh*. Contributors, critics and readers alike would discuss its content the very same evening it came out.[15] In those days, editors of such magazines used to go to the Coffee House to meet budding

[13] Chattopadhyay, *Nana Katha*; Roy, *College Street*, provides a lucid account of the literary *addas* of the writers' duo Gajendra kumar Mitra and Sumathanath Ghose of the publishing house Mitra and Ghosh.

[14] Indrani Sen, 'The School of Small Bites', 11 August 2014, http://www.saveur.com/article/travels/indian-coffee-house?con=india#comment-form.

[15] Das, 'Coffee-houser Adda', in *Kabitar Dwimeru Viswa* (The Bi-polar World of

poets and collect their work. As many writers and poets gathered there, the Coffee House became the place where one could distribute one's new book among those concerned. On Saturdays new issues of little magazines would be distributed freely among those present. This free exchange of work at once paved the way for the combined cultivation of thought, discourse on literature and other forms of art in the Coffee House leading to the construction of new thought—a part of the creative process, the 'fundamental truth behind the whole effort'. The presence of legendary authorities of Bengali literature like Kamal Kumar Majumdar, Binoy Majumdar, Shakti Chattopadhyay and others acted as a source of inspiration to visit the space. For students this became an important space for learning about subjects outside the university syllabus.

The early twentieth century introduced the Bengali literary public to a number of little magazines—alternative and experimental literary magazines that set the trend for the rest of the century. The liberal *Sabuj Patra* (Green leaf, 1914) that revolted against the hold of market forces on literature was followed by modernist *Kallol* (Waves, 1923), traditionalist *Shanibarer Chithi* (Saturday Post, 1924) and more modernist magazines like *Pragati* (Progress, 1927), *Parichay* (Acquaintance, 1931), *Purbasha* (Hope of the East, 1932) and *Kabita* (Poetry, 1935). The modernist magazines were against the established literary traditions including prosody in poetry, voicing new perceptions, and they rebelled against the orthodox way of thinking. The nineteen forties saw *Parichay* being purchased by the Communist Party publication *International* and the publication of many leftist journals like *Arani*, *Chatushkon*, *Samasamoyik* etc.[16] Rabindranath Tagore contributed both to *Sabuj Patra* and *Parichay*, and writing in the latter, he conceptualized little magazines as periodicals operating independently of market forces and concerned

---

Poetry), Kolkata: Saptarshi Prakashan. 174–75; Debi Roy, 'Coffee kimba Sidhupaner Adda', in *Kolkatar Adda*, 2009, 192–93; Ramesh Upadhyay, interview, 8 January 2014; Vallabh Dobhal, interview, 5 October 2013.

[16] Soumitra Das, 'Little Things Mean a Lot', *The Telegraph*, 20 July 2008; the most influential poet of this generation was Jibanananda Das (1899–1954).

about culture and society, and not entertainment. This trend was the beginning of a rich heritage of parallel publication in Bengali presenting new writers and poets, a practice still celebrated with much fanfare in the ICH and other spaces including (since 1978) the Little Magazine Research and Library and the annual fair dedicated to little magazines since 2001. Magazines like *Anushtup*, *Baromas* and *Jijnasa* are known for original research-based essays by eminent exponents of different disciplines.

A considerable part of the crème of Bengali culture patronized the ICH. If the Radical Humanists did not always go to the Coffee House in person, their presence on the second floor office of the Association and the fact that they used the same stairs to go up, and consumed the same coffee as supplied to other customers was enough to cite the association. Similarly, the presence of the young couple of letters Kitty Datta teaching English at Scottish Church College and the economist Amlan Datta, teaching at Calcutta University (CU), was duly observed by many. Among littérateurs, editors like Shailendranath Basu (*Madhyahna* [*noon*]), Tapan Dhar *Abyay*, inexpendible)), Shaileshchandra Bhattacharya (*Bela Abela*) to poets like Ekram Ali, Belal Chowdhury, Nirendranath Chakrabarti, Purnendu Patrea, Alokeranjan Dasgupta, to prose writers Atin Bandyopadhyay, Shibram Chakraborti, Narayan Gangopadhyay, Shyamal Gangopadhyay, Gour Kishore Ghosh, Narendranath Mitra, Dibyendu Palit, Tarapada Roy, Pabitra Sarkar, Syed Mustafa Siraj, painters like Ganesh Pyne, Bikash Bhattacharya and folk littérateurs Dulal Chaudhuri, Mihir Bhattacharya, Jagat Chakrabarti, to jurists like Mukul Gopal Mukherjee were just a few of those who could be seen here often.[17]

An intimate account of the space in College Street Coffee House provided by Debabrata Mukhopadhyay, the artist who was associated with the ICH for more than three decades, helps to understand how the space became a meeting point for practioners of different fields. As soon as Mukhopadhyay turned the ICH into his afternoon office, those who wanted him to design the cover of a book, a placard or a poster, or simply to see him, would go to the ICH. In his own words,

[17] For these and other names see Saha, *College Street*, 2–9.

he did not have any academic education. Whatever he learned, whether in the field of art or culture, he picked up from the *adda* in the ICH, where he spent the best years of his life.[18] It was partly from the ICH that he edited *Darshak* [the viewer], a magazine on fine arts which too had an *adda* of its own, and visitors to the official address of the magazine were treated in the ICH.[19] His involvement with the War of Bangladesh was inspired by his reading of the *Citizen Tom Paine*, a copy of which he had received from the much acclaimed (screen-play) writer Nabendu Ghosh during a Coffee House *adda*.[20] In his turn, this old-fashioned communist for whom the 'only luxury was to visit the Coffee House', often used to sit with younger radical students like Sumanta Banerjee, Nirmal Brahmachari and advise them, instilling a revolutionary spirit among them.[21]

Mukhopdhayay was far from an exception when he was using the favourite social space as his workplace. Nirmalya Acharya, the co-editor of *Ekshan* (Current Times, 1961), a distinguished literary magazine too used the ICH as his office. Acharya lived in a small flat and did all the editing work of the magazine in the ICH. In the words of the poet Sankha Ghosh, "The Coffee House was in fact the office of *Ekshan*".[22] To the chagrin of the ICH workers and other visitors, Biplab Halim, a communist leader used to do the editorial work of a party magazine in the Coffee House. He would spread all his papers on two-three tables even during the peak hours, and spend there from nine to five without ordering any food. Approached by one of the workers, Pheluram Banerjee, another regular customer, requested Halim to confine his activities to one table· Similarly, Sachindra Nath

[18] Mukhopadhyay, *Cofffeer Cup*, 16.

[19] Ibid., 50–51, 80.

[20] Ibid., 57; Mukhopadhyay was not the only artist visiting the space; Ganesh Pyne, a regular at the *adda* at Basanta Cabin in College Street market could be found at the Coffee House too. After the death of Mukhopadhyay in February 1991 a meeting in his memory was organized by his friends and followers in the Coffee House; letter from Shipra Aditya to the General Secretary, ICWCS, 23 February 1991, private archives, Pheluram Banerjee.

[21] Nirmal Brahmachari ex-Naxalite writer and editor of *Purbasha Ekhon*, interview, 17 February 2011.

[22] Sunil Gangopadhyay, interview.

Bhattacharya who began visiting the place as a student of Museology in the 1970s and continued to visit it after he began teaching in the CU recalled preparing most of the drafts of his book *Shilpavastu Samrakshan* (preservation of objet d'art) in the ICH.[23]

That the *adda* at the ICH was a combination of leisure and professional practices can further be extrapolated from the fact that in the early 1950s a group of budding poets gathering there came up with the idea of a new magazine. *Krittibas*, the seminal little magazine for poetry that Sunil Gangopadhyay began together with his friends Ananda Bagchi, Shakti Chattopadhyay, Deepak Majumdar, Sarat Kumar Mukhopadhyay, Samarendra Sengupta and others in 1953, grew out of the *adda* in the Coffee House. In the words of Sarat Kumar Mukhopadhyay, a poet of the nineteen fifties, most of his poet friends were then semi-employed or unemployed. They used to go to the Coffee House in the afternoon and other friends like Mukhopadhyay who had a paid job, would join them in the evening.[24] Initially Shakti, part of a group of students from Presidency College, sat at another table occupied by prose-writers. Sunil, like others in the group was anti-establishment in this phase, and the magazine they brought out reflected this spirit. The purpose of the little magazine was to act as the mouthpiece for new, unknown poets and offer them a platform to publish their work. It is worth mentioning that the editorial of the very first issue of this magazine sought connection with Bengali poets and writers in East Pakistan [now Bangladesh], thus disproving the logic of the Partition.[25] At least twenty poets were associated with *Krittibas* including Belal Chowdhury, a poet from Bangladesh known in the literary circles of both Bengals in the 1950s and 1960s, and a regular face in the ICH, who functioned as an editor of this magazine for some time. During the first phase of *Krittibas* that lasted till 1968, the male-centred *adda* of this group was mainly in the ICH. In this initial

[23] Prabal Basak, 'Coffee and Much More', 2011, http://www.business-standard.com/article/beyond-business/coffee-and-much-more-111073100008_1.html'.

[24] Mukhopadhyay, 'Krittibaser Adda'.

[25] Introduction, *Krittibas,* 1.1, July 1953.

phase, most of the editorial work of the magazine was done by Sunil there. He recalled that there was no office space at his home and that 'one table in the Coffee House virtually served as the office of the magazine'. There were separate tables dedicated to prose (at least two tables), poetry, to writers and poets of *Parichay*, and to theatre around which groups of *adda* at the Coffee House were formed. Members of the CPI and the *Parichay* group could be found at one table. Writers calling themselves the 'Hungry Generation' and the members of *Shruti* and *Ei Dashak* (This Decade) would sit at two other tables. There was such a lively discussion at the table of the poets that it 'attracted a prose writer to our [the poets'] table'—a reference by Sunil made in connection with Shakti Chattopadhyay. Whoever among the friends arrived first, occupied a table and gradually others gathered round. At their daily *adda* in the evening, each member of Sunil's group would have something new to mention in connection with his work. While all of them would discuss their work in seriousness, talking vigorously, they would, at the same, listen to each other's comments and read newly received poems for the magazine at intervals. The selection of poems for a new issue of *Krittibas* was made there on the spot. When someone had a new work published, he gifted a copy to other members of the group and Sunil would distribute copies of new issues of the magazine to the contributors present. The only female member of the group was the late feminist poet Kabita Sinha, who was married to Bimal Roy Choudhury. Pranabendu Dasgupta, another member of this group introduced Nabanita Dev Sen to the Coffee House and the group for the first time in 1956.[26]

As it was the nerve-centre of Calcutta's intellectual world, foreigners interested in meeting the city's cultural elite would visit the Coffee House.[27] After Sunil Gangopadhyay moved to Dumdum, the *adda* would sometimes take place there but Sunil and other poets of *Krittibas* were regulars at the ICH, and even after he went on to join the International Writers' Workshop at Iowa University, much

[26] Mukhopadhyay, 'Krittibaser Adda'.

[27] See Mukhopadhyay, 'Coffee-r-cup', for foreign personalities meeting him there.

of the magazine's editorial work was conducted there. The *adda* of *Krittibas* gradually broke apart after Sunil returned to Calcutta and began working with ABP, a corporate group of publications.[28] Later Sunil began independently a private gathering at his place, which met on Wednesdays, and this *adda* was called *Budhsandhya*.[29] Like *Krittibas*, *Kallol Naba Parjay* [Kallol New Phase] and *Anushtup* (1966), named after a Sanskrit meter, were also conceived during the sessions of *adda* at the ICH.[30]

Sunil Gangopadhyay often met the renowned screen and stage personality Soumitra Chatterjee in the Coffee House. A student of literature, Soumitra was a regular at the ICH where he used to co-edit *Ekshan* together with his close friend Acharya. Even after he became a celebrity following the world-wide fame of the Apu Trilogy, Chatterjee used to visit the Coffee House and his space was respected by fellow visitors who knew he was there mainly for his magazine.[31] It was in the Coffee House that Acharya introduced Raghab Bandyopadhyay to the historian Ranajit Guha.[32] When Shakti Chattopadhyay brought out his weekly poetry magazine, *Kabita Saptahiki*, there was an enthusiasm and competition among the young poets in ICH to bring out magazines on poetry at more frequent intervals with the daily *Kabita Dainik*, and the hourly, *Kabita Ghantik*.[33] Those connected with the literary journal *Parichay* that had its office on the first floor of Basanta Cabin in the College Street market would also participate in the *addas* at the Coffee House.[34]

Not surprising therefore that the ICH provided a unique platform where the youth dared challenge the established literary practices, which saw the emergence of one such experimental group—the Hungry Generation poets.

[28] Sarat Kumar Mukhopadhyay, interview, 29 July 2011.

[29] Sunil Gangopadhyay, interview, 11 February 2011.

[30] Anil Acharya, the founder of the magazine Anushtup who runs a publishing house bearing the same name, interview, 14 March 2013.

[31] Partha Chatterjee, interview, 29 January 2014.

[32] Raghab Bandyopadhyay, interview, 10 February 2011.

[33] Mukhopadhyay, 'Krittibaser Adda', 112.

[34] Partha Chatterjee, interview, 29 January 2014.

HUNGRY GENERATION MOVEMENT

If Sunil Ganguli and *Krittibas* are said to have become part of the establishment after Ganguli returned from the US, there were other instances where there was a close connection between anti-establishment literary movements and the Coffee House *addas*. One such movement was the Hungry Generation Movement.[35] Members of this movement were inspired by the post-WWII Beat generation poets like Allen Ginsberg, Lawrence Ferlinghetti, Gregory Corso and Gary Snyder known for their position against mainstream culture and politics. Defying social conformity and established literary tradition was central to the works of these poets based in New York City, the West Coast, and San Francisco. It may be recalled that Ferlinghetti faced trial in San Francisco on charges of obscenity for publishing Ginsberg's first work *Howl and Other Poems* in 1956 from his City Lights Press. Although dismissed, the case brought Ginsberg and the Beat group immediate fame.[36] The second issue of the New York based journal *Evergreen Review* (Barney Rosset, 1957) carried a collection of works by Ginsberg, Ferlinghetti, Jack Kerouac and other Beat poets.

While on his fifteen-month long sojourn and spiritual quest in India during 1962–63 together with his partner Peter Orlovsky, Allen Ginsberg visited Calcutta and went to the Coffee House to meet among others Shakti Chattopadhyay, Sunil and their friends, including Tarapada 'torpedo' Roy, Utpal Kumar Basu, Sarat Kumar Mukhopadhyay and other poets of *Krittibas*.[37] Ginsberg introduced Sunil and his friends to drugs like marijuana and LSD, then a taboo for the middle class.[38] On Ginsberg's advice, one of Shakti's poems was sent to *Evergreen Review* for publication. Shakti Chattopadhyay was one of the initiators of the Hungry Generation Movement. Designated as a 'challenge....to the eroticism of the

[35] To name a few of the movement, Subo Acharya, Subimal Basak, Shakti Chattopadhyay, Pradip Chaudhuri, Basudeb Dasgupta, Saileshwar Ghosh, Subhas Ghosh, the Roy Choudhury brothers Malay and Samir, interview, Samir Roy Choudhury, 29 July 2011.

[36] For the recent biography of Allen Ginsberg see Baker, *A Blue Hand*.

[37] Deborah Baker, *A Blue Hand: The Beats in India*, New Delhi: Penguin, 2008.

[38] Gangopadhyay, *Ardhek Jiban*, 211–13.

culture and its repressed character',[39] the goal of this movement was to examine the extent to which it could subvert the existing literary and social norms. Rumour had it that Shakti had already been promised the scholarship that Paul Engle, the director of the Iowa Writers' Workshop was trying to arrange, that took Sunil to the US.[40] Although most of the members of the Hungry group belonged to the middle class, they were against the establishment and middle class values cherished by the *bhadralok*. Two major protagonists of this movement, the Roy Choudhury brothers, Samir and Malay, were descendants of the ancient landholders of Barisha, in Calcutta, [41] while Shaileshwar Ghosh and Phalguni Roy, two other important poets, also came from Hindu upper caste families. They identified themselves, however, as reflected in this statement made by Shaileshwar Ghosh, with the subaltern:[42]

> In fact the police knew very well that we came from low class families; and it had become clear to us that we would not be able to spare the ideology of the elite. India's freedom was conditional to the rise of the subaltern (*chhotolok*) [in opposition to *bhadralok*]. Our aim was to achieve freedom from the pressure under which we felt ourselves as useless as old prostitutes waiting in the dark veranda of old monuments of Calcutta. It was in order to reach this goal that we embraced writing.

Members of this group, like their contemporaries, had witnessed the Partition and the accompanying communal riots. But as they saw 'politicians trying to secure power for themselves, and intellectuals selling themselves to the establishment for favour', they got disillusioned with modernity. In their own words, their movement was against the 'conspiratorial existence of materialism' leading to the

[39] Rabindra Ray, *The Naxalites and Their Ideology*, New Delhi: OUP, 2011, 80; for other anti-elite aspects of the ICH see the Chapter Six.

[40] Baker, *A Blue Hand*, 194–95.

[41] Moloy Roy Choudhury, *Chhotoloker Chhotobela* (Youth of the Uncivilized), Kolkata: Charchapad, 2012.

[42] Saileswar Ghosh, *Hungry Generation Andoloan* (The Hungry Generation Movement), Kolkata: Pratibhas, 1995, 41.

birth of bourgeois consciousness.[43] They refused to come to terms with the taste and social values of the *bhadralok* that they considered to be hollow. Their aim was to reveal what 'lay hidden in the depth of modern existence, to disclose all falsehood, not to trust the rubbish called fine arts, not to become a slave of the establishment, to release suppressed sexuality and to use abusive language [slang] and the vocabulary of the subaltern' in their work.[44] The first bulletin of the Movement was published in May 1962. Conceived as a poetry movement, it soon expanded to other branches of literature. The members of the Movement quickly drew attention to their anti-establishment stand by clever moves like sending masks to different dignitaries in Calcutta with the request that they take off their invisible, symbolic masks and use the real ones, or a blank sheet of paper to the editor of the literary supplement of *Anandabazar Patrika*, with the request to publish it as a short story. Eight to ten manifestos of the Movement were published from the ICH, which was their official address.[45]

A powerful spokesperson of this group and a product of *Krittibas* who was also associated with *Kourab*,[46] another experimental magazine focusing on the life of the tribal communities published from Jamshedpur in the 1970s, was Sandipan Chattopadhyay. A strong representative of the radical post-modernist avant-garde experimental vernacular literature, his *Kritodas o kritodasi* [Slaves, m/f], a collection of short stories was a must read for the youth in the 1960s. His writings are some of the best representatives of the existentialist literature portraying the dark sides of life common in the works of Kafka, Camus and Sartre.[47] Although he published his works independent of any established publishing houses, Chattopadhyay joined the Bengali newspaper *Aajkaal* in 1981, and his works featured regularly in that daily as well as in *Pratikshan*.[48]

[43] Ibid., 42.

[44] Ibid., 47–48.

[45] Samir Roy Choudhury, interview, 29 July 2011.

[46] Arup K. Chatterjea, 'Power of Words', *The Telegraph*, 23 July 2007.

[47] See Arka Chattopadhyay, 'Patricide and Historical Neurosis' in Sandipan Chattopadhyay's novel, *Swarger Nirjan Upokule*.

[48] There were factions within the Movement. Saileswar Ghosh for example

Rejected by the Bengali establishment, the members of this group sent their writings to journals abroad and between 1963 and 1966, some of their work saw the light of day in magazines like the *Citylights Journal* published by Lawrence Ferlnighetti and *Kulchur* edited by Rita Hornik. While the 'Hungry' poets continuously attacked the establishment for the emptiness and the falsities it stood for, the press and the entire establishment in Calcutta rose up in rage against this group on the ground of morality. On 2 September 1964, a FIR was lodged against the ten contributors to the eighth issue of the mouthpiece of the Movement bearing the same name. Some of the members of the movement were questioned by the police in the Coffee House.[49] When the police arrested five of them in early September 1964 and a case was lodged against Malay Roy Choudhury for writing a poem dotted with obscenities in that issue, the incident drew worldwide attention from the national and international press reporting on the Movement and the incident. The 20 November 1964 issue of *Time* carried an article on the group and their arrest.[50] Ginsberg also contacted many influential Indian literary and political figures in support of the group.[51] In India, among others Ajneya or Agyeya as editor of *Dinmaan*, and Panishwarnath Renu wrote in support of the arrested Generation.[52]

According to Samir Roy Choudhury, the activity of the Hungry Generation writers spanning the 1950s and the 1960s led to an explosion of little magazines in Bengali. Every time the group brought out a manifesto—which was often not more than a leaflet—there

---

attacked Sandipan Chattopadhyay and others for vacillating between the establishment and anti-establishment each in order to draw attention to himself, Ghosh, *Hungry Generation.*

[49] Saileswar Ghosh stated that he was questioned by the police in ICH because of his poem '*Tin Bidhaba*' (three widows), cited in Uttam Das, *Hungry, Shruti and Shastrabirodhi Movements* (Hungry and other literary movements), Kolkata: Mahadiganta Publishers, 1986, 147.

[50] 'India: The Hungry Generation', *Time Magazine,* 20 November 1964, http://www.time.com/time/magazine/article/0,9171,830799,00.html.

[51] Ghosh, *Hungry Generation.*

[52] Phanishwarnath Renu, 'Bhukhi Pidi Paricharya', *Dhramyug,* 7 March 1965.

were other leaflets in support of or against their position. Much of this took place in the Coffee House.

What is interesting is that although members of this group claimed they were against the middle class, the bourgeois society and the intellectuals that colonial rule produced, their correspondence, statements given during the eight-month court case against them show clearly that very much like the poets of *Krittibas* and others they criticized, they too used the Coffee House, a purportedly middle class space as a point of contact.[53]

The movement touched the Hindi literary world, albeit in a limited nature. Rajkamal Chaudhary, an influential writer of this genre who possibly came in contact with the Roy Chowdhury brothers during his study at Patna and Bhagalpur, spent six years in Calcutta at the time when the Hungry Generation Movement was at its peak. In his poetry and prose he broke all established rules and was the first one to write a novel on lesbianism in Hindi.[54]

While the members of the Hungry Generation Movement called themselves subaltern, it is worth noting that Shashadhar Dutta, the author of the popular series *Dasyu Mohan* belonging to the literary genre known as Battala created by non-elite writers mainly for the underprivileged sections of the society and representing a counterculture vis-à-vis the high culture of the educated *bhadralok*, also used the Coffee House where he would be seen writing.[55]

SHRUTI AND SHASTRABIRODHI MOVEMENT

At least two other literary movements took place in this decade of disillusion that engulfed the first generation of intellectuals after

[53] Ghosh, *Hungry Generation,* 26, 28, 37, 49, 51; according to Ghosh, the revolutionary (Naxalite) leaders of Bengal considered the Hungry generation poets to be reactionary and promised to take action against the latter as soon as they came to power, 89.

[54] Rajkamal Chaudhary, *Rajkamal*; 'Lekin ye bhukhi padi hai kya?', *Dharamyug,* 17 January 1965.

[55] Raghab Bandypadhyay, interview, 10 February 2011; Anirban Mukhopadhyay, interview, 14 August 2011.

Independence. The political opportunism of the leaders coupled with the influx of refugees and the dismal economic situation induced the young generation to question the existing value system resulting in the search of self. Both *Shruti* (the name is an allusion to the Vedas, knowledge of which were transmitted orally) and *Shastrabirodhi andolon* rejected the way the Hungry Generation promoted their movement. *Shruti* believed in freeing poetry from customary rules and changing the form of poetry through the use of single words without punctuation, making poetry visually appealing through a new kind of printing arrangement. Poetry had to be inward looking, devoid of articulation of hunger, sex or other biological urges. Sajal Bandopadhyay, Mrinal Basuchoudhury, Ananta Das, Pushkar Dasgupta, and Paresh Mandal were some of the exponents of this Movement. The first issue of *Shruti* came out in April 1965. Similarly, the *Shastrabirodhi* (literally, against scriptures) movement rejected any received formula of short story writing. *Ei Dashak*, the mouthpiece of the latter movement that stated itself as the 'campus of contemporary literary movement' declared short story to be 'against all conditions' and 'whatever we write'.[56] Members of the *Shastrabirodhi* movement Balaram Basak, Nalini Bera, Jhareshwar Chattopadhyay, Atindriya Pathak, Ramanath Roy, Pushkar Das Gupta, Debarshi Sarogi were regular members of the Coffee House *adda*. Some of them continue to visit the ICH.[57]

SHOTOJOL JHORNAR DHWONI

While most of the poets and writers in the Coffee House were inspired by Leftist ideologies, with the Presidency College as a main centre of the Naxalite Movement in the late 1960s, and the Naxalite student leaders crowding the social space, the Coffee House in the early 1970s had a symbolic value in theoretical disputes on literature.[58] Many aspiring poets supported the spirit of revolution; they dreamed of the

[56] Uttam Das, *Hungry, Shruti, Shastrabirodhi Andolan*, 96–97.

[57] Ramanath Roy, one of the pioneers of the *Shastrabirodhi Andolon*, interview, 4 February 2011; also Sabyasachi Bhattacharya, interview, 20 August 2011.

[58] For the Naxalite Movement see Chapter Five.

student leader Ashim Chatterjee as their hero. Poetry could not be a vehicle of propaganda for the party as some Leftist poets believed, but the question was, how to write poetry that would not reinforce the views of the bourgeois elite. Should literature be limited to the sphere of art, for the sake of literature itself? If poet Shamser Anwar believed in art for the sake of art, Parthapratim Kanjilal, Tushar Choudhury, Ranajit Das, Samarendra Das, Arani Basu, Bhaskar Chakrabarti, Subrata Chakrabarti, Mridul Dasgupta, Kalikrishna Guha, Tushar Roy, Prasun Bandyopadhyay (editor *Punarbasu*), Gautam Chaudhury and others would engage in the ICH in a hair-split analysis of theories and their application. *Adda* was not just small talk or gossip, but creation of new ideas through debate and reflection.[59]

In the years around 1973–74 a group of students, still in their late teens, began using the Coffee House as a place for networking network at the time they began experimenting with creative writing. It was due to poets of this generation that the Bengali little magazine movement reached its height in the shape of *Shotojol Jhornar Dhwoni* (the sound of a hundred streams fountain, henceforth *Shotojol*) in the following decade. Calcutta was the nerve centre of Bengali literature at the time with the publication and distribution system under the control of the established print media based there. With an idea to bring all Bengali little magazines together on one platform, at a time when postcards used to cost 5 paise and an envelope 25 paise, members of this group began communicating with writers and editors of little magazines elsewhere in Bengal. Grammar, techniques and their application in poetry were not the content of the movement. Their goal was to expand the world of Bengali poetry that had begun decentralizing since the 1960s as a result of the youth movements elsewhere in the world, the war in Vietnam and the Bangladesh War of Independence and to bring all little magazines published in Bengali language on one platform. With poets from the suburbia like Joy Goswami from Ranaghat, Anuradha Mahapatra from Medinipur, Subodh Sarkar and Mallika Sengupta from Krishnagar, Ranajit Das

[59] Das, 'Coffee-houser Adda', 118–19. Naxalite student leader Ashim Chatterjee was arrested in Deoghar in Bihar in 1972 and spent six years in different prisons.

from Silchar in Assam and poets like Ajit Bairi, Biswanath Garai, Ratantanu Ghati from marginal groups earning fame around this time, the gap between the metropolis and the countryside was eroding fast. *Shotojol*'s goal was to further liberate Bengali poetry by taking it out of the control of the establishment through little magazines.

According to Prasun Bandyopadhyay and Gautam Chaudhury, many of the meetings of *Shotojol* naturally took place at the ICH, especially when representatives of little magazines based outside Calcutta wanted to meet the initiators of the movement.[60] But as many of their *addas* also took place at Howrah, Halishahar, Naihati, Ranaghat and other bases of little magazines outside Calcutta, the practices carried out in the ICH became connected with those outside the metropolis. The members in Calcutta would be invited to attend meetings/poetry reading sessions organized elsewhere.[61] The attempt at decentralization took the form of organizing an all-Bengali language little magazine conference outside Calcutta. After the initial idea of holding it somewhere in North Bengal did not work out, it was organized at Krishnagar. The two-day conference was attended by three hundred participants including contributors, editors and publishers of little magazines in Agartala (Tripura) and Chittagong (Bangladesh).[62]

Even as poets/writers in Purulia in southwest Bengal were encouraged not to depend on the large distributors based in Calcutta, the movement quickly drew the attention of the established print media that feared it would lose its control and be relegated to irrelevance. Shakti Chattopadhyay wrote an essay entitled '*Ato kobi keno*' (why [are

[60] They also used the staircase of Sanskrit College and the portico of Presidency College for this purpose. Prasun Bandyopadhyay and Gautam Chaudhury, interview, 18 August 2011.

[61] Prasun Bandyopadhyay received an invitation to a poetry reading event organized at Naihati through a postcard announcing the date, time and venue with the warning, 'The reward of absence will be skinning'; ibid.

[62] The conference was inaugurated by a cowherd boy found riding a buffalo near the venue. The *Kaash* (*Saccharum spontaneum*) stick they fixed in his hair looked like a crown; Prasun Bandyopadhyay and Gautam Chaudhury, interview, cited above. It is worth noting here that it was around the same time that magazines like *Kourab* and *Kalamati* published from places outside Bengal were also drawing attention from the literary world in Calcutta.

there] so many poets?). A debate organized at the behest of the weekly *Desh* between Sunil Gangopadhyay and Shakti Chattopadhyay with Shirshendu Mukhapadhyay as the anchor ridiculed the movement.[63]

As noted above, many of the meetings of *Shotojol* took place in the ICH; but paradoxically, by taking Bengali poetry outside the ICH and Calcutta and connecting with poets in distant corners of Bengal and outside it helped expand the network of the connected practices and decentering literary disputes. *Bijalpo*, the literary magazine born in 1990 was also conceived during the *addas* in the Coffee House and much of the magazine's public relations work is still done there.[64]

MOHEENER GHORAGULI

Being located at a comparatively new location of the city, the ICH at Jadavpur never attracted as large a population as its counterpart on College Street. Moreover, the facility of a relatively good and spacious canteen within the large campus of Jadavpur University kept most of its student activities inside. But indeed there were students who went to both places. At a time when the activities of *Shotojol* were linking the metropolis with its hinterland, another group of youngsters with their base at Jadavpur Coffee House was literally rocking Bengal with their popular music band. *Moheener Ghoraguli* (literally Moheen's horses)—the name inspired by a poem of the modernist Bengali poet Jibanananda Das—an experiment in syncretic music, was formed in 1975 by Gautam Chattopadhyay. He was an ex-Naxalite imprisoned during 1970–71,[65] who teamed up with his brothers Biswanath and Pradip (Bula), cousin Ranjon Ghoshal and friends Abraham Mazumdar, Tapesh Banerjee and Tapas Das to form the band.[66] Sharmistha and Sangeeta, the two women who were from

[63] Prasun Bandyopadhyay and Gautam Chaudhury thought it was an attempt to suppress the movement; on this debate see Shirshendu Mukhopadhyay, 'Chole Giyeo Sunil Roye Gelo' (Although Sunil passed away, he is with us), *Desh*, 80.1, 2 November 2012, 23–26.

[64] Bodhisattva Kar, interview, 7 November 2011; Prasun Bhaumik and Gautam Chaudhury cited above.

[65] See Chapter Five for more on Naxalite Movement.

[66] Satadru Ojha, 'Song of the Stallion', *TOI*, 21 June 2009.

the very beginning part of this team, especially in the production of the album covers, later married Gautam and Ranjon respectively. The team usually had its meetings at the residence of Gautam (Mani) in Behala, but when Pradip studying in Bengal Engineering College in Shibpur (currently BESU) joined them, they would meet at the Coffee House in Jadavpur where some of the numbers were composed. 'Our *adda*s were on diverse subjects ranging from engineering, physics to philosophy.'[67] Dwelling on politics, revolution, injustice, begging, love, loneliness and other themes of ordinary life, the songs of the experimental band were inspired by the urban folk movement led by Bob Dylan. The band broke up in 1981 when members of the group dispersed in pursuit of career, to be revived again the in late 1980s and 1990s.[68]

With the consolidation of Left rule in Bengal, writers began assuming an increasingly political colour and literature lost its autonomy and objectivity. As literature began serving particular political ideology, there was no scope of literary discussions in a public space like the Coffee House.[69]

In fact, according to the poet Anirban Mukhopadhyay, one could not talk about Bengali poetry writing without mentioning the Coffee House. An ex-student of Ballygunge Science College in South Calcutta, Anirban never went to the Coffee House when he was in college. He went there by chance when one of his poems was published and acquired fame almost overnight. 'It is a kind of insecurity, a feeling of endangered existence that takes the budding poet to the Coffee House.'[70] Almost the same voice is echoed by Dipankar Bagchi, another poet who goes to both the College Street and Jadavpur outlets of the ICH and maintains that 'the journey

[67] Private correspondence with Ranjon Ghoshal; also Abhishek Ganguly, 'Citybeats: Urban Folk Music in Late—Modern Calcutta', Sarai Reader 02, The Cities of Everyday life, http://archive.sarai.net/files/original/92896f10b6ff9d2887154484b136488c.pdf.

[68] The cover of the album 'Abaar Bochchor Kuri Pore' (Returning Twenty Years Later) brought out in 1995 and shot in situ, Sharmishtha Chakraborty, teacher Ashok Hall, Calcutta.

[69] Abhijit Mukherjee, Sarasija Basu, interview, 16 February 2011.

[70] Anirban Mukhapahyay, telephone conversation, 22 February 2011.

of an aspiring poet begins at the Coffee House'.[71] When practiced at home, writing poetry does not get, according to Bagchi, enough encouragement from the immediate surroundings where creative writing is often ridiculed as a sheer waste of time. Coffee House is the only refuge for such novices. It is here that they come across seniors who have gone through the same phase of angst and hesitation, who take interest in their writing, listen to their problems, read their work and encourage the new generation to continue, all through casual conversations. Again, like Mukhopadhyay, there are students from disciplines other than literature who have ideas but do not have enough hold on the language to articulate these ideas. Editors of little magazines used to meet such authors in the ICH and read their work and help them formulate their ideas and subsequently publish them. Elderly, established poets like Parthapratim Kanjilal welcomed the younger generation to the Coffee House.[72]

Many of the poets connected with little magazines claim that it is still possible to bring out such literary magazines *only* because of the Coffee House. The Coffee House is the place to collect submissions and contact contributors, editors and publishers of little magazines. As she lives partly abroad and partly in Pune, Shukla Ganguli prefers to come to Calcutta in order to collect contributions for her magazine. Often she gets poems which, when she shows around in Coffee House, are recognized by someone or other to be a copy of the work of an established poet.[73] Not only are new issues distributed among friends and well-wishers here, the Coffee House is also where informal get-togethers are organized to celebrate the publication of a new book or in memory of a poet or an activist.[74]

[71] Dipankar Bagchi, ICH Jadavpur, interview, 21 February 2011; Anuradha Mahapatra, interview, 4 February 2011.

[72] Prasun Bandyopdhyay and Gautam Chaudhury, cited above.

[73] Shukla Ganguly, interview, 17 February 2011. The editors of *Purvasha akhon* (Hope of the East now) like the ex-Naxalite Nirmal Brahmachari, who lives in Oslo and visits India regularly, and Biswanath Bhattacharya also use the Coffee House for this purpose.

[74] Monfakira, a group of cultural activists-cum-parallel publishing house organized a get-together in order to pay respect to the memory of the anti-nuclear activist, puppeteer and writer Shyamali Khastgir in August 2011; the same year saw a

From the 1950s to the 1970s the ICH in Calcutta was witness to the different experiments being made with the form and content of literary magazines, of poetry and prose writing outside the mainstream. The idea of such new experiemts questioning the established order was often born during *adda* in the ICH. Consequently, *adda* became the activity that combined momentary leisure with long-lasting trends in the professional and other associated practices of its participants. While most of the times the urban milieu of the ICH was the centre of such *addas*, this in its turn paved the way for discourses over decentering Bengali poetry from the metropolis and its Coffee House. In the words of Bodhisattva Kar, the idea and plan of *Bijalpo*, a literary magazine of the 1990s, was germinated in the Coffee House.

ALLAHABAD: THE PLACE OF LITERARY PILGRIMAGE

The Anand Bhavan and the headquarters of the Indian National Congress at Swaraj Bhavan made Allahabad a gravitational centre of Indian politics drawing big and small political leaders of all hues and shades to the town. Together with Benares and Lucknow, Allahabad was already a major seat of Hindi literature in the erstwhile United Provinces. While most of the Sanskrit and Hindi books came from Benares, these were by and large, in keeping with the old tradition, devotional and religious texts, lyrics and light novels.[75] Lucknow was on the other hand, with at least two major publishing houses—Naval Kishore Press and Ganga Pustak Mala—the largest producer of Indo-Persian and Urdu literary works. Although Benares took the lead in the movement for Hindi as the national language, Allahabad developed as the centre of modern Hindi literature.[76]

---

memorial meeting being organized by the friends of the late poet Bhaskar Chakrabarti. The publishers and booksellers' guild in Calcutta organized a meet in memory of the poet Sunil Gangopadhyay in October 2012 and in memory of the popular vocal artist Manna Dey in 2013. Notice of such meetings are typically circulated orally in small circles and such activities in the space take care of not disturbing the daily business of the ICH.

[75] Srivastava, *Prayag*, 156.

[76] Harish Trivedi, 'Prayagvad in Hindi Writing', in Neelum Saran Gour (ed.), *Allahabad: Where the Rivers Meet*, Marg, 138–45.

The city was also a centre for English newspapers. The *Pioneer* was published thrice a week from 1865 to 1869 when it became a daily and continued at that place till it was moved to Lucknow in 1933.[77] Madan Mohan Malaviya (1861–1946), the freedom-fighter who had been practicing law at the High Court since 1893, founded the *Leader*, the most influential English language newspaper in British India.[78] In addition, there were the *Independent* brought out by Motilal Nehru and *Hindustan Review* of Sacchidananda Sinha. The *Allahabad Law Journal* published by the Law Press, and *Allahabad Magazine* (1907) a monthly, were well known all over India. From the late nineteenth century Allahabad started to grow as a centre of Hindi and Bengali language publications among others by the Indian Press founded by Chintamani Ghosh in 1884, and Ramnarayan Lal. Till the opening of the publication department of Visva Bharati in Calcutta, the Indian Press was known for publishing most of the works of the poet Rabindranath Tagore including *Gitanjali* that brought him the Nobel Prize. The well-known periodicals *Prabasi* (Bengali) and *Modern Review* founded by Ramananda Chatterjee too were printed in the Indian Press. While the oldest vernacular magazine published there had been the weekly *Prayag Samachar*, one of the greatest achievements of the Indian Press under Ghosh was to launch, under the editorship of Mahavir Prasad Dwivedi—who ushered in the age of *khari boli* or the modern Sanskritized Hindi literature—the epoch-making Hindi magazine *Sarasvati*, the organ of the *Nagari Pracharani Sabha* in Benares. Marking a departure from the old tradition of devotional literature to a new genre influenced by English Romanticism on the one hand to Indian nationalism on the other, *Sarasvati* became the vehicle of modernity in Hindi, with Dwivedi as the pioneer of the

[77] Nevill, *Allahabad*, 101.

[78] Both newspapers *Leader* and *Bharat* were published by Bharati Bhandar, later owned by the Birla Group. Note that while the Malviya family of Gaudiya brahmins had originally migrated from Malwa, C. Yajaneswara Chintamani, the editor of the *Leader* during 1909–36, hailed from Vizianagaram in modern Andhra Pradesh. Chintamani was the chief editor of the paper between 1927 and 1936 during which period he was also the leader of the Opposition in the U.P. Legislative Council.

literary movement.[79] Additionally, there was *Bharat*, launched by the Leader group; and *Abhyuday* (1909) and *Maryada* (1910) in Hindi started by Malaviya. Alongside *Sarasvati,* there were *Deshdoot, Balsakha, Shishu* and other widely read Hindi magazines published from Allahabad.[80] At the same time, with journals like *Grihalakshmi, Stridarpan* and *Chand*, Allahabad became the pioneer in women's journalism as far as Hindi was concerned.[81] The National Press of Ramnarayan Lal and Shanti Press of Lala Ramdayal specialized in Hindi text books.[82] Added to this, the presence of Maithilisharan Gupta, Sridhar Pathak, and the legendary figures of the *Chhayavadi* Movement Sumitranandan Pant, Mahadevi Varma and and later Suryakant Tripathi 'Nirala' then dominating the scene of Hindi literature made Allahabad the cultural capital of the Hindi-speaking world. According to Harish Trivedi, it was the unique confluence of this trinity that lent much of the mystique ascribed to the literary atmosphere in Allahabad. [83]

As part of the *Ganga-Jamuni tehzeeb* mentioned above, Allahabad's Urdu literary tradition went back at least to the sixteenth century. In the nineteenth century there were seventy recorded full-time poets—Hindu and Muslim—with Akbar Ilahabadi, arguably the greatest and the first 'postcolonial' poet of Urdu occupying the centre stage.[84] For the promotion and dissemination of Urdu, there was Anjuman-a-Taraqqi-e-Urdu. Among the prominent Urdu publications of the time were the monthly *Al Islam* and the *Kayastha*

[79] This phase was known as the Dwivedi Era (1893–1920). Karine Schomer, *Mahadevi Varma and the Chhayavad Age of Modern Hindi poetry*, Berkeley: University of California Press, 1983, chapters 1–2; this reference owes to Theo Damsteegt, retired university lecturer in Hindi, Leiden University.

[80] Mehta, *Pradakshina,* 148.

[81] While the first two dealt with issues related to women, *Chand* merged those issues with the mainstream nationalist movement, Orsini, *Hindi*, 37, 267–74, and passim.

[82] Some other publishing houses were Hindi Sahitya Sammelan, Sahitya Bhavan Ltd., Hindustani Academy, Chand Press, Hindi Pustak Bhandar; Srivastava, *Prayag Pradeep,* 156.

[83] Trivedi, 'Prayagvad'.

[84] Faruqi, 'Urdu and Persian literature', 147–55.

Samachar (Kayastha News, 1866–1900).[85] Urdu literary production in Allahabad continued to flourish in the twentieth century with Premchand, the great fiction writer in Hindi and Urdu, the noted scholar and critic Sayyid Vaqar Azim, the critic Mujtaba Husain, professor Sayyid Aijaz Husain, writer Sayyid Ehtesham Hussain, and the scholar, critic, and linguist Gyan Chand Jain, to name a few living and working there. The establishment of the *Hindustani Academy* (1927), with its Urdu magazine *Hindustani* edited in its initial years by the poet Asghar Gondvi, and other magazines like *Adeeb* [courteous], *Karavan* and *Fasana* [fiction] further ensured the cause of Urdu literature.[86] Before 1947, this writers' fraternity included those in western Punjab and beyond. Lahore, a city with a mall, hotels and restaurants, had an outlet of India Coffee House that performed the same role of a space for sociability like its sister concerns elsewhere in British India. K.K. Aziz's memoir of that Coffee House is indeed an intellectual biography of the institution. In the post-colonial period it continued as before, as Pak Tea House, frequented among others by Ustad Amanat Ali, Intizar Hussain, Faiz Ahmad Faiz, Saadat Hasan Manto, Kamal Rizvi and others.

From the 1920s through to the early 1970s, Allahabad became a place of literary pilgrimage attracting many authors, a few of whom

[85] H.R. Nevill, *Allahabad: A Gazetteer*, District Gazetteers of the United Provinces of Agra and Oudh, Allahabad: Government Press, 1908, 101, and Srivastava, *Prayag Pradeep*, 162. Beginning as an Urdu language monthly in 1873, the *Kayastha Samachar* was converted to into an English monthly in 1899 to be styled as *Hindustan Review and Kayastha Samachar* in 1905, William L. Rowe, 'Mobility in the Nineteenth Century Caste System', in Milton B. Singer and Bernard S. Cohn (eds.), *Structure and Change in Indian Society*, Chicago: Aldine, 204.

[86] Faruqi, 'Urdu and Persian'; Singh, *Allahabad*, 142–43; Shobna Nijhawan, *Women and Girls in the Hindi Public Sphere: Periodical Literature in Colonial India*, New Delhi: OUP, 2012, xv. The focus of the current work is restricted to Allahabad, but the annual poets' conferences and those of the Sammelan, often organized at a university, offered a common platform to aspiring and established Hindi and Urdu littérateurs spanning entire north India. See for example the exposure and acclaim Bachchan recollected of having received at such meetings, *Afternoon*, Benares (1933) 176; Delhi (1934), 177, Muzaffarpur 196; Bareilly and Fatehpur 214; Amritsar 214; Lahore 258; Jabalpur 349.

not only settled there, but also opened their own publishing houses.[87] For rising poets and writers in Hindi it was considered essential to have the blessings of the pioneers in Allahabad and taking its cue from the existing teashops, the Coffee House became the place where lively *adda*, literary consultations, debates and discussions took place. Krishna Sobti, who would visit Allahabad from time to time, recalled that a glance at the face of the author sitting in the Coffee House was enough to predict what the literary world had made of his latest writing.[88] Allahabad University, known in those days as the Oxford of the East, was a hub of scholars, giants in their field. With writers like Harivansh Rai Bachchan and Raghupati Sahay who were university teachers at the same time, the atmosphere also nourished the literary talent latent in others like Vipin Agarwal, a professor of Physics. Till the 1970s printing flourished like cottage industry in Allahabad and made it the largest centre for printing in northern India bringing publishers from afar to have their books printed.[89]

In this context, Allahabad seems to have been a natural choice for housing the Progressive Writers' Movement in India. After the launch of the mass movements under Gandhi in the 1920s bringing Hindus and Muslims on a common platform, the 1930s saw the demand for Independence becoming a common goal. The success of the socialist revolution in Russia, the rise of nationalism in Turkey, Iran and Afghanistan inspired the intellectuals many of whom had become acquainted with the ideologies of nationalism and socialism during their study abroad. At home, there was a clandestine circulation of socialist literature, and although the two communities began drifting apart, moderates and radicals in the Congress Party joined hands in demand for Independence. By the 1930s there were Leftist thinkers

[87] The Hindi and Urdu writer Upendranath Ashk began his publishing house in 1949.

[88] Krishna Sobti, interview, 28 January 2012; also Ramesh Grover, Rajkamal Prakashan, Allahabad, interview, 23 January 2012.

[89] There were printing presses or composing units in each lane and the cost of printing here was the lowest in the country. Publishers from as far as Bombay, Jabalpur, Bhopal and Delhi visited Allahabad for having their publications printed, Kalia, *Ghalib*, 214–15.

among Indian literary circles inspired by Marxist, Radical Humanist and other ideologies.

The Progressive Writers' Group of young Indian writers was originally formed in London in 1935 with Mulk Raj Anand, Promode Sen Gupta, Dr M.D. Tasir of Lahore, Sajjad Zaheer and a few others.[90] Soon the waves of this movement reached India when Zaheer put forward the idea of starting a progressive writers' movement in India. The discussions he had with Firaq, Ahmed Ali, Ehtesham Hussain, Amarnatha Jha and others led to the formation of the Progressive Writers' Association (PWA). At the first All India Progressive Writers' Conference held in Lucknow in 1936, the decision was taken to have the central office of the Movement in Allahabad.[91] The second such conference when Hindi and Urdu Progressive writers joined the meet was held in Allahabad in 1938 with active support from among others Shyamkumari Nehru and Bishamvarnath Pandey. Maithilisharan Gupt, Josh Malihabadi and Sumitranandan Pant participated in this conference.[92] Jawaharlal Nehru attended this meeting and spoke in Urdu; the movement was blessed by Rabindranath Tagore.[93] Influenced by Marxism, the idea of socialist realism, anti-colonial, anti-imperial and anti-feudalism ideology, the Progressive Writers believed in the purpose of writing to influence social change by inducing reform. The Association deeply impacted the development of modern Urdu literature, Leftist movements and the activities of the Indian Peoples' Theatre

[90] A collection of short stories called *Angare* (1932) set the way for the Progressive Movement as it marked a departure by posing a challenge to accepted literary values and introducing modern themes, Ralph Russell, *The Pursuit of Urdu Literature: A Select History*, London: Zed Books, 1992, 205–8.

[91] Sajjad Zaheer, *The Light: A History of the Movement for Progressive Literature in the Indo-Pakistan Subcontinent*, a translation of *Roshnai* in Urdu by Amina Azfar, Karachi: OUP, 2006; A.G. Noorani, 'Socialists and Writers', *Frontline*, vol. 29.16, August 2012, 11–24.

[92] Zaheer, *The Light*, 118; this was also the time when sectarian politicians were trying to pull the world of the two languages apart by spreading hatred, ibid., 121–22.

[93] Ralph Russell, *The Pursuit of Urdu Literature: A Select History*, London: Zed Books, 210.

Association (IPTA).[94] Most Urdu writers were either members of, or closely affiliated to the PWA. The Movement was an all-India organization, and in the 1930s and 1940s Allahabad became a base for Progressive writers and critics.[95] Amarkant, Upendranath Ashk, Bhairav Prasad Gupta, the critic Prakashchandra Gupta, Sayyid Ehtesham Hussain, Sayyid Aijaz Husain, Sekhar Joshi, Markandeya, Amrit Rai, Ramvilas Sharma, Samsher Bahadur Singh, Lakshmikant Varma and Vijaydev Narayan Sahi, Sailesh Matiani were among the prominent members of the PWA. Writers like Sachchidanand Hiranand Vatsyayan (Agyeya)[96] and Amritlal Nagar who did not live there permanently visited the Coffee House as part of this group whenever they went to Allahabad.[97]

Many writers however felt restricted in their freedom and the strong leaning of the PWA towards political propaganda such that writers like Harivansh Rai Bachchan and Dinkar gave up their membership of the group. The beginnings of *Parimal* (named after a collection of poems of Nirala) went back to the earlier gatherings of a few university students reading out and discussing their own work over tea and snacks, formally organized into the forum on 10 December 1944.[98] *Parimal* consisted of among others, Dharamvir Bharati, Ramswaroop Chaturvedi, Jagdish Gupt (1924–2001), Pravakar Machwe, Raghuvansh, Vijaydev Narayan Sahi, Lakshmikant Varma, and Keshav Chandra Varma. Composed predominantly of local literati, *Parimal* was a literary organization

[94] Rakhshanda Jalil, *Liking Progress, Loving Change: A Literary History of the Progressive Writers Movement in Urdu*, Delhi: OUP, 2014.

[95] Mehta, *Pradakshina*, 158–59; Orsini, *The Hindi*, 36.

[96] Vatsayan (1911–87) was a foremost novelist, short story writer and poet in the twentieth century. He was also the editor of *Dinmaan*, the newsweekly of *TOI* during 1964–71.

[97] Mehta, *Pradakshina,* 159. The writers and poets in the Lahore Coffee House too were deeply influenced by the PWA, Aziz, *Indian Coffee House*.

[98] Before the forum took its formal shape, initial members of the group were the Tandon Brothers Bishan Narayan and Inder Narayan, Mahesh Chaturvedi, Giridhar Gopal, Keshav Chandra Varma, and a couple of other students. Beginning with 10–12 members in December 1944 when it was formalized, the membership of *Parimal* was limited to twenty-one; Varma, *Parimal*, 6, 7–9, 15.

whose members were like an extended family of friends.[99] While Bharati, Sahi and Keshavchandra had been connected with the PWA at some point of time, members of *Parimal*, usually teaching in the University, were considered to be inspired by the socialist ideology of Ram Manohar Lohia.[100] Although the criticism of the writers of *Parimal* group was that they believed in art for the sake of art, it has been pointed out they too were conscious about the purposefulness of literature the Progressives stood for. Moreover, they were open to Western thoughts and experimentation with new techniques. During the twenty-five years of their existence they held about four hundred literary seminars. These seminars were held in other public spaces but much of the literary discussions with writers at large, especially the ideological disputes with the PWA took place during the *addas* at the ICH.[101] 'Roped into' joining the *Parimal* group, Hemendra Shankar Saxena, used to visit the ICH daily along with other members of the group.

The combination of a highly charged political environment, the thriving publishing industry, the University and the High Court, the Prayag Sangeet Samiti (1925), Hindi and Urdu writers ensured constant arrivals and departures of politicians, littérateurs, cultural artists and other dignitaries making Allahabad a place of political, literary and cultural pilgrimage.[102] If the Coffee House in Allahabad was the place where vernacular writers and poets socialized, Lokbharti is said to have been the information centre keeping and providing details regarding the whereabouts of the littérateurs.[103] Located in

[99] Mehta, *Pradakshina*, 158–59.

[100] Ram Manohar Lohia (1910–67) was a member of the Indian National Congress Party, who together with Jay Prakash Narayan, Acharya Narendra Deva and others inspired by Socialism, founded the Congress Socialist Party (CSP) in 1934. He was arrested several times during Freedom Movement. The Socialists left Congress Party in 1947 when the Socialist Party (SP) was founded. In 1952 the SP merged with Kishan Majdoor Sabha to form the Praja Socialist Party (PSP). Much of Allahabad's anti-Congress and anti-Gandhi-Nehru politics was and is still inspired by Lohia's ideology.

[101] Schomer, *Mahadevi Varma*, 146–49.

[102] Varma, *Parimal*, 106–9.

[103] Kalia, *Ghalib*; Krishna Sobti, interview, 28 January 2012.

the same building as the ICH, Lokbharti and Neelabh Prakashan—especially the former as the organizer of literary congregations—seem to have functioned as parallel places of (extended) *adda*. Throughout the 1950s Rajkamal Prakashan, with the help of Dinesh Chandra Grover of Lokbharti organized large literary conferences usually held in public buildings elsewhere in the town.[104] Dinesh Grover recalled the enthusiasm among the participants of the talks and smaller meets organized on the office-floor. The shop did not have many chairs those days; the few chairs that it had would be removed to create space, and writers would sit on cloth rugs spread on the floor. Harivansh Rai Bachchan, Ilachandra Joshi, Pant, Mahadevi Varma, Jaspal, Ramkumar Varma were regular visitors at the gatherings at that place.

Although the literary gatherings organized by Rajkamal-Lokbharti are a thing of the past, a couple of visits to Lokbharati was enough to suggest that it still retains the attraction of what I have discussed in this book as *adda* with gossip as a main ingredient. As I was trying to make appointments with Lalit Joshi and the Urdu writer Asrar Gandhi, Dinesh Grover suggested that I ask them to come over to his office [instead of the Coffee House]. Once these persons came over on the appointed day, Grover ordered coffee from the ICH. While we were talking, Dineshji, a beehive of gossip, took out old photographs of poets and writers gathering in his shop on different occasions; and in no time a pure *adda* ensued with Gandhi, Grover and Joshi conversing about the old days, joined from time to time by Jaiprakash, the son of the late Bhairav Prasad Gupta, working in Lokbharti, with myself an 'outsider' researcher receding to the background. Looking at the old photographs of the place, Joshi recalled an anecdote of his youth that made him a witness to a historic decision being weighed up. He and his younger brother, accompanying their father to the place, were playing *chor-sipahi* (police-thief) at the back of the room in the middle part of the office. Harivansh Rai Bachchan and Pant were talking in that room.

[104] A sum of Rs 20,000 or more was spent annually for entertaining the participants of such conferences with coffee and other delights from the ICH, Dinesh Grover, interview.

Senior Bachchan was discussing if the decision of Amitabh Bachchan to join the film industry was wise. This story took Grover down the memory lane. He recounted how Pant would come to Rajkamal and ask him to get his favourite chicken dishes from the local eatery of Khunnulal's with a note implying that the bill was to be footed by the publisher. Joshi recalled that Pant was so fond of meat that he would stock his fridge with enough supply on October 1 because no meat would be available on October 2, the birthday of Mahatma Gandhi. Consumption of excessive meat was, in Joshi's opinion, the cause leading to the death of Pant. Grover also recalled that Osho, Prithwiraj Kapoor, Harivansh Rai Bachchan (even after he left Allahabad), Namwar Singh and many others, while visiting Allahabad, went to Rajkamal/Lokbharti for an *adda*. Jaiprakash reminisced about the rich ambience of Civil Lines with its congregations of magazines, their editors and writers. But as Grover now kept on supplying coffee, and (by that time Gandhi and Joshi had left while my new interlocutor Doodhnath Singh joined in) got someone to get some *murhi* (puffed rice) which was divided among those present, it soon became clear that his office while supporting ICH, was its rival at the same time as it lured potential Coffee House visitors—many of them Grover's clients—away by offering coffee and a place of small *adda*s in the quiet of his office.

The discussions were stimulated by the coffee from the ICH in the other wing of the building.

THE CROWD AT THE COFFEE HOUSE

Coffee and the Coffee House as we have seen above represented modernity. And like in Calcutta the literati and the literary groups in Allahabad duly graced the ICH by making it part of their leisurely and professional practices. Whenever they had two consecutive periods free, the university teachers would go to the Coffee House.[105]

105 H.S. Saxena, interview, 22 January 2012; later he used to take his student M.M. Das and others to the ICH.

Poets and writers assembling in the Coffee House could roughly be divided into five groups, and although between five and seven in the evening was the usual time when the inter-group engagements would be at their climax, there were many who went there several times a day. Of these groups, the two most prominent were the *Parimal* and the PWA discussed above.

There was a third group led by Firaq that began visiting the Coffee House especially after his retirement, usually accompanied by Ramesh Trivedi, Akbar Illahabadi and other rising poets interested in learning the art of writing from him. Firaq was a regular at the *addas* both in the ICH and Lokbharti. He used to spend considerable time at the ICH, often more than once including at lunch time.[106] According to Dinesh Grover, when Sahay would be seen walking to and fro in the lawn in front humming unmindfully, out of tune, '*kahin aaj kisi se mohabbat na ho jaaye*'[107] or some other popular film song, those present knew that he was deeply immersed in some composition. The importance attached by littérateurs to the gatherings in the ICH can be attested by a sarcastic comment made by Firaq. He was among those who would linger even after the ICH had closed its doors in the late evening. And as he would reluctantly mount the rickshaw, once he was heard lamenting: 'there was someone who deserted his wife and child for the sake of knowledge; and here I am leaving [the source of] knowledge behind in order to go back to my family'—a reference to Gautama Buddha who renounced his family and took to ascetic life in order to acquire wisdom. The Coffee House conversations were in his view a repository of knowledge enriching the experience of the participants.

The major figure in the fourth group was the critic Bishwambhar Manab, whose relationship with the Coffee House was like that between 'wealth and Kuber, the god of riches'. As many contemporaries recall, it was a part of his daily ritual to reach the

[106] K.N. Rao, 'Harivanshrai Bachchan, 27 November 1907–19 January 2003, part 1', 14 January 2008, http://www.journalofastrology.com/article.php?category_id=22&article_id=137&language_code=pt.

[107] 'E Goolbadan, Phoolon ke Mahak', a hit from the Bollywood film *Professor* (1962).

place at 6.00 pm and sit at a table towards the back of the hall below the notice 'spitting is prohibited here' hanging on the wall.[108] The popular memory about him is that whenever he was there, he used to drink one coffee and eat one plain *dosa* but never asked others if they wanted anything, never allowed anyone to foot his bill, and would not even look at others till he was finished with his food and beverage.[109] Vachaspati Pathak would share this table with Manab. When Dinesh Grover would join the group, he would pay for everyone else but Manab. If due to some reason Bishwambhar Manab did not show up at the Coffee House, the table where he sat, would be left unoccupied out of reverence for him.[110]

Finally there was a group of university teachers who usually wrote in Hindi, especially Ramswaroop Chaturvedi, Raghuvansh, Vipin Kumar Agarwal and others. Agarwal was a professor of Physics and a writer.[111] One memorable figure among the scholars was Tribikram Pati (1929–2008), later the vice chancellor of the university who was seen at the Coffee House every day. A Bachelor of Arts in Sanskrit, Pati was a mathematician, and a philosopher known at the same time for his deep passion for paintings and philately. He, like many other Coffee House goers of the time, was famous, down-to-earth, and did not hanker after publicity. He often went to the Wheelers, followed by a visit to the Coffee House where he sat for three to four hours. If he lacked company in the Coffee House, he would drag students to his table and talk about a new book that had just come out.[112]

Reminiscing about Pati, M.M. Das and H.S. Saxena recounted an anecdote. Following Nehru's wishes, a plan was devised in the 1950s to extend the Allahabad station by adding a new line which required

[108] Mehta, *Pradakshina*, 202–3; Dinesh Grover, interview, 23 October 2012.

[109] Ibid., also H.S. Saxena, interview, 22 January 2012.

[110] As a publisher, wherever he sat, Dinesh Grover usually paid the bill. Manab sitting alone must have been odd enough to draw the attention of Anita Gopesh who, as a child of eight, accompanied her father to the Coffee House. She used to think that the others present there boycotted him for some reason; Anita Gopesh, interview, 25 October 2012.

[111] Among other books he authored was *Adhunikta ke Pahlu* (Aspects of Modernity), Allahabad: Lokbharti, 1972.

[112] Lalit Joshi, interview, 23 October 2012.

the construction of a new overhead bridge. The arch-shaped plan of the bridge without a pillar caused during its construction a problem that none of the engineers involved could solve. The engineers were advised to seek the advice of Pati, then on a special UGC fellowship. They found Pati in the ICH, and he found the solution after about an hour of discussion. When asked about his fees, Pati replied 'another coffee please'.

There was, however, no hard line among these groups, and the *adda* overlapping ideological and professional differences kept the gatherings in Allahabad lively. At the same time, as the following paragraph notes, writers could be further categorized on the basis of the pattern of their visit:

> There are some who come every day, while there are others who come at times. The Saturday-ers belong to the latter group. As evident from the label, they come every Saturday, and feel happy by seeking the meaninglessness of money (*arth ka anarth*). This group is led by Bhairav Prasad Gupta. Even the way Congress was defeated in Kerala is nothing compared to the way he was ousted from the field of *Kahani*.[113] Another glittering star of this group is Sri Markandeya. Dushyant, Kamleswar, Markendeya represent a strong combination [within this group]. Wherever they go, they leave an imprint. Yet another member of this Saturday group is Amarkant. [....] Sekhar Joshi, who works in a workshop during the weekdays, joins them on Saturday, when Doodhnath Singh, and Gyanranjan who, because of his beard and his *kameez patloon* could be confused with Sohrab Modi enacting Porus, and Gyanprakash Shukla, will be part of this group. The presence of Vijaydev Narayan Sahi, a daily visitor to the Coffee House among

[113] The reference here is to the elections of 1956 when for the first time a communist government came to power in Kerala. Similarly, the word *kahani*, story, is a pun on *Kahani*, the magazine of the *Nayi Kahani* movement. This is an allusion to the replacement of Bhairav Prasad Gupta by Kamleshwar as the editor of this magazine. Gupta was known for his love of gold and from the office of *Maya* in Muttiganj he would often go to Ranimandi to buy at least one gram of gold. The rumour was that during the India-China War, he deposited all that gold with his publisher who lost no time to gossip about it. This soon became a topic of conversation in the ICH encouraging the peer group pulling Gupta's leg, Kalia, *Ghalib*, 223.

them is a paradox, but due to his effortless behaviour he easily fits in with this group too.[114]

In the words of Dinesh Chandra Grover, *bahas* (debate) was very important to Upendranath Ashk who used to sit at all the tables. Ashk's attempts at 'self-promotion' often made him a subject of ridicule. Once Pant was said to have told a visitor, 'Ashk is a writer of great calibre'. When that person requested him to explain, Pant replied, 'Why, he says it himself!'[115] Some of the weekday visitors who went there again on Sunday mornings formed another group: G.K. Gopesh, Markandeya, Kamleshwar, Naresh Mehta, Dushyant Kumar (1931–75; left for Bhopal in 1954), Doodhnath Singh, Amarkant, and their mentor Bhairav Prasad Gupta who used to instruct others about literary techniques and styles. Giriraj Kishor who lived in proximity to the ICH was also a regular visitor there.[116]

The Coffee House was the place where all the groups got together and where ideologies clashed, discussions took place over casual conversations. The overlapping of the groups is acknowledged by Doodhnath Singh as well. When they began visiting the place, he and his friends were interested in reading and writing, but were beginners, and thus hesitant to sit with the stalwarts. Initially they formed a group of their own. Gradually they started sitting together with members of both *Parimal* and PWA resulting in an overlap. *Parimal*'s Jagdish Gupt and Dharamvir Bharati were his *gurus*; they

[114] Varma, *Aflatoonon*, 3, 10–17; Sanjay Joshi fondly recalled that come Saturday, his father, who would be back from the workshop early, would take a shower and rest a little after he had his lunch, before he left for the Coffee House. This was part of his routine, interview, 14 February 2013.

[115] Ashk's multi-volume memoir details many such encounters. Once, after Ashk expressed surprise at the fact that he received an award for writing play while he hadn't written any play during the previous decade, Ramswaroop Chaturvedi responded, 'it is for this consideration of yours that you are rewarded'. On another occasion at a party hosted by Mrs Sandhu, the M.D. of Rajkamal, when he expressed happiness over the fact that one of his plays had been translated into Gujarati, Nemichand Jain said, 'that explains why the quality of Gujarati plays is deteriorating', Upendranath Ashk, *Chehre: Anek* (Many Faces), 8 vols, Allahabad. Neelabh Prakashan, vol. 1, 69 and 70 respectively.

[116] Gyanranjan, 'Taramandal'.

initiated him into the Coffee House and he often sat with them. At the same time, Prakash Chandra Gupta, a professor of English and member of the PWA was very fond of Doodhnath and through him Singh got acquainted with other writers of the group like Markandeya and Bhairav Prasad Gupta. Encouraged by Dharamvir Bharati and Lakshmikant Varma, he joined *Parimal* but on the very first day had difference of opinion with Lakshmikant Varma. Till Bharati was in Allahabad, Doodhnath remained with *Parimal*. After the former left for Bombay in 1970, he left *Parimal* but did not join the PWA. Later in 1982, together with others he founded Janavadi Lekhak Sangh (JLS, CPI (M)).[117]

While pointing out that there was a good market for the guavas and literature from Allahabad, Keshav Chandra Varma, an active participant of many of the Coffee House *addas*, left a satirical account of the atmosphere there:

> As soon as the evening sets in, writers begin appearing in the Civil Lines. Some go out only on special occasions, i.e. when the birth of some movement has been announced. Gradually they occupy their own tables in the Coffee House. The guffaws let out, and the figures cited by writers sitting around different tables at the top of their voice tell you which movement is currently more forceful and which one has been beaten. Some writers are seen changing their table and joining hands with others at a different table....the number of such writers gives an idea of the increasing and decreasing strength of the movement concerned. Some very young leaders of movements keep on standing outside the Coffee House....while discussing, they begin walking towards [Lucky] Sweet Mart and then go back to the university hostel. Critics mostly sit together with publishers at the last table against the wall of the Coffee House. After having debated the whole evening, when the writers get up, their faces radiate in their own halo.[118]

The reference to the 'young leaders' in the text is possibly an allusion to students who, unlike in Calcutta, were overawed by the

[117] Doodhnath Singh, interview, 23 October 2012.

[118] Varma, *Aflatoonon*, 4.

presence of the relatively older generations comprising university teachers and writers, often their guardian or family friends.

Hindus and Muslim writers writing in Urdu as seen above, facilitated Hindu-Muslim interaction, a continuation of the Mughal ideology of a secular national culture.[119] Urdu had been the language of literature for Hindus, Muslims and Sikhs in undivided Punjab.[120] One characteristic of the Coffee House in Allahabad and Coffee- and Tea House in Delhi was that Hindi and Urdu language writers always shared this platform commonly, a tradition that still continues.[121] There were writers like Ashk who began writing in Punjabi and Urdu before switching to Hindi. Krishna Sobti wrote in a very colloiquial language that was far from the standardized (Sanskritized) version of Hindi. The cross current resulting from the encounter of different ideologies, languages and opinions led to the ushering of a very productive period for both Hindi and Urdu literature. The movement for Hindi as the national language must have ensured, however, that the gatherings were not as smooth as one would have hoped, because it led to agitated arguments among practitioners in the two languages.[122] While persons like Lohia strongly supported the cause of the movement for Hindi, Firaq was known for his anti-Hindi sentiment. ICH Allahabad saw the latter often engaging into heated arguments with Vachaspati Pathak and Ram Vilas Sharma on this issue.[123] Noted

[119] Kavita Saraswathi Datla, *The Language of Secular Islam: Urdu Nationalism and Colonial India*, New Delhi: Orient BlackSwan, 2013.

[120] Russell, *The Pursuit*, 211.

[121] Ashrar Gandhi (writer) and Ashfaq Hussain (critic), interview, 24 October 2012; for Delhi see the contributions to *DTH*.

[122] It has been suggested that Upendranath Ashk's hostility towards his contemporaries was caused by his feeling that as a newcomer to Allahabad and to the world of Hindi literature he was considered to be an outsider and was not taken seriously, Daisy Rockwell, *Upendranath Ashk: A Critical Biography*, New Delhi: Katha, 2004.

[123] Pathak was a veteran publisher and manager of Bharti Bhandar, a concern of the Birlas bringing out *Leader* and *Bharat,* two leading newspapers. Firaq Gorakhpuri's anti-Hindi attitude is noted by Varma in *Parimal*, 61–62; these feelings are captured in his interview too, Anita Gopesh, 'Firaq Gorokhpuri in his moods', *Hindi*, April-June, 87–92, http://www.hindivishwa.org/pdf/publication/hindi_varta_april_june.pdf, 87-92.

Urdu writers and critics like Ehtesham Hussain, Ejaz Hussian, Aqeel Rizvi and Ashfaq Hussain, all belonging to the department of Urdu in the University at different points of time, shared the space of the ICH in Allahabad and took part in those literary and political discourses.[124]

WHAT WAS ALL THAT ADO ABOUT?

Parimal had the tradition of a hair-splitting analysis of a new work presented by its members, to an extent that to outsiders it might appear as a verbal altercation. Yet, when such gatherings ended with tea and snacks, the members of the group interacted as friends and as members of an extended family.[125] This tradition flourished further in the literary discourses in the Coffee House where practitioners of different streams of writing gathered. Sahi and Lakshmikant Varma first talked between themselves in the lawn in front before they went in. This was their normal routine, and it was common knowledge that this was when they planned their strategy to criticize the latest work of a writer.[126] To quote Lalit Joshi, 'The discussions in the Coffee House were so rich that you could learn even from eavesdropping'.

An analysis of some of these conversations shows that, like in Calcutta, the literary arguments and disputes in the Coffee House gave shape to many experimental movements in Hindi as well. One such movement was the *Prayogvad* Movement, the concept of experimentation, also emerging in response to, and parting with the doctrinaire approach of the Progressives. Guided by a deep ethical concern, a 'quest for new values, and a searching analysis of the basic sanctions or sources of values' independent of Western influence, and better known as the *Nayi Kavita* [new poetry] Movement (1943–60), *Prayogvad* encouraged poets to experiment with the form, content and techniques of Hindi poetry in consonance with the changing perspectives of their times. Introducing free verse style with symbols taken from mythology, archaeology, philosophy and contemporary

[124] Asrar Gandhi and Aiyaz Husain (critic), interview, 24 October 2012.

[125] Varma, *Parimal*.

[126] Dinesh Grover, interview, 24 October 2012.

life, the movement reflected a multi-dimensional consciousness in Hindi poetry. The pioneers of this movement were Agyeya, Muktibodh, Shamsher, Raghuvir Sahay, Sarveshwar Dayal Saxena, Jagdish Gupt, Kunwar Narain and Kedarnath Singh.

Another movement connected with the *adda* in the space was the *Nayi Kahani* [new story] movement. In contrast with the social realism in the stories of Premchand, Jaisankar Prasad and others in the 1930s and 1940s, the *Nayi Kahani* movement of the late 1950s and 1960s represented by stories published in journals like *Kahani*, *Nayi Kahaniyan* [new fiction] and *Dharmyug* took its cue from Premchand, added new trajectories and claimed to usher in modernism in Hindi literature. Based on the experience of the cultural and political transition they witnessed, the works of writers like Amarkant, Dharamvir Bharati, Rajendra Yadav, Kamalakant, Markendeya, Bhisham Sahni, Nirmal Kumar Verma and others were closer to real life.[127] The philosophy of the movement was anchored to the socialist ideology while its creative force drew its inspiration from the action and reaction of the real. Together with parallel movements like *Nayi Katha*, *Nayi Alochana* (new discourse), *Nayi Kavita* there was also *Akavita* (anti-poetry) movement, (1965). Using symbols of filth, squalor and sex, poetry belonging to this genre focused on the corruption in political and social spheres. Literary disagreements and disputes between the writers of the 1950s, and those of the 1960s known as the new generation (*nayi peedhi*) also took place in the space of the Coffee House.[128] The stories submitted to *Kahani* would be the subject of indepth analysis in the discussions of the ICH led by Bhairav Prasad Gupta.[129]

[127] The elevation of the status of Hindi and increased demand for literature in Hindi induced some writers of this generation to write for commercial success, Mohan Rakesh, 'Aaj ki Kahani ka Preranasrote', *Hindi Samay*, http://www.hindisamay.com/contentDetail.aspx?id=453&pageno=3'.

[128] Hindi writers of both generations seem to have engaged more with the life of individuals in an urban middle class setting and major religious, social and political problems were not of primary concern. See Gordon C. Roadarmel tr., *A Death in Delhi: Modern Hindi Short Stories*, Oakland: University of California Press, 1972, 1–2.

[129] Dinesh Grover and Jaiprakash Gupta, interview, 12 September 2013.

Both in Calcutta and Allahabad the boundaries between leisurely conversations and literary practices were often blurred in the gatherings of the Coffee House. As most of the writers and poets in Delhi and Allahabad conversed in Hindi, and were part of the same linguistic and publishing world, naturally there was a continuity of the discussions on the literary trends between Allahabad and Delhi.

DELHI: THE CAPITAL OF HINDI LITERATURE

After Delhi became the capital of India and Hindi the national language, the government actively took part in promoting the language inside and outside the country. For the practitioners of the language the importance of the city increased considerably. Already under the British when CP was taking shape as the major commercial hub, several bookshops saw their beginnings in that area. In 1935 the late Lala Shanti Pershad Jain of Delhi opened Jain Book Agency at C-9, CP—a shop since catering to businessmen, corporate houses and lawyers. These were soon followed up by English Book Depot at L-17 in the Outer Circle, Cambridge Book Shop in the Regal Building, Bargain Book Shop and Famous Book Shop in Janpath. Housed in G-Block, People's Publishing House, or PPH, was already importing translations of Communist, children's and other literature to India. Krishna Sobti often bought her English books, gifts for anniversaries and weddings from Bhavnani & Sons in F-Block.[130]

In the evenings writers like Jainendra, Agyeya, Bhagwaticharan Verma, Balkrishna Sharma 'Naveen', Satyavati Malik, Sumitranandan Pant, Vachaspati Pathak and others could be found at the newly founded Rajkamal Prakashan (1947).[131] Prakash Krishna of Lahore opened a book shop in CP after Partition.[132] Joining the fray in the 1950s were 'Panditji's' bookshop on Irwin Road (which later on moved to Shankar Market where it still operates), B.D. Galgotia, Rama Krishna and Sons and New Book Depot in B-Block.

[130] Currently the hotel-cum-restaurant Host is located here, Sobti, 'Marfat Dilli'.

[131] Ibid.

[132] Ranjana Sengupta, 'Delhi's last conquerors', *The Penguin Book of New Writing from India*, 2 vols., Delhi: Penguin, vol. 2, 94.

The first Punjabi printing press in Delhi was begun by Pritam Singh, a migrant from the Indo-Pakistan border who started his own publishing house Navyug Publishers bringing out the literary magazine *Arsee*.[133] The office of Rajkamal at Dariyaganj functioning as the office of the *Nayi Kahani* movement also housed the Akshar Publications. Bharatiya Jnanpith, Hindi Pustak Bhandar, Radhakrishna Publications and Vani Prakashan too had their office in the same neighbourhood. The conglomeration of the publishing concerns brought literary figures like Rajendra Jadav, Jainendra, and Kamleshwar to Daryaganj, thus making it the capital of Hindi literature.[134] From their respective offices, writers would assemble at the Tea House or ICH or both. In short, when the Coffee House was set up, a visit to the place could be combined with a visit to the bookshops in the neighbourhood.

THE PERFORMERS OF THE COFFEE-TEA HOUSE ACT

As I have argued in Chapter Two, in Delhi there was a continuum between the ICH and one of its legacies, the Tea House, not only because coffee was more popular at the latter place, but also because the connoisseurs of *adda* moved between the two places.[135] Many of the discussions at the tables in the Coffee and Tea House in Delhi were enriched by artists, journalists, poets, politicians and writers in English, Hindi, Punjabi and Urdu alike. Long before he became famous, Maqbool Fida Husain was a familiar figure both at Janpath and later at the Tent Coffee House. There were days he would be seen standing on a table in the ICH Janpath and auctioning his sketches for Rs 50 a piece.[136] His Fiat painted with horses parked in the sidewalk near the Tent was a proof that he was in. Another artist regularly seen was Jagadish Swaminathan (1928–94). Theatre

[133] Khushwant Singh, 'Lovable Pritam Singh', *The Tribune,* 28 May 2005.

[134] Kalia, *Ghalib*, 104–05.

[135] Jagdish Chaturvedi, *Connaught Place*, Nayi Dilli: Radhakrishna Paperbacks, 2009; cf. Sanjay Joshi, 'From Coffee House to Kumbh', Weekend films, 2012.

[136] Inder Sharma, interview, 21 October 2012; Sharma recalled that those days fifty rupees meant a considerable sum and hardly a few could dispense with such an amount!

personalities like Habib Tanvir (1923–2009), M.K. Raina (1948–), the pantomime actor Irshad Panjatan were known faces there. According to Panjatan who later became a successful artist in Germany, his success owed a lot to his Coffee House friends who would offer a scathing analysis of his acting in the space. [137] It was in the Tent that many heard the African-American Civil Rights Movement famous 'we shall overcome' recited by Habib Tanvir for the first time.[138]

Like in the ICH in Allahabad and Calcutta, reminiscences of the socialization in ICH Delhi too reveal aspects not only of the *adda*, but of other actions of the participants, and of their character not seen elsewhere. Literary personalities like Vishnu Prabhakar and Mohan Rakesh were regulars at the ICH, first at Janpath, subsequently at the Tent ICH and later at Mohan Singh Place. The poet Ashok Bajpayee, when he was still teaching in Delhi University used to visit the place. Other Hindi writers including Mani Kaul, Kumar Sahani, Srikant Varma, Kamleshwar and many other persons of repute would be seen in the Tent ICH (and alternately in Tea House). A distinct familiar figure in khadi *kurta-pajama*, jacket and Gandhi cap, Prabhakar used to commute daily from his house at Kundewalan to CP, first visiting the Tea House, and in the evening, the Coffee House. The openness of the ICH at its current location with both the public and private sections overlooking a huge terrace, combined with the warm welcome he received from the workers and the gatherings irrespective of their age, position and status were especially appreciated by Prabhakar.[139] Like 'a judge who did not give his verdicts', Prabhakar was known for treating all writers, senior or junior with equal affection and esteem, and distancing himself from all controversies that raged in the social space. Like Firaq in Allahabad, that Prabhakar too attached a lot of importance to the Coffee-Tea House gatherings where visitors could learn from each

[137] Irshad Panjatan, Berlin, interview, 22 July 2012.

[138] Arjun Dev, interview, 6 January 2012.

[139] Tyagi, 'Dilli mein Chaupal', 261; Vikas Kumar Jha, 'Dam Tod Raha Kaffee House Culture' (Coffee House culture is breathing its last), *Rashtriya Prasang* (A monthly news bulletin), 9.2 (June), 12–17, 2008.

other, can be surmised from the fact that he coined these social spaces as 'universities'. Workers of the ICH not only served him coffee before he had even ordered it, if someone had left the space without having paid the bill, they would request him to pay and later recover the sum from the person concerned.[140] Devraj Dinesh and Radhashyam Jadav often accompanied him, joined from time to time by Manglesh Dabral, Hardayal, Trinetra Joshi, Vishnu Khare and Namvar Singh. If Prabhakar is remembered in the Coffee House for his amiability in spite of his fame, Dr Ratanlal Sharma is remembered for the epithet *alochak samrat*, emperor of critics, bestowed on him, often making him a subject of ridicule. Every one present knew who was meant by references like 'the emperor is not here yet', or 'the emperor has not come here today'.[141]

Although almost all writers sniffed around the book and magazine stall at the entrance of the Tea House selling the largest number of magazines in the capital, [142] there were a few like Bhupendrakumar Snehi, Devendra Sharma 'Indra', Hansraj Rahbar, Rajkumar Sharma and Pankaj Bisht who did not visit the Tea House but only the ICH.[143] Like in Calcutta, foreign writers visited the ICH in Delhi. Literary meets at the Coffee House drew rich gem merchants like Vijay Chand Jain whose interest in Marxism inspired him to launch a publishing house for Progressive literature.[144] For writers and poets of different generations and members of the literary movements like *Akavita, Akahani, Nayi Kavita, Nayi Kahani, Pragatishil Lekhak Sangh* (PWA), *Sachetan Kahani* visiting CP was part of their daily ritual. The *Shanivar Samaj*, the Saturday literary gatherings led by

[140] Sanjay Joshi 'Yugsrashta Vishnu Prabhakar', (documentary, 2 parts 2005). Prabhakar was equally affectionate to children accompanying their father to the ICH, Hardayal, 'Tea House', in *DTH*, 507.

[141] Many of the regulars here received such an epithet that described their activity; for example Baldev Vanshi, who took a deep interest in poetry written by himself and by others, was called 'kavi samrat'; Dharmendra Gupta was called 'patrika samrat' because of the great interest he took in publishing and editing magazines at his own cost, Hardayal, 'Tea House', 511–12.

[142] Kalia, *Ghalib*, 71.

[143] Hardayal, 'Tea House', 505.

[144] Yogesh Gupta, 'Yaadon mein Dilli Tea House', in *DTH*, 315–16.

the poet Vishnu Prabhakar had separate tables in the Tea House. Mohan Rakesh was a regular at the Coffee House in Janpath where he would meet Suresh Awasthi and Nemichandra Jain. Together with Kamleshwar and Yadav, Rakesh formed the trio leading the discourse on the *Nayi Kahani* Movement that brought story writing to the centre of Hindi literary genres.[145]

The duo of Devendra Satyarthi and the poet Sudarshan Kumar Asal was a much-discussed topic in the Coffee and Tea House. In his long coat and a long flowing beard, Satyarthi, the collector of Punjabi folk-songs resembled Tagore; eager to read out his stories, Satyarthi always carried a bag full of his unpublished work, and those with patient ears would not only listen to his readings for hours but also pay for his coffee.[146] Tea House gossips included numerous stories about Sathyarthi's search for an audience. In one that was very popular, once when he returned home at midnight, Satyarthi realized that he had forgotten his bag containing the manuscript of a novel at the Tea House. At once he left his abode in Karolbag and walked all the way to CP and began knocking hard on the door. Charanmasi, the worker who used to sleep inside opened the door, and Satyarthi's being a familiar face, asked the reason behind his nocturnal visit. After he confirmed that Satyarthi was the lawful owner of the bag in question, Charanmasi returned it to him. A grateful Satyarthi then responded: "How can I take it back just like that; now that you have done me this favour, you have to listen to the novel as I read out".[147] Asal had a unique way of smoking and shaking the ash off his cigarette. Like Satyarthi, Asal too always carried fresh work along for kind-hearted listeners like Vishnu Prabhakar, Ramkishor Dwivedi or someone else. Unpublished poems of Asal could be purchased for Rs 10 a piece in the 1970s and for Rs 50-100 in the early years of the new millennium.[148] Agyeya, Mohan Rakesh and Srikant Varma were often seen leaning against the railing in front of the Tea House.

[145] Ibid., Kamleshwar, 'Tea House', 75; Prabhakar, 'Tea House', 412.

[146] Sobti, 'Marfat Dilli', 107; Tyagi, 'Dilli', 518.

[147] Kalia, *Ghalib*, 111.

[148] Dwivedi, 'Ek Tha Tea House', 361.

AND THE ACT STIMULATED BY COFFEE

Writers working in different colleges, government offices, and the print media went to CP after office hours. The proximity of the Tea House and the Coffee House created a continuum in the arguments, discussions, and the in-groupism and the spatial practices in the Tea House in Delhi, while decentring the literary discussions from the ICH, took up the cue from it:[149]

> Imagine a very spacious restaurant where writers and visitors of different generations associated with different literary movements sharing the space and chatting over cups of coffee and tea. At one table Vishnu Prabhakar and Devendra Satyarthi of the oldest generation, at another table Mohan Rakesh and Kamleshwar of the middle generation, at a third table Ravindra Kalia and Gangaprasad Vimal, and at yet another table Ibbar Rabbi and Ramesh Upadhyay of the youngest generation. Alternately, Raghuvir Sahay and Srikant Varma of *Nayi Kavita* at one table, Bhishma Sahni and Ramesh Bakshi of *Nayi Kahani* at another table, Jagdish Chaturvedi and Mona Gulati of *Akavita* at a third table, Mahendra Bhalla and Atul Bharadwaj of *Akahani* at a fourth table, Mahip Singh and Manohar Chauhan of *Sachetan Kahani* at a fifth table, Sudarshan Chopra and Bhimsen Tyagi of *Sathottar Kahani* at a sixth table, Omprakash Deepak and Ashok Seksaria of the socialist movement at a seventh table, Ramakant and Rajeev Saksena of the Progressive Movement at an eight table, and a ninth, tenth and successive tables occupied by Mudrarakhsas [pen name of Subhas Chandra Arya], Ramkishor Dwivedi, Yogesh Gupta, Balraj Pant and other writers arguing animatedly with Hindi lyricists, and writers in Panjabi and Urdu.

Although the passage above mentions only two authors at a table, normally many writers and poets writing in English, Hindi, Panjabi and Urdu shared one table, often a political leader like Lohia joining in. Issues related to the nationalist cultural project that saw Hindi being recognized as the national language, were deliberated in the Tea House gatherings in Delhi where Lohia, a strong Hindi

[149] Upadhyay, 'Dilli ka Tea House', 319–20.

protagonist not only vis-à-vis English but the rest of the Indian languages would interact with Hindi writers.[150] While visiting the capital, publishers and writers from other places—Agyeya, Anamika, Upendranath Ashk, Rajendra Singh Bedi, Dharamvir Bharati, Rajkamal Chaudhary, Doodhnath, Sherjang Garg, Gyanranjan, Dushyant Kumar, Nemichand Jain, Rajeev Saxena, Bindaprasad Thakur, Gopal Upadhyay, Bhagawaticharan Varma and others would visit the Coffee and Tea House and form part of these groups.[151] No one was stationed at the same table throughout the evening. Entering the Tea House, one could find a big sofa on the right. This sofa and the chairs around were meant for Dr Ramkishor Dwivedi ('doctor' in the Tea and Coffee House parlance), Vishnu Prabhakar, Kamleshwar, Devraj Dinesh, Mohan Singh Sengar, Mudrarakshas, Sudarshan Chopra, Ramesh Gaur, Bhimsen Tyagi, Harisankar Dwivedi and others.[152] As the visitors critically discussed each other's new work, it was not unusual for two altercating writers to come to blows resulting in one's glasses being broken or having a bloody nose.[153] A reconciling committee would however spring up soon and the fighting writers would be taken to *Sardar ke Dhaba* at the backyard of the building where reconciliation would be sought over food and alcohol. Next day, the same writers would be seen sharing the same table at the Tea House again, because they could not stay away from the engaging *adda* of the Tea House.[154]

[150] On Lohia's language policy see Sudhanva Deshpande, 'Lohia and Language', *EPW*, 44.48, 28 November 2009, 76–78; on the question of Hindi see Alok Rai, *Hindi Nationalism*, Delhi: Orient Longman, 2002.

[151] Kalia, *Ghalib,* 71–72; Sobti, 'Marfat Dilli', 107, 119.

[152] Dwivedi, 'Ek tha Tea House'.

[153] Kohli describes such a skirmish after a contest between two writers in Hindi and Urdu respectively in which the writer in Hindi was defeated, Kohli, 'Bedil Dilli', 151.

[154] Upadhyay, 'Dilli ka Tea House', 319–20. Cf. everyone used to go there (the Tea House): Vishnu ji (Prabhakar), Devendra Satyarthi, Mohan Singh Sengar and sometimes Mahavir Adhikari... Dr Ramkishor Dwivedi, Senger's bosom friend from their days in Calcutta also was there. At one table you could see the Urdu experimentalist Balraj Menra sitting together with Surendra Prakash, Yash, Saroj, Naresh Kumar 'Shaad', Kumar Pashi; at another table there would be Sudarshan

Since the largest gatherings in the Tea House took place on Saturdays, newly published books were presented there. Any poet or writer whose work was just out would eagerly wait for the day when he would take fifteen to twenty copies of the newly published book and distribute it among friends. The distinct ritual that was part of this procedure had an engrossing aspect that deserves attention: [155]

> [On such an occasion] the lucky writer often goes to the place ahead of time and places a copy of the book upside down on each table. Gradually other writers pour in. As they approach a table, they catch sight of the book. They first adjust their glasses and then pick it up, turn over, and after seeing the title, look at the author and ask in an appreciative tone "your new work?" The latter closes his eyes in humility, and nods in a gesture of silent confirmation.
>
> This is followed by an analysis of the book. Comments on the image of the author on the back cover come first in order. Then the short biography of the author below the image is read at a glance. Afterwards, the quality of the paper is tasted by feeling the top of a right folio between the thumb and the forefinger. This is followed by an inspection of the binding....

Chopra of *Sarita* group, Pradeep Pant, Bhimsen Tyagi, Ibbar Rabbi and others. Dharmendra Gupta, Yogesh Gupta and Surendra Malhotra would occupy another table. Others like Harbans Kashyap, Mudrarakhsas, Balraj Pandit, Ramesh Upadhyay, Baldev Vanshi, members of the Akahani, Sachetan Kahani and Akavita group, Mohan Srivastav, Virendra Saksena and Sherjang Garg of Central Hindi Directorate, lyricists Devraj Dinesh, Virendra Mishra, Ramavatar Tyagi, Balswarup Rahi, the satirist and poet Omprakash Aditya, and Ram Manohar Lohia, Omprakash Deepak and Krishna Menon from the political arena were regulars there. Kamleshwar working as a script-writer for *Doordarshan* on Sansad Marg, was part of this gathering, Kamleshwar 'Tea House: Ab Na Rahe Ve Peenewale', *DTH*, 71–72; Dwivedi, 'Ek tha Tea House', 360–61; Hardayal, 'Tea House', 506–7; for the classification of writers in the Tea House see Tyagi, 'Parajit Pidi', 519–20.

[155] Kohli, 'Bedil Dilli', 154. Kohli's position in fact validates the rest of the findings and the position of the current research: difference of opinion among the literary personalities of the Coffee and Tea House was common. Tyagi's piece also illustrates how content of writings was discussed, albeit in a light mood and how Tea House and the fraternity of writers could be a refuge during temporary conjugal discords; for the politics of the space see Gupta, 'Yaadon mein', 313–18.

Following this participant, it would appear that the content of the book was not often discussed in the Coffee and Tea House. That is however contrasted by other testimonies like the following:[156]

> In keeping with the tradition of the Mahabharata or the Rajput heroes, the writers of *Akahani*, *Sachetan Kahani*, *Samantar Kahani* and *Nayi Kahani* and poets of *Nayi Kavita*, *Akavita*, *Samakalin Kavita* and others exercised, fought and came to decisions in the Tea House.

In fact Vanshi's side of the scale gains more weight if we compare other contributions to the volume:[157]

> [Informal] literary meets used to be held in the Coffee House around 1957–58. Premkumar Shastri, Ugrasen, mysef and others used to take part in it. Stories were very often read out there, heated discourses used to take place, discussions were held on different issues. No one used to mind the severe criticism his work was subjected to. Even though there were sharp differences, a sense of affection was also there.

An even more powerful account of the connection between these *addas* and literary practices is provided by another Coffee and Tea House addict:[158]

> It will not be an exaggeration if I say that *adda* (*addebaji* in the original) in the Tea House and later in the Coffee House in Mohan Singh Place contributed to a great extent to my development as a writer. There I got acquainted with old and young writers, journalists of Hindi, Urdu, Punjabi and English. Second, sitting and conversing with them provided me with the opportunity at the same time to read writings by others in their circle. Third, it helped my understanding of the failure and success of the literary movements. Fourth, while praise for my work increased my confidence, criticism made me aware of my lapses and weaknesses. Fifth, and most important, there I made friends who never gave me the occasion to feel lonely in Delhi.

[156] Vanshi, *DTH*, viii-ix.

[157] Gupta, 'Yaadon mein'; also, 'Explicit literary and political discussions take place in the Tea House, movements are born here and strategies to carry them are chalked out and dreams of the end of the opponents are dreamt here', Tyagi, 'Dilli', 263–64.

[158] Upadhayay, 'Dilli ka Tea House', 324.

Backbiting and witty jests formed an essential part of the Coffee and Tea House culture. Different kinds of conversations interspersed with often sarcastic jokes ensured an ambience of fun arousing laughter. The Tea House knew at least three distinct streams of guffaws: Mohan Rakesh's image in the Tea House was one of often bursting out into laughter baring all his teeth. The sound of his laughter could be heard from the pavement outside. The table shared by Keval Goswami, Dharmendra Gupta, Baldev Vanshi and others was noted for ascending and descending sounds of the 'vegetarian' laughter of Goswami and Vanshi. However, the table associated with the most remarkable type of laughter was shared by 'doctor' Dwivedi and others. Unlike Mohan Rakesh who needed a reason to laugh, this 'doctor of the littérateurs, and littérateur among the doctors' who began talking with the catchphrase 'I beg your pardon", could make jokes and laugh just for the sake of it, with no reason at all.[159] On occasions, when the combined sound of the laughter of the 'doctor', Ravindra Kalia and Shyammohan Srivastav seemed to crack the ceiling of the hall, the manager would send a chit through a worker requesting them to calm down.[160] Kamleshwar and Devraj Dinesh continuously shared jokes causing everyone present to laugh 'at varying gears ranging from the first to the fourth'. Each time the level reached the second gear, determined to bring the decibel level under control and improve the state of order in the Tea House, Sikka, the newly appointed young manager of the place, would rush to their table and that led to frequent altercations between Kamleshwar and Sikka. The latter also had a television and jukebox installed in order to divert the attention of the noise makers but the sound box of the former was paled by the combined sound of laughter, and the latter became the victim of an act of vandalism on behalf of an angry customer who missed the target when he aimed at an opponent with the bottle of tomato sauce on the table, but hit the jukebox. Frequent interruption on behalf of the manager was not

[159] Tyagi, 'Dilli mein Chaupal', 263–64.

[160] Sherjang Garg, 'Tea House Ki Yaad Mein' (In Memory of Tea House), in *DTH*, 445.

tolerated and he was transferred to *Kwality* after the 'doctor' sent a note to Daljit Singh, the owner of the Tea House. Notwithstanding the merry-making through jests and laughter, the openness of the Tea House gatherings also lays bare the underlying competition and tension among both established and aspiring vernacular writers and poets in Delhi. The Tea House being the centre where almost all concerned met, the anthology of memoirs on it speaks a legion about the politics of group formation in the Hindi literary world that often governed the appointment of the editor of a reputed magazine or the director of a national organization, the (non-)publication or unjustified criticism of works by authors/poets not belonging to the camp of certain important figure resulting in a continuous search for new forums, mouthpieces, and finally to a fragmentation of interest groups. Like the ICH in Calcutta, the Tea House often witnessed a lack of subtlety in varying grades in the attitude of regulars noted by its chroniclers. Thus a miser or a person exhibiting his wealth but not taking out his purse when the bill had to paid could be forced to pay for all members of the group concerned. While this sweet revenge would be relished for days or months, being asked by a fellow writer to pay for a bottle of alcohol could cause irritation, but could still be ignored. But at times when making fun at the cost of one crossed all limits of decency, or flattering some important figure amounted to insulting another person, this was bound to create a rupture often irreproachable.[161]

[161] For reasons not known, Ratanlal Sharma, 'the emperor of criticism' in the ICH stopped visiting the place. Hardayal concluded that some unpleasant experience must have induced Sharma to stop visiting the place, Hardayal, 'Tea House', 512–13. See Kamleshwar, 'Tea House', and Kohli, 'Bedil Dilli', 154–55 for the ups and downs in the mutual relationship among the patrons of the Tea House. The Patna youth poets' conference held in 1970 saw a group of aspiring writers and poets under the influence of alcohol tearing into pieces the works of Baldev Vanshi among others. According to Neelabh, one of the dramatis personae, there was no particular reason justifying this action; it was part of the total lack of discipline and organization witnessed at the event. Baldev Vanshi recalled a similar act of vandalism when another of his books shared the same fate in the hands of the members of the same group much later in the 1980s. Neelabh, *Gyanranjan*, and interview, 20 October 2012; Baldev Vanshi, interview, 1 October 2013.

The physical blow to the Tea House gatherings came from the capitalist owners of the place.[162] However, a change in the ambience of the Tea House reflected changes in the Hindi literary world since the 1970s when the Progressives, reactionaries, Marxists and radicals began forming strictly separate groups. Individually, writers followed different ideologies in earlier times too. But although there was always some bitterness due to differences of opinion and jealousy leading to the formation of cliques, like in the case of Parimalians and Progressives. Ideological and other differences did not stand in the way of literary disputes and personal relations. But now political allegiance among other things became a marker and different factions of writers began sitting separately. The 1970s saw influential writers in key positions as editors of magazines and heads of elite institutions bestowing awards, favours leading to the cultivation of a godfatherly cult, and allegiance to such figures provided an easy road to instant fame preferable to readers' accolades or critical acclaim of fellow writers.[163] This process seems to have undermined the need to disagree through discussions resulting in fewer and fewer writers visiting the Coffee House.

This account of the association of the ICH-Tea House sociability with literary production in all the cities discussed will remain incomplete if the legacy of the tradition of literary disputes practised here is left out. The conglomeration of such a multitude of intellectuals under the same roof stimulated the imagination of literary-minded persons pursuing other professional careers for whom *adda* in this social space kindled their literary aspirations. We have noted the cases of the medical practitioner Ramkishor Dwivedi, the police officer Vibhuti Narain Rai, and the government official Sriprakash Mishra, writers in their own right, above. The literary ambience of the College Street outlet in Calcutta is kept alive by a group of (retired) government officials, bank employees with a deep interest in literature. When Debatosh Mitra began going to the Coffee House in 1979, he was

[162] See Chapter Seven for more on this process.

[163] Neelabh, e-mail, 23 August 2012; also Chaurvedi, *Connnaught Place,* 30, 91–92, 120, 122.

a solitary visitor. He had heard about ICH from Debidas Basu, his school teacher in Baranagar. An old CPI who supported the workers' movement to begin the Cooperative, Basu, a bachelor, used to have his breakfast at ICH before he went to the school and dropped by again after the school hours. A commerce student who got employment in Dena Bank before he finished his studies, Mitra initially used to buy Alisdair Gray, Milan Kundera and Henry Miller from Rupa next door and Indyana on Shyamacharan De Street. From his office Mitra went to the ICH where he sought a place close to the wall on the left and sat reading. Far from feeling disturbed by the deafening hum of the continuous chatter, it worked as a wall isolating him from the rest of the crowd. He continued this habit uninterrupted till 1986 when attracted by his daily practice, the group of new prose writers like Ramanath Roy and Subimal Basak began talking to him thus drawing him into the networks of writers and editors of little magazines. Mitra began receiving requests for writing essays for little magazines. He brought out a booklet of poems.[164] But he is known in the ICH as someone who reads 'diagonally and horizontally' and who successfully predicted the possible winner of Nobel Prize for literature in the cases of J.M. Coetzee, Orhan Pamuk and Doris Lessing. Amal Bhattacharya, a retired government officer's addiction to the Coffee House goes back to 1961, when he was a student of the Scottish Church College. Later, he brought out the magazine *Pratichhabi*, (reflection) which was published for ten years. He has been commuting from Ichapore in the Suburbia lately visiting once a week on Saturdays.[165]

CONCLUSION

In the opinion of a few, the Coffee House had nothing but some functional value. As a conveniently located popular meeting place,

[164] Debalosh Mitra, interview, 29 November 2014.

[165] Amal Bhattacharya, interview, 4 February 2011. Dilip Kumar Bandyopadhyay, retired geologist, is an award winning writer, especially of science fiction has been visiting the space since 1955 when he joined the Presidency College. While in service, he was posted at different places when he always caught up with the local Coffee House. After his retirement in 1995 he has been a regular again, interview, 25 February 2012.

it only facilitated contact. Even if considered from this conservative point of view that the Coffee House was a space that only facilitated networking among its customers, the Coffee House is in place, because after all, what more can be expected from a public space? Through a closer look at the practices of sociability in this space this chapter has shown, however, that at all the places surveyed, the worlds of *adda*, Coffee House, literature, and publication inter-alia, were intimately connected. In all the cities studied in the current book, there were locations, private and public including the office of several publishing houses, frequented by creative writers, editors, publishers and others connected with the publication industry. Yet the Coffee House became an important place. In the case of Delhi it was complemented by the Tea House where the world of the university with its teachers and students, the literary world with its established, rising and aspirant writers and poets, and the world of publication with publishers, printers, designers, complemented by those with a literary bend of mind came together. While delineating *adda* in Chapter One, I pointed out that the closed intimacy of free chatter within the *adda* circle, whether we call it *adda deoa* (Bengali) or *addebaji* (Hindi), that allows the spontaneous airing of ideas, projects and questions, as if innocently, that subsequently can be taken up narrowly and professionally in other ways. The autobiographical account of Debabrata Mukhopadhyay in the Coffee House of Calcutta is rare in that it documents how the practices of the fine arts, literature, mentoring the younger generation and political action were integrated in the practice of *adda*. Irrespective of the kind of social gathering, the literary *addas* rose above their respective limited scope and became multi-dimensional, open-ended. Similarly, when a young Irshad Panjatan or Saeed Jaffrey's friends critiqued their performance on stage, the *addas* in the ICH did not remain limited to mere leisure but contributed to the perfection of the art they practised. In Calcutta in the 1950s and 1960s, many debates and discussions of the contemporary literary movements took place in the Coffee House. The Coffee House in Allahabad and the Coffee and Tea House in Delhi also witnessed many storms raised over coffee cups regarding the Progressive Movement, the New Poetry Movement, the New Prose Movement, the Anti-poetry Movement and the likes.

Hindi being the national language in independent India, the career opportunities it created in the worlds of media, publication and teaching saw the literati hailing from different states in North India travelling in connection with higher studies and career. While ideas thus travelled back and forth between Allahabad, Calcutta, Delhi, Jabalpur, and Lucknow for example, and as the Coffee House had its outlets in all these cities, it witnessed a continuum in the discourses across the centres of the Hindi literary world in North India.

This is not to claim that the Coffee—or Tea House creates a genius or a talent; but it nurtures the budding poet, the aspiring artist, and connects them with the publisher and the editor—each combining as a reader, connoisseur and a constructive critic at the same time—by bringing them together under one roof and providing the space to interact. Especially for the practitioners of literature, the exposure at gatherings at a public space like the Coffee and Tea House had the potential of widening one's mental horizon, bringing out a dormant talent, and making further cultivation of that talent possible through critical appraisal of, and recognition by others in an informal ambience. As many of those socializing here became successful in their respective field of practice, their association with the space became a benchmark for sociability in the space. Bonhomie among littérateur in the earlier decades was replaced by fragmentation into interest groups since the 1970s affecting the *adda* groups.[166] The next chapter will address the question of the potential opportunity the Coffee House offers in generating public opinion.

[166] See Chapter Seven for more on this.

CHAPTER five

Brewing Discontent Instead of Coffee? Politics and the Indian Coffee House

> And who will lead this revolution? Perhaps Mr Bronstein [Lev Trotsky] sitting over there in Café Central?[1]
>
> There is an ordinary revolutionary, who organises the masses. He starves, gets bashed up, goes to jail....Then there is the VIP revolutionary. He trims his beard, sits in the coffee house, sips the bitter coffee....He violently stubs out the cigarette as if he were battering the bourgeoisie. He crams up revolutionary quotes from Marx, Lenin and Mao. At night he boozes with his friends and mouths those revolutionary quotes. Then he attacks the chicken as if he were mauling capitalism.[2]

Both the epigraphs, one referring to a Marxist theorist in Vienna in the heart of Europe in the pre-Russian Revolution days, and the other pointing to the young leftist intellectuals frequenting the outlets of the ICH in the late twentieth century, ridicule the idea of an association between ideological communications in the coffee house and the organization of a revolution. In doing so, both the statements

[1] The famous response of Count Von Berchtold, foreign minister of Austria-Hungary to Victor Adler when the latter stated that a war against Serbia might lead to a revolution in Russia, even if not in the Habsburg monarchy. A.J.P. Taylor, *Struggle for the Mastery of Europe, 1848–1918*, Oxford: OUP, 1971, xxxiv. Opened in 1876, Café Central was one of the social spaces where intellectuals gathered in Vienna.

[2] Harishankar Parsai, 'Atikrantikari' (The Radical), in *Pratinidhi Vyangya* (Selected Satire), New Delhi: Rajkamal, 95–98.

directly address the issue of the role of integrative communication in the public sphere. Those who spent time discussing politics in the comfortable, convivial atmosphere of the coffee house would not be the same political activists who work with the masses to mobilize a revolution. The last chapter showed the connection between *adda* and literary production; this chapter will try to understand the interaction between rational discussions and the organization of everyday life in the context of the public sphere of the petit bourgeois—the Indian Coffee House. Were the storms raised over coffee cups in the ICH limited to the walls of the Coffee House? To what extent did the face-to-face interaction in the ICH result in consensual mode of action? Is there a link between the participation in the coffee house conversations and policy making at any level in the sense that citizens' right to the democratic practice of deliberations on the basis of common understandings and practical rationality counteract the combined forces of money and power represented by the market and state respectively?

Existing literature on the coffee house elsewhere in the world points out the politically significant role of the institution as a public space, even when operating in totally diverse socio-political environments. In early modern Europe for example, reading, thought and discussion, leading to an exchange of opinion among equals, were important preconditions for the literary public sphere (Literarische Öffentlichkeit) of the coffee house. This later developed into a full-blown political public sphere (Politische Öffentlichkeit) in which early capitalists played the role of catalyst.[3] In this view, prior transformation of social relations from feudal to capitalist, that gave way to the rise of capitalism, the bourgeoisie and the consumer society were necessary preconditions for the emergence of this public sphere. The potential of gossip against an oppressive authority is recognized in social science as a popular crowd-pulling space of oral communication and mobilization of protest.[4] And

[3] Habermas, *The Structural Transformation.*

[4] Ranajit Guha, *Elementary Aspects of Peasant Insurgency in Colonial India*, Delhi: OUP, 1992.

coffee houses have been considered a threat that an absolutist state cannot tolerate.[5] In the mid-nineteenth century, when there was only one newspaper in Ottoman Istanbul, translating fragmented, heterogeneous popular and political gossip-mongering into tangible evidence for examining public opinion, the state espionage system documented the power of private articulation in the public sphere of the coffee house. In post-colonial India, the name of the College Street outlet of the ICH is often taken in the same breath as that of the Naxalite Movement in Calcutta. Similarly, the Coffee House in Delhi is said to have been demolished by the absolutist state under Indira Gandhi, during the Emergency, that viewed the space as a nest of anti-government activism and propaganda.[6] The question is, if civil society institutions of modern associational life promoting autonomy, equality and freedom of entry and exit are accessible only to a small segment of the population, how does the communicative action of the consumers of the Coffee House, the erstwhile nationalist elite, connect to the population outside? Can it possibly be claimed that the ICH has been a sphere mediating between the society and the state in the sense that here 'the public organizes itself as the bearer of the public opinion?'

Although political decisions are usually taken at the higher levels of the state, parliament and political leaders, such decisions are often related to food, rationing and wages, matters concerning the humble daily level of individual, social and practical experiences. The threat of loss of work of the employees of the Coffee Board saw the mobilization of support leading to the reorganization of the social space of labour. What happens when a daily visitor to the coffee house finds out that rational or not, his *adda* over coffee is going to cost more due to a rise in the price of daily necessities like milk and sugar, indispensable for the beverage that stimulates discussions?

I shall first take a cursory look at the way anti-Congress political culture was nurtured in post-colonial Allahabad under the guidance

[5] One of the reasons for repeated closing down of coffee houses in the early Ottoman Empire was that coffee houses were seen as the central place where opposition to the centre was formed and took shape, Kırlı, 'Coffee-houses'.

[6] See Varma and Roy, 'Addebaaj'; and Guha, 'A salute'.

of socialist leaders. This culture was strongly present in the ICH there till at least 1977, and played an important role in the proclamation of the state of Emergency by Indira Gandhi. Thereafter, following the ICH at critical moments when practices in the Coffee House became entangled with larger economic and political issues vexing society, I shall focus in this chapter on the question of the relationship between Coffee House conversations and the mobilization of political opinion. In the post-colonial period, the Price Rise Resistance Movement in Delhi (PRRM, 1964) was the only occasion when a few consumers were able to mobilize a large public protest to voice their demand. This movement, begun at the coffee house on Janpath, gave birth to a new outlet of the ICH in CP. There is a strong belief that the revolutionary spirit of the students participating in the Naxalite Movement in Calcutta and elsewhere in the late 1960s and early 1970s was cultivated in the ICH. A close look at the nature of the spatial practices in the ICH during these key moments will shed light on the role of the ICH as a public space mediating between the state and society.

We have noted in Chapter One earlier that pre-colonial forms of public oration drew the common people to the public sphere. Consequently, the movement for modernity witnessed mass participation in politics at numerous societal levels and at multiple sites. Susanne and Lloyd Rudolph have argued that M.K. Gandhi persuaded intellectuals joining his movement to forsake their urban practices and adapt to the communal life of the ashram. Comprising the rural illiterate, the ashram served similar purposes like the coffee houses studied by Habermas.[7] The multiple sites of public sphere engaging different kinds of public at different levels have continued into the post-colonial period.[8] Launched at a particular historical moment when the Indian Nationalist Movement demanding decolonization was at its height, and acting as an important place for

[7] Lloyd Rudolph and Susanne Hoeber Rudolph, 'The Coffee House and the Ashram: Gandhi, Civil Society, and Public Spheres', in Carolyn M. Elliott (ed.), *Civil Society and Democracy: A Reader*, Oxford: OUP, 2003, 377–404.

[8] Chapter Two earlier and Vivek Bhandari, 'Civil Society and the Predicaments of Multiple Publics', *Contemporary Studies of South Asia, Africa and the Middle East,* 26.1, 2006, 36–50.

socialization for a section of the urban literati, the ICH was never the *only* public sphere.

While it was predominantly a space for socialization, it attracted both Leftist and secular intellectuals because the institution had a history of supporting those who criticized and questioned the establishment. Even during the pre-Partition riots on the streets of Calcutta, Hindus and Muslims shared the social space of the ICH where a neutral atmosphere prevailed.[9] In Delhi immediately after Partition, it was possible for two friends—one a Hindu editor of a newspaper and the other a Muslim journalist—who did not believe in the separatist arguments, to engage in a rational discussion on Partition in the Coffee House. Ram Prasad Chaturvedi and 'Hanif Sahib' were friends from their college days. Like many Hindus and Muslims at the time, Hanif, a Leftist alumnus of Allahabad University was inspired by the ideology shared by Maulana Abul Kalam Azad and Jawaharlal Nehru and was against the idea of the creation of a separate state for Muslims on the basis of religion. In independent India when Chaturvedi became the editor of a Right wing Hindu newspaper, Hanif, a freelance journalist without income, decided to write regular columns in that paper under the pen name 'Desh Bhagat', arguing, in the spirit of the newspaper, that there was no place for Muslims in India. The columns were so popular that the circulation of the newspaper increased, and the columns were debated at ICH gatherings. Both editor and columnist took part in those animated discussions in the ICH, during which the Muslim Hanif would vehemently denounce the 'Hindu' columnist for his fundamentalist point of view and only the Hindu editor, the Muslim columnist and the latter's Christian friend writing about it were aware of the fact. Massey, *Azaadi* before going on to focus on the crucial moments mentioned above, we shall take a brief look at the Coffee House in Allahabad.

Allahabad, and the ICH there, were strongholds of Indian politics. As the birthplace of Jawaharlal Nehru and Indira Gandhi, and the location of Swaraj Bhavan, the venue of important nationalist meetings, the city had a close association with mainstream nationalist

[9] Bandyopadhyay, 'Counter-er Opar theke'.

politics. Five of the country's prime ministers were from the Uttar Pradesh, and many politicians like Madan Mohan Malaviya, Purushottam Das Tandon, Chandra Sekhar Singh, Vishwanath Pratap Singh, Janeshwar Mishra were products of the Allahabad University where they had first lessons in politics as part of the students' movement. Consequently, Allahabad was the centre of political gravity within the state. While it had a strong Congress background, much of the socialist opposition to the single party domination of the Congress Party in the 1950s and 1960s was also generated in ICH Allahabad. And consequently, for a long time it was said that it was ICH in Allahabad that decided whatever good or bad befell the central government in Delhi.[10]

With the responsibility of nation-building on their shoulders, Indian politicians in the early decades after Independence often sought the advice of economists, political scientists and sociologists and others teaching in the universities. Political activists from Congress, Jana Sangh and Communist parties along with university teachers often met and exchanged views in the ICH. Both literary groups, PWA and *Parimal*, catered to variations of Leftist/socialist ideology. In the 1950s and 1960s ICH in Allahabad was witness to inter-party discussions among ideologues of different political parties and university teachers scrutinizing public policy. Enriched by such discussions emerging political leaders would often bring up the issues discussed in the Coffee House in the Parliament. The foundation of the Socialist Party (SP), and then the Praja Socialist Party (PSP), [11] by leaders like Acharya Narendra Deva (1889–1956), Ram Manohar Lohia, Acharya J.B. Kripalani (1888–1982), Jayaprakash Narayan (JP, 1902–79), and Basawon Singh (1909–89)—vocal in their opposition to domination of the Congress Party in Indian politics—augmented the socialist culture of Allahabad. Within the Congress Party, Feroze Gandhi, the husband of Indira and son-in-law of Nehru—who had grown up in Allahabad and was elected to the Parliament from

[10] Ramesh Chandra Grover, interview, 22 January 2012; Dinesh Chandra Grover, interview, 23 October 2012.

[11] The SP had its roots in CSP. PSP split in 1964 gave birth to Samyukta Socialist Party but both factions were reunited to form SP in 1972.

Rae Bareilly—played a dynamic role by drawing attention to the financial irregularities on behalf of business corporations close to the government. His participation in the *adda* of the ICH at Lucknow and Allahabad thoroughly invigorated the discussions at both the places. From the 1950s through to the 1970s anti-Congress dissent in Allahabad was guided by the socialist ideology of Lohia. His was a familiar face in the Civil Lines because whenever he was in Allahabad, Lohia would always pay a visit to the ICH. His attempts at organizing youth made Allahabad a stronghold of the socialist movement with the result that even after his death in 1967, students' politics in the University was closely linked to the SP. The All India Youth Conference in 1974 was held in Allahabad. That the socialist leaders at the Centre tried to feel the pulse of Allahabad is evident from the actions of Narendra, the secretary of George Fernandes, the president of All India Railwaymen's Federation. He would be regularly seen spending a considerable part of the day in the ICH exchanging notes with those present. As he moved from table to table, he took active part in the discussions. Narendra used to pick up ideas and issues and brief his superiors on the conversations in the ICH. Dinesh Chandra Grover who participated in many such conversations in ICH *addas* recalled that debates in the Parliament actually reflected discussions in the ICH. Janeshwar Mishra (1933–2010), popularly called *Chhote* Lohia (Lohia Jr)—an allusion to his long association with Ram Manohar Lohia—was another socialist leader who patronized the ICH. Other local leaders like Saligram Jaiswal, an ex-Congress MLA who joined the PSP, Kalyan Chand Mohiley alias Chhunnan Guru, who had earlier been a member of the Hindu Mahasabha but later became a member of the PSP, and student leaders like Arun Kumar Singh Munna who was elected President of the Students Union in the Allahabad University in 1970, joined the discussions.[12] The Lohiaite Samajvadi Yuvjan Sabha virtually ruled the Students' Union from 1962–70 till their hold was broken in the 1970s by the Indira Congress and by its students' wing, the National Students' Union of India (NSUI).

[12] Neelabh, e-mail, 23 August 2012. Singh became the president of the Youth Congress and then the Uttar Pradesh Congress Committee President in 2002–03.

Niranjan Lal Srivastava, who was a student in the Law Faculty of the Allahabad University during that time, recalled a strong anti-Indira and anti-Congress wave in Coffee House conversations. This happened when the Congress became more and more autocratic under Indira leading to a split in the Party in 1969. Allahabad High Court became the epicentre of Indian politics as the case against Indira Gandhi that ultimately led to Emergency Rule, was lodged and decided there. Throughout late 1974 and early 1975 when the movement led by JP was at its height, a fierce criticism of the Indira government's undemocratic measures went hand in hand with latest developments in the court case. On 12 June, Justice Jagmohan Lal Sinha's announced the verdict that Mrs Gandhi's win in the 1971 parliamentary elections when she stood from Rae Bareli was the result of a rigged ballot.[13] Subsequently, Mrs Gandhi's lawyer Justice Khare from Srinagar appealed to Justic Sinha to put the verdict in abeyance. On 25 June, Justice V.R. Krishna Iyer, vacation judge of the apex court, gave her a conditional stay. The same night the Emergency was proclaimed. During the days in between, the prevailing mood was one of anger and anxiety mixed with occasional outbursts of emotions that reached its climax with the proclamation of the Emergency.[14] This atmosphere of criticism soon changed as top Opposition leaders were put behind bars. At a time when Sanjay Gandhi influenced decisions taken in Delhi, criminalization and violence became the hallmark of local politics. The anti-Indira sentiment, however, died hard. And when Indira Gandhi visited flood-affected Allahabad in 1978, the year after her historical defeat in the national elections, the students of the AU planned a black flag demonstration against her.[15] The political vibrancy in the AU campus ended when students and goons formed

[13] These included the appointment of Yashpal Kapoor, the PM's private secretary and a government official as her election agent violating the Representation of People's Act, 1951.

[14] Interview of Niranjan Lal Srivastava by Akshat Lal Srivastava, 14 June 2014.

[15] When she disembarked her car to reach out to the flood-stricken, the flags were, however, not raised, Zafar Agha, 'Indira Gandhi might have sent gorgeous bangles to Musharraf', *Tehelka*, 2 November 2001.

a Sanjay Gandhi loyal brigade by introducing a culture of violence in student politics.[16]

With the foundation of the Bharatiya Janata Party in 1980, anti-Congress politics took a different turn. While Hindu-Muslim polarization dominated national politics in the 1980s, the beginnings of the caste-based politics were made through the foundation of the Bahujan Samaj Party (BSP) in 1984 by Kanshi Ram. The normative discussion in the Coffee House lost its force with the emergence of a new type of grassroots politics in rural Uttar Pradesh. Then came the demolition of the Babri Mosque which saw the civilians of Allahabad joining in protest at the ICH.[17] Doodhnath Singh and the JLS were vocal against this barbaric act of violence. Vibhuti Narain Rai, then posted in Allahabad, underlined the plight of the Muslims in his novel *Shahar Mein Curfew*, (the town under curfew, 1988) based on the 1980 communal riots in Allahabad.

While conversations on politics could be part of any *adda*, ICH linked activism and rational debate on larger social issues involving the civil society thus compelling the political machinery to take desired action. This is exemplified in the movement that temporarily shook Delhi in 1964.

THE PRRM

The movement against rising prices begun at the Coffee House on Janpath is an example showcasing the role of the coffee house as a place for garnering mass support for a public cause. If the workers of the Coffee House regained their place in the city after their existence was threatened by the closure planned by the Coffee Board of India, the citizens of Delhi fought in 1964 to regain the social space they thought belonged to them, now threatened by forces of capital. The Delhi edition of *The Statesman* of Saturday, 19 September 1964

[16] Glimpses of the violent student politics in Allahabad can be found in Pankaj Mishra, *The Romantics*, New York: Anchor Books, 2001 and P.K. Mehrotra, 'Sex and the small town', in *The Last Bungalow*, 321–29.

[17] Doodhnath Singh, interview, 23 October 2012; Sriprakash Mishra, interview, 24 October 2012; Niranjan Lal Srivastava, interview, 26 May 2014.

carried an image of the prime minister (PM) Lal Bahadur Shastri who in his parliamentary address reaffirmed his decision to stick to the Nehru line in coping with the ongoing food crisis in the country. The price of essential commodities in the capital had been spiralling during the previous few months compelling the PM to devote fifty minutes to the issue. Occupying the central place on the page was the four-column photograph of the Coffee House in Janpath, with the accompanying story, 'The customer turns in Delhi'. The Coffee Board had handed over the Janpath outlet of the ICH to the Puri family who owned the building. Since 1958, the place was run privately by the four sisters-in-law of the family where the ex-workers of the Board continued to work. Like every other day, Rajendra Kapoor, a special correspondent of the Urdu daily *Tej*, had taken two cups of coffee in the Coffee House on the morning of 18 September.[18] When he asked for the bill, he noticed that he would have to pay ten paise more than usual because the price of coffee per cup had been increased from 45 to 50 paise. Including the sales tax, he was charged for Rs 1.05. Already stretched financially due to rise in the prices of daily necessities, Kapoor, betrayed at this unwelcome gesture, let out a cry, *et tu coffee house!* and informed his friends present about the rise in the price of coffee. As someone said: "This is the last straw", another person stood up and made a forceful plea for boycotting the coffee house. What followed, according to the staff reporter, was something the coffee house experienced for the first time in its life. All of a sudden a 'Please keep silent' signboard put all noise to a stop and drew the attention of the then present customers to a spontaneous speech on boycott. Subsequently, everyone walked out of the Coffee House, some without footing the bill, and began picketing in front. They informed approaching customers of the increased price and requested them to stay away from the Coffee House and even put up a notice with that request. This continued till about 1.00 pm when the regulars went back to their customary seats, ordered just 'boiled' water, but tipped the workers before leaving the place. Those willing to pay the increased rate were a minority. In the evening too there was no other

[18] I owe this reference to Vishwa Bandhu Gupta of the daily *Tej*.

gossip or discussion of national or international news. Some visitors talked of the incidents in the morning as others collected signatures on a petition to the authorities to permit customers to picket outside the Coffee House. This was the first time that some consumers in Delhi began a resistance against the rising prices they had been quibbling about. Would the management revert to the earlier price? Would the picketers step down and change their stand? The reporter covering the incident was not sure.[19]

A review of the situation in the preceding period shows that there had been an upward trend in the prices of commodities since at least the commencement of the Second Five Year Plan (1956–61), and the failure of the harvest in 1962–63 had pushed up the prices by 8 per cent between April and October 1963. Wheat, pulses, mustard seed and sugarcane had a bad harvest during the winter of 1963–64, and the post-harvest prices rose by 3 per cent.[20] There had been a record crop of groundnut and the groundnut oil price was low during the first half of the year boosting the export trade. Failure of the *rabi* linseed, mustard, rapeseed and sesame crop resulted in a scarcity. The total output of foodgrains during 1962–64 was lower than in 1961–62 registering a shortfall of more than 20 million tons though the import of foodgrains increased from 4 million tons in 1962–63 to 6.27 million tons in 1963–64.[21] Earlier, prices of agricultural produce used to fall and rise seasonally in response to a bumper crop and crop failure respectively. The situation had worsened due to hoarding and black marketing, and prices now showed an upward stickiness. The price regulatory strategies of the government were overshadowed by the machinations of the parallel economy through black marketing and smuggling. Between June 1963 and June 1964 prices of food articles had increased by 13.4 per cent.[22] In August

[19] The management had called in the police but the police only kept a watch on the picketers. Rajender Kapoor was stopped from entering the coffee house and the waiters were asked to supply water only when order was placed for coffee, *The Statesman*, 21 September 1964.

[20] S.K. Nath, 'The Economy in 1964–65', *The Economic Weekly*, 27 February 1965, 403–06.

[21] Ibid.

1964, Lohia, the socialist leader of the Opposition, initiated talks with the two factions of the Communist Party and Jana Sangh to form a joint front in order to force traders to sell wheat, rice and other essential commodities at a reasonable price. Although the rightist faction of the Communist Party and the Jana Sangh were not sure about this plan, the Leftist Communists had no hesitation to join Lohia, and to entrust him with the organization of the plan. The price of essential commodities in the capital was further spiralling during the previous few weeks, and some restaurants had already revised the prices in view of the trend. In the first week of September the Delhi administration announced an action plan to resist price rise. The Delhi government was to set up a central consumers' council. This council, together with 56 subsidiary councils in the 56 wards of the Delhi Metropolitan Council planned to launch a three-pronged attack on the trend of rising prices. The councils under the respective local councillor would work as watchdogs to resist any spurt of prices in the area. Second, the councils would organize peaceful picketing of shops that raised the price, and third, a price list of essential commodities and a list of shops where fair-priced goods would be available would be supplied to the consumers. There was thus a general public awareness regarding the urgency to take action against rising prices.

The agitation in front of the Coffee House resumed next morning following the display on the pavement of new clippings of incidents of the previous day including slogans like 'Peaceful boycott', 'Unity is strength'.

As the picketing continued, Kapoor was helped by Shammi Kichlu, his Kashmiri friend and Inder Verma, a chemist,[23] who procured a commercial coffee filter and coffee was served by engaging a caterer at 25 paise a cup in the parking lot outside the Coffee House that remained deserted. As the 19 workers of the Coffee House had no

[22] The prices of both wheat and edible oils had increased by 27 per cent, those of rice by 9 per cent (in addition to the 15 per cent the year before) and of sugar by 12 per cent. Manuja Kesari, 'Behind the price spiral: rise in money incomes, the prime mover', *The Economic Weekly*, (July, special no.), 1964, 1293–96.

[23] Keshav Malik, interview, 23 November 2012.

customer to serve that day, the protesters made sure to collect enough tips for them.[24]

On 20 September, the third day of the boycott, about hundred regulars gathered in front of the building and coffee was being served from the pavement stall now called the 'little coffee house', and over a cup of coffee offered in this way, new members of the committee were enrolled. Verma named this spontaneous protest of the consumers the Price Rise Resistance Movement (PRRM) that momentarily appointed an action committee called the Price Rise Resistance Committee (PRRC) with nineteen members. Membership of the Committee could be purchased for one rupee. That day the PRRC held a meeting in an adjoining lane at 3.00 pm when the decision to form a sub-committee was taken that would keep a watch on the coffee house and request visitors to boycott it. The Committee wanted to make sure that coffee would be made available at a cheaper rate, and at the same time launched an extensive crusade against price rise in general. It was further decided that championing the cause of consumers, the Committee was to remain strictly non-political.[25]

On the fourth day of the resistance, although no one urged visitors not to go to the coffee house owned by the Puris, customers in general boycotted the place. With Ram Manohar Lohia, S.M. Joshi, the chairman of the Samyukta Socialist Party and B.K.P. Sinha, a Congress MP and a large number of men and women paying for membership, the number of members exceeded 400 that day, evident that the movement spread beyond the regular coffee house goers. That day the Indian Coffee Workers' Cooperative Society (ICWCSL), already running the ICH in the DU campus, became part of the consumers' movement by helping the solitary caterer to supply coffee. In a leaflet entitled 'why pay more today', the PRRC tried to raise awareness among consumers on the issue, calling upon them to join the committee:[26]

[24] Uma Vasudev recalled that it was Inder Verma who made the selling of coffee on the pavement possible, interview, 22 October 2012; also 'Coffee house boycott goes on', *Sunday Standard*, 20 September 1964; 'It's Coffee on the Pavement Now', *The Statesman*, 20 September 1964.

[25] 'Much Coffee but Little Gossip', *The Statesman*, 21 September 1964.

[26] 'V.I.P.s Join Price Rise Resistance Body', *The Statesman*, 22 September 1964.

> You and I are consumers. We pay for what we buy. Whether it is coffee or other commodities, we must not buy them at [an] ever increasing rate [that] the profiteer fixes in order to maintain his ever increasing profit. If we pay more today, we have to pay still more tomorrow. Our refusal to buy things at higher rates today shall bring down the prices tomorrow. So don't pay more today than what you paid yesterday.

The PRRM thus crossed the threshold of the Coffee House and appealed to the prevailing general discontent regarding the persisting peril of rising prices. That the movement had already created a stir in different quarters, was evident on 22 September. It was the day Subhadra Joshi, who had played an active role in the formation of the coffee workers' cooperative, and Begum Anees Kidwai, both Members of Parliament, purchased membership of the Committee, bringing the new total to over 600. The new members included film comedian Om Prakash and his four assistants who were in Delhi for a shooting and happened to be on the spot. The coffee house remained empty for the fifth consecutive day when the PRRC decided to set up a new coffee house, a rival to the one run by the Puris. To this end, the Cooperative Bank promised a loan of Rs 50,000. The Committee announced that it would collect another Rs 50,000 through the sale of shares. It was decided to send a deputation on behalf of the PRRC to Gajraj Singh, the president of the New Delhi Municipal Corporation (NDMC), requesting a suitable location for the proposed coffee house. The Institute of Cooperation readily permitted the PRRC to make use of its office premises in the Theatre Communication Building at the heart of CP. The by-laws for the establishment of the proposed Consumers' Cooperative Coffee House were also drafted on this day.

In spite of rains on the morning of 25 September, a crowd of more than 200 journalists, social workers, politicians and foreign tourists gathered in front of the Coffee House to resume their agitation. Ground coffee was now retailed at the pavement stall. The deputation to the president and vice presidents of the NDMC was able to extract a promise that the procedure of granting permission required for the opening of the proposed coffee house would not be delayed. Moreover, the movement received an additional impetus when Ashoka Mehta, the then Deputy Chairman of the Planning Commission who had been to a hairdresser nearby, was cajoled to drink coffee standing on the pavement together with others. On expressing his sympathy for the movement, Mehta was sweet-talked to pay for membership.[27] The movement reached its climax the following day, 26 September, when the six-man delegation of the PRRC meeting the PM was asked to prepare a detailed note on the working of the restaurants in the capital on the basis of which instructions would be issued regarding the standardization of all restaurants in the city. Meanwhile, the All India Federation of Hotels and Restaurants (AIFHR) appointed a three-member committee to inquire into the rise in the price of coffee. The president Mr Ram Pershad made a call to all hotels and restaurants not to raise the price of foodstuff and beverages arbitrarily. It was also stated that the price of coffee could be raised only after consulting the Federation, and hotels and restaurants found guilty of raising the price unjustly were to be expelled from the Federation. To top the happenings of the day, the consumers' coffee house was launched in the evening in a tent, earning it the epithet of *Shamiana* or Tent Coffee House, adjoining the Theatre Communication Building. Rajender Kapoor had the honour of drinking the first cup of coffee at 27 paise (inclusive of a 2 paise sales tax!) in the new coffee house.[28] The day after there was yet another milestone when the Union Minister of Housing and Supply M.C. Khana became a member of the PRRM and assured of his help in finding a better location for the proposed consumers' cooperative coffee house in CP.

The tremendous success that the movement saw in a short span of time, including reaching the PM's office, could be attributed to the incident taking place in the heart of the capital and also because many political leaders were familiar with the coffee house from their

[27] 'Mehta Joins Anti-price Rise Movement', *Hindustan Times*, 26 September 1964.

[28] 'PM for Standardization of Delhi Restaurants', *Hindustan Times*, 27 September 1964.

student days. The involvement of journalists in the movement from its inception ensured the quick publicity it received and influenced the fate of the coffee house run by the Puri sisters-in-law. Two central columns of *The Statesman* of 28 September announced: 'Price resisters win battle: coffee house reverts to old rates'. The boycott forced the management of the coffee house the night before to revert to the price of coffee before the agitation began. In a statement, they declared that the decision had been taken 'pending standardization, classification and fixation of prices by a committee as suggested by the PM'.[29] However, the most important factor behind the popularity and increasing strength of the movement seems to have been its championing the cause against price rise plaguing urban life. The movement instantly struck a chord with the general public because it was an issue everyone understood. As we shall see, the PRRM made consumers outside the coffee house aware of their right to protest through peaceful resistance. The movement was successful in having a parallel coffee house set up where coffee would be available at a low price, demonstrated that a consumers' resistance movement could be effective and legitimate. While requests for information, help and guidance in starting similar movements began to come in from Ambala, Chandigarh, Jaipur and other places in Punjab and Rajasthan, hundreds of men, women and children were reported to be visiting the 'Parisian style' coffee house in CP.[30]

The letters sent to the media in the wake of the Movement bear testimony to the fact that the news of the PRRM had spread far and wide blurring the distinction between the public and the private. The news was being followed by sections of the population including housewives, who had to bear the brunt of the increase in the price of daily necessities.

On 30 September the PRRM had a record 1800 members. Consumers at large now wanted to protest against increased prices at other restaurants in CP and sought the guidance of the PRRM. On that day the PRRM decided to launch an enrolment drive among

[29] *The Statesman*, 28 September 1964.

[30] Ibid.

housewives and other sections of the public to check the rise in prices of other commodities such as grains, *vanaspati ghee* and vegetables.[31] In an interesting move, the same day the Price Committee of the Delhi Administration recommended the introduction of partial state trading in grain as a measure to check the price rise. The Committee urged the Central Government to fix the price of rice, wheat, grain and pulses in the producing states so that they could be regulated in Delhi. It also suggested the amendment of the Foodgrains Licensing Order to facilitate stricter control on the licensing of warehouses.

If the objective of the PRRM was limited in scope, it took an entirely new turn when the spirit of the movement was taken over by residents in some other parts of the city. Residents of Vinay Nagar, Munirka, Kamala Nagar, Netaji Nagar and Paharganj protested against the increased price of milk, potatoes and other vegetables and took initiatives to sell these commodities at an affordable price in their respective neighbourhoods. Encouraged by political leaders at local and national levels, citizens at Green Park, Hauz Khas, Lodi Colony, Rajendar Nagar, R.K. Puram and other neighbourhoods also took to the street raising their voice against price rise and setting up small open-air outlets for daily necessities.

In spite of having received a positive response from different quarters, the movement however, soon began showing signs of weakness. While it remained a middle-class agitation, differences of opinion and lack of coordination among the PRRM members became apparent during the 11 October meeting especially with regard to the organization of the movement and the nature of the proposed coffee house. In a letter sent to the editor dissociating himself from the movement, Rajendra Kapoor noted that the two main goals of the movement had been that consumers should, as a class, rise against the arbitrary rise of prices, and that there should be a coffee house where coffee would be available at an inexpensive price. The massive response from citizens all over Delhi proved that the movement had served its initial purpose. However, due to the interference of business and political interests, there was a rift in the

[31] 'Price Resistance Movement to be extended', *The Statesman*, 1 October 1964.

movement that complicated matters.[32] It is also remarkable that the steps taken by the consumers of the coffee house and outside remained confined to the populist measure of targeting small vendors. Apart from the letters to the editor of *The Statesman* noted above, none of the other newspaper reports showed that there was an attempt to mobilize public opinion that led to the worsening of the situation, like black marketing, hoarding, and smuggling. Similarly, there was no protest against the attempt of politicians trying to hijack the citizens' movement.

Kapoor's wish, like that of many coffee house visitors, was soon fulfilled. With the active help of the Union Home Minister G.L. Nanda and M.C. Khanna, Minister for Work and Housing, on 13 November the ICWCSL was formally allotted the accommodation to run the new coffee house in the premises of the Theatre Communication Building. The ICWCSL made an agreement not to raise prices without consulting the committee of consumers.[33] When nearly two months after the movement had been launched the pavement coffee house moved to Theatre Communication Building on 16 November, it was indeed a spectacular show. As he sipped his last cup of coffee on Janpath, a young 'coffee addict' held a victory torch in his other hand, symbolizing the victory of consumers. Piloted by two scooters and four men on foot, he went round CP, and was received by a jubilant crowd of 2000 citizens in front of the illuminated *shamiana*—the Tent, in the premises of Theatre Communication Building. Amidst slogans, cheering the consumers' movement and the PRRM, poetry in Hindi, Punjabi and Urdu was recited accompanied by the *shehnai*. M.C. Khanna inaugurated a new outlet of the ICH.[34] While the Minister stated that the consumers' movement had the blessings of the PM and the Home Minister, the PRRM declared that this was not the end, but just the beginning of the movement that was to continue.[35]

[32] Rajendra Kapoor, 'Perils of PRRM', *The Statesman*, 2 November 1964.

[33] 'PRRM's coffee-house to move on Monday', *The Statesman*, 14 November 1964.

[34] Since 1958, as pointed out above, the coffee house on Janpath was run privately.

[35] 'Poetry Ushers Consumers' Coffee Indoors', *The Statesman*, 17 November 1964; 'Kerb coffee-house in new premises', *Indian Express*, 17 November 1964.

In what followed it was however clear that there was a dissension within the ranks of the PRRM. The general body of the committee wanted the ICWCSL to be entrusted with the management of the proposed coffee house, while the secretary was in favour of a business lobby that had infiltrated the Committee, with the aim of sharing the spoils. A majority of the members of the Committee felt that the secretary was working against the spirit of the movement. They suspected that, in order to influence the decision to be taken at the meeting of the Coordinating Committee on 8 November, he wanted to restrict entry to the meeting by not issuing membership cards to all members of the PRRM. Consequently, the meeting was called off and the secretary along with his two assistants were suspended.[36] As the two factions of the Committee failed to reconcile their differences during the following days, the movement petered out once the momentum was lost.[37]

The PRRM served the immediate purpose of regaining the social space where it was once again possible to carry on *adda* over a cup of coffee without having to pay much. The ICH lost to private enterprise in 1958 now reopened its doors at a new location as the Tent. But begun on the spur of the moment following a spontaneous act of protest by an ordinary journalist, the way the PRRM drew the attention of the rank and file in the capital, made the coffee house comparable to the Speaker's Corner in Hyde Park, the 'lawful free assembly' where everyone had the right to mount a soapbox or ladder to deliver a free speech and criticize social injustices.

THE NAXALBARI MOVEMENT IN CALCUTTA AND ICH

If the rise in prices of daily necessities sparked off the PRRM in the Coffee House in Delhi, in the late 1960s and early 1970s the ICH on College Street, Calcutta witnessed many student customers with a rebellious streak mobilizing support for their cause in the place. Guided by the idea of a social revolution, they engaged in the anti-establishment movement known as the Naxalite Movement. Home

[36] 'PRRM Secretary Suspended', *The Statesman*, 7 November 1964.

[37] 'Janpath Price Resisters Remain Divided', *The Statesman*, 10 November 1964.

to the strong tradition of an anti-colonial revolutionary movement, Bengal had been apathetic towards mainstream Congress politics ever since the expulsion of Subhash Chandra Bose from the Party. While there was a large number of unemployed educated middle class, post-famine and post-Partition Bengal had to cope with the rehabilitation of refugees. The 1950s were a decade of hope that the expectations raised by the transfer of power would be fulfilled. With clouds of frustration over the lack of economic growth, inadequate supply of food grains and unemployment casting a grim shadow over the country, the 1960s represented a decade of dreams that had remained unfulfilled.[38]

Ashim Chatterjee. Chatterjee alias 'Kaka' studied in Presidency College. As a student leader of Bengal Provincial Student Federation (BPSF) in Presidency College, he formed the Bengal-Bihar-Orissa Border Regional Committee CPI (ML) as a separate faction and became a part of the College Street area during 1960–68. He was at the head of the angry students' protest against the college authorties paralyzing normal activities in the neighbourhood. Many recall that as school students they heard his name while commuting on bus or tram as the organizer of students' strikes and blockades that used to cause regular traffic jams in the region. Chatterjee and other urban students often visited the Coffee House but went to rural Bengal in order to mobilize peasants. He was arrested in the wake of the repressive measures and was incarcerated in different prisons of Bihar during 1972–78. After his release he formed the Communist Revolutionary League of India.

Economic disillusion coupled with militant trade unionism helped the cause of the labour movements during this period. Due to internal differences regarding electoral politics there were several ambiguities such as whether to align with the progressive section of Congress or to strive together with Jana Sangh and the Muslim League in order to break the Congress monopoly as well as the party's position on

[38] Rabindra Ray, *The Naxalites and Their Ideology*, New Delhi: OUP, 2011, 122–23.

the India-China War of 1962. This led to the Communist Party of India (CPI) split in 1964, with the radical section of the party forming the CPI Marxist (CPI-M).[39] The Leftist parties in India had been observing from a distance the effects of Long March and the success of the revolution through the mobilization of peasants in China under Mao Tse Tung. There were ideological differences among communists regarding the use of violence, and further on the issue of the split in the international communist world between the Bolshevik and Maoist camps, represented locally by the CPI and the CPI-M respectively. A further split at home saw both the parties branded as revisionist by a few, giving birth to a third party (CPI-ML, Marxist Leninist)—the most radical and inspired by Mao in 1967.[40]

Presidency College, the Calcutta University Arts Department and the ICH together formed a hub of student politics during the 1950s and 1960s and many political protests took place at College Square.[41] Presidency College with its sprawling lawn, the portico, the new building and canteen became the venue of meetings for student leaders of different colleges and was the heart of at least three student movements in the 1960s: the Food Price Resistance Movement of 1966, Presidency College Movement (1966–67) and the Naxalite Movement.[42] Naturally, most of the debates and discussions that began in the university premises, continued at the tables of the ICH across the street.[43]

[39] K. Damodaran, 'Memoir of an Indian Communist', *New Left Review*, 1/93, Sept-Oct. 1975.

[40] For an analysis of these differences and the situation leading to the formation of CPI-ML, see Ray, *The Naxalites*, especially chapters 3 and 5.

[41] Sumanta Banerjee, *In the Wake of Naxalbari: Four Decades of a Simmering Revolution,* Kolkata: Sansad, 2009, passim.

[42] Biswanath Das, *Presidency College-er Itibritto* (A History of the Presidency College), Kolkata: Thema, 2011; Anil Acharya (ed.), *Shat-sottorer Chhatro Andolan* (Students' Movements of the 1960s and 1970s), Kolkata: Anushtup, 2008.

[43] The death of 80 people due to police firing during the Food Movement of 1959 had seen the students participating in it. The movement against the increase in the price of tram tickets in July 1965 was led by students who began picketing on the streets. Ordinary citizens joined the movement spontaneously by refusing to pay the increased fare. This was followed by another mass movement during March-April 1966

Concerned with the state of the society, students followed national and international developments with great interest. Since 1947 there had been lingering dissatisfaction over the unchanging socio-economic condition of the rural poor. In Bengal, in view of the primordial dependency of the agricultural labourers, share-croppers, poor peasants and artisans on the big landlords, the CPI, and the CPI (M), had been mobilizing the peasantry and demanding the distribution of surplus vested land illegally occupied by landlords. The formation of the United Front Government in Bengal in February 1967—an alliance of fourteen political parties including the CPI and CPI (M)—had aroused hopes among the landless poor for more land reforms enabling quick distribution of vested surplus land. These hopes were not fulfilled as on the one hand the landlords took recourse to legal and illegal measures to postpone such distribution, while the CPI (M), in its attempt to consolidate its power, drifted away from its initial promise on the other.[44] As leaders like Charu Majumdar, Kanu Sanyal, Jangal Santhal and others decided to intensify mobilization by encouraging peasants to engage in direct action against landlords in order to bring an end to oppression, a rift within the CPI (M) became inevitable. The spirit of socialism had a great appeal among the youth who looked to the peasants' struggles in China and Vietnam for inspiration. Not only did they distrust India's role in the Indo-China War of 1962, the news of the Vietnam War, the radical students' movement in Paris and the Prague Spring of 1968 deeply moved them. It was believed that changes in rural society could be brought about through an agrarian revolution that would empower the peasants against the landowners, the class enemy.[45] After police firing on the peasants in the village of Naxalbari

---

demanding the supply of food-grains and kerosene. The waves of all these movements touched the university students and the Presidency College. In 1968 about 50,000 students took part in the anti-McNamara demonstration in West Bengal; interview, Raghab Bandyopadhyay.

[44] Banerjee, *In the Wake*, 105–06; Achintya Gupta, *Akjon Naxalpanthir Ardhek Jibon* (Half the Life of a Naxalite), Kolkata: Neo Camp, 2009, passim.

[45] Ashim Chatterjee, 'Goondader Goondamir Daay Bortabe Chhatroder Upor?' (Will Students be held Responsible for the Activities of the Anti-Socials?), *ABP, 14* May 2013.

in North Bengal in 1967 had given birth to the movement bearing that name, young urban students engaged in guerrilla warfare in retaliation for the violent attack on unarmed peasants by the establishment.

The communist leaders in Bengal since the early twentieth century had developed the perception of 'being declassed' that involved deriding middle class identity and *bhadralok* sensibility, as seen among the Hungry poets and writers in Chapter Four. This perception was part of the Indian communists' conviction of the necessity of complete identification with the peasant and the worker.[46]

Guided by the notion that they could change the existing structure of the rural society of which they had no practical knowledge, many bright students of Presidency and other colleges went underground in order to raise consciousness among peasants of their rights and help them organize against feudal landlords, the class enemy. Ashim Chatterjee and his friends' work among peasants Gopiballabhpur in Midnapore. Soon however the students were disillusioned by the hard reality. 'We had a dream, but the dream was devoid of reality....it was a great beginning, but the measures we took in order to reach the society were wrong', (*Dipanjan Roy Chowdhury, interview, 26 July 2011*). The disillusion of the urban students in rural surroundings is portrayed by Dilip Simeon in his semi-autobiographical novel where students of Delhi University leave the campus for the hinterland in order to work among peasants and workers. *Revolution Highway*, New Delhi: Penguin, 2010; Achintya Gupta's account is a testimony to the difficulty middle class students faced in coping with the hard life in the prison, *Akjon Nakshalpanthir Ardhek Jiban* [Half the Life of a Naxalite], Calcutta: Neo Camp, 2009, 109, 127, 132–33, 135.

Dissidents within the CPI (M) supporting the Naxalbari Movement were led by students of Presidency College who formed committees and held meetings at the regional and national level in support of the peasants' struggle encouraging rebellion among the

[46] Rajarshi Dasgupta, 'Marxism and Middleclass Intelligentsia: Culture and Politics in Bengal, 1920s–1950s' unpublished Ph.D. thesis, University of Oxford, 2003.

CPI (M) ranks in other states.[47] By 1969 revolutionaries in different states had consolidated their position in Telengana and Srikakulam in Andhra Pradesh,[48] Mushahari in Bihar, Lakhimpur in Uttar Pradesh, and in Calicut, Trichur and Trivandrum in Kerala. Incidents of occupation and forcible harvesting of crops, or the organized fight for better wages and acts of reprisal directed against landlords and money-lenders during 1967–69, showed that the earlier sporadic outburst of peasant rebellion was developing into organized armed struggle in an attempt to overthrow the government and seize power.[49]

From their knowledge of coffee houses in Europe, students associated the Coffee House with radical anti-establishment subversive movements.[50] Since Presidency College was one of the main centres of the Naxalite Movement, the ICH, dominated by Naxalite students, gained a symbolic significance in this conflict.[51] But what did the revolutionary students seek in the comfort of the Coffee House? Although the struggle of the workers against the Coffee Board may be termed as class struggle, the concern of the students in this context was improving the lot of rural society, and political activism of sympathizers of such movements—the struggle of the rural poor against landowners led them to the field.[52] Moreover, the strategy for action could be chalked out/discussed in the public space of the ICH, where it might be overheard.[53] The PRRM did not dream of changing the existing social order like the students in the late 1960s did. How can we link the Naxalite Movement with the ICH?

Writing about student groups in ICH in the 1950s, one memoir observed that Presidency's students were each other's best teacher; through discussion, debate and gossip difficult theories would be

[47] Banerjee, *In the Wake*, 114, 126–27; Ray, *The Naxalites*, 99.

[48] Since 2014 Telengana forms a new state.

[49] Banerjee, *In the Wake*, 155–56.

[50] Ashim Chatterjee, interview, 24 July 2011; Dilip Simeon, interview, 28 February 2012.

[51] Das, 'Coffee-houser Adda', 119.

[52] Ashim Chatterjee, interview, 24 July 2011.

[53] Ibid.; Ritajyoti Bandyopadhyay, interview, 6 June 2013.

clarified, one would come to know about essays in reputed journals in India and abroad, and learn how to stunt others.There were three dividing lines among student groups: one such line was between those who could afford only coffee and those who would have cutlet in addition, and the second distinction was between the all-female and all-male groups. But the most crucial division was between those belonging to the Students' Federation (SF, since 1970 SFI) and anti-SF groups for whom a few tables were always [unofficially] reserved. While the anti-SF group used to discuss girls, marks obtained in tests and career, SF groups engaged in discussion mainly on two themes: books and politics. There would be heated debates on anything from Kafka to Cuba, Engels and Jibanananda Das, impressionism to folk painting, American imperialism to 'the tragedy of Africa'.[54]

In the words of the student leader Ashim Chatterjee aka 'Kaka', a leading personality behind the Movement, there was no such place as the Coffee House in the neighbourhood where students could just sit and refresh. Before 1968 the canteen in Presidency was not at all attractive[55] whereas across the street there was the Coffee House where 'creative persons' from different media like fine arts, literature, theatre and politics discussed conflicting ideologies and consequently, there there was a continuous flow of ideas. It was there that he met the engineer poet Binoy Majumdar, and asked him about the most complex 'mechanism' in the universe. Majumdar replied 'it is the equation of a straight line that beginning at one point continues into the space'.[56] This kind of interaction expanded their horizon and broadened the thought pattern—experiences needed for the birth and development of new ideologies. 'That was possible only in the ICH.'[57]

[54] Bharati Roy, *Ekal Sekal: Panch Prajanmer Katha* (These Days, Those Days: Tells of Five Generations), Kolkata: Ananda, 2008, 178–79; although separate groups sat at separate tables, discussion among members across the tables seems to have been possible; see the testimony of Ashim Chatterjee.

[55] Ashim Chatterjee, interview, 24 July 2011; Sankha Ghosh, interview, 14 February 2011.

[56] Ashim Chatterjee, in 'Coffee House Coffee House', Bahirbanga archives, 4 May 2012, https://www.youtube.com/watch?v=lTIM6-IDSPU.

[57] Raghab Bandyopadhyay and Ashim Chatterjeeon, interviews, 10 February 2011 and 24 July 2011 respectively.

A similar view was held by another Naxalite student of the time: 'if you wanted an introduction to contemporary urban Bengali culture, you had to go to the Coffee House'.[58]

College Street was the most important street in the politics of the time, and this politics became the politics of the Coffee House. Although the Congress Party and the CPI (M) combined in their attack on Naxalite ideology, student leaders and members of opposing political parties did not consider each other as adversaries; notwithstanding the ideological differences, they could engage in *adda* on contemporary art, film or world literature.[59]

The phase between the conflict among the communists prior to the Naxalite political action was also abuzz with activity. The induction of students into political groups as well as the printing and distribution of posters and handbills had to be planned, in between the *addas* in the ICH. Animated discussions on matters related to student politics among student leaders of different parties from the colleges continued to keep the atmosphere charged.[60] In the same way, a few Naxalite student leaders would be seen there every day with a fresh group of students who had just joined the university. In the course of daily interaction, while gaining trust of fresh students through friendly conversations about their life, study among other things, student leaders would inform and attract newcomers to the ideology they believed in.[61] Friendship was made in this way; but this was also how the ideology behind the Movement was disseminated and new members recruited in the ICH for the cause. For organizing

[58] Dipanjan Roy Chowdhury, a student of Presidency during 1961–64 participating in the Naxalite Movement since 1967; later he taught at the same college, interview, 26 July 2011.

[59] Ashim Chatterjee, interview, 24 July 2011; and Dipanjan Roy Chowdhury, interview, 26 July 2011.

[60] The protagonist in an aubiographical fiction meets *Kaka* for the first time in ICH, Gupta, *Akjon Nakshalpanthi*, 32; Alok Kumar Bhattacharya, who has been visiting the space since 1966, got acquainted with the Naxalite ideology in the Coffee House. He participated in the Movement and was among the arrested, spending 1971–73 in the prison, Basak, 'Coffee'.

[61] Partha Chatterjee, interview, 29 January 2014.

large meetings and actualizing the ideology however, students and leaders met elsewhere outside the Coffee House.[62]

Pradip Dhar, who lived close to College Street, studied at the Hindu School and then at Presidency, knew the ICH since his school days, where he used to spend a considerable part of the day. While in Presidency, he was attracted to the radical ideology. Being an easy-going person, he was very popular with the senior and junior students, and soon became an indispensable activist of CPI-ML. Students in groups were entrusted with different tasks; and at the end of the day they all met in the ICH.[63] Pheluram Banerjee was one of the students attracted to the radical ideology of the Naxalites. He came from a family of priests and their house at Maniktola Crossing in central Calcutta is at least three hundred years old. The Shiva temple on the ground floor of their house attracted no less than the famous Rani Rasmani and the religious leader Ramakrishna. His father had a *tol* (a traditional school for learning Sanskrit). He began attending political meetings during his high school days. While in college, as a member of the BPSF, he joined the students' union of St. Paul's College and the Presidency College Union (1965–66). Later as the general secretary of St. Paul's College Union (1967–68) Pheluram participated in the Naxalite Movement. According to him, many students affiliated to BPSF including those who turned radical used to visit the Coffee House which thus became a hotbed of political discourse. 'As you climbed up the stairwell, the wall was seen covered with revolutionary posters and slogans promising revolution and change; you were inspired to participate in such change.' He would busy himself with political activism during the day. In between those activities he would drop in at the ICH for coffee and a chat drinking

[62] Large meetings involving 25–30 activists could not be organized in ICH (without a microphone it would be impossible to convey any important message to such a large group) and after the canteen in Presidency was opened, strictly political meetings would take place there, or in the lawn of the College, Ashim Chatterjee, interview, 24 July 2011.

[63] Till recently, Dhar was still a regular at the ICH. The annual blood donation camp organized by the ICH was at his initiative, Pradip Dhar, interview, 23 July 2011.

as many as seventy cups of coffee a day. There were days he did not return home and spent the night in the Coffee House together with the workers. Communist leaders like Anil Biswas, Biman Bose, Subhash Chakrabarti never went to the Coffee House, but student activists from different colleges and members of different political parties would meet there.[64] Senior students of the Presidency College with similar ideological concerns often accompanied Banerjee to his house. According to him, during this time his house was transformed from the meeting place of spiritual leaders into a 'political *akhara*'. The initial proposal of students' union activities—for example a *Bharat Bandh* (all-India strike) or *Bangla Bandh* (strike in Bengal)—could be discussed in the Coffee House, among other places. The plan would be passed to other college unions. The ICH was used as a point of connection, a kind of post office where news could be disseminated orally, letters distributed and news-bulletins circulated. Equally important were the debates on the party line, as student leaders and members following different political ideologies used to meet there. If there was a students' agitation in one college, the message first reached the Coffee House, and from there it circulated to other colleges.[65] Raghab Bandyopadhyay, then a student, used to go to the ICH as an active member of the Naxalite Movement. Naturally the subjects of discussion with fellow radicals such as Ashim Chatterjee, Dipanjan Roy Chowdhury and Ranabir Samaddar among others included politics. National and international political issues often dominated the agenda of the *adda* even when members of *Hindol*, the little magazine Raghab edited, joined the table. What is also important to note in this connection is that discussion in the ICH was open and public.

[64] Debabrata Mukhopadhyay, who sympathized with the Naxalite students and was all along an eye witness to the happenings in the ICH named some of them: Saibal Mitra (poet), Ashim Chatterjee, Dipanjan Roy Chowdhury, Nirmal Brahmachari, Achintya Gupta, Dipen Bandyopadhyay, Raghab Bandyopadhyay, Pheluram Banerjee, Biplab Halim, Amal Datta, Arati and Ajit Saha and many other leaders and workers, *Coffeer-cup*, 42.

[65] Pheluram Banerjee, interview, 12 February 2011. Banerjee is a member of the Coffee House Consumers' Forum; Ashim Chatterjee, telephone conversation, 12 March 2012.

Although the Coffee House etiquette was maintained in general, such public gatherings and discussions of students were not always peaceful. In an autobiographical fiction, the then general secretary of the students' union of Vidyasagar College, an active participant of the Naxalite Movement, reminisced about those turbulent years of his life. One day, after the protagonist Anup had openly criticized the content of a leaflet written by a Naxalite leader, he was approached by a few members of the Left-allied Presidency Consolidation Group (PCG) in the Coffee House where his right to criticize the leader was questioned. They left after he pacified them by pointing out that as a follower of the same political ideology he had the right to criticize. Soon however, another group of students went up to him, and they too introduced themselves as belonging to PCG, and discussed the same issue with Anup for more than an hour. Within half an hour after the second group left, came yet a third group who insisted that Anup accompany them to the Presidency College to discuss the issue. At this, the protagonist pointed out that he had already discussed it twice and that they could continue to discuss in the Coffee House itself. Since they were adamant, Anup however felt compelled to accompany them. As soon as they entered Presidency College, he was violently assaulted.[66] In another incident members of the PCG tried to beat up 'Kaka' who successfully averted the attackers by pushing a chair in between.[67]

The fire of revolutionary ideology quickly spread to universities in other parts of India and in DU a group of about thirty students of St. Stephen's College began militant activism under the student leader Arvind N. Das. There too, much of the discussion in the preparatory

[66] Nirmal Brahmachari, *Anuper Diary* (Anup's Diary), Kolkata: Naya Udyog, 2006; Saibal Mitra, Anil Acharya (eds.), *Shat Sottoren Chhatro Andolon* (Student Movements of the 1960s and the 1970s), 3 vols, Kolkata: Anushtup, vol. 1, 262–66.

[67] Thinly built *Kaka* taught others the usefulness of this defensive strategy, interview Dipanjan Roy Chowdhury, 26 July 2011; cf. the gambler Subhas Chandra Bose (70 years, a regular since the early 1960s), recalled that he was sitting with the owner of the Arya Pustak Bhandar, a Naxalite in the ICH one day, when there was a police raid. Bose was asked about the identity of the young Naxalite and he replied they were friends, interview, 2 February 2011.

phase took place in the *addas* in the Coffee House, as documented in an autobiographical fiction:[68]

> The excitement of 1968 continued for some months. The Science Faculty Coffee House.... was [the] breeding ground-cum-watering hole for Mohan's friends and other radicals who congregated there to discuss Vietnam, world revolution and strategies for overthrowing the Indian state. Other activities included gossip, eating coffee-jelly with cream [....] and yearning for sex objects from the nearby women's college to walk in.

Although this 'idyllic' description of students discussing revolutionary politics confirms the position of the epigraphs to this chapter, this narrative is an account of the dilemmas that shook the world of the students. They went underground with the conviction that they could help the underprivileged in rural areas and returned disillusioned. The author Dilip Simeon, Rabindra Roy, Awadhesh Sinha and Rajiv Kumar were among the fifteen students who, guided by the spirit of revolution, left the university and went underground. Some of them went to villages to create awareness among the poor. The reality on the ground, the difference between the world of the urban middle class youth used to a comfortable life and that of the rural poor, often resulting in a communication gap, opened their eyes to the limitations of the ideology.

Throughout 1968–69 when radical ideology had students in Calcutta and Delhi under its charm, Naxalism remained like a 'distant drumbeat' in Allahabad, and Neelabh, then a university student, recalled having heard only once, from his friend Devi Prasad Tripathi, about an upheaval in Naxalbari.[69] It was only when he went to attend the Young Writers' Conference in Patna in 1970 that he came to know

[68] Simeon, *Revolution*, 25–26, also 29–32 for an idea of a few of the revolutionary literature they read and discussed in ICH. Many students from other universities travelled to Calcutta and the office of Thema Publishing near Lake Market was a meeting point where Naxalite students from other places like Rana Bose, Utpal Sen studying in St. Stephen's in Delhi would meet their counterparts in Calcutta, Nandini Dutta, e-mail, 9 May 2014.

[69] Neelabh, e-mail, 8 September 2012.

more about it after Phanishwarnath Renu approached the podium to read out an open letter addressed to the socialist leader Jayaprakash Narayan (JP), who, then encamped at Mushahari in Bihar, was trying to pacify the Naxalites there.[70] That was the turning point, after which Neelabh and his generation moved more and more towards Marxism before coming to sympathize with Naxalite ideology. Although he and his friends with Naxalite leanings would go regularly to the ICH, unlike in Calcutta or Delhi, the ICH Allahabad never became a place for the congregation of local Naxalites who had their office in front of Swaraj Bhavan.[71] Those who wished to engage in critical discussion of radical ideas would prefer to go to meet other Naxalites in Delhi or Patna.[72]

This first phase of the Naxalite Movement in Bengal known for its politics of indiscriminate killings and other acts of violence was ruthlessly put down by the state in 1971–72. CPI (M), that had formed a part the United Front government of Bengal, covertly sanctioned this measure. After this government was dismissed and President's Rule decreed, Operation Steeplechase was launched on 1 July 1971 that saw Naxalite leaders arrested or killed one by one[73] In the early seventies the College Street area, like many other neighbourhoods of Calcutta, became a permanent zone of a triangular conflict for control over the area among the Congress, CPI (M) and the Naxalites. Skirmishes between the police and the revolutionary students in front

[70] Neelabh, *Gyanranjan*, 15. Like in many other other rural areas, that area too witnessed agrarian clashes including forced harvest on behalf of the peasantry often encouraged by Naxalite students. JP had agreed to intervene in what was considered 'the Naxalite challenge' in Mushahari, Muzaffarpur district, Bihar, see Arvind N. Das, *Agrarian Movements in India: Studies on 20th Century Bihar*, London: Frank Cass & Co., 1982, 32–35.

[71] This office still functions from the same place and the members sometimes go to ICH if they have to meet someone or on occasions when members of CPI-ML from other places visit Allahabad to meet them, Ramayan Ram, current leader of the CPI-ML students' union, Allahabad University and state secretary of AISA, e-mail, 13 June 2013; Ramayan Ram, interview, 12 September 2013.

[72] Neelabh, e-mail, 8 September 2012.

[73] Christophe Jaffrelot, 'The State and the Maoist Challenge in India', *Les etudes de CERI*, no. 175, September 2011, 1–38 (9).

of the gate of Presidency College, spilling over to the ICH across the street, became common. Revolutionary activists and intellectuals used to occupy a few tables of the Coffee House in the evenings, especially on Saturdays. The iconoclastic irreverence of the revolutionaries displayed in the destruction of the original photograph of Tagore hanging on the north wall was indulgently overlooked by seniors and others present.[74] There were occasions when, alarmed at news of an imminent police raid, regular visitors and workers of the ICH helped students escape through the staircase at the back of the building.[75]

As the students were already familiar with the ICH, its workers and other customers, there was widespread support for this group of bright students, who, influenced by the radical ideology, were ready to sacrifice their private life and career. Consequently, Naxalite students continued to use friends, sympathizers and workers there to pass on messages to members of their group.[76] Sometimes CPI (M) leaders Saroj Mukherjee or Sushital Roy Chaudhuri would come in person or send their followers with a message. The rooftop of the Coffee House was a place where the revolutionary students used to hide hand-bombs (*peto* and *patka*). They would hurl these hand grenades at the police from the rooftop, and either hide among the crowd in the main hall of the ICH or escape through the stair-case at the back.[77] There were occasions when regular visitors like Debabrata Mukhopadhyay had to intervene physically in order to save the students from reactionary forces. In his own words, he felt it was

[74] Mukhopadhyay, *Coffee-r cup*, 40; Das, 'Coffeehouse-er Adda', 119.

[75] Zahir Hussain, interview, 31 July 2011; Subhas Chandra Bose, gambler, interview, 2 February 2011; also Mukhopadhyay, *Coffee-r cup*; Das, *Kavitar Dwimeru Viswa*, 171–72.

[76] For example the Naxalite poet Ajay Sen who, being chased by the police in Howrah had left his ancestral house and was staying in College Street was a regular at the Coffee House where he, would narrate stories of his encounter with *goondas* of other political parties in the area in an 'aggressive body-language', and in case of violence, would protect fellow poet-sympathizers of revolutionary ideology Das, 'Coffeehouse-er Adda', 119–20. After he was freed, the Naxalite leader Kanu Sanyal who used to live in North Bengal would come to the Coffee House in order to meet fellow ideologues and friends, Basak, 'Coffee'.

[77] Mukhopadhyay, *Coffeer cup*, 42–43.

his obligation to offer at least temporary protection to those honest, self-confident students who had left their home and were being chased by reactionary forces and political opponents alike. He wanted to instil a humanist ideal and cultural consciousness especially among those confused students who had deviated from their political ideal and were following the path of self-destruction.[78]

Located in the heart of student political activism, the Coffee House was a natural choice for students to relax, seek diversion, discuss their concerns, ventilate their grievances, and above all, make friends. For the Naxalite students, the real field of action was outside the Coffee House; but they used the place to argue, to clarify their viewpoint, to interact with intelligentsia outside the university, to persuade, thus making the Coffee House a site for mobilizing support and recruiting new adherents to their ideology. The Leftist artist Debabrata Mukhopadhyay's memoir cited above is a rare testimony to how the social space helped the cause of the Movement by nurturing this interaction, and when it was necessary, by offering them protection.

THE LIBERATION WAR OF BANGLADESH

If post-Partition migrants to Delhi in 1947 found solace in the meetings at the ICH Queensway, the porous boundaries on the eastern part of the subcontinent ensured that there was a constant flow of people especially from the east to the west. Bengalis on both sides of the border tried to rise above the Partition imposed by political forces exemplary in the attempts of *Krittibas* at the ICH to offer a common platform to Bengali poets in both West Bengal and East Pakistan discussed in Chapter Four. Separated geographically

[78] Mukhopadhyay's efforts in the ICH in this respect had active support from other regulars like Debabrata Chakrabarti, Manab, Jishu Chaudhuri and Gopal Haldar. Sharing the table with him were among others the university teacher Anathbandhu De (the economist), Rabindra Mukherjee, Ashim Chatterjee, Dipen Bandyopadhyay, Sumanta Bandyopadhyay and Bhavani Chaudhuri, *Coffee-r cup*, 41; Gupta, *Akjon Nakshalpanthi*, 82–84; Rudraprasad Sen Gupta, theatre personality, interview, 21 August 2011.

from West Pakistan by the landmass of the Indian subcontinent, and belonging to a different cultural world, East Pakistan was economically exploited by the centre of power in West Pakistan. Already in the early 1950s East Pakistan had tried to assert its cultural identity through the Language Movement protesting against the imposition of Urdu on a Bengali speaking population and on 21 February 1952 a massive students' protest in defence of Bengali had met police violence resulting in the death of a number of students. When the elections won by the Awami League under Sheikh Mujibur Rahman in East Pakistan in 1970 were ignored by the administration in West Pakistan that refused to allow Rahman to form a government, Rahman declared independence in the spring of 1971 followed by a nine-month struggle for liberation during which the Pakistani army massacred about three million people and carried on violence against women on a large scale. In a renewed flow of migration, about ten million refugees, including many intellectuals, fled to West Bengal in India. There was a widespread sympathy in West Bengal participating in the moral struggle for the liberation of Bangladesh, and both Calcutta and the ICH on College Street played a crucial role in this process. The office of the exile government of the Peoples' Republic of Bangladesh formed in April 1971 was located at 8, Theatre Road (now the office of the Consulate of Bangladesh) and the radio station of this government operated from a secret address in Calcutta.

The day after Samir Dasgupta, poet and assistant editor of *Amrita Bazar Patrika* brought the news of the military crackdown in East Pakistan to the Coffee House, Debabrata Mukhopadhyay, who had been guided by the fictionalized biography of Thomas Paine, and others, formed a group of volunteers who travelled across the border and established direct contact with the freedom fighters to offer relief goods. The first group going to Bangladesh included Mukhopadhyay, his muse artist Shipra Aditya, Mihir Sen (writer), Umaprasad Maitra (film director) and an acquaintance familiar with the border region. The decision to leave for East Pakistan was taken instantly in the Coffee House and Mukherjee and Aditya informed their respective family by phone that they would be away for a few days. In order not to lose time, on their first trip Mukhopadhyay and his group could take only a bag full of hand-bombs the Naxalite students had stored back in the terras of the ICH. On another occasion they carried cotton blankets and medicines for first aid arranged by Ashok Dudhoria, then a student in the Calcutta University. Dudhoria hailed from a business family, and as he expressed his desire to join Mukhopadhyay on the trip, the latter insisted that Dudhoria arrange for the relief goods. Mukhopadhyay himself travelled several times with relief material provided by the Bangladesh War of Liberation Relief Association set up by the University of Calcutta. The group he set up used to collect hand-bombs and guns and send it through commuters secretly to the freedom fighters. Taking advantage of the lenience of the Border Forces, that group would cross the border carrying relief goods and medicines. Many refugees from East Bengal migrating to Calcutta had small shops or found employment in the informal sector in an around the College Street area since the pre-Partition days. Many of the book stalls on the pavement were owned by them. There was a wave of sympathy for Bengalis on the other side of the border in the entire College Street area and ICH became a camp where young students, poets and other intellectuals fleeing the Pakistani army to West Bengal and heading for Calcutta gathered.[79] Among Bengalis from across the border who made the Coffee House their temporary workplace were Al Mahmud (poet, 1936–), Zahir Raihan (writer and film-maker, 1935–72), Ahmed Sofa (poet, translator and writer, 1943–2001), Sikandar Abu Zafar (poet, 1919–72), Nirmalendu Goon (poet, 1945–) and M. R. Akhtar Mukul (writer and radio journalist, 1929–2004). Raihan's documentary 'Stop Genocide' on the torture and violence unleashed by the Pakistani army was planned in the ICH with indirect support from Mukhopadhyay and others. Many connoisseurs of the Coffee House had themseves arrived in the city as refugees. When Bengalis across the boundary engaged in a second war against authoritarian repression, their co-brethren in West Bengal spontaneously extended support independent of the government, and the Coffee House became a site to mobilize support for this effort. Shukla Ganguli, whose family migrated to Calcutta in the wake of

[79] See Mukhopadhyay, *Coffee-r cup*, 53–60.

the new political turmoil, and began visiting the Coffee House as a college student, noted that in those day the entire College Street area was a support zone for people from Bangladesh. Each time the Football Club of East Bengal would defeat Mohun Bagan—the two traditional rivals from colonial times representing East and West Bengal respectively—the entire neighbourhood including the Coffee House would don red and yellow, the colours of the East Bengal club.

THE EMERGENCY

The discussion above bears testimony to the fact that during the initial decades after 1947 time and again the social space of the Coffee House was used by its occupants to give voice to their protest against the existing socio-political order including single political party dominance at the centre, and even beyond the national boundaries. The government under Nehru tolerated that perhaps because during the nationalist struggle he himself had been a symbol of the Left and secular force within the Indian National Congress. The ICH was a stronghold of Leftist ideologues, many of whom took part in that struggle, just like Nehru and other leaders at the helm of the country after Independence. Also, till some time before the Emergency rule, there had been no state vigilance in the ICH.[80] The demolition of the Tent ICH in CP during the Emergency is usually ascribed to the fact that it was considered a Leftist bastion and a 'hotbed of dissent', that the PM Indira Gandhi and her son Sanjay Gandhi could not allow continue.[81] What went on at the ICH that could have been conceived as a threat to the Emergency government? Was it at all possible during that time to openly take an anti-government stand in the public space of the Coffee House? We shall cast a brief glance at the opposition to the Indira-led government in the early 1970s that led to the proclamation of the state of Emergency in 1975.

[80] Inder Malhotra, interview, 24 November 2012.

[81] See Varma and Roy, *Addebaaj shahar*, 184; Guha, 'A salute'. This indeed guided the popular belief in 1975–76, Uma Vasudev, interview, 21 October 2012; Narayani Gupta, e-mail, 2 August 2013; also Coomi Kapoor, *The Emergency: A Personal History*, New Delhi: Viking/Penguin, 2015, 76.

The politics of allegiance and the selection of chief ministers encouraged by Mrs Gandhi since the late 1960s resulted in widespread criticism among the Opposition and the media regarding the way the office was being used for the personal political interest of the PM and her followers. In states like Gujarat and Bihar, elected Congress governments had failed to cope with the problems of food scarcity and rising prices that had led to unrest among students and other sections of society. In Gujarat internal strife for power within Congress in the face of severe economic distress resulted in the rallying of students, trade unions and urban middle classes against the elected Congress government in 1973. Supported by the opposition parties like Jana Sangh, Congress (O) and BLD, this movement saw the launch of *Nav Nirman Juvak Samitis* (Youth for Reconstruction Association). The youth in urban Gujarat began a movement of protest demanding the dissolution of the state government—a movement that continued in the face of the deployment of BSF, CSF and finally, the Indian Army. In the end the Gujarat Assembly was dissolved and President's rule imposed in the state in 1974.

The early 1970s also saw the Sarvodaya leader and Gandhian political ascetic JP, a hero of the nationalist movement, launching a grassroots struggle advocating massive cultural, economic, social and political reforms. Narayan had renounced party politics in 1954 and started living following the principles of the Gandhian ascetic Vinoba Bhave. He urgerd Nehru and other Congress leaders to leave politics and called for a 'saintly politics' for the strengthening and preservation of democratic values in a 'party-less democracy'. The *Sampurna Kranti* or Total Revolution Movement that JP began in the 1970s aimed at decentralization of power, village autonomy and a more representative legislature. With his base in Bihar, JP devoted his energy to organize Students' and People's Struggle Committees to check corruption and other social evils in order to introduce a new value system and a new social order paying special attention to religious minorities, backward classes and tribes. With the Vidyarthi Parishad, the student wing of the SSP in the lead, massive demonstrations attended by the youth including male and female students demanded the dissolution of the ineffective and corrupt state government and peacefully obstructed all government work. The central government forcefully arrested demonstrators, resulting in mob violence and strikes. The Student Action Committees formed by non-communist students, launching demonstrations throughout the state, received support from the communal Jana Sangh, Congress (O), CPI (M) and other opposition parties. As the majority of the chief ministers in states with a Congress government had been selected personally by the PM, Indira Gandhi, the dissatisfaction with corrupt state governments now targeted the Centre. By the end of 1974 the leaders of the opposition—widely congruent groups like Jana Sangh, Congress (O), SSP, BLD, and other regional parties together with Sarvodaya leaders formed a twenty-member National Coordination Committee that endorsed JP's programme of Total Revolution and urged him to launch a nationwide popular protest against the Centre. In crowded public meetings organized in different states, JP approved of the extension of his movement to Gujarat, Haryana, Uttar Pradesh, West Bengal and Andhra Pradesh. His movement thus turned into a Grand Alliance openly confronting Mrs Gandhi and her supporters within the Congress. During an all-India convention organized in Delhi in April 1974, a non-party organization called Citizens for Democracy was formed with the intention of creating a pressure group as a watchdog for ensuring the autonomy and independence of the judiciary, press, radio, and the bureaucracy.[82]

While pressure from these agitational movements mounted, the government was faced with yet another challenge in the form of the All India Railway Strike of 1974 (8–27 May), called by the All India Railwaymen's Federation then headed by the Socialist Party leader George Fernandes. As services came to a halt with more than a million railway workers on strike, and protest throughout the country, the government felt cornered in the face of opposition from all sides.

The Coffee House was, as the earlier chapters have shown, the venue where artists, political activists, university teachers, trade unionists, social workers among others met. For a section of the

[82] Ajay Gudavarthy, *Politics of Post-Civil Society: Contemporary History of Political Movements in India*, New Delhi: Sage, 2013, 39.

erstwhile connoisseurs, however, the Tent did not have any charm, and 'it meant nothing', so they would go to Embassy restaurant.[83]

The launch of the Tent alias the PRRM ICH in the premises of the Theatre Communications Building (TCB) in 1964 symbolized the victory of the lifeworld or the power of integrative communication based on practical rationality in the public sphere of the ICH. In its turn, like its predecessor, it attracted hundreds of visitors daily. The hutments of the erstwhile WWII barracks in the TCB housed government offices like the publication department of the Ministry of Education, state emporia, Hindi Bhavan, citizens' forums such as *Sampradayikata Virodhi* Committee (committee against communalism), the Quami Ekta Trust, and privately-owned offices like the Student Travel Information Centre.[84] From 1955, the secretariat of the Sahitya Akademi too was housed there till 1961, when it moved to Rabindra Bhavan.[85] Being at the heart of the metropolis, with the Parliament, government and newspaper offices, All India Radio and fine arts academies within a short radius, the Tent ICH soon became a place where intellectuals, especially outside academia could gather. The socialist ideologue Ram Manohar Lohia with his followers (popularly known as 'his widows' after his demise), Inder Kumar Gujral (till he became a minister in 1967), Chandrasekhar, formerly a PSP leader who joined Congress in 1964, and the Jana Sangh leader Atal Bihari Vajpayee, the latter two familiar with the ICH in Lucknow, were regular faces here. Political leaders used to celebrate their birthdays at this place.[86] Journalists would

[83] Inder Malhotra, interview, 24 November 2012;

[84] In 1971 the emporia moved to their current location on Baba Kharak Singh Marg.

[85] D.S. Rao, *Five Decades: The National Academy of Letters in India, (1954–1994)*, New Delhi: Sahitya Academi, 2004, 19. Since 1961 the three national academies, Sahitya Akademi, Sangeet Natak Akademi and Lalit Kala Akademi are housed in this building at the Mandi House crossing. In 1961 the literary magazine *Sahityiki* under Jainendra organized a three-day literary meet in Hindi Bhavan, Theatre Communication Building, Shyam Vimal, *Sahityikon ke Pratikrudh Varas*, in *DTH*, 430.

[86] The Congress leader Brij Mohan held his birthday party at the Tent ICH, Prabhakar, 'Tea House', 411.

crowd the Tent every morning for shop-talk and political gossip.[87] Functioning partially under a large tent, the ICH was not equally well-lit at all places and had a more open character. This open character of the Tent made it a meeting place for persons of different walks of life, including many ordinary people besides gamblers, racers and shady people producing counterfeit passports. Leftist students and writers like Aalok Dhanwa, Mangalesh Dabral, Viren Dangwal, Girdhar Rathi, Ibbar Rabbi, Sayeed, Asgar Wajahat, inspired by the Naxalite ideology and JP's call for total movement, would crowd at Tent, the ICH at Mohan Singh Place and the Muslim 'Panditji's tea shop.[88] A considerable section of the customers, especially vernacular littérateurs, moved between the Tent, and the Tea House across the street, Embassy in D-Block, among other places. The medley of this multifarious crowd bestowed the space its unique ambience, and for university students 'it was such an interesting place that one would make time to be there at a certain time of each day or at least a couple of times a week'.[89]

This ambience of the Tent as a place of free and open conversations changed abruptly during the Emergency. How did the journalists and littérateurs, who, as seen in the previous chapter, evidently had a great time in the ICH in the earlier period, experience the Emergency? As to what was going on in the Tent during that time, Rajinder Puri, allegedly the 'most powerful political cartoonist of the time'—who was a severe critic of the Nehru Dynasty and had antagonized Mrs Gandhi through a series of cartoons that suggested a constitutional

[87] Rajinder Puri, cartoonist, interview, 5 October 2013; Inder Malhotra, interview, 24 November 2012; G.V. Krishnan, 'The Emergency: When the Media Went Without Power', 2008, http://www.indiaofthepast.org/contribute-memories/read-contributions/the-unforgettable/105-the-emergency-when-the-media-went-without-power-by-g-v-krishnan, Krishnan was a reporter with *Hindustan Times* at that time.

[88] Mangalesh Dabral, 'Maani Paida Karta Jeevan' (A Purposeful Life), in Premshankar Singh (ed.), *Smaran: Viren, Ghaziabad, Navarun*, 2016; Pankaj Bisht and Anwar Rizvi, interview, 17 October 2012. Bisht (66) has been a loyal customer of ICH since at least 1968. Together with fellow writers making a group that would vary between ten and fifteen, Bisht visited alternately both the outlets almost daily between 1969 and 1975.

[89] Basudev Chatterjee, Chairman, ICHR, interview, 6 January 2012.

breakdown[90]—responded. Soon after the Emergency, a warrant was issued on numerous journalists including him, forcing him to go underground. This warrant was withdrawn after three months, when he resumed his visits to Embassy, which was also under surveillance. He would go there just for a cup of coffee, spend some time and go back home. After the Emergency rule ended in 1977, Puri became the founding General Secretary of the Janata Party. Accoring to Pankaj Bisht, a writer and editor of *Samyantar*, it was a common knowledge that the place was under surveillance. There were some ICH regulars who were being tailed by intelligence agents. He himself was visited three times at his home and office by officials of the Central Bureau of Investigation (CBI) and Intelligence Bureau (IB) who inquired into his activities including the nature and purpose of his visits to the ICH. Among ICH visitors with whom Bisht was personally familiar, two persons were arrested. One of them was the socialist Girdhar Rathi, editor of *Pratipaksh*, the weekly brought out by George Fernandes, and the second was the Naxalite DU lecturer Vinod Khurana. A few of his friends had left Delhi, and assuming that their earlier contact with the Naxalite Movement would lead them into trouble with the government, a few others went underground. In order to avoid a face-to-face encounter with the police, most of the radicals had stopped visiting the ICH.[91] In a series of political arrests that began even before the Emergency had been officially proclaimed, JP, Moraji Desai, Charan Singh, Raj Narain, Vijayaraje Scindia, Jivatram Kripalani, L.K. Advani and many other leaders of the Opposition, including those from Jana Sangh and RSS were put behind bars. Over a hundred thousand arrests of important journalists were made during this period.[92]

Many poets, artists and writers—some of them followers of the Congress Party—continued to visit the Tent as usual. Contemporaries

[90] E.P. Unny, 'The Combative Cartoonist', *Indian Express*, 16 February 2015, http://indianexpress.com/article/opinion/columns/the-combative-cartoonist/.

[91] Pankaj Bisht, telephone conversation, 2 August 2013; Khurana was, however, not a political activist.

[92] Francine R. Frankel, *India's Political Economy, 1947–2004: The Gradual Revolution*, New Delhi: OUP, 2011, 546.

noted that in spite of the repressive measures adopted by the government, the Emergency was generally accepted by a large section of the population.[93] M.F. Husain, who had incurred the displeasure of the Congress high command, was seen one day with a large bill-board-like image of Indira Gandhi portrayed as the ten-armed goddess Durga slaying JP. It was placed at the entrance of the ICH, where it would attract immediate attention. Pankaj Bisht mentioned that this blatant attempt to placate the PM was criticized in ICH.

It is thus evident that there was a general feeling of anxiety and insecurity, coupled with dissatisfaction over the imposition of censorship on freedom of expression among writers and others who met at the ICH. After Emergency rule was proclaimed, Chandrajit Yadav, the Coal and Mining Minister, invited writers regular at the Tea House and ICH to his house for tea one evening. No one knew who the other invitees were, but many established names of Hindi literature were present. Once they were there, it became clear that the idea was to garner writers' support for the Emergency. Among the writers present were Jagdish Chaturvedi, Dharmendra Gupta, Rajeev Saxena, Ganga Prasad Vimal, Mahip Singh, Baldev Vanshi and other members of the *Bharatiya Lekhak Sangathan* (Indian Writers' Association). Questioned about their silence regarding the Emergency, the writers raised the issue of the freedom of press and the imposition of censorship. Following this there was an argument between Singh and Yadav.[94]

On the request of a few journalists and writers at the Tent ICH, the acclaimed writer Vishnu Prabhakar wrote an open letter to Indira Gandhi congratulating her on her birthday, which was published in a daily:[95]

[93] Khushwant Singh, noted that the initial impact of the Emergency was good; schools and colleges reopened, work in factories was going on in full swing, price of essential goods was under check and black marketers and smugglers were rounded up, *Indira Gandhi Returns*, New Delhi: Virgin Books, 1979, 71; also Vishnu Dutt, *Indira Gandhi: Promises to Keep*, New Delhi: National, 1980, noted that the Emergency was synonymous with arbitrary rule, and there were certainly excesses, 'but at its best the period was a demonstration of the hard state..., many steps were taken that furthered the interests of the nation and particularly the poor....', 79–80.

[94] Mahip Singh, interview, 3 October 2013; Chaturvedi, *Connaught Place*, 163–67.

[95] Prabhakar, 'Tea House', 410–19. The places referred to in the letter were Swaraj

Dear Indira ji,

It is your birthday today, I have heard. Birthday is supposed to be very sacred. You are familiar with [the ideology of] the person who reared you in his lap, with the place where you grew up. You studied at Santiniketan. You have attained a remarkable height [....].They call you by the epithets such as *Ranachandi*, *Maha Bhairavi*, and *Durga*. Mr Vajpayee for example called you *Ranachandi*. I shall call you by these names only when it will be possible for me to live with dignity under you.

With due respect,

Jürgen Habermas has described the undermining of the sphere of public communication by modern state machinery through censorship as 'shamming of communicative relations'.[96] The space of normatively regulated communication through sociability on the basis of shared values is encroached upon by the apparatus of the state. This letter symbolized the spirit of 'free speech' in a time when the public sphere of rational communication based on values and common understandings was severely truncated. This letter does not voice the protest of a weathered citizen against the loss of his essential democratic rights to freely express his opinion, interact on common issues with others in public. Apparantly, as a response to this communication, CID agents shadowed Prabhakar for a few days during his early morning walks to Rajghat. Fellow writer Ramesh Gaur intervened to use his influence with the Agency through friends to make sure that Prabhakar was left untroubled.[97] That Husain, Prabhakar and a host of others still crowding both outlets of ICH and the Tea House were not disturbed thereafter suggests that like

Bhavan and Anand Bhavan in Allahabad known for the nationalist meetings attended by freedom fighters including Mahatma Gandhi. The allusions to Mrs Gandhi are different forms goddess *Durga* assumed during her fight against buffalo-demon, *Mahishasura*.

[96] J. Habermas, *The Theory of Communicative Action*, 2 vols, vol.1; *Reason and the Rationalization of Society*, vol. 2; *Lifeworld and System: A Critique of Functionalist Reason*, tr. Thomas A. McCarthy, Boston Mass: Beacon Press, 1984–87, vol. 1, 91, 341; vol. 2, 101, 387.

[97] Prabhakar, 'Tea House'.

the press, the average intellectuals discussing politics in the Tent or the so-called 'coffee house politicians' remained under self-imposed censorship during Emergency rule, at least in public.[98]

The mood among the journalists was not much different elsewhere. Inder Malhotra who was in Bombay working with the *TOI* heard the news on the morning of 26 June on BBC radio. The streets were empty. As he went to his office and talked to the chief editor Sham Lal about having the news out in the evening newspaper, the police arrived at their office with the news of the imposition of the ban.[99]

These narratives are especially important because just as they portray the tension among the citizens, they also bear testimony to the fact that the state was closely following the Coffee House and its inmates. What should be remembered in this connection is that in a public space like that of the ICH, an unfamiliar face immediately attracts attention, and as seen in Chapter Two, leaders of regular groups do their best to keep 'outsiders' at bay. Members of groups at different tables may not have personally known each other, but regular visits to the fixed place made the faces familiar. 'Such and such person was not a member of our table' implies 'he was there, but as part of some other group.' While conversing with members of one's own group, drinking coffee, or smoking, regular customers constantly—consciously or not—observed others also occupying the social space they were familiar with. Discussion on a particular subject brought members of different groups into direct contact depending on shared interest or knowledge. But this apart, there may be numerous occasions of casual interaction while entering the place, asking for change, or matches to light a cigarette, in the restroom or while leaving the building. Besides, the multitude gathered at the place, the buzz created by the simultaneous chatter still has an

[98] Regular visitors of the ICH were aware of the movements of persons supposedly working for intelligence department, Varma and Roy, *Addebaaj*, 184; Bisht stated that all visiting the ICH and Tea House were anxious about the presence of the intelligence in both places.

[99] Inder Malhotra, interview.

imposing impact on any outsider visiting the place *alone*, or for the first time.[100] Consequently, a newcomer visiting the ICH is bound to feel intimidated and betray his/her discomfort. Considering all this, any investigating agent visiting the ICH for surveillance, would find himself placed under the scanning gaze of the ICH regulars. Ramachandra Guha, a student at the DU during the Emergency, spotted a middle-aged man wearing spectacles and donning a dyed goatee in the ICH in the campus suspected to be a spy of the Research and Analysis Wing (RAW).

The awareness of the presence of intelligence on the part of the regulars in the Tent would determine the subjects of conversation under the Emergency rule. Guha noted that the student occupants of the ICH at DU during that time—mostly followers of Jana Sangh—not only conversed in a hushed tone, but the subjects of their conversation carefully 'eschewed' politics and dwelt on romance and sport.[101] Inder Malhotra commented that Indian secret agents were so 'flat-footed' that if they followed someone, it became obvious. Open, intra-group and inter-group debates and discussions on political ideologies attracted the Naxalite students in Calcutta and Delhi to the ICH. There seems to have been little scope for such open-ended communications in the Tent under the Emergency. Although it retained its function as a post office for the secret dissemination of news and rumours,[102] the available narratives of the period suggest that open discourse leading to the formation of public opinion witnessed during the PRRM or the Naxalite Movement could not be repeated under the prevailing circumstances.

On the eve of the Emergency, JP addressed a massive rally at

[100] Arnab Roy from Koochbehar in north Bengal, Ph. D. student, Imperial College, London, interview, 22 August 2011.

[101] Guha, 'A salute'; cf. 'The subjects of conversation among the writers sitting in the Tea House changed (during the Emergency). We began having the feeling that every third person sitting there was an agent of the CID', Singh, 'Tea House', 293; they would also speak in a symbolic language in the Tea House and the ICH, Baldev Vanshi, interview, 3 October 2013; Kapoor, *The Emergency*, 75–76.

[102] K. P. Sasi, 'K. Damodaran: An Unfinished Chapter', *Dissident Left*, 18 March 2012.

Ramlila Maidan in Delhi on 25 June, where Mrs Gandhi's opponents called for her resignation and launched a massive pacifist movement of non-cooperation with the government. Preparations for the imposition of the Emergency, a dark spot in the history of Indian democracy, began with attempts to choke the voice of the press by shutting down the electricity connection of the entire block on Bahadur Shah Zafar Marg in CP housing newspapers like *The Statesman* and *The Indian Express*, *The National Herald* and *The Times of India* on the night of 25 June 1975. Power supply was resumed only two days later. The same night saw the arrest of JP.

Emergency rule saw a blatant aggression on the personal integrity of individuals taken into custody under the Maintenance of Internal Security Act (MISA) and detained indefinitely without trial.

The case of Inder Mohan, a class I gazetted officer in the government of India and a social worker not affiliated to any political party since 1955, who was arrested because of his objection to the scheme of demolition of the Muslim colonies near Jama Masjid, and after initial confinement together with criminals, sent to Tihar Jail, exemplified the working of the Emergency, Uma Vasudev, *The Two Faces of Indira Gandhi*, New Delhi: Vikas, 121–28, 144, 154–61. Kuldip Nayar, one among numerous journalists arrested, detained and tortured, wrote about his case in *The Judgement,* New Delhi: Vikas, 1977, especially 125–33; in Calcutta Gour Kishore Ghosh, the JP-ite journalist was arrested from the Coffee House and little magazines operating from that place had been asked by the police to use self-censorship, Mukhopadhyay, *Coffee-r cup*.

The invocation of Article 352 of the Indian Constitution gave Mrs Gandhi extraordinary powers to influence police forces to detain protestors and strike leaders. Although clueless journalists speculated in the ICH on 26 June about the course politics was going to turn, with the subsequent code of ethics set for newspapers and the re-organization of the press, the Emergency was successful in drastically curbing the freedom of the press and removing chances of reports on any of the excesses being published.[103] What is interesting is that except for about three dozen journalists who rose in resistance, the rest caved in and surrendered their liberty by submitting to the draconian law issued by the Ministry of Information and Broadcasting. The situation was, in the words of Minoo Masani, 'in the nature of a nightmare, but it was neither a Fascist or Communist dictatorship; rather a limited form of authoritarianism....'.[104]

It was only after the Emergency was lifted that critical news began pouring in. Even a jurist like Soli Sorabjee, then a senior advocate of the Supreme Court of India, contemplated publishing anonymously his pamphlet on Emergency and its impact on the press, points to the general climate of fear created by the arbitrary arrests, dismissals, transfers and indefinite detention without trial that accompanied the unprecedented and undemocratic authoritarianism.[105] This fear seems to have gone a long way to frighten the public and we can assume that the public discussions in places like ICH during Emergency were lukewarm.

Aware of the larger schemes of demolition, resettlement and rebuilding that characterized Delhi since the Emergency, Varma and Roy suggested that Sanjay Gandhi was bent upon demolishing Tent ICH because of the dissentious nature of the discourse here. The other reason in their view was that beginning at CP, the Parliament Street runs along the parliament and ends at Aruna Asaf Ali Marg, with Jama Masjid still a couple of kilometres away. It is because of the colony at Turkman Gate that Lutyens had not been able to extend the imperial gaze up to Jama Masjid. Sanjay Gandhi was determined to remove the shanty colony at Turkman Gate as it blocked the view of Jama Masjid. The

[103] Soli Sorabjee, *The Emergency, Censorship and the Press in India, 1975–77*, London: Writers and Scholars Educational Trust, 1977; Nayar, *The Judgement*.

[104] Minoo Masani, *Against the Tide*, New Delhi: Vikas Publishing House, 1981, 357, 358–61; cf. Sorabjee, *The Emergency*, 15–24; but for the trials and tribulation faced by a journalist couple during this period see Kapoor, *The Emergency*.

[105] It was published under his name because meanwhile the Emergency had been lifted; see Michael Scammel's foreword Soli Sorabjee, *The Emergency*.

Tent ICH blocked precisely this view, and so its removal became an essential part of his project. "It is of historic coincidence that Tent [ICH] had the same fault of being at the crossing point where the Parliament Street connects with the CP and blocking the gaze that wanted to look beyond". This connection is far-fetched and the authors forgot that Tent ICH was in the premises of the Theatre Communication Building which perhaps formed more of a block and was part of the demolition project. Moreover, Narayani Gupta pointed out that Aruna Asaf Ali Marg runs south-south-east of the CP and that she was not aware of any plan of having an undeterred view of the Jama Masjid from the Parliament House, and in fact till recent times one could have such a view from the CP end of Minto Road anyway; e-mail, 2 August 2013.

The Emergency, however, did not put a stop to the underground activities of the Congress (O), RSS and other opposition parties. Production and distribution of underground literature such as the weekly all-India magazine *Lok Sangharsh* (People's Conflict, printed in both Hindi and English) and the local *Jana Vani* (People's Voice) began in July 1975. These bulletins were copied in different centres in Delhi and distributed in the adjacent states. The RSS was especially successful in printing and circulating literature in Hindi on its role in the Opposition including the speeches by the members of the Opposition in the Emergency session of the Parliament in July 1975. With its extensive network of volunteers organized at the grassroots level, the RSS actively resisted Emergency and the countrywide *satyagraha* launched by leaders of the underground movement that saw thousands of agitators participating and courting arrest.[106] Similarly, there were protest activities in states with non-Congress governments, and members of different ages and affiliations carried out a series of explosions throughout the country between 23 October and 30 December 1975. Moreover, the Socialist Party leader George

[106] For the underground activities of the RSS see Christophe Jaffrelot, *The Hindu Nationalist Movement and Indian Politics, 1925 to the 1990s*, New Delhi: Penguin, 1999, 272–77; also Coomi Kapoor, *The Emergency: A Personal History*, New Delhi: Viking/Penguin, 2015, 130–33 and passim.

Fernandes, in spite of the warrant for his arrest, evaded the police and remained untraced for almost a year (Fernandes was arrested on 10 June 1976). Travelling and coordinating underground resistance throughout the country, Fernandes used his contacts with socialist leaders in the West to publicize the news on the excesses during Emergency and issue anti-Emergency statements in the Western media.

In a private communication Chander Mahadev, formerly a journalist with *The Indian Express*, and *TOI*, informed me how he and his friends including Gautam Varma, the son of the late Congress (O) leader Ravindra Varma were deployed by resistance leaders that included erstwhile members of Congress (Indira) and leaders of the Khadi Village and Industries Commissions in undermining the Emergency. Chander and his friends, casual, 'dope-smoking' Nizamuddin or 'Niza Town' boys meeting at the Tent, Cellar in Regal building and elsewhere were not under the lense of the IB. They worked from 7 Jantar Mantar, the office of Congress (O) where they set up the editorial office of the underground resistance newspaper *The Subterranean Sun*. They would meet resistance leaders at Jantar Mantar and Gautam, the major link to the think-tank would be given a part rupee note as a code for identification. The students met leaders like Kedar Nath Sahni, Surendra Mohan, Ravindra Varma and Subrahmaniam Swamy who appeared in disguise in the *Shamianą*. These leaders decided on the content of the newspaper and gave the students signed articles to be published in the cyclostyled editions. On one occasion Chander met George Fernandes dressed up as a coolie when the latter was staying at a hideout in New Delhi railway station. During another instance Ravindra Varma turned up disguised as a hakim with a long flowing beard, and after the meeting at the Coffee House, Chander and his friends dropped Varma at the Hamdard Dawakhana in Daryaganj. It is an irony that within three decades after the Empire had been forced to leave India, 50 British MPs from the House of Lords were now said to be making monthly contributions towards the publication of this organ for the restoration of democracy in India. The idea of the demolition of the Tent as an act of revenge on behalf of the authoritarian regime in view of the underground activities carried on by the Opposition is appealing to both the establishment and the anti-establishment. But the Tent was one of many other places where such meetings took place. Its demolition, in my view, was related to another project with far greater consequences for a larger section of the population of Delhi. Since the Tent ICH was in the premises of the Theatre Communication Building, the demolition of the latter as part of the proposed facelift of the capital sealed the fate of the Tent. Moreover, the nature of the ICH as a public space as evident from my research, and the spatial practices there during the Emergency as detailed earlier strongly suggest that there was no place for open dissent in the Tent during the Emergency. Even after the Tent was demolished, the Tea House (closed in 1984) and the outlet at Mohan Singh Place attracting many critics of Emergency, continued to operate. In addition, there was the Coffee Home on Baba Kharak Singh Marg—an initiative of the Government of Delhi—that would attract a few of the ICH regulars after the Tent ICH was taken down.

What is interesting in the context of the Tent ICH is that, little is said about the fact that for the Delhi Government, the location of the Tent ICH was a temporary solution. As noted above, already, when he allotted the Tent to the PRRC, M.C. Khanna, the Minister for Housing, had promised a better location of a more permanent nature. The Theatre Communication Building itself had already been marked for demolition. The memory of the resistance movement leading to the opening of the Tent ICH in 1964, being too fresh, perhaps stood in the way of closing it down. After the shopping complex at Mohan Singh Place on Baba Kharak Singh Marg next to the Regal Building was launched in 1968 to house the temporary stalls that had been set up in the area after Partition, the ICH had been allotted a permanent space there some time in 1969–70.[107] The importance of places like the ICH as a space for socialization can be gauged from the fact that already since then, in addition to the Tea House and the Tent ICH across the street in the inner court of CP, the outlet at Mohan Singh Place was also functioning. Being located at the very

[107] Gurnam Singh, interview, 7 January 2012; Pankaj Bisht and Anwar Rizvi, interview, 17 October 2012.

centre of the CP, the Tent could be reached from all directions. As it remained open from 9.00 am to 11.00 pm, allowing visitors the choice to sit either inside or stand outside, under the tent, or in the small part under the concrete roof of the Theatre Communication Building, or even in the open area in front. Things went on like this till the state of Emergency was imposed.

Meanwhile, the early 1970s saw the entry of Sanjay Gandhi, the younger son of Indira Gandhi into politics. Mrs Gandhi's fear that the Leftist elements she had brought into her government were trying to dominate her, and would in the long run overthrow her, inspired her to set up Sanjay as the right wing counterpart of the Left. As Sanjay Gandhi—a champion of social inequality and neo-liberal capitalism—began manoeuvring like an administrator, architect, politician and town planner, a perfect match of him could be found in Jagmohan Malhotra. Popularly known as Jagmohan, who as the vice-chairman of the Delhi Development Authority (DDA) had been the architect of the Delhi Master Plan that envisioned the modernization and regeneration of Delhi, now played 'yes man' to Sanjay Gandhi. A recent article emphasized the role of Jagmohan, an admirer of Baron Haussmann, Le Corbusier and Lutyens, as 'the master planner' who dreamed of the social and spatial transformation of Delhi into a seat of high culture, a city for the middle class, free of the poor.[108] One of the pet schemes Sanjay put forward was the non-political issue of the beautification and modernization of Delhi. This project included plans such as the demolition of slums and unauthorized makeshift colonies of the poor, widening of roads, improvement of the sewage and transport infrastructure, promotion of cleanliness and family planning. This was exactly what Jagmohan had dreamed of. When the Programme Implementation Committee comprising the top brass of the Delhi Government and the Delhi Corporation formed in August 1975, and set to the task of demolition and resettlement under the direct supervision of Sanjay Gandhi, the

[108] Sushmita Pati, 'Jagmohan: The Master Planner and the Rebuilding of Delhi', *EPW*, 49.36, 6 September 2014, 48–54; Jagmohan, *Island of Truth*, New Delhi: Vikas, 1978, 174.

'sensitive concern for the human condition became a peripheral one'.[109] What followed was a ruthless implementation of programmes of demolition and resettlement in the name of development. Thousands of poor families were forced to leave their shanty homes, which were razed to the ground, forcing them to migrate to other areas without any offer of an alternative accommodation. The map indicating the key sites of demolition reminded Emma Tarlow of a bombardment plan rather than one of development, and her study of a single resettlement colony showed that the inhabitants were from as many as 80 different locations throughout the capital. Nearly 700,000 people were dispersed outside the city, and more than 160,000 men were sterilized.[110] The bulldozing of the Theatre Communication Building and the Tent ICH has to be considered against this larger plan of beautification and modernization, what Gupta has termed as 'thoughtless and unnecessarily hasty efforts of technocrats to decongest (and dehumanize) this area'.[111] In view of the human tragedy resulting from this drastic facelift of the capital, the demolition of the Tent ICH becomes inconsequential.[112] That the movement led by JP petered out and could not be resuscitated in the post-Emergency period lay in its inherent contradictions, not because the Tent had been demolished.[113]

Scholars like Sudipta Kaviraj and Arvind Rajagopal have pointed out that the Emergency marked a watershed in Indian history. By

[109] Vasudev, *The Two Faces*, 120.

[110] Emma Tarlo, *Unsettling Memories: Narratives of the The Emergency in Delhi*, London: Hurst & Co, 15–16.

[111] Gupta, *Delhi*, 180.

[112] Nayar, *The Judgement*, 87–88; Vasudev, *The Two Faces*, 134–38, 142–44, 164–67; for the coming into being of a particular resettlement colony, see Emma Tarlo, 'Welcome to History: A Resettlement Colony in the Making', in Véronique Dupont, Emma Tarlo and Denis Vidal (eds.), *Delhi: Urban Space and Human Destinies*, New Delhi: Manohar, 51–74; and Tarlo, *Unsettling*; for some of the architecture in the 1970s and 1980s see G. Menon, 'The Contemporary Architecture of Delhi: The Role of the State as Middleman', in Véronique Dupont et al (ed.), *Delhi: Urban Space and Human Destinies*, New Delhi: Manohar, 145–56.

[113] Cf. Frankel, *India's Political Economy*; Jaffrelot, *The Hindu Nationalist Movement*.

monopolizing the communicative space represented by mass media during this period and by replacing the Nehruvian model of state-backed developmental economy with the market-oriented liberal economy, in the period after the Emergency, the categories of culture and community became points of reference for political intervention, leading to a major reorientation of the model of governance.[114]

Jagmohan was very much a representative of this liberal economic sentiment. Faced with the charges of excesses committed during the Emergency by the commission of inquiry set up in 1977, he defended 'what was done in Delhi' during this period as *development* and not 'demolition'.[115] In recapitulating the saga of the triumph of the system of instrumentality over the system of integrative communication on social issues in laying the foundations of Ninth Delhi, Jagmohan 'the doer' could conceal his liberal agenda by taking a dig at his critiques:[116]

> ...was it wrong to shake off lethargy, eliminate "gossip café" from our offices, relieve the tyranny of Kafkaesque world of papers, full of sound and fury, signifying nothing? Is it not correct that the speed attained during the emergency should be normal if we have to extricate ourselves from the vicious grip of *poverty and underdevelopment... Can we be really free if the gap of our productivity and that of the developing world goes on widening*?

The 'gossip café' was of course an allusion to the ICH. Ironically, to those who had been a part of the resistance, the demolition was an acknowledgement that they had posed a real threat. But the vision of a 'modern', air-conditioned underground market with a park above in the heart of the city received a vigorous administrative and capitalistic push as part of the developmental project aimed at making the capital free of the poor. The 'ugly' barracks from the 1940s, together with the makeshift Tent had no place in that plan.

[114] Sudipta Kaviraj, 'A Critique of the Passive Revolution' in *EPW*, n. 23.45–47 (1988) Special Issue, November, 2429–44; Arvind Rajagopal, 'The Emergency as Prehistory of the New Indian Middle Class', *Modern Asian Studies*, 45.5, 1003–49.

[115] Jagmohan, *Island of Truth*, New Delhi: Vikas, 1978, 1, and especially the chapter 'Demolition or development?', 57–76; emphasis added.

[116] Ibid., 111–12; emphasis added.

CONCLUSION

Social practices can only be understood in their articulations with historical events. The epigraphs to this chapter sneer at the idea that coffee house sociability can be linked up with active political action. I have argued above that the average 'everyday interaction' of the petty bourgeois who patronized the Coffee House for his leisurely *adda* had the potential and did link up the 'system' with the 'lifeworld' through institutional and normative interactions.[117] The reader would recall, that small teashops in colonial India played an important role by accommodating *adda* and sympathizing with the revolutionary cause. In the same way, the informal ambience of the ICH indeed facilitated sociability among its customers. But as the customers in their individual capacity brought up social issues and articulated their opinion in public, the social space was transformed into a public sphere. The social practices of the urbanites at the coffee and tea houses in modern India combined both these realms.[118] Consequently, if in the post-Partition period the Coffee House in Delhi rose above the logic of Partition by publicly criticizing the divisive politics based on religion, in newly independent India personalities like Acharya Narendra Deva, Ram Manohar Lohia, Acharya J.B. Kripalani, Janeshwar Mishra and others kept the discourse against anti-single political party dominance alive. The ideological discussions inspired by them generated and mobilized public protests and anti-state movements. While the casual conversations in the Coffee House were interspersed with discussions of a normative character, it also

[117] Sherry B. Ortner, 'Theory in Anthropology since the Sixties', Nicholas B. Dirks et al, *A Reader in Contemporary Social Theory*, Princeton, NJ: Princeton University Press, 1994; Asutosh Varshney, *Ethnic Conflict and Civic Life: Hindus and Muslims in India*, New Haven: Yale University Press, 2002.

[118] Cf. Public sociability is combinable with the civic perspective of the public sphere, Jeff Weintraub, 'The Theory and Practice of Public/Private Distinction', in Jeff Weintraub and Krishan Kumar ed. *Public and Private in Thought and Practice: Perspectives on a Grand Dichotomy*. Chicago: University of Chicago Press, 1997, 1-42, 23–25.

shows that at least till the late 1960s the state allowed citizens certain freedom to openly express their anti-state sentiments and pay attention to that critique, which is remarkable in view of the world politics during these decades of the Cold War. This was also a time, when the consumer counted every paise he paid for his purchase, and a 5 paise increase in the price of a cup of coffee in the Coffee House was enough to give birth to a movement that was not confined to the coffee-drinkers or the customers of the Coffee House alone. As this increase was part of a general rise in prices of all essential commodities that affected all households adversely for some time, it appealed to ordinary citizens in different parts of Delhi who voluntarily participated in the PRRM and organized an alternative to what they found unacceptable. The Movement was also able to mobilize political support obliging the government to heed to their demand by curbing prices of essential commodities in general, and by setting up a new outlet handed over to the ICWCS. While allowing political leaders to hijack what began as a citizens' initiative, the members of the PRRM also failed to take a common stand against market forces. Consequently, the Movement failed to create a common forum of a more permanent nature but not before it had demonstrated the potential of the public place of the ICH as a site of mobilizing protest, and a mediating point between the system on the one hand and the life-world on the other.

Both in Calcutta and Delhi, the years preceding, and during the early phase of the Naxalite Movement, young students inspired by the radical ideology engaged in open democratic debates and discussions that helped them to get acquainted with the world outside the academia. In Calcutta, their interaction with others helped them to garner wider support for their cause outside the Party from other occupants of the place including senior members like the artist Debabrata Mukhopadhyay and the semi-literate workers who sympathized with their cause, and helped them in different ways. Their spirit of courage and sacrifice not only inspired generations of poets, it still acts as a source of inspiration for both cultural production and political activism.

Launched as a direct result of the PRRM, the Tent naturally embodied the public sphere. The repressive measures adopted by the government during the Emergency meant, however, that there was no scope for free and open discussion on politics or the generation of publlic opinion in the public space of the ICH. The arrest of the main leaders of Opposition, numerous political activists, journalists and others for indefinite period of time induced other political activists to go underground. In my view, this seriously undermined the role of the Tent Coffee House as a public sphere. The Tent had been from the very beginning a temporary location and pulling down of the Tent was unavoidable as it stood in the premises of the TCB, its demolition being inspired by the alliance of administrative-capitalist forces that design and redesign space, and in this case, planned to 'modernize' and 'beautify' the capital.

The politics of authoritarianism and allegiance at the centre and state since this time resulted in an apolitical attitude in society in general. In recent decades however, thanks especially to the revolution in the communication world and the expansion of the mass media the level of political awareness has undergone a transformation.[119] This has created new sites of public sphere. Does it signify that the ICH has become redundant as a site of public sphere? A radical change in the nature of politics and the quality of the political leaders since the Emergency meant that politics became more and more dependent on narrow ideologies such as caste, party, region and religion. As elsewhere in the world, the failure of the political Left to come up with a viable option to the aggressive global capitalism, fundamentalism and the increasing economic disparity between the rich and poor resulted in a disillusion with the Leftist parties. Consequently, the public sphere of integrative communication is increasingly undermined. There has been an overall degeneration of the debates on public policy and one of the consequences of these processes is that a considerable section of the urban middle class has since grown apolitical. For sections of the urban middle class, the ICH is still a place where they can get together both as an individual, and

[119] Bhandari, 'Civil Society'.

as a member of the civil society.[120] The outlets in Allahabad, Calcutta and Delhi host gatherings and meetings that intersect the so-called conflicting worlds of everyday interaction and associational practices including engagement with popular debates retaining the potential of concerted political action.[121]

[120] The Allahabad ICH is still visited by local wheeler dealers like Ashok Vajpayee, the former SP MLA Radhey Shyam Bharti, Jagpat Dubey (the former personal advisor to Jawaharlal Nehru and Indira Gandhi who is a regular from the last 35 years), Jan Morcha sympathizer Bimal Chand Mohiley, (son of Chunnan Guru), Avadesh Dwivedi, and hardcore BJP supporter and member of the prestigious Hindi Sahitya Sammelan Vibhuti Mishra. Interview, Ramchandra Jaiswal (60 years, a regular during the last 30 years), D.S. Bhandari (65 years, a regular since the mid-1970s) and S.K. Jaiswal (60 years, visiting the place for the last 15–20 years) 22 January 2012; also Sutirtho Patranobis, 'This Allahabad coffee house brews politics', *Hindustan Times*, 25 April 2007.

[121] See Chapter Seven for recent developments in this connection.

CHAPTER SIX

How Public is the Public Space of the Indian Coffee House?

Set up in the 1930s, the chain of the ICH was to some extent similar to the public sphere Jürgen Habermas described. Like the bourgeois public in the Habermasian public sphere, the petit bourgeois in the public sphere of the ICH had the tendency to claim the place as its own and their attempts at delineating a boundary within this space were often quite obvious. The gentlemen at 5CA did not mind revealing their ungentlemanly self during their *adda* in the place. At the same time, the late colonial and post-colonial India Coffee House was different from its early modern European counterpart in that it became a ground for the struggle of the working class, when they took up the challenge of being robbed of their work and living space, and successfully encountered the coffee capitalists. This chapter seeks to understand to what extent the space of ICH is accessible to different segments of the public usually termed as 'private'. The previous chapter saw how the spatial practices at the Coffee House linked up the private world with the public space. This chapter will take a close look at a few different social groups of the public and their relationship with the ICH in the cities covered in this book. I consider, however, these 'other' segments of the public not as a 'counterpublic', but as segments of the public kept out of the public sphere and exploited by traditional forces guided by feudal and patriarchal values of society. I argue here that the association of this public in different capacities, whether it is women, or members of the working class, is not to formally represent the respective gender or class; nor do these groups consciously lay claim on the public. But embedded in life outside the Coffee House, the practices involved nonetheless make them part of the social space.[1] The Coffee House is thus a zone where overt and covert exclusion of different natures is constantly being questioned by emerging social practices.

The bourgeois rational sphere Habermas presented was inhabited only by men. Relegated to the private realm, the lived experience of women for example was excluded from the coffee houses presented as a place of male conviviality. The proletariat too was conspicuous by its absence from this domain of the bourgeois elite.[2] Geoff Eley emphasized that the absolute state was not the only concern of the bourgeois public; they were equally vocal on the need to contain the popular element in the public, and that the public sphere was 'always constituted of conflicts'.[3] Oskar Negt and Alexander Kluge have labelled the struggle of the proletariat as the counterpublic sphere, constantly threatened by hegemonic forces that use exclusionary techniques by imposing high culture, and systematically suppressing any force that might lead to the creation of an alternate horizon of experience of the non-bourgeois, sub-cultural and even the fascist. While the bourgeois public depends on the forces of production, the counterpublic sphere takes over the left-over of the bourgeois public sphere.[4] The coffee houses in Ottoman Istanbul had a carnivalesque, multi-dimensional character, and as the venue of theatrical performances, story-telling, shadow

[1] Acting in individual capacity a female visitor of the ICH can be a Maoist or feminist or lesbian or all three at the same time, networking with members sharing similar affiliation, ideology etc. But women visiting the space do not follow a common political agenda just like Muslim patrons do not frequent the Coffee House to talk about their religious identity. Moreover, ethnic minorities are not seen coming to the ICH as a group but with friends and like-minded citizens across religious boundaries.

[2] Habermas notes the existence of a separate plebian public sphere but according to him the only occasion when it assumed a crucial role was during the French Revolution after which it became insignificant, *Structural*, xviii.

[3] Eley, 'Nations'; Markman Ellis, 'The Coffee-Women, the Spectator and the Public Sphere in the Early-Eighteenth Century', in Elizabeth Eger and Charlotte Grant (eds.), *Women and the Public Sphere*, Cambridge: Cambridge University Press, 27–52.

[4] Negt and Kluge, *Public Sphere*.

theatre and literary production, attracted the rank and file of the society, predominantly male.[5]

Feminist writers like Fraser, Landes and Ryan have underlined that women's relationship with the public has historically been most problematic and tenuous.[6] Joan Landes has argued that in opposition to the prevalent woman-friendly salon culture that was being described as effeminate and aristocratic, the new republican public sphere in France under the Jacobins pursued a manly, rational culture and campaigned for the adoption of virtuous manners in appearance and speech that turned it into a gendered space.[7] In a powerful essay, Nancy Fraser holds that the public of the bourgeois public was never the only public. The civic, cultural and professional associations and clubs were meant exclusively for the bourgeois male who saw themselves as the 'universal class', and thus bracketing inequalities, used these networks as springboards for asserting power. They typically denied access to the traditionally marginalized social groups like women, other status and ethnic groups. These excluded groups, according to Fraser, formed a multitude of public spheres she termed as' 'subaltern counter public' of nationalist public, elite women public, working class public and popular peasant public, and consequently, the bourgeois model of public sphere was never real but a hegemonic masculinist concept created with the purpose to legitimate the emergent form of class domination.[8] Others again have noted that women were not entirely absent from the early modern coffee houses. Not only that many coffee houses had women

[5] Yasar, 'The Coffee-houses', 9.

[6] Mary P. Ryan, 'Gender and Public Access: Women's Politics in Nineteenth Century America', in Craig Calhoun (ed.), *Habermas and the Public Sphere,* Cambridge: MIT Press, 1992, 259–88.

[7] Joan B. Landes, *Women and the Public Sphere in the Age of the French Revolution,* Ithaca: Cornell University Press, 1988.

[8] Fraser, 'Rethinking the Public Sphere'; Fraser's 'subaltern' is based on Gayatri Chakraborty Spivak's 'Can the Subaltern Speak', while 'the counterpublic' on the 'Counter-public Sphere' in Rita Felski, *Beyond Feminist Aesthetics: Feminist Literature and Social Change*, Cambridge, Mss.: Harvard University Press, 1989, 94, Felski again drew upon Negt and Kluge's work cited earlier.

as keeper or worker, and even though the spatial organization of the place clearly demarcated the woman's space from that of the gentlemen, women and the feminine figured in the coffee house in many other ways. In comparison with alcohol, coffee was an effeminate drink, poured by the woman of the house. Since the housekeeper of the coffee house in Europe was a woman, and women often lodged in a private part of the same tenement of which the coffee house was a public part, the coffee house instituted the public imitation of a private home.[9]

THE COFFEE HOUSE AND ITS ENVIRONS

College Street in Calcutta, also known as *boipara* (neighbourhood of books, old and new) is not only at a central juncture leading to different busy commercial areas, it is also at the cross section of a variety of formal and informal economic activities that take place throughout the day and night. The booksellers with their permanent and makeshift establishments vending their ware draw customers from all classes of the society. For many customers of the ICH, permanent clients of some of these book shops, a visit to the place is combined with a glimpse at the latest arrivals. Those connected with the academia represent only one facet of the whole. The lanes and bylanes here, as noted above, are dotted with workplaces ancillary to book production, like bindery and printing, drawing a large section of the clientele of the that form the backbone of the book industry.[10] Workers of such places are not to be counted among the customers

[9] See for example the description of an English coffee house-cum-lodge where not only the keeper was a woman, the occupant of one of the rooms too was a woman taking temporary refuge there, M. Voltaire, *The Coffee House or Fair Fugitive: A Comedy of Five Acts,* London: Printed for J. Wilkie, 1763; for the Blurred Boundaries of the Private and the Public in the Coffee-house, Emma J. Clery, 'Women, Publicity and the Coffee House Myth', *Women: A Cultural Review*, 2.2, 1991, 168–77; Cowan, *The Social Life*¸ 251–52; for the feminist public sphere, modeled on the public sphere of Habermas, Felski, *Beyond Feminist Aesthetics*.

[10] Ashok Sen, 'The Bindery Workers of Daftaripara', Occasional papers no. 127 and 128, CSSSC; also Roy *College Street,* especially v. 1, ch. 16, and passim.

of the Coffee House; but the latter have a close business relations with them, often meeting them at the ICH.

Soon after the College Street Coffee House closed its doors at 9 pm, the College Street market is taken over by wholesalers unloading truckloads of vegetables and fruits feeding into different markets in the city and its suburb. On Tuesdays, a floating population consisting of daily passengers from places outside Calcutta, with orders from booksellers in the interior requisitioning their week's stock, visits the bookshops in the area. The ICH being the *only* public building with public facility and a free entry in the entire College Street area, many of these weekly visitors find their way to the ICH in order to relieve themselves.[11] The middle class description of the *adda* in the ICH naturally does not take this population into consideration.

In the 1960s, the ICH used to vend coffee among the booksellers on the pavement, a practice discontinued for some time now.[12] Currently, bookstalls in the same building like Rupa, Chakrabarty, Chatterjee & Co., and in the immediate vicinity. Like *Ekushe* further down Bankim Chatterjee Street, that has a small *adda* of its own, sometimes get coffee when they have customers or visitors.[13] The fact that from 1958 onwards the outlets of ICH are run by members of the working class, is perhaps the reason why the thresholds of class boundaries can be constantly compromised here by the life experience of those occupying the space inside, and of those around the outlets.

[11] Ritajyoti Bandyopadhyay, interview, 6 June 2013; it is a fact that most old-fashioned eateries such as Putiram, Favourite Cabin and the *sherbet* shop Paramount in the neighbourhood do not have any toilet. During the field research for this work I asked the female owner of Dilkhusha at MG Road crossing, if there was a toilet for customers to use. She thought I needed to use the toilet, and hurriedly pointed to the public pay toilet further down the road. Public rest room is further available at College Square, but one has to pay in order to use the facility, and if an alternative is available, it is normal that people will opt for that; note that small tea houses emerging in small towns in China in the first half of the twentieth century already had a toilet, Wang, *The Tea House*, 286.

[12] Roy, *College Street*, 105; ICH in Bangalore still follows this practice.

[13] The owners of the cigarette shop and the two bookstalls on either side of the entrance can be seen using the rest room of the ICH; the workers often supply the owner of the book-stall coffee on the spot.

As consumption of coffee or tea often goes together with the intake of tobacco, many coffee and teashops in India had an adjacent cigarette shop, just as they are there now. Almost all such cigarette shops are known for allowing customers—student or otherwise—to buy on credit. Many customers at Trivandrum preferred to have a *paan* or betel leaf after they had their coffee, hence there was a mobile *paan* vendor catering to their need.[14] The livelihood of the owner of such places is closely associated with the ups-and-downs of the coffee/tea-shops they serve and by obliging generations of clients, they too have become a part of the establishment, like in the case of the ICH.

There are cases when this association with the ICH provides members of this group with an opportunity to climb up the social hierarchy. Many old-timers of ICH Calcutta fondly remember Ismail Chacha who began a cigarette shop with a small wooden cupboard facing the entrance at the foot of the staircase in the building. A migrant from East Pakistan, Ismail began this shop sometime in the early 1950s.[15] It was common for boys growing up and attending school in the neighbourhood of the ICH, to have their first cigarette purchased from this shop. This was the only shop in the immediate neighbourhood with stocks of not only cheap brands like Charminar, but exclusive brands like 555, an attraction for university students especially in the beginning of the month when they had just received their monthly allowance.[16] After Ismail passed away sometime in 1972–73, his sons Kader and Khalek took over the shop. When they wanted to sell the shop and return to their village in Bangladesh, it was taken over, in 1990, by Bangshi Nandi who now runs the place together with his brother-in-law Swapan Kumar Dinda. Bangshi, originally from Hughli,

[14] At Anna's arcade this mobile shop was replaced by a small fixed shop in the early 1990s.

[15] The shop has been renovated and refurbished. Goods for sale are displayed in a cupboard with see-through glass doors fitted with aluminum frame. This is also a place to top-up the balance of cell-phones. The latest addition to the stock of their wares are books, Swapan Kumar Dinda and Bangshi Nandi, interview, 12 and 15 July 2011 respectively.

[16] Bodhisattva Kar, interview, 7 November 2011; Ritajyoti Bandyopadhyay, interview, 6 June 2013.

used to stay with his relatives in Thanthania in north Calcutta. He dropped out of school during the tumultuous years of the Naxalbari Movement when he thought attending school did not make much sense. He was familiar with Ismail and his sons, whom he visited at the shop. Currently, they pay Rs 350 as rent for the shop-space to Bhabi Properties, the owner of the building. As cigarette began losing its popularity due to the government's anti-tobacco campaign, the brothers-in-law started exploring other areas including selling books, chocolate and candy, incense sticks, pre-paid sim cards etc. They have a long-term relationship with many ICH customers who still buy on credit. Asked about their income from the shop, the current owners evaded the question with a smile, but Dinda added later that the income was sufficient to feed and clothe them (*kheye pore chole jaay, didi*). The profit from the shop has enabled them to construct a brick-house in their ancestral village where their children attend school. Responding to the question pertaining to the relationship of his shop and other shops with the ICH, Dinda replied that they were all so busy with their own small businesses, managed by single persons, that they did not have the time to take a break and go to the Coffee House:

> It is not because it is expensive that we cannot go there. Everything has become more expensive.... A packet of cigarette that used to cost 10 rupees now costs 25 rupees, so the Coffee House is not an exception; but even if the Ganga flows close-by, you do not have the time to take a dip.

In other words, he does not sit in the ICH to have a cup of coffee. Yet, he goes upstairs to the ICH at least twice a day, at around 11.00 am, and again when Bangshi takes over the charge after 6.00 pm, to chat with the workers many of whom have become his friends, and in order to use the restroom. Does he think it is possible for him to sit upstairs in the hall and order a cup of coffee? It should be possible as many other small traders indeed visit the Coffee House, but he would rather share the back-space together with the workers and drink his coffee there than to place an order with them and have it brought to him.[17]

[17] Bangshi Nandi, interview, 12 July 2011.

Tapan Pramanik and Kamal De, owner of Bankim Book Stall and Sarada Book Shop on the left and right respectively of the entrance of the ICH, have coffee occasionally brought to them when someone visits them. Although very much aware of the importance of the place, as they have seen many celebrities visiting the ICH, they seldom have the opportunity to go up.[18] Apart from the owners of the cigarette shop, the owners of the book stalls lining the pavements of the streets in the neighbourhood are often familiar with the customers of the ICH, but have no direct connection with the Coffee House.

The sudden displacement accompanying Partition forced many members of the middle class to begin afresh from a very humble beginning across the border. Uma Vasudev recalled Sudarshan Seth, the young refugee from Pakistan whose family was able to convert all their belongings into a gold bar hidden among *chapatis* packed for the journey across. He began a small pen shop in front of the ICH, Janpath, and eventually became an established businessman. Customers of the Tea-House in Delhi noted the *paan* shop at the entrance. One additional attraction of these inconspicuously small shops was that they not only sold on credit, but if a customer was for some reason in sudden need of petty cash, the owners were a never-failing quick source of money at hand. From Krishna Sobti and Uma Vasudev in Delhi to Sunil Gangopadhyay in Calcutta, the customers of the ICH fondly remembered the humble owner of the respective shop as part of the institution of the ICH.[19] This tradition continues even now, as students and other familiar customers in College Street regularly approach Swapan Dinda when they need petty cash.

The people outside the ICH at Allahabad, especially the owner of the *paan* shop and the unofficial keeper of the cycle-stand in front, are quite conscious of the heritage of the ICH and the intellectual

[18] It was Pramanik, who informed me about the little magazine *Coffee House*. He sold me the Book Fair 2011 issue of the magazine and was instrumental in putting me in touch with its editor Ashok Raychaudhuri.

[19] Uma Vasudev and others would often borrow money from Sudarshan. In Calcutta Sunil Gangopadhyay recalled buying cigarette from Ismail on credit; cf. the *paan-beedi* shop owner adjacent to the Tea House in CP used to lend money to the writer Kamleshwar, 'Tea House', 76–77.

atmosphere inside. The *paan* shop at the entrance of the Coffee House, run by Shashimohan Dubey was started in 1972 by his father, the late Chintamani Dubey, a poor brahmin from Thattapur village in Akbarpur.[20] After Chintamani passed away, Shashimohan gave up his job at a cooperative bank and decided to take over the shop. He has been able to replace the old mud house in his village with a brick one, and his children are being educated.[21] Sardaprasad Dubey, a brother of Chintamani and currenty the keeper of the cycle-stand, according to a few, runs this business illegally. The area in front of the Coffee House is leased by the ICWCSL and Sardaprasad is supposed to pay a part of his income to the cooperative, but he does not. Sardaprasad showed me how on one occasion he held the hand of the former PM Viswanath Pratap Singh during one of Singh's visits to the Coffee House.[22] He does not go inside the ICH himself, but all the visitors including political leaders know him and often buy him coffee.[23] While bad blood marks the relationship between the uncle and nephew, the latter evidently cherishes his position at the elevated seat of his stall, which allows him to keep an eye on all

[20] Renamed Ambedkar Nagar by the Chief Minister Mayavati in 1995.

[21] Before he began the *paan* shop, Chintamani was the keeper of the cycle stand. Shashimohan informed me that the bank was not in a good shape, which guided his decision to make this switch and does not regret it.

[22] Sardaprasad Dubey, interview, 17 January 2012; I saw Rustam Gandhi (family of Feroze Gandhi) shaking hands with Sardaprasad; cf. Rajender at the DSE coffee house recalled he had often seen the former PM Manmohan Singh when the latter was teaching there; that time he 'did not know Singh was so important', Rajender, interview, 28 Februray 2012.

[23] Sardaprasad lives alone in a rented place in Allahabad, while his wife lives in the *dehaat* (village). He earns his livelihood by charging the visitors to the ICH for their vehicles parked in front of the ICH. There is no fixed charge as such but usually he takes 10 rupees for a car, 5 rupees for a scooter (but would also take 2 rupees). He has three children and at the time I carried on this field research, his daughter was studying M.A. in Kanpur, elder son was in Gujarat studying BA while working part-time, and the younger son was studying MA in Awadh University, Sardaprasad, interview, 21 January 2012; the retired university teacher Manas Mukul Das who introduced me to the ICH Allahabad, was visiting the place after a long time. As he saw Sardaprasad Dubey, a person he had known since he was a university student, he discreetly pushed a ten-rupee note in Dubey's hands.

those passing the front end, and he mocks at his uncle as the latter approaches owners of parking vehicles—cars, motorbikes and cycles, for his due. Individually, both are thick and thin with the workers-cum-owners of the ICH who share coffee with them in the privacy of the kitchen. The air these persons put on when they talk to a stranger demonstrates that they are the repositories of information as to the whereabouts of the Coffee House and its visitors.[24] They give their political opinions, exchange pleasantries and their thoughts on the condition of the city and politics at different levels as they serve their customers.[25]

The legacy of the ICH has often worked against the interest of the cooperatives. The popularity of the concept of the Coffee House gave birth to public places of various magnitudes offering coffee and

[24] P. T. Pradeep, the secretary of the Coffee House Allahabad in January 2012 told me that these two members of the Dubey family were very much involved in the internal politics of the ICH. The officiating secretary of the outlet was suspended on the charge of corruption and Pradeep had been transferred to Allahabad to take over. But he was an outsider, while other members of the cooperative were local recruits and had been there for a long time. So the deposed secretary, together with others wanted to see him gone, and were being supported by the *paan* shop owner and the cycle-stand keeper who were using their political muscle. By October 2012, Pradeep was indeed transferred, and the local employee, who had been suspended on the ground of corruption, was in the meantime reinstated as the secretary.

[25] While this is a personal observation on my part at all branches of the Coffee House visited, this was confirmed at Allahabad by Anita Gopesh. During my stay at Allahabad, Shashimohan offered me a *paan* at least once a day. As he would prepare the *paan*, he would take the time to make a small talk and inquire about the progress of my work. I would ask him whom he had seen during the day, and what news he had. One day he told me there was someone waiting for me inside. I was surprised as I had no appointment at that time, and saw among others a large group occupying two tables joined together. As I did not know anyone of them, I went out and asked Dubey what he meant. He replied that the local political leader Ashok Vajpayee was there along with his clout. Cf. 'the *paanwallah* at the entrance of the Tea House ....can inform at any time when Nagarjun is to visit the place, if [Mohan] Rakesh is sitting there or has already left, if....Ramesh Gaur has received any payment for any work, since when....Sarveswar Dayal Saxena has not visited the place, what are the new projects of Jagdish Chaturvedi, why ...Jawahar Chaudhary, Ajit Kumar and Dr Devishankar Awasthi have become less frequent here, why Prayag Shukla is separated from 'Rani,' or when the next issue of *Das kahaniyan* is due', Kalia, *Ghalib*, 70.

South Indian snacks in competition with the original institution. In Allahabad, till the end of 2012, the Amber Coffee Shop on M.G. Marg was a small concrete structure on the sidewalk of the main road comprising just the counter with an espresso coffee machine. Beginning in 1971, the shop welcomed its guests with a few chairs scattered here and there in front, selling instant coffee and snacks. This café was demolished on the eve of the *Purna Kumbh Mela* in 2013 as part of the beautification and street-widening drive that removed the road-side stalls encroaching upon the pavement area,[26] but is now located in the building housing offices and small shops in front of the ICH. Sipping coffee in front of this stall, customers could chat with those enjoying the hospitality at the New South Indian Coffee House a few paces away owned by Verghese, an ex-employee of the ICH. When he retired, instead of going back to his village in Kerala, Verghese decided to open this stall. Not that these places offer coffee (instant Nescafe) at a cheaper rate than that of the ICH, but many customers of the ICH could be seen sitting under the tree and enjoying coffee from a glass just because it is more convenient and pleasant sitting under a leafy tree (never mind the drain). Youngsters prefer to sit outside because the ICH is dominated by *dadalog*, the grandfatherly generation. Since they thrive on customers many of whom visit the ICH too, they belong to the same matrix, although they lure away new customers with the claim that theirs is the real 'Indian Coffee House', and they have a symbiotic relationship with the ICH.[27]

Moving further north to Delhi the same trend of association with the ICH providing opportunities in career building exists. Anthony (age 59) from Kerala joined the ICWCSL in Delhi sometime in 1972–73. He quit this job at the ICH in Delhi School of Economics (DSE) in 1979 when, together with a friend and a capital of Rs 6,000 he

[26] The makeshift stalls in front of the market on the other side of the street, together looking like a market, were also demolished during this time.

[27] P.T. Pradeep said when he was transferred to Allahabad he was dismayed to discover that if at the end of a busy day the ICH would run short of for example *sambar*, instead of preparing it fresh in their own kitchen, the workers would just go to the South Indian Coffee Shop with a pan, and ask for some!

had received from home, he left for Bombay to set sail for the Gulf, a popular destination for people from Kerala looking for opportunities outside the country. This friend was unfortunately run over by a train near the Bombay railway station compelling the traumatized Anthony to abandon the plan. Upon his return to Delhi with the corpse of his friend, he went back to the ICH in DSE. In the early 1980s, a few members of the Delhi University Teachers' Association (DUTA) asked him if he would take over the charge of the canteen in Venkateswara College. Gradually, he was able to expand his business by taking over the canteen in Ramjas College, and begin an independent catering business. Currently, he owns a house in Delhi and his son, who has an MBA degree in hospitality management, has joined him in the business while his daughter is a doctor, practicing in Dubai.

The story of Ambarnath Gupta (age 62), popularly called *dada* (elder brother) of the coffee house in DSE, is quite similar to that of Shashimohan Dubey in the sense that unlike most of the other ICH workers, they belong to a middle class family and have had access to education.[28] Gupta's father had been a central government employee in Delhi but since Gupta was not interested in studying, he joined the ICH in 1964. Initially, he worked as *masalchi* in Chandigarh, Delhi and Simla and became a member of the ICWCSL upon completion of his probationary period. Gupta said he knew V.K.R.V. Rao, the director of DSE who later became the vice chancellor of Delhi University, very well.[29] In 1984 when the Institute of Economic Growth (IEG) celebrated its silver jubilee, Rao was there for the last time when Indira Gandhi was invited on the occasion. When she came to the campus, her driver went to the ICH 'to get coffee for madam'. Gupta recalled carrying the coffee for Mrs Gandhi and handing it to her in person.[30] During his long career at the ICH in

[28] Ambarnath Gupta, interview, 28 February 2012; Sanjay Srivastava, Professor, Department of Sociology, Delhi University, interview, 12 June 2013.

[29] Rao, the director of DSE during 1948–57 and Vice Chancellor of DU during 1957–60, was a Union cabinet minister during 1963–69.

[30] This was shortly before she was assassinated; Ambarnath Gupta interview, 28 February 2012; I am grateful to Roma Chatterjee of the Department of Sociology, DU for introducing me to *Dada*.

the campus, Gupta not only came to know several economists and social scientists with whom he still has a social relationship, but also as a fellow member of a Bengalee Club in Kashmere Gate.[31] The members of the faculty helped him in filling up the home loan form and because he did not have the cash needed to make the down payment for purchasing house, they collectively made sure that he had the amount he needed for this purpose.

When the Coffee Workers' Cooperative decided to close down the DSE outlet in 1996, the then director K.L. Krishna offered Gupta the chance to take over and run the place.[32] He formed a partnership with Mr Chandran and has since carried on the business on a 50:50 partnership basis. It was then that they introduced the *thali* system for lunch. When I did the field research, Gupta was still in touch with many of the ex-students, some of whom later became teachers in the university.

The legacy of the ICH is also seen in the way Gupta recruited his employees. He had twelve employees mostly recruited by him through his networks of kin and neighbours from his native place in Medinipur, West Bengal on contract basis. In the informal labour market, the employment offered by Gupta served as a springboard for new recruits who learned Hindi while working with him, and could later move to better restaurants in Delhi.

This account of the connections with the ICH providing the public around it with opportunities for climbing up the socio-economic hierarchy will remain incomplete if I do not introduce the reader to Anandhan of Trivandrum. Every regular patron of the Anna's Arcade outlet was of opinion that a history of the ICH had to take Anandhan into consideration.[33] My inquiry about Anandhan revealed that previously he had a mobile *paan* shop he used to carry on his

[31] Kaushik Basu, Surjit Bhalla, Sukhamoy Chakravarti, R.K. Das, Veena Das, Mrinal Datta Chaudhury, Ashok Lahiri and Prannoy Roy, were some of the persons named by Gupta. In case there is a function at home, Gupta takes care of the catering; in case of a death he would supply manpower. When he hears that some retired academic has passed away, he cannot help feeling very sad.

[32] Popularly known as KL, Kosaraju Leela Krishna retired from DSE in 2000.

[33] Calvin Miranda, Nandu, Shashi Kumar, interviews.

shoulders, but now he has a shop near the shopping mall further down the M.G. Road near Statue Junction. From the vague reference to the the place, it seemed that he perhaps owned a stationary *paan* shop. But in fact I found him to be the owner of a rather fancy looking 'duty paid shop' manned by three persons selling cell phones and accessories in a shopping mall catering to the lower middle class. He admitted to having sold *paan* in front of the old ICH but later he came to own four cell-phone and other electric appliances shops in Trivandrum. He used to know all ministers, secretaries, under-secretaries and officials, filmstars, and other celebrities who would buy *paan* from him as they left ICH after having coffee. Among them was the Malayali actor Mohanlal who used to visit the place since his college days for his favourite *masala dosa* and coffee, a practice he continued even after he became famous. Rumour has it that Anandhan used his contacts to manoeuvre his way up. However, when asked if any of the VIPs helped him build his business, he was clearly irritated, as if it put a veritable question mark on his capability and reputation and that he did not need anyone's help in either setting up or growing his business! His somewhat mysterious behaviour led me to further inquire about him at the ICH when I came to know that Anandhan had allegedly been a smuggler, and had contacts with VIPs in the state. One of his sons was studying in Dubai while his daughter was preparing for her graduate examinations.

Although Anandhan's relation with his former clients is not clear, it becomes apparent from the discussion above that the ICH has a symbiotic relationship with a section of the society usually described as the 'counter-public'. While the workers as members of the cooperative run the Coffee House, it allows the adjacent *paan* and cigarette shop-owners, direct and indirect access to the place and its politics. Association with the ICH thus provides an opportunity to the humble member of the working class to negotiate his position in the informal labour market, and in the larger society in general.

Naturally, the public of the ICH contains the private in different ways. The outlets in the large cities pull workers who, coming from the village, have no place to stay in the city. Given their meagre salaries for sustaining themselves and their families back home, often many could not afford to rent a room elsewhere in the city. Consequently, in many outlets, after the working hours are over, the main hall is transformed into a communal bedroom for the workers. So the workers not only own the cooperatives, they consider the place as their home. Regular patrons of the place, especially students who spent a larger part of the day in and around the Coffee House often did not mind sharing with the workers the same facilities available to the latter.[34] The sharp distinction between the public and the private is stated to be a legacy of early liberalism and the rise of the centralized state.[35] Constituted of the private worlds of the working class, the public sphere of the Coffee House is inclusive of the private sphere too.[36] Focusing on the participation of women in this public place, the next section will dwell on the question of the private and the public in some more detail.

WOMEN AND THE PUBLIC SPACE OF THE COFFEE HOUSE

There is a fast increasing corpus of literature on the role of women in the public. As noted in the introduction to this chapter, scholars in the West have severely criticized the bourgeois public sphere of Habermas, where women were relegated to the private. This section will consider the role of the ICH in facilitating women's access to the public, reflecting in its turn, the role of women in this public space. Some background information on women's engagement with the public in the late nineteenth and early twentieth centuries India is in place here in order to understand the context.

Partha Chatterjee has argued that anti-colonial nationalist discourse in Bengal was constituted in and by the hegemonic

[34] As a student activist, Pheluram Banerjee spent many nights in the College Street outlet, Pheluram Banerjee, interview, 12 February 2011; Neelabh, e-mail, 17 August 2012.

[35] G. Mahajan and H. Reifeld (eds.), *The Public and the Private: Issues of Democratic Citizenship*, New Delhi: Sage, 2003, 11; Gupta in the same volume attests that the public and the private are antithetical to but affirmative of each other; D. Gupta, 'The Domesticated Public: Tradition, Modernity and the Public-Private Divide', ibid., 56–74.

[36] Cf. Calhoun, *Habermas,* 7.

male dominance that not only denied women any autonomous subjectivity, but also relegated women's question to be decided in the 'inner space' of the middle class home.[37] With their autonomy in that domain, women engaged in the literary public sphere, but politics remained a male bastion. However, Chatterjee has also demonstrated that the production of Bengali theatre adopting the conventions of popular narrative performance on the public stage targeting especially the English educated middle class, had a broader reach, and was able to create a popular public culture with women where the illiterate folk formed an important part of the public.[38] In her researches on women's education and access to the public in colonial Bengal, Tanika Sarkar has dwelt on the blurred boundaries between the public and the private. Formal education brought women a status equivalent to that enjoyed by widows and immoral women (prostitutes). Women's issues dominated the public sphere throughout the colonial period, initially on the question of widow-burning and later through the appearance of women in public and their participation in the literary public sphere.[39] Recent researches on the appeal for women to Gandhian ideology underlines the movement's emphasis on interrelatedness of all people, irrespective of gender, that enabled them to project the personal relationship into the public sphere while the public space penetrated the personal, thus removing the sharp distinction between the public and the domestic space.[40]

[37] Chatterjee, *The Nation*, especially 136–37.

[38] Chatterjee, *The Black Hole of Empire: History of a Global Practice of Power*, Princeton: Princeton University Press, 2012, ch. 8; for Bengali theatre in colonial Bengal see also Sarkar, *Rebels, Wives, Saints: Designing Selves and Nations in Colonial Times*, London: Seagull, 2009, ch. 4.

[39] The conjoining of the public and the private in modern Bengal has been extensively explored by Tanika Sarkar, *Words to Win: The Making of Amar Jiban, A Modern Autobiography*, New Delhi: Kali for Women, 1999, and *Rebels, Wives, Saints*; Chattopadhyay, *Representing Calcutta*; David Arnold, *Everyday Technology: Machines and the Making of India's Modernity*, Chicago, IL: University of Chicago Press, 2013.

[40] Shashi Joshi, 'Indian Nationalism: Feminism, Mass Movement and Gandhian Ideology', in Malashri Lal and Sukrita Paul Kumar (eds.), *Women's Studies in India: Contours of Change*, Shimla: IIAS, 2002, 223–41.

In Chakrabarty's analysis of the early twentieth century, there was a structural opposition between the domestic space and that of *adda* resulting in the creative endeavour of the Bengali intellectuals being undertaken in a 'homosocial space....With a sense of....phallic solitude'.[41] Chakrabarty's attempt at writing women off the public space, including that of *adda*, has been described as one of the most successful instances of cultural exclusion on behalf of the middle class Bengali male.[42]

Notwithstanding the large-scale entry of women in the formal and informal sector of the economy, and the positions of authority enjoyed by some women in politics, the role of women is economically, politically and socially determined by patriarchal authorities.[43] The hierarchical inner structure of the political parties in India allow little room for women to influence party politics, and when it comes to the question of capturing or staying in power, the question of women's representation is sacrificed in favour of party interests. Leftist movements, in spite of their support of the women's cause, were shy of offering them priority. This indifference is part of the wider arena of social values and practices as well as the representation of women in politics.[44] Recent researches of Sen have drawn attention to the systematic gender gap as far as opportunities are concerned; women's progress is marked at the same time by caste, class and community.[45]

[41] Chakrabarty, *Provincializing Europe*, 211.

[42] Chattopadhyay, *Representing Calcutta*, 185.

[43] Nirmala Banerjee, 'Analysing Women's Work Under Patriarchy', in Kumkum Sangari and Uma Chakravarti (eds.), *From Myths to Markets: Essays on Gender*, New Delhi: Manohar, 1999, 321–37.

[44] Malathi Subramanian, 'Women in Indian Politics: Participation and Representation', in Malashri Lal and Sukrita Paul Kumar (eds.), *Women's Studies in India: Contours of Change*, Shimla: IIAS, 2002, 242–61; for hindrances on the way of women's representation on the elcted fora, Vidya Munshi, 'Political Participation', in Jasodhara Bagchi (ed.), *The Changing Status of Women in West Bengal, 1970–2000: The Challenge Ahead*, New Delhi: Sage, 2005, 81–95; Mallarika Sinha Roy, *Gender and Radical Politics in India: Magic Moments of Naxalbari (1967–1975)*, London etc.: Routledge, 2011; Naxalite activist Krishna Bandyopadhyay's reminiscences 'Naxalbari Politics: a Feminist Narrative', *EPW*, 2008, 43.14, 52–59.

[45] Samita Sen, 'Towards a Feminist Politics: The Indian Women's Movement in a

Feminist scholars and activist groups have been vocal about the silence of the law with regard to the deep-rooted nature of normalization of sexual violence and the acceptance of impunity in South Asian society.[46] Concern regarding the sexual purity of women often uses the concepts of purity of class and caste as a dual source of oppression to reinforce patriarchal hegemony. The non-consensual, non-egalitarian relations often shockingly explode into the public arena in India revealing the unresolved double standards regarding the gender question never thoroughly interrogated in public.[47] The notion of male right over the female body is indiscriminate about age, caste, class or religion. In fact, attention has been drawn to the fact that notwithstanding the multi-faceted development in women's liberation achieved in the past hundred years of reducing the male-female relation to the confines of the bed, feminist discourse in the Hindi literary world focuses on the female body as suspect, weak and vulnerable.[48] It is important to remember this power structure as we take a closer look at the gender relationship, experienced in the different outlets of the ICH.

THE PIONEERS IN CALCUTTA

Unlike the teashops described in Chapters One and Two, from the very beginning, the ICH opened its doors to women. In the outlets in Calcutta there was no segregated space allocated for family or

---

Historical Perspective', in K. Kapadia (ed.), *The Violence of Development: The Politics of Identity, Gender and Social Inequality*, London: Zed Books, 459–525.

[46] Navsharan Singh and Urvashi Butalia, 'Challenging Impunity in Sexual Violence in South Asia: Beginning a Discussion', *EPW*, v.47.28, 2012, 58–63.

[47] Gruesome details of several cases of sexual violence against women drew the attention of the world to India while research for this book was on. On domestic violence see e.g. B. Purakayastha, et al, 'The Study of Gender in India: A Partial Review', *Gender and Society*, 17.4, 2003, 503–24; and Kumkum Sangari, 'Settled Alibis and Emerging Contradictions: Sex Selection, Dowry and Domestic Violence', *EPW*, v. 47.34, 2012, 39–48.

[48] Archana Verma, 'Stree Vimarsh Ke Mahotsav', *Kathadesh*, 2010, in response to the statement of Vibhuti Narain Rai that feminine discourse had been rduced to a 'grand celebration of infidelity'; also Kshama Sharma, *Stritvavadi. Vimarsh: Samaj aur Sahitya* (Feminist Discourse: Society and Literature), Nayi Dilli: Rajkamal, 2008.

women. A few female students of Presidency College began visiting the Coffee House in the late 1940s, especially university students from outside Calcutta staying in girls' hostels had the opportunity to taste their newly acquired freedom more freely in comparison with their day scholar friends.[49]

Asked if the Coffee House was a gendered space, the poet Sankha Ghosh, a student of Presidency in1949 and regular in Coffee House in the early 1950s, recalled that there was a separate *adda* of the men's common room, and the women's common room in Presidency College. There was a canteen in the college as well; but it was so small that he never entered the place as a student. The Coffee House was then known as the 'common room of Presidency College', and during 1950–54, Ghosh went there daily, often spending eight hours on end. The University of Calcutta (CU) had just introduced co-education at the post-graduate level. 'In the 1950s the ratio of male-female students in the university was 50:20, and almost the same ratio could be found in the Coffee House. You cannot call the place a gendered space', he recalled. His female friends used to visit ICH often, albeit few in number. In some cases, the romance that began at the ICH ended up in wedlocks. In fact, his own romance began at that very place and he proposed to Pratima, his wife, there.

Pratima Ghosh, an academic who taught at Berhampur College in Murshidabad, had graduated from a college in Jalpaiguri in North Bengal and joined the CU as an M.A. student in 1952, and was a classmate of Sankha Ghosh. In a personal interview she recalled that female students were fewer in those days compared to male students. Outside the university, the ICH was the only place where she could freely sit with her friends and talk over a cup of coffee. They had classes mostly between 11.00 am and 3.00 pm. When she used to

[49] Mixed groups were to be found in pre-independent Lahore and Lucknow too. The veteran CPI leader and activist Satyapal Dang who was born in Sheikhupura in pre-Partition Punjab had met his wife Vimala at ICH Lahore Gurcharan Das, 'In Praise of Unselfishness', *TOI*, 18 February 1998; for female students of Isabella Thoburn College in Lucknow visiting ICH with their male friends, see Hyder, *River of Fire*; Bhuvan and Rekha, the protagonists of Agyeya's *Nadi Ke Dweep*, set partly in the early 1940s Lucknow, meet in the ICH there.

go to the ICH with her friends after her classes in the afternoon, it would be always full, '*dole dole meyera jeten*'(several groups of women would go there) she recounted; and though girls usually had separate groups, some boys and girls would sit in mixed groups.[50]

Who were these women who went in groups to the Coffee House?

Since the number of women with access to higher education was comparatively limited in the 1950s, one has to consider this statement cautiously because even the opportunity to pursue higher education alone was not enough for visiting a place like Coffee House for leisure.

Contemporary fiction and films portray women of the middle and lower middle classes refugee families earning livelihood further blurring the lines between the private and the public. In order to help her family, an unmarried woman in Jyotirindra Nandi's novel *Baro Ghar Ek Uthon* (Twelve Families and One Courtyard, 1959) decides to look for ways of financial independence. Similarly, Shaktipada Rajguru's *Meghe Dhaka Tara* (The Cloud-Clapped Star 1960), immortalized on screen by Ritwik Ghatak we see the young Nita sacrificing her own happiness in order to support her family and losing her love to her younger sister in the process. In the case of such families, even if girls are encouraged to opt for higher studies in order to ensure economic security for the future, or women had to seek employment in order to lighten the economic burden on the patriarch in the family, the question of visiting the Coffee House would not arise. In Satyajit Ray's *Mahanagar* (The Big City 1963) Arati, the middle class housewife of a traditional family with live-in in-laws, is forced to take the job of a door-to-door saleswoman (we do not know about her academic qualifications) when her husband Subrata, a clerk, loses his job. After an initial feeling of embarrassment, Arati becomes confident in her role as the family's only breadwinner, but she is aware at the same time that she is disrupting traditional family roles. When her boss makes a disgraceful remark about his Anglo-Indian employee who has meanwhile become a friend of Arati's, the latter condemns him for his unfairness and, impulsively quits her job when he refuses to offer an apology to his wronged employee. In

[50] Pratima Ghosh, interview, 11 February 2011; also Roy, *Ekal Sekal*, 174.

her work on middle class refugee women of south Calcutta, Rachel Weber has argued that womens' participation in the public, instead of creating two exclusive domains of the private and the public, saw an extension of the domestic sphere to the public arena. Women joined political activism in the role of a mother, who protects her home. [51] Other scholars have reiterated this argument more recently.[52] These women portrayed in films/fiction, or the refugee women interviewed by Weber did not visit the Coffee House.

In Chapter Two I have argued that connoisseurs of the Coffee House from the 1940s onwards claimed that they belonged to the middle class. But the term (just like *bhadralok*) concealed the actual economic condition of the families ranging from landholders (Tapan Raychaudhuri) to that of an ill-paid school teacher (Sunil Ganguli). There were men like Bhetki who were permanently or temporarily unemployed. There were a few, who were dependent on the generosity of the better off members of the group. By contrast, it is easier to place their female counterparts in the Coffee House in the early decades. Compared to the men, their female counterparts seem to have come from a more comfortable and sheltered milieu. At least initially, female students pursuing university education came from the elite and well-off families, they received a larger allowance as pocket money, often the only source of refreshment their male friends in the group could rely on.[53]

Up to the 1970s, there was a social taboo on free mixing of the sexes in public. Partha Chatterjee recalled that more than a decade after co-education was a fact, in the mid-1960s male and female students used to sit separately in Presidency (but shared the same table in the Coffee House). Uma Das Gupta, who attended Presidency

[51] Rachel Weber, '(Re)creating the Home: Women's Role in the Development of Refugee Colonies in South Calcutta', in Jashodhara Bagchi and Shubhoranjan Dasgupta (eds.), *The Trauma and the Triumph: Gender and Partition in Eastern India*, Kolkata: Stree, 2003, 59–79.

[52] Gargi Chakravartty, *Coming Out of Partition*, New Delhi: Srishti Publications, 2005.

[53] Rudraprasad Sengupta, interview, 21 August 2011; cf. the fictional character Prem Burli, a rich Punjabi female customer of the ICH, buying coffee and snacks for her friends and others, Bhattacharya, *Albert Hall*.

(1960–62), and CU (1962–64) reminisced that the female students sat in the first couple of rows in the class. Their English teacher Amal Bhattacharya would encourage male and female students to sit together.[54] With reference to Nira, the fictional woman to whom many of Sunil Ganguli's poems were addressed, it has been noted that the name was a reconstruction of the words *nari* (a woman) and *rani* (a queen), both beyond the reach of the average Bengali middle class male.[55] The poet Kavita Sinha was the only female member in Sunil's *adda* group in the ICH. Once, when Nabaneeta Dev Sen walked up to their table in the afternoon looking for the poet Pranabendu Das Gupta, it became news. The thrill of excitement felt when she gave a pinch of sugar from the sugar pot on the table to each present at the table was such, that it was remembered and recorded even more than four decades later.[56] The following excerpt from the memoir of the Leftist artist Debabrata Mukhopadhyay is a testimony to the male chauvinism with regard to the presence of women in the space:

> Coffee House was then the common room of Presidency College in the afternoons. The college was by that time already a co-educational institution. ...It was around this time that one group of boys regularly used to take part in an *adda* in Coffee House centring one such girl. We, members of an *adda* group sans women, felt a little jealous. We called this girl "queen bee". One day I caught her in a sketch I made.[57]

Gender-based discrimination in public (and private) spaces persists in the new millennium, and is not limited to India; even outstanding scholar-writers face it everyday in myriad ways, and the fact that the presence of attractive and smart female visitors in the ICH attracted

[54] Uma Das Gupta, interview, 26 December 2011; in Allahabad too female students in the university entered the classroom as a group, sat in an area specified for them and left the room as a group. That however did not stop in the way of romance, Mehrotra, 'Partial recall', 23.

[55] Biswajit Roy, 'Je Purush Alajjo Drishtite Meye Dekhe, Take Dokhol Korte Chaay Na', *ABP*, 7 March 2014.

[56] Mukhopadhyay, 'Krittibaser Adda'.

[57] Mukhopadhyay, 'Coffee-r Cup', 64; Pratima Ghosh went to study M.A. in 1952 and the scientist Anjali Mukherjee who began her Ph.D. that year, had already studied B.A. in that college.

a lot of male attention, suggests that at least initially, women in the Coffee House were perhaps not many in number.[58]

The ICH at College Street, however, was a place that in the 1950s and the 1960s provided young adult women of established families a space where they could be on their own and develop their self-identity. Participation in discussions, initially among women, but then increasingly more among mixed groups, prepared them for participation in the larger world. The ICH helped them in extending their practice of sociability to the public. In this respect the Coffee House was different from most of the neighbourhood teashops visited by only men.[59] Consequently, the ICH was a safe destination for young women from *bhadralok* families. According to my female interlocutors, once inside the ICH in Calcutta, everyone received similar treatment, and the workers of the place made no gender-based discrimination, a practice that still prevails.[60]

Pratima Ghosh and her female friends never had any negative experience in the Coffee House. The atmosphere, friendly in the beginning, felt homely after a few visits when the workers knew the students and students knew the workers by their name. While money was a perennial problem with the men, for female students, the Coffee House specialties were one of the attractions of the place: [61]

> Coffee House was precisely the place we needed for relaxing, having good food, especially the thick omelette they used to make then with cheese, tomato etc.; or just for having coffee. There were tables where visitors would be animatedly discussing political issues; there were

[58] In response to my question regarding the presence of women in the ICH, Sunil Gangopadhyay informed me that a raving beauty in her youth, Gayatri Chakravorty (Spivak) who joined Presidency College in 1956 was the 'queen bee' sketched by Mukhopadhyay; consider also the comments on Uma Vasudev in Delhi.

[59] The difference in the infrastructure of the two sets of spaces has been noted in Chapter Two.

[60] Currently, if a patron finds an empty chair at a table (s)he is lucky and has to wait till a worker comes to take order. Depending on how busy the moment is, discrimination may be made here on the basis of (non) familiarity which determines when a visitor is asked if (s)he wishes to order something.

[61] Pratima Ghosh, interview, 14 February 2011.

> other tables where students would chat … an excellent, extraordinary place where you could go no matter how your mood was, and discuss issues accordingly.

Bharati Ray, who later became the Pro-Vice Chancellor of Calcutta University and a member of the Upper House in Parliament, was another female student of Presidency in the early 1950s to frequent the Coffee House.[62] The groups in the place according to her were usually mono-gendered, but the boundaries were fluid and that female and male students did not sit next to each other, did not stand in the way of romance.[63]

Just like their male counterparts who were overwhelmed when they discovered this new social space in the city, female interlocutors contacted in connection with the current work seemed to have been totally swept off their feet in their first encounter with the place. They cherished the memory as they talked about the days when a trip to the ICH was part of their routine. In order to understand this, one has to look at the social background of the young adult females of middle class families visiting the ICH or other places for socializing until the 1980s. Girls in middle class families in (and outside) Bengal generally had a protected life until they left secondary school, and entered college. Schools followed a strict discipline, and attending a girls' school already determined the gender of friends. Visit to a neighbour, or a friend's house, and an occasional movie together with friends were mostly the adventures a girl was allowed to undertake on her own. This changed entirely when the same girl went to a college as a young adult: the transition from school life to college life was their passport to freedom.[64] Indeed, even as college and university students women had to return home before dusk. But during the college hours, together with the time it took to commute between home and the college/university, one was practically free. In between

[62] Her father was in the Bengal Civil Service, Roy, *Ekal sekal.*

[63] There was no restriction in looking at members of the other sex across the tables leading sometimes to hilarious situations, and the male-female boundary in ICH was falling apart already when she visited the space, Roy, *Ekal sekal*, 176, 178.

[64] Uma Das Gupta, interview, 26 December 2011.

classes there was often a period or two free; and as the statement of Pratima Ghosh shows, students were free after the classes were over. Visits to the Coffee House was part of this newly acquired freedom that inspired the young women to explore different parts of the city as a part of exploring themselves.[65] When the waves of the feminist movement reached Calcutta in the late 1950s and 1960s, the Coffee House was the place where women could smoke freely. What was unthinkable in the college or university premises was normal in the Coffee House. Not only was the ICH the only public place where young Aparna Sen and others would be seen smoking; this was the place where young women could argue, and mix with members of the opposite sex for hours on end without the practice being decried.

If Pratima and Sankha Ghosh were one of the first couples here, soon the Coffee House seems to have become a place where potential young couples could safely court. A couple drawing attention in the place in the late 1950s was the would-be famous theatre personalities Rudraprasad Sengupta, the actor-director of the theatre group *Nandikar*, and the late Keya Chakrabarti, at that time both students. Their romance had a long, tumultuous period of courtship full of uncertainties during which much of the time spent outside individual homes was spent in each other's company at the Coffee House.[66] 'Looking back, it seems surprising now', Sengupta recalled, 'that there were so many women around in the Coffee House'. In the early 1960s, Uma Das Gupta (then Roy) used to sit in a mixed group together with Ram Roy, Malini Bose and Mihir Bhattacharya, students of the English department, in connection with the college magazine *Sanglap*. Later she would sit there together with the late Ashin Das Gupta, the newly appointed lecturer in Presidency College, the person she had met through a common family friend, and would marry later.[67]

[65] Ibid., Swati Lal, interview, 21 February 2011.

[66] Rudraprasad Sengupta, interview, 21 August 2011; cf. Dipanjan Roy Chowdhury, interview, 26 July 2011.

[67] Uma Das Gupta, interview, 26 December 2011; her batchmates Malini Bose and Mihir Bhattacharya too got married. Krishnanath Nandi (retired principal of Charuchandra College, interviewed on 24 August 2011) of the batch of 1959 also met his would be wife Shipra Chakrabarti in the ICH. They both studied in Presidency;

When she joined Presidency in 1966, the historian Tanika Sarkar, the daughter of Professor Amal Bhattacharya teaching there, went to the ICH on the first day of her college. In the beginning, she went with friends from her school, but very soon, the *adda* group became a mixed one, and the ICH was the only place in the neighbourhood for that purpose. As the college was the nerve centre of the Naxalite Movement, it affected the academic atmosphere there, and students would spend most of the time in the ICH. She became the core member of a mixed group that included Dipesh Chakrabarty (currently teaching in Chicago) of the Physics department. Literature, what happened in the class, and the teachers of different subjects, were the oft-discussed subjects. Dipesh used to write poems and lyrics and read out one everyday, which they would discuss.

That female students had their separate groups in the Coffee House is clearly evident from the 1950s through to the end of the 1980s. But gradually, an increasing number of female students had access to the ICH and by the mid-sixties mixed groups became common, and male and female classmates began addressing each other informally as *tui*. Krishna Bandyopadhyay, who joined Presidency in 1967 and subsequently joined the Naxalite Movement the same year, was a regular at the Coffee House until 1970 when she became a whole-timer and began working in rural Bengal. Whenever she had to see someone outside her college, she used to make an appointment at the Coffee House.[68]

Swati Lal, who joined Presidency College in 1973, cherished a similar pleasant memory when she related to the ICH. She had already heard a lot about the place from her father and other relatives, and had a romantic notion about the place even before she went there. In her experience, the ICH was something of an anomaly, a circus:

> The entrance [of the Coffee House] on the ground floor was dark....A thick cloud of smoke hanging in the air in the hall upstairs, and the buzzing sound of everyone talking at the same time deafened you.

---

she was in the department of English, and he was a student of Economics and had to attend his classes in the B.T. Road campus; but these are just a few examples.

[68] Krishna Bandyopadhyay, interview, 19 August 2011.

> You saw the workers moving around in their starched white uniform against this background.

Together with her girlfriend Chandra, Swati used to go to the place almost every day. There were ten female and six male students in her batch studying English as a major. Those young men were not very enthusiastic about the ICH,[69] but male students from economics and other subjects would sit in mixed groups with Swati and others. The three years she was in college, she discussed a sundry of subjects with her friends in the ICH, which worked as a forum where they could go on discussing the new things they learnt during the forty minutes' class in the college:[70]

> The discussions in the Coffee House were building blocks for the future.

Rupa's bookshop is in the left wing of the same floor as the ICH. Swati and her friends would save money to buy books. After buying new books, they would sit in the Coffee House together, to look inside the books:

> The flavour of coffee, new books and cigarette blended together, spoke of life in that place....the smoke, the noise were trivialities one had to ignore in order to experience the sphere of the Coffee House; something worth the trouble.

Swati emphasized repeatedly that the ICH was her passport to the world of adults, the key to adulthood:[71]

[69] Including Ananda Lal, her classmate and later her husband.

[70] Swati Lal, interview, 21 February 2011.

[71] Ibid., emphasis added; the role of the ICH in furthering the cause of women's liberation was emphasized by Partha Chatterjee in the interview he gave to this author. Keshto was favourite among female students in the late sixties too, interview, Tanika Sarkar. Keshto, the colloquial for Krishna, the mythical character from the *Mahabharata* who in his youth in Vrindavan was known for flirting with young women and for his liaison with Radha, a married woman, was not the original name of this Muslim worker. But once he had brought his Anglo-Indian girl friend to the Coffee House. None of the regular visitors could place her and when asked, the worker only grinned but remained silent. Since then he was named Keshto; Mukhopadhyay, *Coffee-r cup*, 37.

> It was very special; you went in, Keshto [their favourite worker] told you—*without the intervention of a guardian*—that there was a place free; a table you could sit at.

Coffee House was a place parents and other relatives were familiar with; the crowd, the haze of smoke, and the continuous, deafening buzz created an unique ambience. Shukla Ganguly, whose family migrated from the then East Pakistan in 1971, has almost a similar memory of the place. New in Calcutta, she attended Bethune College (1976–79) in Bidhan Sarani for her Bachelor's degree. The memory of the Naxalite Movement still haunting the collective memory of Bengalis both she and her elder brother, the latter studying engineering in Jadavpur University (JU), were asked by their parents to stay away from the ICH; yet both of them separately found their way to the place with their own group of friends, discreetly disobeying that injunction. Shukla recalled that together with her friends from Vidyasagar and City College, they would get off the bus near M.G. Road and walk in mixed groups toward the ICH. A few of the women in the group used to smoke.[72]

From Pratima Ghosh in the 1950s, Uma Das Gupta, Tanika Sarkar, and Krishna Bandyopadhyay in the1960s, to Swati Lal and Shukla Ganguly in the 1970s, women visiting the Coffee House considered their experience as an extension of the freedom that came with entering the university. In the view of Ghosh, Lal and Ganguly, the interactions with semi-familiar and non-familiar (male) persons in ICH prepared them for their later participation in larger public arenas. The practice of cross-gender sociability in the ICH that these women participated in, paved the way for young unaccompanied women to practice sociability in a public place, not experienced in

[72] Shukla Ganguly lives in Pune where she brings out a Bengali magazine. None of the siblings divulged the secret to their parents but exchanged notes on their experience in secret. For mixed group *addas* elsewhere in the city in the 1970s and 1980s, see Chattopadhyay, *Representing Calcutta*, 182–85; according to a few interlocutors, women stopped going to the Jadavpur Coffee House after smoking was banned in the outlets of ICH, Abhijit Mukherjee, interview, 21 February 2011; however, few of them can be still spotted there smoking together with male friends in the corridor.

the pre-ICH teashops. This is more significant than the number of women in the Coffee House in the 1950s and the 1960s.

As far as women in the ICH are concerned, a breakthrough in the Calcutta elite domination came in the late 1970s when poets and writers from the suburbia and the interior began visiting the place. Among them was the poet Anuradha Mahapatra from Medinipur, the editor of the little magazine *Bangoposagar*, who currently lives in Calcutta. By the time she began visiting the place, women were indeed coming in large numbers, and mixed groups of male-female students had become common, but women were definitely fewer in number compared to men. Anuradha married the poet Somak Das but the couple had different sets of poets and writers each interacted with, and preferred to visit the ICH separately.[73] Biswa Mandal, a poet and the librarian of Ashutosh College in Calcutta and the poet Kaushik Mitra, both known as the poets of the 1980s agreed in that male chauvinism was very much there in the Coffee House, reflected in the pattern of the visits of the two sexes. Up until now, women come as student, and also, as long they are not married. Once married, women would stop visiting. Trapped within obligations, often in combination with family and work, one lost the spirit in a system, that was, according to Mahapatra, still feudal. Sexism in the Coffee House notwithstanding, the place had been also a platform for debating and questioning, among other issues, the role of women in public space.[74] In a meeting organized by the poet Parthapratim Kanjilal in the 1970s, Shakti Chattopadhyay commented that women were not capable of writing poetry. Animated arguments followed for days in the Coffee House and Mahapatra did not talk to Chattopadhyay for years.[75] Mahapatra notes that with the passing of time that space of debate has eroded because at every step in life political allegiance is the first and the final word.[76]

The 1970s was also the time, when, at least a section of the Calcutta *bhadralok*, men and women, began distancing themselves

[73] That is the way I met them in the ICH.

[74] Biswa Mandal and Kaushik Mitra, interview, 4 February 2011.

[75] Kaushik Mitra, interview, 4 February 2011.

[76] Mahapatra, interview, 4 February 2012.

from the ICH. The culture of bloodshed and violence begun by the Naxalites and continued by the tripartite struggle for the control of the College Street area by Congress, CPI (M) and CPI-ML, while taking the city by horror, had partly stripped the area of its glamour. This was followed by the period of Emergency when only those who had no reason to fear, went to the Coffee House. On the other hand, as the schedule of the CU including classes and examinations continued to be disrupted—a legacy of the students' movements of the 1960s—an increasing number of students began to spend more and more time in the ICH, among them a large section from the suburbia, including women.[77]

That the Coffee House had meanwhile caught the imagination of ordinary women outside Calcutta, will be clear from one example.[78] Kumudini Roy, a resident of Burdwan, visited the ICH a couple of times in the late 1980s.[79] In late 1990, she left her home temporarily in order to protest against the marriage her parents were going to arrange for her. She took shelter in a women's hostel, began attending a morning college while teaching in a primary school during the day—following the sage advice of the hostel's matron. She did not know anyone, had no social contact when she began visiting the ICH regularly in 1991 in the evenings. In her own words, at that time, the Coffee House was everything to her. At that place she became familiar with the Radical Humanist Association, became a member of the Red Cross and the Save Narmada Movement, began writing for little magazines, and had a brief stint with the Maoist Movement in the late 1980s. After she was convinced, that she would not be married off, she went back home. Since then, she travels to Calcutta every Friday, visits the Coffee House on Fridays and Saturdays and usually goes back on Sundays. Visiting

[77] Swapan Kumar Chakravorty, the director of the National Library in Calcutta, who was a student of English in Presidency during 1972–75, found the atmosphere in the College and the University extremely male-oriented. The academic staff in good departments like Economics and Physics were all-male. In comparison, the Coffee House was full of women, Chakravorty, interview, 15 February 2011.

[78] For more on recent trends in the place, see Chapter Seven.

[79] This is not the real name of the person.

the Coffee House, she has joined many protest actions, including the civilians' protest against police firing on innocent villagers in Nandigram in 2007.

I have seen Ms Roy in the ICH during all my research trips. Of course she has unquestioned access to this public space, but I have also noticed a subtle hostility in the way she is sometimes shunned from certain tables. It is clear that she is a familiar face at that place; but she is not welcome everywhere. This kind of exclusion is, as we have seen in Chapter Two, part of the politics in the space, and as nothing further is said on either side, my role is nothing more than that of an observer. What is important in this case, however, is that she finds here what she seeks; and therein rests the significance of the Coffee House as a public space: beginning with the women of mostly elite families in the 1950s, it has helped a woman like Kumudini to negotiate her space in the public on her own terms.

DELHI

That young, ambitious and enlightened women used this public space without a male escort also holds true for the ICH on Janpath but the Coffee House public there did not hesitate to call them names:

> I remember the regulars: Surojit Sen, (English newsreader), Saeed Jaffrey (actor) and Reggie Carrapiet, as well as Roshan Menon—all from AIR; Dr Charles Fabri, Richard Bartholomew and his wife Rati, Veda Thakurdas, the first principal of Miranda House, poets Jaipal Nangia and Rakshat Puri, Uma Vasudev, Michael Overman of the Little Theatre Group and his wife, dozens of journalists, painters, budding politicians and struggling writers. Men and women mixed freely. We smoked like chimneys and argued for hours.[80]

Uma Vasudev, who had been in her mid-teens during the Partition and had a busy life as a university student playing tennis, learning Bharatnatyam, and editing *Surge* (later *Surge International*), used to go around in her own car freely. Her male contemporaries in the ICH

[80] Reginald Massey, e-mail, 16 July 2013.

called this ravishing beauty a '303'.[81] There were very few women seen alone in public spaces, [82] but Vasudev visited the ICH on her own as well as with her male friends and colleagues, with whom she used to 'hold court'. She would move in and out of the place several times a day in between her other obligations elsewhere, and since she had to talk to the contributors of her magazine to discuss the nitty-gritty of journal production, she would sit anywhere depending on the space available and the purpose of the visit. If she wanted to read something, she preferred to sit in one of the cabins. She would often also sit in the main hall when she would share the first table in the centre (as one entered the ICH) with Inder Kumar Gujral, then a civic contractor, Surinder Nihal Singh of *The Statesman* and Inder Malhotra (TOI), Ajit Bhattacharya and Rakshat Puri, also journalists, and they would all discuss politics animatedly. 'Were you aware of the sexist sobriquet you received at the place? Did you have to face any other sexist comment there? How did you cope with the issue at that time?' To this query of mine Mrs Vasudev responded that she never felt uncomfortable at that place, nor did she ever pay much attention to the sexist comments. There was one idler, also a regular at the ICH. He would brag to his friends that he had 'done it' with her (Uma Vasudev). When asked where, he replied that it was in the cloakroom of the Gymkhana Club. There was another person, a young journalist working with HT who had fallen for her and sent her a 90-page long letter, 'but people of this kind are there everywhere'.[83]

This aside, both Inder Kumar and Nihal Singh, when joined by their wives, just like Agyeya and Kapila Vatsayan, Richard and Rati Bartholomew and Satish Gujral accompanying his family, would always sit in the family cabin.[84] There were women, who went there because they had different kinds of pretensions of wanting to be seen in the company of well-known personalities and therefore would

[81] The reference here is to the 303 British Rifle using .303-inch (7.7 mm) calibre introduced in 1888 and widely circulated in the Empire especially during WWII.

[82] Sethi, 'Delhi-o-Delhi'.

[83] UmaVasudev, interview, 21 October 2012 and 17 July 2013.

[84] Jatinder Sethi, 'Delhi-o-Delhi: Memories of 1950s', Academy of the Punjab in North America, http://www.apnaorg.com/articles/sethi-2/.

also sit in the cabin. But women like Uma Vasudev, Roshan Menon, Krishna Sobti, Veda Thakurdas, Kapila Vatsayan participated in the general discourse and added to the quality of the discussions in the *adda*.[85] Social and political activists like Subhadra Joshi who took an active part in the formation of the cooperatives, belonged to this latter group.[86]

Notwithstanding the long association of female writers with the Hindi public sphere for many of them writing in the 1970s was still neither a full-time occupation, nor an art to talk about.[87] They would secretly write poems as well as prose and keep them hidden among the *sarees* in their wardrobes. At an opportune moment, they would send it to some editor's office by book post. Seeking a more direct contact with an editor by phone or through letter would earn them ill repute (*apyash*). Mamta Kalia reminisced that it was her friendship with Ravindra Kalia that not only gave her the courage to change that situation, but a sea of confidence that taught her to love not only him but also herself.[88] Working for *Akashvani* (AIR) was glamourous for women in the Hindi-speaking world, and as we have noted above, Roshan Menon visited the ICH together with her colleague Reggie Carapiett. At a time when discourses on tradition, modernity and comtemporaneity were not limited to literature, the ICH in CP, like Alps, Gaylord and other places that offered space to romantic couples often invited undue attention. Still, writers like Mridula Garg occasionally visited both Coffee and Tea House.[89] But Mamta Kalia's

[85] Reginald Massey, e-mail, 17 July 2013.

[86] Aruna Asaf Ali, Kamaladevi Chattopadhyay and Subhadra Joshi were a few among such pioneers.

[87] Orsini, *The Hindi Public Sphere*; Nijhawan, *Women and Girls*.

[88] Mamta Kalia, interview, 22 November 2012; also Kalia, 'Kitne Shaharon Mein Kitne Baar: Dilli', *Tadbhav*, http://www.tadbhav.com/site/tadbhav_issue_25/kitnea sahar_delhi.pdf; some of the female writers Kalia mentions in this connection are Mannu Bhandari, Indu Jain, Shenhmayee Chaudhari, Kirti Chaudhari, Nirmala Jain, Anita Aulak, Kanta Bharti, Monica Mohini, Mira Mahadeban, Mona Gulati and Prabha Dixit.

[89] Mridula Garg, 'Betartib Diary', in *DTH*, 296–312; see for example Jagdish Chaturvedi's account of his affair with Mona Gulati in Chaturvedi, *Connaught Place*; also Hardayal, 'Tea House', 508–9; Jagdish Chaturvedi and Ramesh Bakshi used to go to the Tea House with their respective fiancé, *DTH*, 509 and 520 respectively.

memoir about women in the literay world is a testimony to the limited access of the average middle class women to public space.[90]

The portrayal of women visiting such public spaces in Hindi fiction confirms the sexist attitude their male counterparts cherished about them. Rajkumar Saini's novel *Khidki Se Jhnakta Hain Kaun* begins with the ICH in CP where the protagonist Yugmukh, a 'jack of all trades...' writer, spends his evenings. Writers following different political ideologies engage in a discussion on the political situation and the qualities of politicians of the past and present times. Two women join the group midway. Aradhana, a rising poet who has come to Delhi from Jaipur in search of a career and is a translator with the Government of India, and Veena Talwar, a well-known but 'seductive' poet of the Anti-poetry Movement who looks like a fair complexioned *yogini*. She spends six months of the year in the US, and the rest of the time in India. Veena does not sit in the group; as she walks in, she stands close behind the chair of Yugmukh in a way that her bosom touches his head; he turns his head as if to hide his face in her chest. Veena does not join the group, but asks Yugmukh to accompany her to the air-conditioned Standard.[91]

Since Veena is supposed to be familiar with the lifestyle in the West, it is assumed that she is not shy of displaying her emotions in public. She has no intention however to share the public space and use the rare occasion (since she is not in Delhi often) to participate in the literary discussion, which would have been normal for a poet. Instead, she distracts the attention of the gathering, and Yugmukh does not ask her to join the group. They leave for the comfort and privacy of Standard, where their conversation lacks both imagination and romance.[92]

It is remarkable in this context that apart from Krishna Sobti, the other female contributors to *Dilli Tea House* do not write about the Tea House or ICH, but about their general experience in the

[90] Kalia, 'Kitne Shaharon'.

[91] At Standard she orders coffee and cutlet for both. By the time Yughmukh drops her and reaches home, he is however drunk, Saini, *Khidki*, 16–19.

[92] Ibid., for a more positive depiction of women in coffee-tea houses see for example Agyeya, *Nadi;* and Dushyant, *July Ki Ek Raat*, Delhi: Penguin, 2013.

Hindi literary sphere. The social horizon of female literary figures writing in Hindi at least till the 1980s did not, in general, include the conviviality of the coffee and tea house available to their male counterparts.[93] Unlike the Coffee House, the Tea House in Delhi was very much a male-dominated area. In the words of Mangalesh Dabral, the atmosphere in Tea House was sexist. Mamta Kalia, who used to accompany her husband to the Tea House occasionally, noted that the ambience of the place was not encouraging for women to be there. 'Not that the entry of women was forbidden at that place, but they were not welcome. Sometimes women would accompany a male member of the family, father or husband, or a friend. Women usually did not go there alone, and I did not think of myself important enough to consider that going to the Tea House was absolutely essential'.[94]

ALLAHABAD

The ambiguity as to the position of women in the public is often further underlined by the physical structure of the ICH. The creation of a private or 'Ladies and Family' section in the outlets of the ICH[95] goes back to the time when it was not very common for women to go out and share the same space in the presence of unfamiliar men. Calcutta was perhaps the only city where such demarcation had never been made in the ICH. The continuation of the spatial segregation based on gender in current times might be interpreted as a fundamental contradiction of the very notion of the public space. For one thing, most of the written or unwritten rules followed in the

[93] Anita Rakesh writes mostly about Mohan Rakesh while presenting glimpses of the literary world she experienced, 'Antim Basiyat', *DTH*, 15–29; Mannu Bhandari's piece in the same volume is an analysis of her role in Hindi literature, 'Ek Sahityik Tukka', *DTH*, 275–88; note that in Allahabad Mahadevi Varma would go to Lok Bharati and Rajkamal, but not to the ICH, Dinesh Grover, interview, 23 October 2012.

[94] Kalia, 'Kitne shaharon'; cf. false plaits- and flower-plaits sellers, present in front of all restaurants in CP would not be seen in front of the Tea House because young girls did not usually go there, Kalia, *Ghalib*, 69.

[95] Calcutta and Simla are the two cities I have visited where the ICH does not have a section segregated for this purpose.

outlets of the ICH have not changed since the 1950s. Second, in Delhi in spite of the demarcated area for family and women, most of the female visitors also sit in the general section.[96] Usually, only when there is no space in the general section or the terras, would visitor sit in the family section. But in places like Allahabad, Trivandrum and Trichur for example, even when accompanied by men, women would sit in the segregated section—in the case of Allahabad in an altogether separate building a few steps away.[97] In such cases, having a separate section is a part of the business strategy; otherwise, the outlets would lose a considerable section of the customers making use of this option.

How important the agency is, can be very well illustrated with the example of the ICH in Allahabad. From Shyam Kumari Nehru, Sarala Devi Chaudhurani to Mahadevi Varma in the early twentieth century through to Neelum Saran Gour and Anita Gopesh in the late twentieth, to Seema Azad and Sandhya Navodita in the new millenium, Allahabad has had a strong tradition of women in the public sphere.[98] Both Gopesh and Gour are teachers in the University, and prolific writers in Hindi and English respectively. Navodita has a nine-to-five job in the Defence Accounts Department, is a feminist poet and a social activist while Azad is the editor of a literary magazine.

The recollection of memories by the regulars at the ICH Allahabad in its peak years suggests that the literary community there was a close-knit one. Although there was a separate family room in order to draw women and families to the eatery, in the 1950s and the 1960s, many of the writers went with their wives to the ICH and

[96] Anwar Rizvi and Pankaj Bisht pointed out that earlier, especially young women, if they came on their own, would be directed to the special zone. These days they have more freedom, and sit anywhere they like, and they smoke.

[97] Each time I entered ICH at Anna's arcade during the first week of my one month stay in Trivandrum in December 2011, and the first couple of days of my visits to the ICH Allahabad, one or other worker pointed out the Ladies' section to me.

[98] While Gour and Gopesh are from Allahabad and teach in the university's department of English and Chemistry respectively, Navodita is a poet and social activist, Navodita, who went to study in the university in 1998 from Bareilly is a poet and social activist. Azad is a columnist and editor of the little magazine *Dastak*.

sat in the general section. When introduced to the friends in the Coffee House, a newly married writer's bride would be welcomed by sprinkling a few drops of coffee on her head to have her baptized into the tradition.[99] Upendranath and Kaushalya Ashq, Ramswaroop and Sushma Chaturvedi, Ravindra and Mamta Kalia, Vijay Dev Narayan and Kanchanlata Sahi, Keshavchandra and Sarojini Varma, Raghuvansh and his wife, sat together in the general section of the Coffee House.[100] Not that all women present there were highly educated, but that never forbade them from visiting this public space, radiating the convivial atmosphere of *adda*. Wives of writers were *bhabhis* (sisters-in-law), and sharp arguments with brethren literati would be concluded by friendly, sincere exchanges in which the younger writers would affectionately demand a treat with delicacies made by the *bhabhi*.[101]

At the same time, however, a conservative tradition has strongly regulated the public sphere in the city.[102] The University known to be the breeding ground for the civil service, the High Court and other government offices attracted many artistocratic families with roots in the hinterland where segregation of the sexes was the rule of the day even in the private space of the home. In the new urban setting of Allahabad, members of such families did socialize with Europeans and Anglicized Indians like the Nehrus and Saprus, but the practice of *purdah* was strictly maintained to the effect that women of traditional families were, for example, not allowed to attend parties held at Anand Bhavan. After they began actively participating in the public life in the city some of these modern men, like the late Asharfilal

[99] Hemendrashankar Saxena, interview, 22 January 2012.

[100] Quite a few of my interlocutors recounted a touching anecdote in this connection. Mrs Kanchanlata Sahi often accompanied her husband Vijaydev Narayan to the Coffee House on Thursdays. After he passed away, she used to visit the place on every Thursday at the same time, sit at the same table where she earlier sat with her husband, and drank a cup of coffee, all alone. She did not want any one's company during the time she spent there; interviews, H.S. Saxena; Dinesh Grover; Anita Gopesh.

[101] Doodhnath Singh, interview, 24 October 2012; Anita Gopesh, interview, 25 October 2012. Gopesh recalled that Mamta Kalia's (b. 1940) generation was the last to accompany their husband to the Coffee House in Allahabad.

[102] Prakashvati Pal, *Lahore Se Lucknow Tak*, Allahabad: Lokbharti, 2009, 79–80.

Srivastava campaigned against the *purdah*, and the system was abolished in a few private spaces, including the Srivastava family.[103] When the patriarch of such a family, often a member of many civil society organizations, organized tea parties at home, male and the female guests gathered, and socialized in segregated groups.

It was then necessary to have a segregated seating arrangement for both sexes in order to attract members of such families to the Coffee House. While the first generation of the Coffee House customers in Allahabad, a part of the nationalist elite, were accompanied by their spouses, this pattern of women sharing changed in the 1970s as the next generation of lawyers, writers and poets, often the second generation in Allahabad, began socializing in the place. The second generation customers like Neelabh did not take their spouses to the Coffee House. Occasionally when someone took his wife along, they would sit in the family section, and if a friend happened to be there around the same time, he would join, but this was far from a regular practice.[104] Anita Gopesh, another second generation Allahabadi who had often accompanied her father to the ICH as a child, and attended the university during 1975–78, went to the ICH as an adult together with her female friends, and sat in the family section. Even when she went there with her brother, they would always sit in the family section. Similarly, Gauri Saxena who used to go to the Coffee House along with her brother and sit in the family section, maintained that although her brother pretended to be protective, she thought he wanted to take the opportunity to revel in the beauties occupying other tables in that section.[105]

[103] Mrs Gomti Srivastava (87) of the princely state of Sohawal, married to the late Asharfi Lal Srivastava of the landholding family of Kaushambi. Asharfi Lal studied LL.B. in A.U. and entered government service in Allahabad where Mrs Srivastava has spent 65 years of her life, interviewed by Akshat Lal Srivastava on 14 June 2014.

[104] Neelabh, e-mail, 8 September 2012; cf. Amrita Chatterjee who went to Allahabad as a PG student in 1974 and has since been living there teaching at St. Joseph's College since 1977, 'Lawyers, doctors, businessmen etc....weekenders....noontime guys....It is a rare man who will take his wife and family to the Coffee House. If he does, he will not meet up with his friends at that time. He will sit in the family parlor....why do men go to the Coffee House sans wives?', Amrita Chatterjee, e-mail, 10 June 2013.

[105] Gauri Saxena, interview, 22 January 2012; without the knowledge of what Gauri

In a town where everyone knew everyone, news moved fast, and romantic escapades could end up in a most awkward situation, teaching others a lesson.[106] After she started teaching, Anita Gopesh went to the Coffee House together with Mamta Kalia, Doodhnath Singh and her own contemporaris like Asrar Gandhi, but she was one of the exceptions. As another interlocutor put it:

> When we had to go on dates we chose to go to less crowded places like Ginza in Chowk. It was cosy, pleasant and did not have many people around. There was also Madras Café near Balson's Chemists. The landscaped Haathi Park with its little ponds and artificial hillocks was another favourite haunt. Some students frequented Macpherson Lake too.[107]

So, while the general section of the ICH in Allahabad became a predominantly male terrain intolerant of women, there was scope of

---

had said, Anita Gopesh almost echoed her, 'When[...] my brother, more protective [of me], accompanied me to the Coffee House, I would sit in the family room [....] perhaps he used it as an excuse to marvel at the beauties at other tables', interview 25 October 2012.

[106] Ravindra Kalia compared the social setting in Allahabad with that of a joint family where the birth of a child of the youngest brother long time after his wedding leads to amused whisperings among the relatives, Kalia, *Ghalib*, 223; Neelabh recalled a situation in which one of his classmates was seen with two women of 'doubtful reputation' in *burqa* in the family section. This young man's father ran a shop in the Subhas *Chauraha*, a major thoroughfare nearby. The news reached him and in no time he was seen rushing to the Coffee House on his motor bike which was followed by a severe reproof accompanied by light physical abuse of the young gentleman and a hurried disappearance of the ladies in question from the scene providing sheer amusement to the onlookers but also sending a message to the younger generation present. The reader does not have to speculate much to guess that eventually this news too circulated quickly. For a sartorial account of the concept of romance among the youth in this city see, Palash K. Mehrotra, 'Sex and the Small Town', in *The Last Bungalow*, 321–29.

[107] Balson's was near the Anand Bhavan on the road past the Bharadwaj Ashram in the direction of Kamla Nehru Hospital, and was a place for clandestine dates in the 1970s and 1980s. The Ganga and Yamuna banks too provided lovely surroundings for romance. One of the popular games was to have contests over who could throw beer bottles farthest into the lake, Neelum Saran Gour, e-mail, 27 May 2013!

clandestine dates at least elsewhere in the town. With the Anglicized elite as its main patrons, El Chico across the road had never known such segregation. Similarly, as the city kept expanding, especially in the wake of economic liberalization, there were newer places where city-bred youngsters could get together in mixed groups, but the practice of orthodoxy dies hard, and the trend of gender segregation in the Coffee House continues.[108]

That Allahabad is not an exception but conforms to existing norms among sections of the society in smaller cities and towns, becomes evident from my experience in the outlets in Trivandrum and Trichur. When N. P. Chandrasekharan, the director (News & Current Affairs) of Kairali TV told me that he wanted to introduce me to his wife and daughter, we made an appointment to meet at the Spencer Plaza outlet of the ICH, where I was carrying out the field research. I had met Chandrasekharan before in his office nearby, and on the given date, I was waiting for them in the general section keeping an eye on the entrance. After about twenty minutes had passed, I decided to peep into the women's section and found out that the Chandrasekharan family had reached the place before me. They thought it would be natural for me to sit in the segregated section, and decided to wait for me there. Many young female students of the Trivandrum University prefer to sit, however, in the general section, either alone for a quick bite, or in mixed groups. Women's socialization practices in a public space like the ICH is thus very much related to the place of the woman

[108] Unless she has to meet elderly writers like Doodhnath Singh or Asrar Gandhi, Sandhya Navodita goes to the ICH often together with male and female friends, but always sits in the family section, e-mail. Gopesh also noted that whether in the ICH or elsewhere, her contemporary male writers and play directors would sit together/work with female colleagues and writers, but would not bring their wife along even when a play was staged. Working women often did not have leisure time as they also had children and household work to take care of. Changes in the parameters of the value system resulted in a lack of interest on behalf of women in the partner's activities. In recent times Gopesh noticed a lot of insecurity in marriages, and a double standard, especially among men, who frowned at the wife taking too much freedom. Strong female personalities were lacking in the city. Married women made a lot of compromise and educated women did not have the same high esteem of the less educated women of earlier times; Anita Gopesh, 25 October 2012.

concerned in the local social setting, and the seating arrangement in the outlets varies greatly depending on the social world of the agency at a particular location.[109]

ACCOMMODATING THE LESBIAN, GAY, BISEXUAL AND TRANSGENDER COMMUNITIES (LGBT)

There is a willful and purposeful resistance to acknowledging the existence of sexual minorities like gay, lesbian, bisexual, and any other gender relationship falling outside the socially accepted heterosexual relationship, criminalized and oppressed with multifarious implications on the society.[110] According to one source, in the 1970s when Leftist movements in India were strong and the society was open to new ideologies, the LGBT community in Delhi revived *Farsi* as a code language for communication among themselves. There was a table with the code name 'red rose' in the ICH at Mohan Singh Place where members of this community met and talked in *Farsi*. Since red was the colour of communist parties, outsiders associated the name with communist ideology.[111] With the spread of AIDS in the 1980s, the forum disappeared for some time only to reappear in the 1990s when many NGOs began addressing the issues, intending to change the given societal attitude towards transexuality and same sex relationships. In Delhi about 35–40 LGBT members united to form a 'Thursday's Forum' that met once a week at the ICH, later five to six times a year. They had been to Barista, one of the new café chains in urban India since the mid 1990s once, but did not like the ambience there. Many of them were familiar with the ICH from their university days, and knew it as an anti-establishment place where it was not necessary to conceal one's identity. A similar place with the

[109] The outlets at Thampanoor, near the railway station, and the one at the Secretariat do not have a separate family section.

[110] Ashok Row, 'Gay and lesbian movement', letter to the editor, *EPW*, October 12–19, 1996, 2770; except for a brief period between 2009 and 2013, homosexuality in India has been a punishable crime under Act 377 of Indian Penal Code.

[111] Himadri Roy, 'Farsi: The Lost Language of Gay Delhi', 20 May 2013, website, http://www.gaylaxymag.com/exclusive/farsi-a-lost-language-of-gay-delhi/.

possibility of holding an uninterrupted meeting was not available anywhere in central Delhi.[112] They did not announce the meetings publicly but the name would indicate where they sat. The workers were informed of these meetings and any newcomer asking about the group would be directed to the concerned tables.[113] There are similar NGOs active in Calcutta creating awareness about the LGBT community. There are a few teachers who have undergone sex change and come to the university and Coffee House with their new identity. Similarly, lesbian students connected with the SAPPHO, (a support group for lesbian, bisexual and transgender women) used to meet at ICH when they wanted have discussions without being ridiculed.[114]

CONCLUSION

This chapter began with the idea to examine the accessibility of different sections of the public to the Coffee House, usually associated with the middle class. Middle class consumers indeed form the clientele of the ICH. But the fact that the cooperative is run by members of the working class, creates an informal ambience to allow a number of others from their peer group engaged in different kinds of informal labour, even when they do not have any business relationship with the place, access to it. Thus, the weekly commuter from the suburbia buying books for shops in his small town, the owner of the *paan*-cigarette shop, and the cycle stand keeper develop a close relationship, both with the workers and the customers, which make them part the place in different ways. The proletariat in this public space does not want to create a 'counterpublic' sphere for itself; nor does it aim at the 'left-over' of the petit bourgeois. Often the association in the public sphere offers these marginal individuals to climb up the

[112] Gautam Bhan, Indian Institute for Human Settlements, telephone conversation, 27 January 2012.

[113] These meetings continued till 2003 when they found a space of their own. Again, during the six weeks prior to the First Pride Parade (held simultaneously in Bangalore, Chennai, Delhi and Mumbai) on 29 June 2008 they met at the ICH for discussing the organization of the Parade.

[114] This was before they had their own meeting place in South Calcutta.

social ladder and improve their socio-economic condition with the ultimate goal to be assimilated into the mainstream. Sometimes this transition takes place within the lifetime of a person, as illustrated in the cases of Anandhan in Trivandrum, Anthony and Gupta in Delhi. Especially remarkable is the case of Anandhan whose alleged connection with the underworld on the one hand and the elite on the other has transformed his fortunes from that of a mobile vendor to mid-sized business entrepreneur. The variegated nature of the public at this place encourages the traditionally ostracized social groups to use to the public space as a springboard to help explore their self-identity and in finding and establishing their foothold in the public as equals.

Representation of gender in the public space concerned demonstrates a spatiotemporal divergence, not entirely related to class, but guided by the customary practices of social groups visiting the place in a given city at a given time. Progression of time has not brought about any unilinear pattern of change. Sexist comments in Delhi and Calcutta in the 1950s and segregated space for women and family in ICH Allahabad and Trivandrum until now confirm that the socio-cultural capital of the agent embedded in the social practices at large is important in contributing to the structure, and that gender, as a category, does not have an emancipatory potential in itself.[115] In a city like Calcutta where there has never been any segregated space for men and women, after the initial uneasiness the presence of women caused among the young men, the groups became more and more mixed till friendship across genders was not frowned upon and mixed groups became common in the 1960s and the 1970s. In spite of the demarcated zone for family and ladies, the same can be said about Delhi, where groups in all the three sections are in practice gender neutral, although elderly male groups usually occupy the tables in the general section and elderly couples visiting the place just for refreshments, might prefer to sit in the demarcated section.[116] In the

[115] Cf. for example the essays in Tanika Sarkar and Urvashi Butalia (ed.), *Rebels, Wives, Saints: Designing Selves and Nations in Colonial Times*, London etc.: Seagull, 2009.

[116] Similarly, Gurnam Singh, single, may be found reading a newspaper sitting at one of the tables in the ladies' section.

ICH in Allahabad and Trivandrum however, maintaining the public-private boundaries was the norm for some, and was continuously reproduced through every day social practice. In metropolises like Calcutta and Delhi, women defied the boundaries and formed part of the general public, sharing the common space with them.[117] In Allahabad, after the initial period when the cosmopolitan nationalist elite occupied the place, women and men shared the common space. But the coexisting tradition of delineating the public from the private gained ground in the post colonial period. This suggests that the structure as such cannot induce a change and is closely related to the cultural capital of the agent. Viewing women as part of the private reduces the place to an extension of the private domestic space and blurs the distinction between the public and the private. Persistence of the myths and symbols of the autonomous, generalized male ego among the section of the population frequenting the place visibly points to the resilient dichotomy between the public and the private.[118] That the public-private boundaries remain unchanged in the ICH in some places is indicative that these markers remain unchanged in the social world the agents represent. It is necessary to unpack and understand the world of these myths and symbols entrapping both the sexes that in their turn determine the role of women in the public sphere.

[117] This is often dictated by the availability of space in the general sections.

[118] See for example Fraser, 'Rethinking', 131; Seyla Benhabib, 'The Generalized and the Concrete Other: The Kohlberg-Gilligan Controversy and Feminist Theory', in *Praxis international*, 5.4 (January), 402–24.

CHAPTER seven

The Middle Class and Coffee Houses Old and New

Those *addas* we had at the Coffee House are no longer there
Where did those sunlit afternoons go, they are lost forever now
Nikhilesh is in Paris, Mohidul in Dhaka and there is no news of them
D'Souza from Goa who played guitar at the Grand is now long buried
Disappointment in love led to Roma Ray languishing today in a mental asylum
While Amal is suffering from terminal cancer, life was not easy on him at all

Those *addas* we had at the Coffee House are no longer there
Where did those sunlit afternoons go, they are lost forever now

Sujata seems to be the happiest today with a wealthy husband
Everything about her is expensive from her jewels to her cars
Nikhilesh Sanyal was the artist who ended up doing ad work
While D'Souza sat in silence listening to us his eyes spoke their own words
We sat at that one table for hours on end, Charminar cigarettes dangling from our lips
Those *addas* we had at the Coffee House are no longer there
Where did those sunlit afternoons go, they are lost forever now [1]

... Everything has changed
the paint on the walls, the discussion, the posters

[1] Lyrics Gauriprasanna Majumdar, a regular in ICH College Street in the 1950s, music Suparnokanti Ghosh, artist Manna Dey. I am grateful to my friend blogger and translator Ruma Chakravarti for translating the lyrics for use in this book, http://www.mp3haat.com/2013/03/manna-dey-coffee-houser-sei-addata-mp3.html.

yet no one raises an eyebrow
new friends are made
adda and debate continue
those days of our dream are perhaps rushing back
the breeze carries the tidings
Amal's son has picked up
the guitar left behind by D'Souza[2]

The first citation from a song recorded in 1983 presented glimpses of the characters—a group of seven friends from the Coffee House—their lives in the past and in the present. The image of the production and reproduction of *adda* in the Coffee House that the song presents is significant. The *adda* the narrator used to have with his friends at the Coffee House was a part of their daily routine and irrespective of the workload or the condition of the weather outside, they made it a rule to meet there. During the three to four hours spent in the place, they would have animated discussions on the poems of Vishnu Dey or the paintings of Jamini Roy while smoking Charminar all the time. The refrain laments that *that adda*, those golden sunlit afternoons—cherished moments in contrast with the ups and downs of life—are things of past.

The lines in the second citation are from the sequel to this hit number cited in Chapter Two. Both numbers were performed by the renowned artist Manna Dey. If the earlier number was about what was lost, the second track cherishes hope. In spite of the changes in the personal lives of the members of an *adda,* life did not stop; the next generation picked up the thread from where the previous generation had left it. This chapter wishes to cast a look at what happened to the real life Amals and D'Souzas who patronized the *adda* culture in the Coffee House and the impact of the process on the place and the gatherings there. Academic analyses and media reports underline the deep structural impact on Indian economy in the aftermath of the economic liberalization since the 1990s. The foreign direct investment (FDI) encouraged by the liberalization process created

[2] *Swapner Dingulo Chhilo shei Coffee-housei* (The days of our dream were in that Coffee House), lyrics Shamindranath Roy Chaudhuri, music Suparnokanti Ghosh.

new forms of employment in the cities generating the rise of a new section of the urban middle class. One of the market segments that underwent profound changes since that time is the coffee-retailing sector. There was emergence of new indigenous coffee café chains on the one hand, and the entrance of multinational café chains in the Indian market on the other. The rise of the new globally mobile middle class inclined towards Western lifestyle including the consumption of coffee at the new urban places, distinguishing itself from the rest on this basis, facilitated this development. All this has supposedly made the ICH irrelevant.

The figures published by the Coffee Board indicate an increase in the domestic consumption of this beverage in the new millennium. While the consumption remained static at an annual 55,000 to 60,000 metric tons between 1981 and 1999, by 2010 it crossed 100,000 metric tons. However, the prognosis of the Board with regard to the internal coffee market is said to be a bit too optimistic and should be taken with a good pinch of salt. For the year 2010–11 for example another source suggested 70,000–75,000 metric tons as a more acceptable figure.[3] While the quantity sold inland has increased, in view of the population explosion, how far of it is actual growth is yet to be analyzed.

But does the new café culture imply that the outlets of ICH are counting their days, waiting to be replaced by the glamourous, spic-and-span competitors, as often predicted?[4] The earlier chapters are a testimony to the different kinds of interaction the ICH facilitated up until the 1980s. What have the new coffee cafés added to the urban scene and what has been the impact of the changes in the political economy since the 1970s on the socio-economic groups visiting the place? Does the old tradition of *adda* and debate at the ICH continue

[3] V. G. Siddhartha, interview, 2 December 2011; also Bhaswati Bhattacharya, 'Drink it the Damn Way We Want: Some Reflections on the Marketing and Consumption of Coffee in India', in Bhaswati Bhattacharya and Henrike Donner (eds.), *Making the Indian Consumer: The Politics of Advertising and Identity Formation 20th Century India*, Delhi: OUP, 2017.

[4] Stuart Freedman, 'The Palace of Monkeys and Memory', http://www.stuartfreedman.com/texts/story.php?nodeID=609.

in spite of all changes, as cherished in the lyrics in the sequel number of the popular song cited above? If it indeed does, and if at the same time the new coffee cafés are the places for the globalized middle class to display their exclusive status, who are the Romas, Sujatas, Mohiduls and Amals in the ICH now? Do they represent the same sections of the middle class, as in the earlier times? With the received wisdom about the new middle class in mind, and on the basis of oral research among past and present connoisseurs of the ICH—and to some extent among the visitors of the new MNC-run coffee cafés especially Café Coffee Day (CCD), this chapter will address the question whether the new coffee cafés have made the ICH irrelevant. Although both the songs referred specifially to the College Street outlet, the analysis will focus on all outlets studied in the book.

THE NEW COFFEE CAFÉS

Consumption of coffee in India in the real sense of the term is said to have begun in the early 1990s.[5] The media and market surveys ascribe this to the opening up of the Indian economy and the rise of the new urban middle class. Like in the 1930s when the export-oriented industry was forced to consider the domestic market due to a crisis in the external market, the pressure this time too was exogenous. Brazil's refusal to yield to the export quota fixed by the International Coffee Agreement determining the quota of export for producing countries led to a crisis in the international coffee market which ended the Agreement in 1989, actually forcing the industry to look at the domestic market again. This coincided with the economic liberalization. The long monopoly of the Coffee Board over the marketing of coffee, purchased at a rate below the market price through the pool system, ended in 1992, when the Board allowed small coffee growers for the first time to sell 30 per cent of their crop in the open market. In 1993, the Free Sale Quota was increased to 50 per cent, and finally in 1995 small growers with holdings of less than 10 hectares were totally freed from any obligation to the

[5] V. G. Siddhartha, owner CCD, interview, 2 December 2012.

Coffee Board.[6] The entrance of global coffee brands and café chains like Costa Coffee, Lavazza (taken over by Barista), Gloria Jean, and lastly, Starbucks, together with the phenomenally growing homegrown multinational Café Coffee Day (CCD), promise the consumer a novel experience. As part of a tie with a local operator, the MNCs are supposed to source coffee locally. The air-conditioned, sleek locales furnished with comfortable, tasteful furniture, satellite televisions and wi-fi connections, represent the trend of the day. In sharp contrast to the bygone era when cappuccino could be sold as espresso, the customer now gets to know the difference between a cappuccino, café au lait, café Americano, frappe and all other hot and cold beverages being sold under exotic names having little to do with coffee. The latest temptation consumers are exposed to in this context is the possibility of tasting single origin coffee, [7] or, say, at Berries and Barrels in Bangalore, to opt for a bottle of imported wine instead of coffee.[8]

Although MNCs like, Costa Coffee, Gloria Jean, Starbucks and others entered the growing Indian market, the winner so far is the homegrown CCD which is supposed to have brought a 'paradigm shift in the café space in India…[and]…has raised coffee from a brew to an experience'. Inspired by Chibo, the largest importer of coffee in Germany, CCD is the retail outlet of the vertically organized coffee conglomerate, Amalgamated Bean Coffee Trading Company Ltd. (ABCTCL), a part of the holding company Coffee Day Enterprises Pvt Ltd sourcing coffee from 10,000 acres (4,800 ha) of coffee estates it owns in South India. As of January 2016, CCD has a total of 1,423 outlets in 209 cities of India, 590 Coffee Xpress and Coffee Day Take Away outlets at metro stations, airports and other places

[6] Rob Jenkins, *Democratic Politics and Economic Reform in India*, Contemporary South Asia Studies 5, Cambridge: Cambridge University Press, 1999, 132.

[7] There are two outlets of CCD in India called Square in Bangalore and CP in Delhi. It is claimed that one can taste unblended coffee originating at one particular estate, indigenous or foreign at such outlets.

[8] Berries and Barrels is a vertically organized company serving coffee grown in their own plantation. I am grateful to Ms Roop Rashi, Finance Officer at the Coffee Board of India for drawing my attention to this outlet and arranging my visit to this place.

that offer coffee on the go, in addition to varieties of premium coffee available at exclusive outlets labelled Lounge and Square to pamper the connoisseur. Involved in all aspects of coffee making and selling, from plantations to roasting, grinding, packaging, retailing and exporting, not to mention selling the brew as well as its accessories, CCD has 'done for coffee what Amul had done for milk'.[9] CCD has also made its foray into the international coffee shop market, with five outlets in the Czech Republic and two in Vienna.

Whether it is CCD, Costa Coffee, Lavazza or Starbucks, the newly emerging cafés operate on a very different principle from that guiding the creation of the chain of the ICH in the 1930s. The ICH was created with the idea to introduce the consumers to a new brew at a nominal price affordable by a large section of the middle class. The interior of the outlets was inspired by the Irani cafés, and photographs of nationalist leaders indicated that the institution was rooted in Indian culture. True, the customers viewed them as representing modern Western culture and transformed the place meant to be a restaurant to a social space for leisure. Ironically, the now septuagenarian institution has long lost its glamour. Its outlets with their dark, uninviting interior, old, stained mica-topped tables and plastic chairs (or torn sofas) attract tourists as an oxymoron, a remnant of the past. The liveried, not-so-professional workers, who bring the order placed by A to the table of B, in a hurry drop the cutlery on the table, or take away the empty cup without caring to ask if seconds are in order, form part of the heritage of the Raj.[10] No one will confuse such outlets to have any connection with the current global culture. The very same arguments of 'heritage', 'history', 'past

[9] V. G. Siddhartha, CCD, interview, 2 December 2011. At the time of the interview there were 1000 kiosks at railway stations and 400 stores selling coffee powder. The company has a large stake in Sical Logistics Ltd through Tanglin Retail realty development, also owns a financial services firm and a luxury resort in Chikmagalur, Karnataka.

[10] These maladies are, however, not unique to the ICH, but seem to be common in restaurants in the post-globalization First World too; See Roberto A. Ferdman, 'The Most Annoying Restaurant Trend Happening Today'; *Washington Post,* 23 June 2015, web site, http://www.washingtonpost.com/blogs/wonkblog/wp/2015/06/23/no-you-may-not-clear-my-plate-the-most-annoying-restaurant-trend-happening-today/.

glory', 'blessed by the visit of celebrities', once used in favour of the pre-Coffee House days small tea-shops and cabins against the 'upstart' Coffee House, are used currently in defence of the Indian Coffee House in order to denounce the new 'upstart' coffee houses like Barista and CCD which lack matching pedigree.[11] By contrast, the new cafés project themselves as part of a global enterprise, uniquely available nearer home. The search for Costa India on the web leads to the website of the enterprise in the UK, and the description 'Costa Experience' as 'voted the nation's favourite for the third year in a row' purposefully blurs the time-space distinction.[12] Once inside its well-lit and air-conditioned confines, the interior decoration with comfortable seating makes the customer feel he or she is in London, Rome, Paris or New York.[13] Posters on the walls inform the customer about the product; one gets to know that the cup of coffee one gets is ethical from bean 2 cup, organic, and tastes exactly the same no matter, where on the earth one is. Built around themes changing per season, the menu of these new places invent terms, which, although often far-fetched from coffee, sound as 'cool' as the cafés appear to be. In addition to serving food and beverage, these outlets often offer internet access, thereby promoting cyber culture. In CCD, the in-house magazine with the latest in the world of coffee and fashion captures the imagination of the consumer—mostly urban middle class youth in the 18 to 35 age group—the target clientele of the company.[14]

[11] Dipankar Das Gupta, ICH Kolkata, interview, 25 January 2011; and Subhas Ganguli, ICH Kolkata, interview, 22 July 2011; Ram Shastri, ICH Delhi, 6 January 2012; Asrar Gandhi, Allahabad, interview, 23 October 2011.

[12] http://www.costa.co.uk/experience/#/1/nations-favourite.

[13] Naina, student of the Hindu College, DU, interview, 5 October 2013; cf. 'When you enter a Starbucks Coffee House in India, you immediately find yourself back in any local Starbucks in the US', in Peter Kohli, 'Can Starbucks Coffee Succeed in India?', 12 November 2014, website, http://www.nasdaq.com/article/can-starbucks-coffee-succeed-in-india-cm413135.

[14] V. G. Siddhartha, inerview; according to a recent study, 65 percent of Barista's visitors belong to the age group 15–30, the majority being students and urban professionals, IIPM, 'Barista vs. Café Coffee Day', http://www.iipmthinktank.com/functions/marketing/compartive.pdf. The elderly often do not feel at home in these new cafés. Not only that they feel unwanted here, the pre-packaged food and the

Working on this principle, CCD claims their cafés to be a 'brick and mortar social community network' where people can express themselves in a friendly atmosphere and where a 'lot can happen over coffee'.[15] The established coffee café chains like Barista, CCD and Costa Coffee did not feel deterred by the debut of the iconic Starbucks (with Tata Coffee as its partner on a 50:50 basis) in the Indian market in 2012. CCD, according to Ramakrishnan K., the chain's marketing president, follows the principle of different pricing across different rental points determined not by competition but by the customers.[16] In addition to the cafés, CCD has a number of more lavish establishments. Its outlet *The Lounge*, offers a wide range of food and beverages targeting a 'more mature and affluent group of customers', and *The Square*, with its 'premium range of cafés showcasing a boutique of brewing systems and single origin coffee beans from different parts of the world caters to the absolute connoisseur and the well-travelled'.[17] The anytime, anywhere coffee experience is offered at the Xpress outlets serving coffee to mobile customers through kiosks at different strategic locations where the customer can have 'coffee to go' such as at petrol pumps, metro and train stations, shopping malls, university campuses and other public spaces.[18]

---

pricey coffee put them off. 'McDonald will never allow the space and opportunity to gather the same way as the ICH does'; 'if you ask for salt at CCD, the waiters respond with a blank gaze; they serve pre-packed food', Prithwish Saha, ICH College Street, interview, 4 February 2011; Ram Shastri, ICH CP, interview, 6 January 2012.

[15] The motto of CCD.

[16] Sunanda Jayaseelan, 'CCD Unfazed by Foreign Competition, Will Lead the Market', Business Broadcast News Pvt Ltd, http://www.btvin.com/article/read/news/2932/ccd-unfazed-by-foreign-competition--will-lead-the-market, 12 October 2015; Starbucks that launched its first outlet in Mumbai in early October 2012, priced its coffee at Rs 80 for a small offering, Rs 165 for a large one, and cold coffee between Rs 120 and 200. The CCD sells hot coffee at about Rs 100 and cold coffee at about Rs 150 (cost at CCD, South City Mall, Calcutta, February 2014).

[17] According to a source that wanted to remain anonymous, all coffee served at the outlets was of indigenous origin.

[18] For the marketing strategy of CCD see M.S. Raju and Domnique Xardel (eds.), *Marketing Management: International Perspectives*, New Delhi: Tata McGraw-Hill, 2009, 361–68.

The café culture in its current global form is new in the US too. In the interview she gave me, art historian Tapati Guha Thakurta who was in Princeton in the mid-1980s, could not recollect there being a café culture among the students in the campus.[19] It is thus evident here that there is indeed a very close connection between public culture and global cultural flows as pointed out by Carol Breckenridge.[20]Who then, are the customers of these places?

THE MIDDLE CLASS: NEW VERSUS OLD

India's 250 million strong and still growing middle class is economically the most dynamic force of the world.[21] As modern capitalism entered the phase when economic focus in the core countries shifted from production to consumption, and to the maximization of consumption, it progressed side by side with the maximization of exploitation of producers elsewhere in the globe.[22] Much of the public debate on economic liberalization in India has centred, however, on the rise of a new transnational urban middle class with a specific pattern of consumption and its impact on the growth of the Indian economy.[23] This section of the urban middle class—termed as the new middle class—equipped with cultural and educational capital benefitting from the process since has engaged in a politics of hegemony, which, although projected as a unifying element representing the middle

[19] Although begun in 1971, Starbucks had only six stores and one espresso bar in Seattle in 1986 but by the early 1990s the rage for coffee had spread and while there were 150 espresso bars and cafés in Seattle alone, there were 40 such outlets in Chicago, and people in New York were showing interest in good quality coffee, Florence Fabricant, 'Americans Wake up and Smell the Coffee', New York Times, 2 September 1992.

[20] Carol Breckenridge, *Consuming Modernity: Public Culture in a South Asian World*, Minneapolis: University of Minnesota Press, 1995. viii.

[21] This estimate is based on Leela Fernandes, *India's New Middle Class: Democratic Politics in an Era of Economic Reform*, Minneapolis: University of Minnesota press, 2006, xiv.

[22] George Ritzer, *The McDonaldization Thesis: Exploration and Extensions*, Sage, 1998; Zygmunt Bauman, 'Consuming life', *Journal of Consumer Culture*, 1.1, 2001, 9–29.

[23] Raka Ray and Amita Baviskar (eds), *Elite and Everyman: The Cultural Politics of the Indian Middle Classes*, New Delhi: Routledge, 2011, 8–9.

class, is marked by illiberalism and exclusion in favour of projects promoting the interest of the elite.[24] The economic reforms saw five million Indians travelling to the West as tourists annually, while at home, satellite television and real time broadcasting of shows have exposed urban Indian youth to the lifestyle of the youth across the world. The launch of new branded goods in multi-storeyed shopping malls and plazas, further highlights a new lifestyle encouraging the consumption of coffee. Gandhi's notion of austerity and Nehruvian socialism, that long stood in the way of conspicuous consumption was shaken off as an outdated ideology. During the last few decades, trends in the pattern of consumption have been changing so fast, that a scholar could find her own work on the subject, written in the early 1990s, a 'historical document' within a span of ten years.[25]

A number of academic works on the middle class have underlined that with broad shared interests in education as a means to claim and conform to the middle class status, claimants of the middle class category increasingly belong to a variety of ranges of economic standards, castes, communities, consumption practices, status and values.[26] Following Varma's definition of the middle class, there are 300 million aspirants, 300 million climbers, and 150 million consumers.[27] But Mazarella has argued that the 250 million strong consuming middle class was a figure pumped up by Indian executives in order to attract foreign investment.[28] Further, all these works emphasize the

[24] Leela Fernandes and Patrick Heller, 'Hegemonic Aspirations: New Middle Class Politics and India's Democracy in Comparative Perspective', *Critical Asian Studies*, 38.4 (2006), 495–522.

[25] Rachel Dwyer, '*Zara Hatke*: The New Middle Classes and the Changing Forms of Hindi Cinema', in Henrike Donner (ed.), *Being Middle Class in India: A Way of Life*, London: Routledge, 2011, 184–208.

[26] Sanjay Joshi, *Fractured Modernity: The Making of the Middle Class in Colonial North India*, Delhi: OUP, 2001; Henrike Donner and Patrick De Neve, 'Introduction', in Donner (ed.), *Being Middle Class*, 1–22.

[27] Pavankumar Varma, *The Great Indian Middle Class*, Delhi: Penguin, 1998, 171; Ramprasad Chakravarthi, 'India's Middle Class Failure', Prospect, no. 138, 30 September 2000.

[28] William Mazarella, *Shoveling Smoke: Advertising and Globalization in Contemporary India*, Durham (etc.): Duke University Press, 2003, ch. 8.

growing inequality even among the sections of the middle class in the aftermath of the economic liberalization. Fernandes's study shows that the new Indian middle class in the forefront of the economic liberalization seeks to create a distinctive social and political identity by conspicuously absorbing the fruits of the process.[29] Dwyer points out that while they are very prominent in India's public culture, they prefer to be identified as 'upper class' as opposed to the 'middle class' that in the Indian context refers to lower middle classes. The distinct identity and status the new middle class claims is based to a large extent on a lifestyle in which the culture of consumption plays a major role. In Mazarella's analysis, this class is guided by 'aspirational consumerism' in that it believes that the pleasure of consumption is a symbol of individual and national progress.[30]

By using the data including those provided by Market Information Survey of Households, E. Sridharan has conceived the middle class in the post-1991 period as consisting of five subclasses on the basis of annual income per household: the high income group middle class (drawing more than Rs 1,40,000); the expanded middle class (Rs 1,05,000–1,40,000); middle class (Rs 70,001–1,05,000); lower middle class (Rs 35,001–70,000), and lower (Rs 35,000).[31] If the globalized upper class rich, keen on distinguishing itself from the rest, opts for the'same anywhere in the world' ambience and luxury of the global café chains, the average ICH consumer—as in earlier times, and now, is—typically a person unable to afford this luxury on a regular basis. While some of the elderly visitors (established writers and [retired] university teachers) are rich, and some students from well-to-do families would visit ICH in addition to more 'modern' and savvy places, the bulk of the Coffee House visitors belongs to the 'expanded middle' and 'middle' segments of the Indian middle

[29] Leela Fernandes, *India's New Middle Class: Democratic Politics in an Era of Economic Reform*, Minneapolis: University of Minnesota Press, 2006, xviii.

[30] Mazarella, *Shoveling Smoke*, 101.

[31] E. Sridharan, 'The Growth and Sectoral Composition of India's Middle Classes: Their Impact on the Politics of Economic Liberalization', in Baviskar and Ray (eds.), *Elite and Everyman*, 27–57.

class. It is in place here to remember which section of society the first generation of the ICH clientele constituted.

THE OLD CONNOISSEURS OF THE COFFEE HOUSE

The first generation consumers of the ICH consisted of a large number of newcomers, especially those displaced from east or west Pakistan in the wake of Partition. If not staying with a relative, students stayed in a hostel or mess, offering food and lodging, at a reasonable price. Initially in Calcutta, young male members from such backgrounds met up in their own mess, in a park, a teashop or a restaurant, but eventually many of them later began gathering in the ICH. The cultural elite leaving west Pakistan for Delhi were economically better off than their eastern counterparts, although here too many migrants had to begin humbly anew in order to adjust to the new situation. The north Indian *bhadraloks* had read about coffee, and were especially aware of the ambience of coffee houses and salons in the West where the intellectuals gathered; but coffee had so far been an exotic commodity, a monopoly of the colonial elite, available in exclusive hotels and restaurants very often beyond the reach of these *bhadraloks*. For a considerable section of the Coffee House goers in the 1940s and 1950s, affordability was as important as ambience. Albeit fractured, as Joshi pointed out,[32] the modern, nationalist Indian middle class had some shared cultural repertoire that made it look homogenous;[33] but this appearance of homogeneity is a fiction fraught with problems.

One of the traits reflected in socialization within the ICH was penury, often guided by straitened circumstances and the need for extreme caution in parting with money. In Calcutta, there were

[32] Sanjay Joshi, *Fractured Modernity: The Making of the Middle Class in Colonial North India*, Delhi: OUP.

[33] Sumit Sarkar, *Writing Social History*, Delhi: OUP, 1997; Stephen Legg, 'Gendered Politics and Nationalized Homes: Women and the Anti-Colonial Struggle in Delhi, 1930–47', in *Gender, Place and Culture*, 10 (2003), 7–27; Christophe Jaffrelot and Peter Van der Veer (eds.), *Patterns of Middle Class Consumption in India and China*, Delhi: Sage, 2008.

visitors dependent on their well-wishing, better off patrons for the payment of coffee, and in Delhi, the moment of the payment of bills, for a large group, could be an embarrassing one. Conspicuous consumption was not part of the lifestyle of the earlier generations. Finding sponsors for coffee and cigarettes was often as important an aspect of visits to the Coffee or Tea House as the much sought after *adda* in the place. In the words of Gyanranjan, one did not need much those days; it was possible to spend the whole evening in the ICH with four *anna*s in one's pocket. It did not matter if someone did not have even that amount, no one asked for it. From the manager to the workers, everyone, was sure that it would be paid some or the other time. Gauri Saxena in Allahabad, Sunil Gangopadhyay and Swati Lal among others in Calcutta stated that spending money on food outside home was something unthinkable.[34] In all the cities studied, the capacity of the ICH to accommodate a large number of customers in an informal ambience, the price differential in comparison with similar places and the hospitality offered by the liveried workers allowing an unrestricted use of the social space without the obligatory consumption of food, made the ICH very special to the middle class who did not otherwise consume the exotic beverage. Popularly it is believed that the tradition of the high profile *adda* lost its importance somewhere in the late 1970s or early 1980s when the place stopped being associated with the production and reproduction of culture, and since that time, the outlets have gradually been reduced to mere eateries. What happened to the first generation of the ICH visitors, and if it is true that they withdrew themselves from the ICH, who were and who are the second and later generation of occupants of the place?

In Calcutta, at the time when the Coffee House was at the climax of its glory, mainstream Bengali culture began projecting the ICH

[34] Gyanranjan, telephone conversation, 12 July 2013; Interviews with, Sunil Gangopadhyay, Swati Lal, 21 February 2011, Gauri Saxena, 22 January 2012; Radha Prasad Gupta talked of the culturally cosmopolitan lower middle class in Calcutta, see his interview in Lina Fruzzetti and Ákos Östör (eds.), *Calcutta Conversations*, New Delhi: DC Publishers, 2003; for the unostentatious interior of a teacher's room in Allahabad in the early 1960s see Gour, 62.

as a benchmark of a valorized *adda*, an ongoing process in which the popular song *Coffee-houser shei addata aj ar nei*, cited in the beginning of this chapter, plays an important role.[35] With Manna Dey at his romantic best, the number produced an imagery of the place in the collective memory of Bengalis, and irrespective of their age and location, those even far removed from Calcutta could visualize the Coffee House and the social and cultural practices produced there. For a long time after Dey passed away in November 2013, the song kept being circulated in the digital media. What is remarkable is that although the last couplet of the song [not cited here] clearly indicates that the process of the production of *adda* and of the social space is ongoing, the nostalgia about the past essentializing the lost cosmopolitan urban culture of which Coffee House *addas* form a part, dominates the collective memory.[36] So much so that the sequel to the favourite number recorded in 2002 describing the then current situation of the remaining members of the group and announcing a reunion in the Coffee House—partially reproduced in the epigraph to this chapter—went practically unnoticed.[37] The production and circulation of the symbolic meaning of the ICH as a place for a glamorous *adda* of the cultural icons of Bengal still holds sway. This is an ongoing process in which journalism plays a significant role. The following lines represent a fantastic example of such production:[38]

[35] See the references especially in Chapter Two. Around the time Gaurisankar Bhattacharya wrote *Albert Hall*, he wrote another fiction entitled *Shravani* (1962). The character bearing the same name grew up in Siliguri in North Bengal began visiting the Coffee House with her friends after she joined the University of Calcutta as a student, 50–61.

[36] Arnab Roy from Coochbehar, a Ph. D. student, had a notion about the highly intellectual ambience of the Coffee House. Once he began visiting the space and made friends it became clear to him that the Coffee House reflecting the essence of Bengali culture was a myth—he thought it tried to uphold a typical urban (upper) middle-class/caste high culture. But back in Coochbehar he would boast that he had been to the Coffee House; interview, 22 August 2011.

[37] Both the versions are available on YouTube; while the first song has been uploaded by several persons and one video has as many as 1,293,523 views and 3,586 likes, the second number has 6,415 views and 65 likes (as on 2 April 2015).

[38] Kasturi Basu, 'The Flavours of Another Era', *The Hindu*, 29 January 2006.

> Old timers recount how Satyajit Ray would sit in a corner [at ICH College Street] drawing a scene from a forthcoming film and Manna Dey break out into an impromptu song while trying to compose the next couple of lines or explain the song sequence to Soumitra Chatterjee, who despite his failing health and advancing years, still drops in....

Regarding Ray's *adda*, Radha Prasad recalled that their group met only for a short while in College Street because they preferred 5CA. Moreover, as seen above, Ray visited the ICH before he became fully engaged in the production of films. Soon after he finished college (Scottish Church 1937–38 and Vidyasagar 1938–41), Manna Dey accompanied his uncle, the famous vocal artist Krishnachandra Dey to Bombay in 1942 where his musical career began. In a telephone interview he gave to the current author, Dey stated that although they lived in north Calcutta, as a student he *never* went to the ICH and visited the space *only* when he was felicitated by the ICWCSL for his contribution to the publicity of the space, and a couple of times again in connection with a television serial partially shot at the ICH. He liked the lyrics of *Coffee Houser shei addata*, and recorded it.[39] But fiction is far more powerful than truth; and after the song became a hit, everyone began talking about Dey and his fictitious visits and *adda* in the Coffee House. Similarly, Chatterjee's appearance in the ICH in the new millennium would be once in a blue moon.

Ironically, such representation neglects that when most of these icons were regular visitors to the ICH, they were either students, or in the early phase of their career—employed yet undecided about the future—toying with different creative ideas. More important, did they owe their fame, talent to the Coffee House? But the more the nostalgia, the more the ICH has been presented as a cultural, fetishized icon from the past. Consequently, following the logic of classic dualism, as opposed to the earlier times when quality was the benchmark of the *addas* in the Coffee House, the place is now considered to have faded into nothing.[40] In an essay entitled '*Coffee*

[39] Manna Dey, telephone conversation, 11 February 2011.

[40] Rakhi Chakrabarty, 'Much has changed. The brew of high-brow intellectualism, aesthetic thresholds crossed, fire of young revolutionaries on a mission to change the

House ta i ar nei' (Even the Coffee House does not exist any longer) the eminent poet Subodh Sarkar, after surveying ICH College Street in person where he could only overhear a few trivial (fictitious) conversations of university students from Presidency and Jadavpur on their career plans, informs the reader that even the place associated with *adda* no longer exists. He takes the reader back to the golden past of Albert Hall, once blessed by the presence of Rabindranath Tagore and the likes, and associated with cultural landmarks:

> Let me give two examples. Kamalkumar Majumdar is reading the script of the film that will later win the heart of the world, and telling his lanky friend that it is rubbish.[41] We have to rewind little further. Entering the Coffee House in colonized India, we see a young boy sitting there; his wrists, as strong as thunder, are capable of chasing the British away (*kabjite tar British taranor bajro*). He dreams [of a free India]. While sipping infusion, he is explaining to his fellow revolutionaries how armed struggle can be the only way to get rid of the British. The name of that youth is Subhas Chandra Bose. The history of the Coffee House is in fact the history of the Bengalis since 1876. The history of *adda*; the history of the fall, repentance, and rising up....
>
> ....What has become of the Coffee House, the birthplace of bright students-turned into Naxalites that for the last five decades advertised the restless intellectuals, writers and politicians! Where have the arguments of the argumentative Bengalis that Sen wrote about gone? What happened to discourse and ideology? The Coffee House did not anymore deliver figures like Camus, Kafka, Neruda although

---

world, a rainbow of idealism, dreams of the youth, living bohemian fantasies, easy familiarity with the famous, simplicity of celebrity, have all faded away....The mythic Indian Coffee House was once a meeting place of freedom fighters, bohemians and revolutionaries. Today its crusty high ceilings and grimy walls ring with deafening student conversation...', in 'Calcutta Coffee House Phoenix Will Rise', 1 October 2009, website, http://www.hardnewsmedia.com/2009/10/3272; Express News Service, 'Brewing Nostalgia in Coffee House with a New Flavour', 13 April 2009; Jhimli Mukherjee Pandey, 'Coffee House: Changes Brews for Cash Infusion', *TOI*, 22 January 2013.

[41] The script of the film *Pather Panchali* (song of the road) and the lanky fellow was Satyajit Ray.

> Foucault and Derrida left some traces here. But now discussions on chit funds dominate the tables in the Coffee House...sitting at one corner, lost in his spiritual world, the poet Binay Majumdar, an engineer from B.E. College murmuring to himself his poems on Gayatri (not Spivak yet) oblivious of the world—this scene will not return to the Coffee House.[42]

It is not clear what the connection between *adda*, and which fall, repentance and rising up of the Bengalis the author refers to; nor is he aware of the fact that when the ICH was launched in Calcutta, Subhas Chandra had already left India; so he could not have been seen sipping coffee with his colleagues at ICH College Street. 'Tradition creates its own enemy', Sarkar argues, and 'like *Chandimandap* is replaced by Facebook, physical copy of a book by digital book, the Coffee House has been replaced by coffee shops'. He goes on to show how and why different outlets of CCD and other new coffee shops, 'icons of globalization' are more attractive to the middle class. In an attempt to prove that everything now happens in this new type of place, he cites the example of two young film directors finding the idea about their film during *adda* in such places.

The reader will notice that unlike the reminiscenses of Radha Prasad or Kumar Prasad discussed above—half of this long quotation showcasing the 'rise' and the rest the 'fall' of ICH—the piece does not tell us what the author and his peer group did in the place, and why they stopped patronizing the ICH. However, he himself admits later in the same article that the presence of acclaimed senior poets and writers acting as a major source of inspiration was a prime reason behind visiting the place when he was an aspiring, young poet. Looking back, Sarkar recalls his last visits to the ICH with Bratya Basu before the latter became the minister of education in the state, and summarily states that he found the *adda* in the place not attractive

[42] Unfortunately, even a poet like Sarkar cannot resist the temptation of the cult that revels at the familiarity with the fact that poems addressed to Gayatri Chakravorty Spivak by Binay Majumdar were written in the Coffee House. But also see Gayatri Chakravorty Spivak, *An Aesthetic Education in an Era of Globalization*, Cambridge, MA: Harvard University Press, 2012, 271–74.

any more.[43] Perhaps the *adda* at the place deteriorated because his generation deserted the Coffee House? Did Sarkar's generation simply stop visiting the place because the *adda* was not attractive any longer or are there deeper socio-economic reasons behind their not finding the Coffee House attractive? Moreover, was this trend limited only to Calcutta?

A few general trends noted since the late 1970s affected the popularity of the Coffee House in all cities concerned. Dispersal of members of *adda* groups due to personal/professional reasons affected the groups and their *adda* as a whole. Although the ICH in College Street has remained in the same building since it was launched and is most of the time still crowded, there is a discontinuity that needs to be followed in some detail. Some interlocutors pointed out that the students of Presidency College do not visit the ICH any longer. Students of this college were however never the only students visiting the place, and constituted only a part of the clientele consisting of government and bank employees, idlers, poets and writers, university teachers, petty traders of the locality and others. Students from Presidency, Sanskrit, Vidyasagar, Bangabasi, Surendranath, St. Paul's, Scottish Church and other colleges shared the space with others, as they continue to do now. Some who visited the place as students in the late 1940s and 1950s, on having found employment in another part of the city or outside, stopped visiting the Coffee House. After Sunil Gangopadhyay returned from the US, he joined the ABP Group and concentrated on writing prose. He moved first to a different house in the northern and then to the southern part of the city, where he began a private gathering with his friends and fellow writers. Satyajit Ray's *adda* at 5CA ended after the incredible success of *Pather Panchali*.[44] Work took Shankha Ghosh out of Calcutta and later

[43] Bratya Basu personally was never a fan of the Coffee House or the *adda* at the space. In an interview given to the current author he stated that those who did not have anything else to do, whiled away their time in *adda* at the space.

[44] Robinson, *Satyajit*, 356; subsequently this adda shifted to the drawing room Ray's residence, Swagato Das Gupta, 'Ray-barir Adda' (The adda at the Rays'), in *Kolkatar Adda*, 226–31.

he joined the Jadavpur University in south Calcutta from where it became difficult for him to commute to College Street. But he began frequenting the Jadavpur outlet. As he became more preoccupied with the film industry, Soumitra Chatterjee did not have the time to visit the Coffee House any more. Keya Chakrabarti, a regular visitor, died in an accident in 1977. After Rudraprasad dedicated all his time to theatre, he had to gradually stop visiting the ICH. The Bengali band *Moheener Ghoraguli*, which often met at the ICH in Jadavpur, broke up because a few of its members followed their own careers and moved out of the city.[45] Rudraprasad Sengupta expressed it in the following way:

> ...when I felt like a home-less, I used to go the Coffee House. It was my second home. When I got married, had a home and decided on my career, the Coffee House was not needed any longer.[46]

In the aftermath of the political turmoil during the Naxalite Movement and its violent suppression in the early 1970s when Siddhartha Shankar Ray set up volunteer squads of criminals, attempts were being made on behalf of both Congress and CPI (M) to capture the area through local goons, some of whom would be seen occupying the ICH. This created an atmosphere considered not congenial for a friendly *adda* and discouraged some from visiting the place.[47]

The flight of students from the city was another reason why the ICH lost some potential patrons. Earlier the intermediate, undergraduate and post-graduate studies in CU allowed students to be connected with College Street for at least five to six years. Delay in the final examinations of colleges under CU since the late 1960s to the detriment of students resulted in the loss of one academic year. This marked the beginning of an exodus of bright students from the city to Delhi University, Jawaharlal Nehru University (JNU) and other institutions. By the 1980s attending universities in the West

[45] Private communication with Ranjon Ghoshal.

[46] Rudraprasad Sengupta, interview, 21 August 2011; cf. Sibnarayan Ray, 'Ponchasher Doshoke Paikparar Adda', in *Bangalir Adda*, 13–22 for breaking up of their adda due to changes in the life situation of the membersof the group.

[47] Pradip Dhar, interview, 23 July 2011; Prithwish Saha, interview, 4 February 2011.

for the pursuit of higher studies further took many young students out of Calcutta.[48]

The boundaries of the city had been expanding since the refugees began setting up colonies in the outskirts of Calcutta during and after the Partition. The pressure created by the increase in population led to the extension of the city's boundaries towards the south into neighbouring districts. Beginning with Salt Lake, the development of new satellite residential-cum commercial hubs of Garia, new Garia, and lately the New Town Rajarhat complexes far away from central Calcutta saw the middle class moving to those areas from where commuting to College Street was difficult.[49]

In Delhi, every time the ICH changed its location, it lost a considerable part of its clientele who dispersed into smaller groups seeking alternative spaces for meeting. We have seen above that when the Tent ICH opened, many patrons of its predecessor at Janpath stayed away. The popularity of the Tent ICH however picked up soon, and judging by the criteria that attracted the clientele to the ICH, the Mohan Singh Place outlet could have taken over, but for other developments taking place in the capital during the time is covered in detail in Chapter Five. The time that saw the beginning of the beautification and modernization of Delhi that took down the Theatre Communication Building housing the Tent, also marked the beginning of the expansion of metropolitan Delhi. Gurgaon was developing since the early 1980s. The soaring price of real estate in ever-expanding Delhi coupled with the rise in the prices of daily necessities compelled many to leave their rented dwellings in the city to move away to newly developing residential quarters across the Yamuna.[50] Mahip Singh went

[48] Arunabha Bagchi, 'The Turning Point', *The Statesman,* 7 January 2011; Gautam Bhadra, private communication. The flight of city based students for better opportunities elsewhere is applicable to Allahabad as well, Akshatlal Srivastava, e-mail, 24 May 2014.

[49] Nityapriya Ghosh, interview, 26 February 2012; Prithwish Saha, interview, 4 February 2011; Bodhisattva Kar, interview, 7 November 2011; Samir Roy Choudhury, interview, 29 July 2011.

[50] Baldev Vanshi, telephone conversation, 19 June 2012 and interview in Delhi, 3 October 2013; Mamta and Ravindra Kalia lived in Lajpat Nagar before they left

to live in Gurgaon, Baldev Vanshi left for Faridabad, Krishna Sobti began living in Mayur Vihar. With increasing pressure of population on an insufficient infrastructure of public transport, commuting to CP from these neighbourhoods remained tedious up until the launch of the metro.[51] Moreover, neighbourhood markets like the ones in Greater Kailash that began in the 1950s and 1960s grew into extensive shopping complexes while on the other hand CP, in spite of the newly built underground Palika Bazaar, lost its popularity. This process was accelerated since the economic liberalization followed by the growth of malls in different sectors of Delhi in the 1990s.

At a time when CP was losing its attraction, the owners of the Tea House dealt a deathblow to the place. Initially negligence in maintenance was visible from the leaking sewage of the toilet where one had to stand on a wet floor. Division of the property led to a division of the space and half the area was used to launch Cellar, the first discotheque in Delhi, with a [beauty] parlour attached to it. The empty space at the back of these new additions was used to open a vegetarian eatery. Separated from the rest by a wooden partition 'standing like the Berlin Wall', and much reduced in size, the Tea House now had only one door left. This situation continued till one day a notice declared that the space was closed for renovation, to be reopened only as a clothing store.[52]

In Allahabad, the ICH never attracted students in a large number. In the view of Ramesh Grover of Rajkamal Publishers, as far as writers and poets are concerned, there prevails a stillness in Allahabad. The regular Coffee House gatherings gradually lost their attraction because writers began leaving the town to seek better employment opportunities elsewhere.[53] Harivansh Rai Bachchan had left for Delhi in 1955 in order to join the Ministry of External Affairs. Dharamvir Bharati left for Bombay in 1960 when he

for Allahabad; they went back to Delhi but do not go the Coffee House any longer, Mamta Kalia, interview, 22 November 2012.

[51] This point was reiterated by Pankaj Bisht and Satish Sharma.

[52] Kohli, 'Bedil Dilli', 154; Mahip Singh, 'Tea House', 296.

[53] Cf. The cultural and institutional facilities available in Delhi are missing in small towns, the poet Ashok Vajpeyi cited in Sadana, *English Heart,* 26.

became the editor of *Dharamyug* (Age of Duty). Many of the second generation writers meeting at the Coffee House like Gyanranjan, the Kalias and Neelabh among others left Allahabad in the course of the 1980s and 1990s.

In addition, the intrusion of a mass media culture into the middle class drawing room through telecasting mega serials, and especially live telecasts of (cricket) matches via satellite transmission created a deep impact on the concept of leisure, and the way leisure time was spent.[54] The technological advance in the post-Independence period and especially the period since the late 1970s witnessed an enormous expansion of the world of media influencing the practices of leisure.[55] The 1980s signified a major breakthrough in the advertising world. By combining the public service paradigm with that of consumption, advertising removed the contradiction between pleasure and obligation.[56] Still a luxury commodity in the 1970s, a television broadcasting globally oriented programmes became an indispensable utility product in a modern urban household by the turn of the millennium.[57] It was not necessary to leave the house for a leisurely *adda*; in a nuclear family setting a few friends could gather in the house of a common friend and watch a match together and an *adda*, beginning with cups of coffee or tea gradually replaced by glasses of rum or whisky, became common.

While recreation in private places with or without the television was a factor, increasing acceptability of alcohol as part of changing lifestyles became common among the writers and poets in all the cities studied.

Most of the old coffee houses in Europe had a bar and consumption of alcohol was common in those coffee houses as well as in the early coffee houses in India. Pubs were a common scenario in Indian metropolises appealing to the modern, urban upper middle class

[54] Sabyasachi Bhattacharya, interview, 20 August 2011; Rabin Mukherjee and Prithwish Saha, interview, 4 February 2011; Pankaj Bisht, interview, 17 October 2012.

[55] Arvind Rajagopal, *The Indian Public Sphere: Readings in Media History*, New Delhi: OUP, 2009.

[56] Mazarella, *Shoveling Smoke*.

[57] Ibid., Rajagopal, *The Indian Public Sphere*, 15–17.

who gradually replaced the European and American clientele. The Coffee Board seems to have kept the middle class values in mind and consequently the outlets of the India Coffee House did not serve any alcohol or alcoholic beverages.[58] Reproducing the European coffee house culture, the Indian cultural elite was happy to emulate the intellectual aspects of that culture, but true to normative middle class practices did not necessarily associate the space with the consumption of alcohol. In Calcutta there were a few for whom the consumption of alcohol was not a choice for various reasons. However, the old middle class was not entirely averse to alcohol.[59] Regular visitors of the ICH would sometimes smuggle in small bottles of rum in their pocket. Mixed stealthily with the infusion or black coffee they drank, the charm of enjoying a prohibited pleasure undetected by the public was double.[60] Alcohol was and is *not* by far a part of the ICH culture and a drunk Shakti Chattopadhyay or Benoy Majumdar was more an exception and nuisance than the norm.[61]

For many established and aspiring poets and writers who were against tradition and wanted to make a statement through their lifestyle, use of alcohol (and drugs) was common.[62] In Calcutta, a visit

[58] Cf. The aged school-teacher Ambikacharan cannot find any similarity between the coffee houses he has read about in Russian novels and the College Street Coffee House he encounters, Bhattacharya, *Albert hall*, 75.

[59] The foundation of Surapan Nibaroni Sabha (Association for the prevention of the consumption of alcohol) by the social reformer Ramtanu Lahiri bringing out two monthly magazines *Well-wisher* and *Hitosadhak* (Benefactor) are testimony to how rampant the consumption of alcohol was among the educated Bengali in the nineteenth century, Shibnath Shastri, *Ramtanu Lahiri o Tatkalin Bangosamaj* (Ramtanu Lahiri and Contemporary Bengali Society), Kolkata: Rubi, 2003, 278.

[60] Somak Das for rum in the ICH College Street; for consumption of alcohol among the visitors of the ICH and Tea House in Delhi, *DTH*, 363, 413 and passim; on consumption of alcohol in Allahabad, Neelabh, e-mail, 23 August 2012.

[61] Clientele at both the outlets at CP in Delhi and College Street, Calcutta have been able to convince the management that it is necessary to overlook the consumption of tobacco in order to ensure a constant flow of visitors. At Jadavpur however smokers keep to the prohibition and use the corridor in front for smoking.

[62] Saratkumar Mukhopadhyay 'Or Netritwo Parokshe Swikar Kore Niyechhi' (Indirectly we accepted his leadership), *Desh*, 80.1, November 2, 35–38, 2012 on his consumption of country liquor together with Sunil Gangopadhyay and Shakti Chattopadhyay at a shop in Shyambazar at night.

to the ICH was followed by some—including the legendary Kamal Kumar Majumdar—by a visit to Khalasitola, the den of country liquor, a hot spot where the rank and file of the society came face to face. On their visit to Calcutta, foreigners like Ginsberg and George Chadoul wanting to experience the 'real' Calcutta were taken to Khalasitola.[63] Watering holes within the budget of the middle class were Chhota Bristol—*chhota* or small because it was close to a hotel bearing the same name—and Olympia Pub (reopened as Oly Pub).[64] 'Hungry' Samir Roy Choudhury saw no conflict between the Coffee House and Khalasitola—the littérateurs he knew easily folded the one into the other adding yet another dimension to the literary space. But poets and writers associated with *Kaurab* like Tushar Roy who went to the Oly Pub, would not go to the Coffee House.[65] It is pertinent in this context to note that, if *Krittibas*, the seminal literary magazine of the 1950s was conceived in the Coffee House, when Sunil decided to organize *Budhsandhya*, the idea of this 'Wednesday evening' get together at his residence was conceived in a bar.[66] The writer Shirshendu Mukhopadhyay stayed away from the *adda* of *Budhsandhya*, because after a while the participants would be high due to unlimited consumption of alcohol, and as a teetotaller Mukhopadhyay would not know what to do.

Similarly, there were a number of writers in Delhi who considered the consumption of alcohol a necessary condition for success as a writer.[67] There were some who would first have a peg or two at Gaylord before visiting the Tea House. The renowned Urdu lyricist and poet Naresh Kumar Shad was known for openly mixing alcohol with the half-finished glass of water on the table.[68] Other visitors of the space could sneak out for a slightly different kick in a nearby

[63] Mukhopadhyay, *Coffee-r Cup*.

[64] Prithvijit Mitra, 'Enjoy a Drink with a Dash of Nostalgia', *TOI*, 5 December 2010.

[65] Samir Roy Choudhury, interview, 29 July 2011.

[66] Subodh Sarkar, 'Shudhu Raja i Nei' (Only the king is not there), *ABP*, 7 September 2013.

[67] Hardayal, 'Tea House', 508.

[68] Dwivedi, 'Ek tha Tea House', 365–66.

dhaba or to one of the fancy restaurants offering alcohol and return to their table at the ICH.[69]

In Allahabad too drinking in public was not commonly accepted and alcohol was consumed in private gatherings till bars began emerging in the 1970s.[70] Yet, many Hindi writers took to drinking alcohol at the time and began smoking as a token of revolt against the purist attitude prevalent at home and outside. The 'Hungry' writer Rajkamal Chowdhury, who would begin looking for a patron for the supply of alcohol early in the morning, would find inevitably someone by the end of the day.[71]

One of the reasons behind writers not coming to the ICH any more since the 1980s was the increasing acceptance of the consumption of alcohol as part of life. Earlier it was not widely accepted, and not so openly practiced.[72] Commenting on Hindi writers, Neelabh informed that earlier when they were young, the consumption of alcohol was taboo, so he and his friends would have to consume alcohol stealthily. Once they had their own family and separate establishment, that was not an issue any longer and gradually the charm of alcohol replaced that of coffee.

Related to the changes mentioned above, are changes in the literary world since the late 1940s. Much of the creativity in the fields of fine arts and literature in the 1940s as reflected in the works of the writers of PWA and IPTA were inspired by the Leftist ideology of addressing real life issues. As shown above, such actors and writers

[69] The best documentation on the relationship between alcohol and Hindi-Punjabi-Urdu writers I have come across is in the memoir of Ravindra Kalia's literary journey in *Ghalib Chhuti Sharaab*. Although Kalia writes about himself, he is seldom seen consuming alcohol alone. The anthology on the Tea House in Delhi is a further testimony on this issue. See Vanshi, 'Sahityik', 220; Prabhakar, 'Tea House', 413; consumption of alcohol was becoming a part of the mannerism in the Hindi literary world of Delhi in the 1970s, Hardayal, 'Tea House', 508 and passim.

[70] In Allahabad there were shacks selling country liquor. From the Coffee House visitors like Narendra Deva would go to those places. In Delhi Ashok Sakseria and Mahendera Bhalla would go to Wankura near the Cottage Industries Emporium, Neelabh, interview.

[71] *DTH*, 75; Neelabh, interview, 17 October 2012.

[72] Kalia, *Ghalib*, 23.

actively supported the cause of the ICH. But both these organizations lost their significance by the late 1940s due to a conflict between the hardliners and soft-liners in the Communist Party of India. Further ideological conflicts led to the fragmentation of the Left as noted in Chapter Five. In his memoir Neelabh Gyanranjan argued that the existing literary movements in the 1970s failed to address the real social issues or impress upon the younger generations. Emergence of institutions of national academies and prestigious awards led to the formation of interest groups around influential figures leading to factionalism that stood in the way of open ideological discussions.[73]

Upendranath Ashk's *Chehre Anek* (Many Faces) documented the cynicism of a writer who thought he was not being taken seriously by his peer group. In the words of his biographer, that he published much of his work himself, was guided by the idea that he was unfairly attacked or deceived by his fellow writers. He also developed a combative attitude in order to deal with negative criticism which he answered with countercriticism and personal attacks.[74] Like their political counterparts, influential writers were not averse to power. Consequently, the later generations, while 'posing to be revolutionary in their writing, were more interested in seeking favour in order to secure their own career'. This attitude helped the commercialization of literature. It kept 'the business running so that the cooperative did not intervene'.[75] In contrast with the animated discussions in the Coffee and Tea House that decided the fate of writers and their creation, new writing in Hindi, important or not, is said to have landed in a black hole of indifference.[76] According to Dinesh Grover and Arindam Ghosh, in spite of the high rate of publishing, readership has declined. Issues like art and society considered important in earlier times are not considered important under the changing economic forces

[73] Neelabh, *Gyanranjan*.

[74] Rockwell, *Upendranath*, chapters two and five.

[75] Bharatbhushan Agarwal, 'Dilli se Patrachar', in *DTH*, 249–59 (255); cf. 'The ground of Hindi literature became so brackish after 1980 that those trying to flourish on it afterwards could produce only weed', Sunita Jain 'Bah Dilli', 471; also see Chapter Four.

[76] Vanshi, 'Bhumika', *DTH*, x.

encroaching upon the space of literary discussions and activism.[77] Keshav Malik resented the little space available for art and literature in the newspapers. Previously there was scope for a serious contribution in the weekly magazines of the newspapers; currently that space has been taken by information on commodity and lifestyle.

The consolidation of the Left rule in Bengal left no space for open criticism. This was followed by a trend of writing for the establishment on the one hand, while on the other, under the changed political circumstances much of the Leftist rhetoric lost its meaning.[78] Currently, not only is the ideology of revolution lost, privileged by an understanding with the changing political top brass, instead of addressing the real issues the elite pay lip service to the mantra of transformation, and in the process have lost their credibility. Nourished by the fruits of globalization, they are more concerned about awards, trips to national and international destinations and seminars.[79]

The influence of the corporate world on art, literature including little magazines has been able to suffocate the free spirit in the opinion of many. In Calcutta, Anuradha Mahapatra, Bishwa Mandal, Parthapratim Kanjilal and Ashok Roy Chowdhury were vocal about the corporatization of literature including the space of the little magazines where much emphasis is given to the physical get-up vis-à-vis the content has become inconsequential—with the exception of a few select titles.

While the cumulative result of all these developments was the gradual moving away of erstwhile patrons from the Coffee House, the factor that facilitated the changing lifestyle of the petit bourgeois throughout India was the attempt by the government of India to bridge the gap in payment between public private, and service sectors by increasing the salary of government servants. From the fourth Pay Commission (1970–73) onwards, the successive increases in the

[77] Novelist, playwright and script writer Ashgar Wajahat cited in Anonymous, 'Decline in Literary Activism: Hindi Writers', http://www.outlookindia.com/news/article/Decline-in-Literary-Activism-Hindi-Writers/789506.

[78] Abhijit Mukhopadhyay, Sarasija Basu, interview.

[79] Sumanta Banerjee, 'Poribartan: Transgression Masquerading as Transformation', *Frontier*, 44.23, 18–24 December 2011.

payment elevated the standard of life of the middle class, reaching its climax in 1991.[80] Earlier, there was a distinction between the cultural elite and the wealthy and the former had embraced the Indian Coffee House at a time when they were insecure and in financial distress. The revisions in the pay scale blurred this distinction and put the cultural elite at par with their global peer group.

It is necessary to consider these developments against the backdrop that since their inception, and especially since 1958 when the outlets of the ICH were taken over by the regional coffee workers' cooperative societies—apart from time to time additions to the menu—the structure of the ICH has indeed remained unchanged.[81] The article by Subodh Sarkar cited previously may be considered as an admission that [under the changed circumstances] the *adda* in the Coffee House lost its attraction.

While over the decades some of the *adda* of the Coffee House has thus been decentered, what is often forgotten in this context is that the first generation of the ICH visitors had begun almost from a void. Whether in Calcutta, Delhi or Allahabad at the time the chain was launched there was *no* alternative to the kind and magnitude of the outlets of the ICH. Not only that, it was part of the regular social practices for 'typical middle class families' to visit the Coffee House, as seen in Chapter Two, for many of the connoisseurs of the place, the day seemed wasted without at least one visit to the Coffee House.[82]

[80] Siba Sankar Mohanty, 'Governance of the Indian Economy under UPA Rule-3: The Happy Middle Class and the Salaried Members in the Government Sector', http://lokkatha.com/150/index.php/11-general-articles/economics/724-the-happy-middle-class-and-the-salaried-members-in-the-government-sector%7CGovernance.

[81] It is interesting to note that the new look of the ICH College Street after it was revamped at the initiative of the government of West Bengal and the private concern Bengal Shelter during 2009–10 remains a contested issue. Veteran ICH visitors see it as an 'old prostitute trying to attract the customer with a new make-up', or Bodhisattva Kar, 'we have been contesting the high culture of Calcutta in the ICH; finally the coffee house has become Sonagachhi (a well-known red light area in Calcutta)'; cf. Sarkar, 'Coffee House-tai'.

[82] Prama Mukhopadhyay, 'The Religion of Resistance', Cultural Cartographies of Media: Andoloni Bangali part II', 13 December 2014, http://mltspaces.blogspot.in/2014/12/andoloni-bangali-part-2.html; also Chapters One, Four and Six.

With the expansion of the metropolitan area, cities like Delhi and Calcutta have been decentered since, followed by the rise of new educational institutions, places of association and recreation. In CP alone for example in comparison with the few places that have been closed like Gaylord and Standard many more cafés and restaurants catering to the national and international clientele have emerged.[83] The renovation and development of Hauz Khas Village and other areas of Old Delhi are a case in point. The university campus in Jadavpur in south Calcutta enticed students and teachers away from College Street.[84] Comfortable bookshops in other parts of the city decreased the importance of the College Street area as the only source for all kinds of books. If in Allahabad there were the pavement coffee shops and the elitist El Chico, in Calcutta in the 1980s, the Academy of Fine Arts with the newly built Nandan complex became a major place for the youth to spend time.[85] The then chief minister Buddhadev Bhattacharya, who as a student of Presidency used to visit the ICH, used the large Satyajit Ray archive room in the complex

[83] Pankaj Bisht, 'Muft Bazaar ke Daur mein Kaffee Haus' (The Coffee House in the Age of Liberal Economy), *Samayantar* (Changed Times), July 2009, 34–36.

[84] For example Sankha Ghosh; the couple of letters Supriya and Sukanta Chaudhuri left the Presidency College for the JU. In Delhi after JNU was established, there was an outlet of the ICH in the campus for a few years. There was some contact with the Tent ICH through students following radical left ideology, but the distance from CP and the problem of transport stood in the way of a closer contact that could be seen in DU and College Street. Even when they are in the neighbourhood of CP in connection with active politics, radical student factions from the JNU usually go to other places for refreshment; interview Rajan Pandey, Ph. D. student and the AISA Delhi State Secretary.

[85] Sankha Ghosh, interview. Both the places have canteen offering tea and snacks of good quality. During 1995–2010 Nandan was the venue where the Calcutta International Film Festival was inaugurated; an annual little magazine festival is held at the Nandan premises since 2001. For *adda* in this complex see Basu Chaudhuri, 'Palte jaoa somporker galpo'. Haldiram's at the crossing of Jawaharlal Nehru Road and Jagadish Chandra Bose Road is a big food joint in that neighbourhood. In College Street itself Food Junction, an upmarket air conditioned restaurant opposite the Medical College and Chini's, a pavement stall selling for example a plate of noodles at Rs 10 came up in the 1990s. Students who found the Coffee House expensive, would go to Chini's (now extinct), interview, Ratnabir Guha.

in the evenings where he would meet Sunil Ganguli and others, and proofread his own work.[86]

Currently, the modern coffee cafés form only a tiny segment of the endless array of new structures in urban India for the new middle class youth to hop from one place to another.[87] While they compete with each other for a clientele who have no brand loyalty, unlike the ICH in earlier times, each café forms only one of the many possible destinations including malls, fine arts and theatre complexes, restaurant chains, theme parks and other attractions that have since been launched and that structurally exclude the poor and underprivileged. Chaitali Mukherjee and Dhruba Mandal—a couple I kept in touch with during the fieldwork in 2012–14—are a typical example of this new middle class. Chaitali's father lost his job in the private sector leaving the family finances in a bad shape, and throughout her student life, Chaitali had to be careful about every rupee she spent. Circumstances changed for her, when she passed M.Com. and got a permanent position in a semi-public concern. Her boyfriend Dhruba, a software engineer, was a member of the underprivileged section of the society, and a second generation of climbers. I met them at CCD in the South City Mall and at Mani Square, but these were the only two of the places they visited. They turned up their nose at the mention of the ICH; the interior did not attract them at all.[88]

[86] Mohua Das, 'The Unthinkable: A Nandan Minus its Mascot', *The Telegraph*, 1 January 2011.

[87]Ankita Biswas, Arijit mukherjee, Sonali Roychoudhuri, Olympia Saha and Shouvik Sen, form a group of 22 fresh engineers graduating from an engineering institute in Beleghata, Calcutta. In the opinion of these five, multiplexes are more attractive for their generation because they offer a package—you can do shopping, watch a movie, have some food. When they watch a movie, it is usually at the South city Mall (Lake Gardens) or Mani Square (Salt Lake), 15 July 2011.

[88] Names changed on request. They also went to City Centre in New Town, Highland Park, Riverside Mall in Howrah and Westside among other places. For lack of brand loyalty among the new customers, see Sourajit Aiyar, 'Starbuck's Strategy for India: Is it a Winner?', Market Moving News and Views, http://www.marketmoving.info/starbucks-strategy-india-winner/; also WARC Case Studies, 'Loyalty Level Low in India', http://www.warc.com/Content/News/N29042_Loyalty_levels_low_in_India.content.

A few of my interlocutors agreed that as soon as they had more disposable cash in pocket, they would stop visiting the ICH. Jo Paul, a third year engineering student at College of Engineering, Trivandrum deserves special mention in this connection. Jo wanted to be an IAS officer. He would like to go to CCD regularly, but the 'paltry' sum he received as scholarship, and the Rs 2000 he received from his father for study coupled with all the other costs, including hostel charges in the city, did not permit such luxury. Wearing an ordinary synthetic polo shirt and a pair of polyester trousers, he liked the idea of wearing branded clothes. Jo could not wait for the time he would have plenty of money to spend on clothes and other consumption goods. 'It would be good if Café Coffee Day raised the price of their items; if they don't, I shall go to another expensive chain.'[89] If Jo was cherishing his dream for the future while sipping coffee at the ICH, some admitted that although they once as students, used to visit the ICH earlier, as young professionals with more disposable income they preferred the decent, neat ambience of CCD.

Chandrayee Ghosh, working on her Ph.D. thesis in physiology from CU was a regular at the ICH College Street as a student. When I met her at the South City Mall on 24 August 2012 she was there with her friend Pritam Sarkar, MCA. In Chandreyee's view while the lifestyle and mentality of the middle class had changed, the ICH had not: 'it was always crowded; it took long before the sloppy workers came to take the order and then to actually bring the coffee'. Pritam, an accountant by profession, added that heritage cannot be sold unless it comes with modern comfort and facility. If the Coffee House had to survive, it had to be 'packaged' and 'marketed'.

During his research on Calcutta Ritajyoti Bandypadhyay of the Centre for Social Science Studies in Calcutta noted that as soon as they had more floating income, post-doctoral humanities students of JU in the late 1990s and later deserted the ICH and began visiting the airconditioned restaurants that had opened in the region in the wake of economic liberalization. Interviewed in Göttingen, Bandyopadhyay succinctly emphasized the socio-economic aspect of the changing

[89] ICH Anna's Arcade, Trivandrum, interview, 4 December 2011.

practice, 'As a student I did not have enough money to spend, and I went to the ICH. Now I am earning in Euro, so after I return, I shall go to Barista, CCD and Starbucks'.[90] Like in earlier times, the ICH caters to the average middle class as long as the latter operates on a shoe-string budget. Once it is possible for the customer to climb up the social ladder, one can dissociate oneself from the ICH. Once the familiarity with the place is lost, the Coffee House *adda* loses its attraction.

IS THE TRADITION OF *ADDA* FINALLY DEAD?

I began this work with the suggestion that while introducing the consumer to the new beverage, the ICH facilitated sociability in the form of *adda*. Dipesh Chakrabarty already drew our attention to the fear among the Bengali elite that like many other traditions, *adda* too was under threat.[91] Subodh Sarkar's article cited earlier confirmed the death of *adda*. Changing society and the increasing pressure for building a career is supposed to have a deep impact on the practice of leisure. Earlier, students had the scope to go astray, to spend time in *adda* and other leisurely pursuits. At a time when the pressure of competition forces students to focus on their career, when as part of the global capitalist system young people especially in the service sector use odd hours for earning livelihood, lack of leisure keeps more and more people away from public spaces. Moreover, digital network sites and video games provide a much sought after possibility of virtual interaction. While this is a concern expressed mainly by the elderly,[92] students too admit that a full schedule during the semester, coupled with assignments, such as mid-term and

[90] Bandyopadhyay, interview, 6 June 2013.

[91] Chakrabarty, 'Adda'.

[92] Parthapratim Kanjilal, interview, 17 August 2011; Raghab Bandyopadhyay commented that earlier students had the opportunity to 'waste time'; Sandipan Deb and Ashis K. Biswas, 'Much Adda About Nothing', 19 June 1996, http://www.outlookindia.com/article/Much-Adda-About-Nothing/201561; Peter Trachtenberg, 'The Chattering Masses', *New York Times*, http://www.nytimes.com/2005/05/15/travel/tmagazine/the-chattering-masses.html?_r=0.

end of-the-term tests, and planning in advance for the next step in career indeed take up most of their time. Yet, the youth in the cities covered insist that the increased pressure notwithstanding, they try to make time for *adda*. The importance of adda may have decreased and modes of *adda* have so changed that they do not have to spend hours on end at once place every day—thanks especially to the digital media. The digital media provides discussion forums, chat sites resulting in an increasing communication on the virtual world. In spite of all these engagements, they try to find time in between and after classes, and especially during weekends for an *adda*.[93] In all the three cities, there are students who get together at least once a week for an extended *adda*.[94]

The question of leisure-time and the withdrawal of the former patrons is related to the quality of the mode of leisure in question. As the article of Subodh Sarkar *adda* has become an inconsequential 'chat'; unlike in earlier times when it involved serious discussion on important subjects, the content of *adda* in the ICH now is light. However, already in the 1950s, when the Coffee House *addas* were at their climax, we find concern regarding the deteriorating quality of *adda*. In the novel *Albert Hall*, the aged school-teacher Ambikacharan, who was familiar with the Hall in its previous incarnation and was visiting the place after one and a half decades, could not get over the shock at the transformation of the space on seeing the Coffee House. In common with regular customers, one of whom—true to Coffee House tradition—offered him coffee, he sat and tried to comprehend

[93] Rahul Chakravarti, P.G. (Economics) final year, PU, interview, 15 February 2011; Jayjayanti Banerjee, Purba Hossain, Lumbini Sharma B.A. Ist year (History); Dithi Mukherjee, B.A. final year (history) P.U.; Akshat Lal Srivastava, e-mail. See also the web forum Allahabad Civil Lines Nostalgic memories that even proposed holding an online *mushaira*.

[94] Malini Bhattacharya, an aspiring Bengali prose and short story writer/translator who used to visit the space during 2005–07 as an M.A. (English, CU) with her batchmates in a mixed group at least twice a week, interview, 9 March 2011. Dithi Mukherjee B.A. (History, PU) 2011–14 goes for an *adda* with friends studying history and political science at least once a week. Dithi used to visit the ICH more after she joined the university; these days their *adda* is more in the courtyard of the College; Akshatlal Srivastava for Allahabad.

the change and observed the *new* generation in the *new* place. As he heard the ongoing conversation at the table he shared:[95]

> A wave of laughter rose in Ambikacharan's mind. The times had changed entirely, he thought. There was *no substance in the conversation of the present day youth* .... his laughter changed into a heaviness of the heart.

Nostalgia about the loss of *substance* in the *adda*—like many other things of the past on the basis of the parameters of one's own experience and times—was there even at a time when there were separate tables for discussing poetry, prose, theatre-producing and reproducing culture in the ICH. However, it also shows that Ambikacharan was *unfamiliar* with the group, and judged them by the fragments of the conversation he overheard.

Adda as a leisurely social practice, however, does not always have to be 'at the highest level' or even 'productive'. As reiterated earlier, *adda* is a break from everyday familial and workplace monotony and can very well be an end in itself. It becomes problematic only when a public space like the Coffee House,—especially in Bengal, is seen as representing only the normative. As shown in Chapter Two, the *addas* of the cultural elite, as gleaned through their own reminiscenses, could be quite un-*bhadralok*-like, falling well below the symbolic value attached to them.

To my question as to what their 15-member student group did at the lengthy Sunday meetings in the *Baradari* (pillared-pavilion) of Baluaghat on the banks of the Yamuna, Akshatlal Srivastava informed me that while the basic idea was to rejuvenate themselves by getting rid of the tension of routine, they discussed books, local, national and world politics, and issues related to the Allahabad Heritage Society which he managed together with others. He also read out his poems to his friends for their opinion. What kind of books did they discuss? The books included Shakespeare's plays, Paul Coelho's *The Alchemist*, the oeuvre of Salman Rushdie, and while *Pride and Prejudice*, *Lolita* and *Gone with the Wind* were all-time favourites

[95] Bhattacharya, *Albert Hall*, 93; emphasis added.

with the female members of the group, Jaswant Sinha's biography of Mohammad Ali Jinnah was especially debated, according to Akshat.[96] Asked what the subject of their *adda* was, the weekly *adda* of the courtyard in Presidency, Dithi Mukherjee, a third year student who also visited the ICH with her friends, responded 'everything; from literature, philosophy, physics, meta-physics, politics to paranormal activities'.[97] In spite of all outwardly changes, the social meaning of *adda* seems to have remained unchanged.

THE CURRENT VISITORS OF THE COFFEE HOUSE

Just as the dissociation from a large section of the middle class is a crucial marker of the distinct class identity and taste of the upper class, appropriation of an idealized social behaviour as marker of taste becomes essential for another section of the middle class. The association with the Coffee House as a cultural marker is so strong that for a section of the city students and those from the suburbia and towns in the interior going to study in Calcutta, the place has remained an indispensable point of reference.[98] One part of the students at the ICH is from areas across the Hugli commuting daily to the city in connection with higher education.[99] Another part of the student population seen

[96] While many members of the group met almost everyday, the Sunday sessions lasted for four to five hours; e-mail, 13 March 2015.

[97] Interview, 27 February 2015.

[98] Shukla Ganguly, interview; Ritajyoti Bandyopadhyay went from a school in Murshidabad to study in JU. While following additional classes in Presidency College, he would visit the ICH. Sandip Chattopadhyay went from a suburban school to attend the Presidency College. For both Raiajyoti and Sandip it was common to visit the ICH with friends from the school and others, while spending time with classmates would be usually somewhere outside the ICH; also Manini Bhattacharya.

[99] Aradhana Murmu (Kamardanga), Bipasha Maitra (Dasnagar), Pallabi Das (Uluberia), Debalina Mondal (Sankrail) and Nazneen Mallik (Andul) all study in the Sanskrit College but commute daily from their respective place across the Hugli, interview, 22 August 2011. Cf. in addition to the students of DU, a large part of the students coming to the ICH in CP are from IPU in Dwarka; in general the students of JNU do not go to the ICH. Members of student unions, even when they are in the neighbourhood of CP, they go to places other than the ICH, interview, Rajan Pandey,

in the ICH especially around lunch hours comes from the outskirts of Calcutta—be it the Ramakrishna Mission College in Narendrapur in the 24 Parganas or the students of the numerous engineering and IT institutes mushrooming in Beliaghata, Salt Lake, Anandapur and other areas of greater Calcutta. Many come in large groups of ten to twelve once a month and combine it with the purchase of books or other errands they might have to take care of in the College Street area. The numerous reproductions of the myth of the lost *adda* and the lost glory of the Coffee House have made these students aware of the 'heritage' and historical value of this practice in the ICH.

Students from outside Calcutta are not new to the ICH. In the case of the erstwhile patrons, who went to College Street and the CU almost every day for the purpose of study/work, and for whom a visit to the ICH was part of a broader range of social practices as many of them were otherwise involved in literary or political pursuits in the neighbourhood. They visited the place in between classes, and made it their 'home outside home'. What is new is that the ICH is not embedded in the daily life of many of the current groups studying in dispersed autonomous institutes who visit the place once in a while. They do not associate themselves with either the neighbourhood or the workers of the place. For various reasons, although they are knowledgable about the high culture associated with the ICH, they are not entirely familiar with that culture, and feel insecure about it. Representing different institutions, there is no common bond or purpose linking such heterogenous groups studying engineering, information technology and the like, and consequently, their groups in the ICH are usually self-contained.[100] Unlike in earlier times when

Robert Raman. However, I have come across a few students of JNU at ICH CP as part of civil society organizations.

[100] A group of students from the Institution of Information Technology Beliaghata were not familiar with other groups of students occupying the space; 'We are students of commerce, we have not studied literature', interview, Surajit Saha, Shoubhik Banerjee, Parameswar Ghoshal, 1st year, Umesh Chandra College of Commerce, CU. They knew the place since they were in class IX students in a school in suburban Belur, interview, 24 August 2011; some faces in the space were familiar to them, but they too kept to themselves.

only high caste saree-wearing Hindu female students patronized the place, female students from the traditionally underprivileged groups and the minority sections of society represent a new phenomenon.[101] Another recent development is that many female students spend time here in the evenings whereas earlier students and especially girls were supposed to return home before dark. Yet another aspect that differentiates the present from the earlier generations is that students currently visiting the ICH in general have more disposable cash and spend it on food in the place.

Consequently, a part of the urban cultural elite associates the ICH and its *adda* solely with such groups because not only have members of such groups not acquired the taste to partake in the normative discussions expected in the space, since they travel a long distance, consumption of food is a part of their visit to the ICH. As this social practice is not based on the acquisition of a distinct taste, it is frowned upon by the urban elite as a characteristic of the lack of 'good taste'. Bodhisattva Kar recalled that as students if they saw someone eating in the ICH, they would sarcastically refer to 'sat-tar local' implying that visitors who ate at that place were from outside Calcutta and would catch the 7.00 pm local train to return. Sarkar too criticizes the post-colonial outfit of the Coffee House that has transformed it into an ordinary restaurant whose lifeline is the cheapest available coffee and cutlet and attests to the popularity of CCD, which had even the Coffee House legend Sunil Gangopadhyay under its spell.[102] Apparently aware of the rights of the workers, this view however does not take into consideration that if the ICH accommodates only the regular *adda* groups who spend hours at a stretch without any intake of food the already distressed survival of the cooperatives will

[101] This observation relates to the Coffee House in College Street where it was easier for me to identify the surnames. Interview Aradhana Murmu, Debalina Mandal, and Nazneen Mallik, students of Sanskrit College, 22 August 2011 and Zarnain Hossain and Zubin Nawaz, students of Jaipuria College, interview, 24 October 2014. According to the regular visitors of the space, female students with a head-scarf are a very recent trend in the Coffee House, interview Prithwish Saha.

[102] In 'Coffee-house-tai ar nei'; for an entirely different view of the institution see Todhunter, 'The Indian Coffee House'.

be further in danger.[103] Moreover, such a view ignores the fact that from Buddhadeva Bose to Suniti Kumar Chatterjee, great figures associated with different *adda* groups, did not see any conflict between the pastime and eating snacks. Furthermore, ambience apart, sale of an increasing assortment of food items forms an important part of the marketing strategy of CCD and other globalized café chains.[104]

In Delhi, the diverse nature of the public in the Tent Coffee House seems to have been discouraging for a section of the middle class patronizing the ICH at Janpath. The PRRM had gone a long way to publicize the institution as a place offering a cup of coffee at a throwaway price. Being centrally located at CP, and open on all sides, Tent was a perfect meeting place, far more public in nature than its precursor, that attracted different kinds of public. Consequently, the disenchanted erstwhile patrons began going to Embassy, the India International Centre (IIC), the Press Club and the like. Like Embassy and IIC, the new spaces of leisure drew some of the old, and in the process acquired the new middle class patrons, but they are *essentially* different from the ICH. While Embassy has always catered to the

[103] According to Angshuk Bhowmik (25), a journalist with *Bengal Post* and a third generation Coffee House connoisseur who first visited the space when he was a student of Hindu School, the business of the cooperative depends on this floating population from the outskirts of the city, interview, 25 August 2011. The urban-rural tension can be noticed in Allahabad as well. When asked about the absence of students from the ICH Asrar Gandhi, Vaidurya Pratap Sahi and Akshatlal Srivastata, my informants at that place responded that more than three-fourth of the student population in the university was composed of students coming from the rural eastern UP who were not familiar with the culture of the city and the ICH. But to the question if they—the *Allahabadis*—ever visited the ICH with their peer group while in school or college, Gandhi responded that his visit to the space as a student was not frequent and Sahi confirmed that he had never been there just in order to spend some time together with his friends like his counterparts in Calcutta or Delhi. Akshatlal stated that students preferred to visit 'cool'places.

[104] V.G. Siddhartha, the owner of CCD told me that a considerable part of the profit of CCD came from the sale of food, interview, 2 December 2011; Rahul Sachitanand and K.R. Balasubramanyam, 'How Starbucks and Café Coffee Day are Squaring up for Control of India's Coffee Retailing Market', The Economic Times, 8 June 2014, http://articles.economictimes.indiatimes.com/2014-06-08/news/50420986_1_cafe-coffee-day-amalgamated-bean-coffee-india-s.

section of the well-to-do middle class, IIC with its closed membership is an elite institution and a gated community, more like an exclusive European Club of the colonial times, catering to brown sahibs in the post-colonial period.

Many of the erstwhile Coffee House visitors in Delhi—and to some extent the regulars from other cities—now go to the IIC. The appointments I had among others with Vijay Dutt, Inder Malhotra, Trilochan Singh, Uma Vasudev and Alka Raghuvanshi (she had heard about the ICH from her father and uncles), was at this Centre. Some of them, like Malhotra and Vasudev, followed the ICH to the Tent but stopped visiting it since it again moved to Mohan Singh Place. SPD with his group of friends, many politicians and journalists began going to the the Embassy. There were different tables for members of different political parties, and tables for journalists. Discussions across the tables were common. Harmit Singh, a photographer who had been out of the country for a number of years, found ICH at Janpath gone after he returned in 1973. He tried to a join a few of the journalists who were going to the Tent. But open on all sides, Tent was 'like a *baraat*'. So he began going to Embassy. Asked about the price differential between the two places, he chuckled 'we had moved up…we moved up'. This interview also took place at IIC. On being pointed out that it was a closed club, he said 'it is; it is'. Tapan Raychaudhuri did not like the ICH on College Street any more but felt at home at the IIC. The lifestyle of the cultural elite has changed to such an extent that the rundown outlets of the ICH, managed by workers, are no longer an option for this section of the middle class.

The fragmentation of the middle class is an aspect evident from the current ethnographic research in that the two sets of coffee houses in question—the MNC-run cafés on the one hand and the unkempt ICH on the other—largely cater to the upper and lower segments of the middle class respectively.[105] Global café chains attract, in addition to the new middle class, a section of the old cultured middle class.

[105] When it was pointed out that students of the JU visited the ICH near the campus, Gautam Bhadra responded, 'tahole oder pocket-e paisa nei'—then surely they do not belong to the well to do; for different classes of people visiting the two sets of coffee houses see Shobhan Saxena, 'The Capital Bean Stalkers', *Tehelka*, 11 December 2014.

The ICH, on the other hand, attracts those segments opposed to the idea of a globalized culture and those who are financially not in a position to afford the new social spaces.

In order to understand the relationship between the middle class and the Coffee House, it is important to bear in mind that in addition to expressing the gratification for sharing the cherished place of cultural heritage and thus validating the claim to middle class aspirations, the economic factor is equally emphasized by interlocutors in *all* the places visited in connection with the current study. From Delhi to Trivandrum, a large section of the students who make the ICH their second home, a few might visit Barista or CCD to satiate their curiosity about the new coffee cafés, but their finances will *not* permit them to visit those establishments often, let alone regularly. They are aware that the service in the outlets leaves much to be desired, and that with every passing day the structure increasingly reveals its vulnerability vis-à-vis the aggressive world of the multinationals contemplatively calculating the real estate value of the buildings housing these institutions. Maladies of the outlets are as clear as daylight. Almost all media reports point to the miserable condition of the structure with its furniture, kitchen paraphernalia and poor service.[106] Complaints about the deteriorating quality of the coffee and the food are aplenty; workers now do not hesitate, especially during busy hours, to rush the visitors especially if they are not consuming any food. They do not want to work on regular shifts, but fight for overtime that brings in some extra cash as bonus; they often demand tips and are ever eager to serve foreigners visiting the space.[107]

There is an occasional overlap in that there are customers familiar with both types of cafés. It also shows that they are aware of the pros and cons of both types of structures. Ankita Biswas, Arijit Mukherjee, Sonali Roychoudhuri, Olympia Saha and Shouvik

[106] Freedman, 'Palace of Monkeys'.

[107] Shyamal Basu, Sabyasachi Bhattacharya, interview. In the new relocated outlet on Church Street in Bangalore, customary patrons feel the pressure on the workers, and if they are not consuming food, they understandingly do not spend more than an hour or so in order to make space for those who consume.

Sen—fresh graduates from an engineering institute in Beliaghata, Kolkata—are of opinion that the new structures including the coffee cafés pose no threat to the ICH, because (1) the lack of pretension the ICH represents is attractive to many who would never go to the multiplexes; (2) the people going to the ICH are *not* the type of people visiting the multiplexes or new coffee cafés; (3) these new places do not have the heritage status that the Coffee House has; (4) they do not have the informal ambience of the ICH; and (5) most important, as experienced by Jo Paul in Trivandrum, the new cafés and restaurants are very expensive.[108] In Delhi too there are those familiar with both types of structure. Naina, a DU student working part-time with an NGO meets her different peer groups at different locations. When she is meeting representatives of sister organizations, she makes an appointment at one of the outlets of CCD. Usually they have a coffee and such meetings of three to four persons last for about an hour on an average. But when she has to recruit other students for her own NGO, she would have to meet large groups of students whom she meets at the ICH: 'there you do not have to pay attention to how long you occupy a table. You can order coffee, and if necessary food without having to worry that it is going to cut a hole into your pocket'.[109] Then there are others ranging from students to professionals like Joy Das, Snigdha Ghosh and Manab Pal, MCA students at an institute near Minto Park, Jayjayanti Banerjee, Purba Hossain, Lumbini Sharma B.A. (History) students from PU and Nilanjan Datta of APDR who consider CCD too expensive to be a part of their everyday life. They will visit CCD once in a while, but their association is with the ICH where they can be themselves without having to worry about either time or spending too much.[110]

[108] Interview, ICH Calcutta, 15 July 2011.

[109] Interview, CCD Khan Market; cf. the accounting consultant Suresh Ramasway in Calcutta too took one set of his clients to the ICH, while he accompanied those from the corporate sector to Taj Bengal.

[110] On 15 January 2012, I came across a group of ten students at ICH CP. Vinayak Joshi, Pranab, Sukrit and Rohit Bajaj from DU, Akash, Zeeshan Bashir, Kartik Joshi, Abhinav Pathak and Rohit Sharma from GGSIPU and Nitish Bharadwaj from Garhwal University. They were regular visitors of the place where they celebrated birthdays

Gautam Shenoy (30 years) of Bangalore passionately stated that although he visited the CCD sometimes, it was during the conversations at the ICH that he had made most of his friends. Whether for gossip or for serious discussions, he preferred the ICH. On the other hand, those seeking solitude amidst the chattering masses, also make their way to the place. Suhas Entur (28 years), the young electronic engineer repatriating to Bangalore from Australia, living on his savings and not yet sure about the future—not willing to spend too much in the fancy cafés around including Koshy's he was pretty familiar with, spent some time every day in the ICH on Church Street. Suhas was an avid reader interested in political science and philosophy.[111]

These findings corroborate recent sociological research underlining the heterogeneity of the middle class.[112] This is not to claim that the part of the middle class visiting the outlets of the ICH belong to the groups entirely excluded from all benefits of economic liberalization. That students visiting the outlets can afford to buy food on a regular basis is an indication that even this section of the aspiring middle class is better off compared to earlier times.[113] But the conflicting concept of 'good taste', and claiming distinction through dissociation from, and

---

and on that day were celebrating Rohit's birthday there. According to Rohit, 'CCD is more for elite couples from the metropolitan Delhi where the etiquette is different and everyone speaks English. Here you can choose a seat you like and talk. You have to call the workers to take order and if they take time to bring the coffee, it does not matter. The place suits our pocket, and where will you get this abundance of space—about 4000 square feet—in CP?'. Similar views regarding the setting of the ICH and the moderate pricing of food 'the cheapest in CP' was shared by Aditi, Ishita, Yama, Kshitish, Pallav, Puja, Richa, Rahul—another group of students from DU and Swamy Ramaswamy Memorial University, Ghaziabad.

[111] Cf. 'The Coffee House thoroughly enjoyable when in a jovial mood, a safe refuge in turbulent moods', Malini Bhattacharya, interview, 9 March 2011.

[112] Ruchira Ganguly-Scrase and Timothy J. Scrase, *Globalisation and the Middle Classes in India: The Social and Cultural Impact of Neoliberal Reforms*, Abingdon, Oxon [etc.]: Routledge, 2009; Mark Liechty, *Suitably Modern: Making Middle-class Culture in a New Consumer Society*, Princeton, NJ: University Press, 2003; Mazarella, *Shoveling Smoke*; Donner and de Neve, 'Introduction'.

[113] Basak, 'Coffee'.

association with the social space in question, together with the differeing positions with regard to the economics of new and old cafés point to the stratification among segments of the middle class continuously shaping and reshaping their identity through social practices.

Nostalgia's rose-tinted view not only laments the iconized, mythic past, it fails to recognize what is there. The attempt to objectify the ICH as a place of 'cultural memory' ignores the fact that 'social memory' is still being produced and reproduced there.[114] The Coffee House, as the frequently cited Manna Dey numbers suggest, has the potential as a place of assembly and the social practice of *adda* that it is not always devoid of 'good taste'. In all the cities the Coffee House has been functioning as a parallel establishment providing space to different kinds of public usually not seen in the new coffee cafés. For a large section of the ordinary urban middle class including political and social activists, brokers, canvassers, idlers, journalists, poets, writers and other professionals, the young unemployed and the retired pension-holder, there is no alternative to the ICH where 'the old become young and the young become old'.[115] Like the Ghoshes, Kumars and Singhs of the 1950s and the 1960s, even now there are urbanites nourishing similar critiques about the life in the city that takes them to the ICH breathing life, as expressed by Anurag Dixit, a young language trainer and poet:[116]

> In this city [Delhi] people carry on their business during the day. At the end of the day, we are all alone; *hollow*. It is this feeling of *hollowness* that brings people to the Coffee House. Here they see similar *hollow*, *lonely* people sitting next to them, or at the next table. A conversation begins between strangers. They become familiar, and friendship begins. This is possible only in the Coffee House.

This confirms the scenario envisioned in the epigraph to this chapter. New generations of connoisseurs have found their social

[114] Jan Assmann, *Das Kulturelle Gedächtnis. Schrift, Erinnerung und Politische Identität in Frühen Hochkulturen* (Munich, 1992), 56.

[115] Dushyant, *July ki ek Raat*, 24, 27.

[116] Dixit began visiting the ICH in 2009, interview, 5 January 2012; emphasis added; also Supriya Sarma, student of English, Ramanand College DU, 5 January 2012.

space in the ICH. Due to the changes in the Hindi literary world and the fate of the Coffee House discussed above, the large unscheduled literary *addas* of the Coffee and Tea House in Delhi came to an end. Attempts to remodel CP began in 2000 and with the opening of the metro which has turned out to be the most convenient mode of public transport, the area has regained some of its popularity.[117] It is since that time that ICH is increasingly visited by a younger generation of middle class students of DU, Guru Govind Singh Indraprasth University (GGSIU) in Dwarka and others who have been discovering this place just as the middle class students in the pre and post-Independence days did. These students use the large terrace of the ICH for their *adda* that often include discussions related to their study and career, rehearsal for a college play, recent socio-political issues and sometimes take all those present by surprise by breaking into song, impromptu.[118] When the mass support for the anti-corruption movements led by Anna Hazare and Baba Ramdev took thousands to the street altering the contours of the second UPA government, many students began coming to the ICH, CP in order to discuss and follow what was going on. They are not the only age group looking for an alternative to the globalized culture the modern cafés represent. Mayank Austen Soofi, a journalist and writer of alternative guidebooks on Delhi went to the capital from Nainital in the mid 2000s.[119] Fascinated by the multiple layers coexisting in the capital, and searching for an alternate face of the city, he began recounting obscure aspects of Delhi in the blog *Delhiwalla* that earned him fame. He felt that the history of the ICH as an institution made it unique. At the time I was carrying on the field research, he was organizing the Delhi Proustian Club in the ICH in Mohan Singh

[117] Christiane Brosius, *India's Middle Class: New Forms of Urban Leisure, Consumption and Prosperity*, London: Routledge, 2010, 54; in fact all Indian cities are in the grip of the mall culture; Neelabh, 23 August 2012.

[118] Personal observation. One trend noted during the field studies was groups of management students being coached at ICH CP while at Jadavpur a university professor was known to give private tuition at the space. In both cases retired university teachers were using the space for private tuition.

[119] At the time of the interview Soofi used to write for the *Mint Lounge*.

Place. The Monday evening meets were announced on his blog, and on the appointed day there were always a few present to take part in the literary discussion that followed. The day I chanced upon the group, Muqtadir from Karnataka studying law in Delhi and Manish, a student of the National Law School in Bangalore and Soofi himself were the participants. Both the students were familiar with Soofi's blog. Beginning with what is Proustian in Proust, the conversation touched inter alia Wordsworth, Orhan Pamuk, Rabindranath Tagore, the difference between the cities of Delhi and Lahore, and of course the Coffee House.[120] A few elderly Lohiaite socialists there were joined by numerous large and small civil society organizations like People's Union for Democratic Rights (PUDR) and, Save Sharmila Irom Campaign.

This normative practice coexists with the mundane. Summer or winter, senior citizen Gurnam Singh (78) begins his day at Mohan Singh Place. After an initial coffee over which he reads the newspaper, he orders his lunch. His long association with the place has made him a familiar face and most of the time he is seen talking to a few others sharing the table with him. He would have two to three cups of coffee, lunch, and snacks in the late afternoon before leaving the ICH at around 7.00-7.30 pm to have a dinner at a dhaba—a fixed arrangement—and go back home. While all this can be enjoyed for Rs 125–150 which may be a paltry sum for many, but Singh is afraid that if the Coffee House closes its doors, customers like him will have no place where they can spend extended hours of the day, and be among other familiar people.[121]

In Calcutta in the early 1980s when the original Dey number lamented the loss of the *adda*, there were poets like, Partha Pratim Kanjilal, Utpalkumar Basu, Kalikrishna Guha, Ramanath Roy, Debarshi Sarogi and those of the seventies and eighties like Ranajit Das, Somak Das, Anuradha Mahapatra, Prasun Bandyopadhyay, Bhaskar Chakrabarti, Gautam Chaudhuri, later joined by Bishwa

[120] Mayank Austen Soofi, interview, 27 February 2012.

[121] Just to name a few in other places: in Bangalore Gautam Shenoy, K. Chandrasekhar, S. Balakrishnan, M.S. Vijay Kumar, Dattatreya, Mr Kochhar; in Trivandrum Shashi Kumar, Calvin Miranda and Nandu.

Mandal, Bodhisattva Kar, Prasun Bhaumik, Dipankar Bagchi among many others using the space for literary production. The younger generation among these poets and writers still meet there on a regular basis.[122] Throughout the 1990s there was strong criticism of the CPI (M) government in Bengal in ICH College Street. Till shortly before he fell ill prior to his death in 2011, the ex-Naxalite writer and human rights activist Saibal Mitra was a regular at the ICH. The playwright Chittaranjan Ghosh and his group would be seen at the College Street Coffee House till 2000 on Sunday mornings. Asked what their Coffee House *addas* were about, Malini replied[123]

> [We] talked about varied topics ranging from course syllabus to latest film releases....After a certain point of time it inevitably turned to heated debates regarding the then political scenario the aftermath of which is continuing even today...The Coffee House has always been a place where we have read out poems and stories which we wrote or which we found interesting...We often used to write poems collectively. One person used to compose the first line and the person sitting next followed her/him keeping in sync with the central idea and the rhythm of the poem. This continued all around the table till a whole poem was composed.

The political scenario in question was the police firing in the villages of Singur and Nandigram in March 2007. Malini recalled that the civilians' protest march against the police atrocities included a group representing the Coffee House. The books they read and discussed in the space included *Love in the Time of Cholera, Death in Venice*, *Murder in the Cathedral*, *Shadow Lines, Inheritance of Loss*, *Purva-Paschim* (East-West, Sunil Gangopadhyay) and *Fera* (Return, Humayun Ahmed) among other titles.

When I carried out my field research, young poets there eagerly awaited the visits of Utpal Kumar Basu at the ICH. For the literary world and for students the Coffee House is like an open stage and in the opinion of the poet Shankha Ghosh, and Anil Achraya, the editor of the little magazine *Anushtup* as long as literature forms an important

[122] Prasun Bandyopadhyay, interview; Gautam Chaudhury, interview.

[123] Malini, interview, 9 March 2011.

part of Bengali culture, the Coffee House and the *adda* it generates will remain important as its indispensable part.[124] Similarly, in the same way as old Naxalites used the space, students following CPI (M)-Liberation ideology met there regularly to discuss and disseminate their ideology. ICH College Street is still a space where a student from a small town in North Bengal newly arriving in Calcutta can approach an established scholar like Sumita Chakravarti—through a person regular in the space known to both—for information or suggestion; a young student interested in LSM talk with the aged political activist Krishna Bandyapadhyay seen either discussing the latest issue of *Khoj Akhon* or *Sanhati* with the young activist Nisha Biswas, or strategies with human rights activists of APDR. Uttam Purakait, Suranjan Midday, Ranjan Laskar, Barendra Mandal and Sahin Sarwar may be busy in discussion with young contributors to the next issue of *Ujagar*. At Jadavpur the septuagenarian Dhruba Bhaduri can be seen exchanging notes with the poet-scholar Dipankar Bagchi. Since such meetings are not organized, there is a chance that the day the students are in the Coffee House, neither Professor Chakravarti nor Mrs Bandyopadhyay is present there. One comes to know when she is likely to meet Bandyopadhyay; and the other student will get the contact details of Professor Chakravarti.

On a small scale, long-time connoisseurs now belonging to the elderly generation living in Allahabad continue to visit the place. Ehtehsam Husain, Asrar Gandhi, Shahnawaz Alam, Doodhnath, Sriprakash Mishra are a few of the writers who still visit the Coffee House from time to time. A visiting writer is still taken on a 'pilgrimage' to the ICH while poets and writers of the younger generation occasionally meet at the space for an *adda* over coffee. But the ICH Allahabad has remained a bastion of the elderly, with students and the youth visiting the space once in a while either lured by the South Indian delicacies there or accompanying outside visitors to the town.[125] In addition, there exists a younger generation of

[124] Anil Acharya, interview, 14 March 2013.

[125] Ramayan Ram, Sandhya Navodita. When asked about the future of the ICH if it fails to attract students, Asrar Gandhi assured that once they were old, the students

Allahabadis conscious of the literary heritage of the place who take an interest in the ICH.[126]

To underline the relations of the ICH vis-à-vis the middle class once more, while the structure of the Coffee House has not changed, due to the convoluted larger changes in the socio-economic pattern affecting the aspirations, lifestyle of a section of the middle class patronizing it through 1940s to the 1970s has stopped visiting the location.[127] Consequently, there is a continuum in the memory of loss; but at the same time, as a meeting place of diverse kind of public, there is a continuity maintained by a few old groups loyal to the place, joined by constantly changing groups of new patrons.

THE POLITICAL ECONOMY AND THE COOPERATIVE

Just as there are sections of the middle class turning to places like the ICH for leisure, there are sections of the poor, still dependent on the employment the likes of the coffee workers' cooperatives promise. Recent research on the Indian political economy has highlighted the co-existence of two contrary Indias dividing the population that can be best described in the age-old parlance of the haves and the have-nots. The euphoria regarding the growth of the Indian economy following economic liberalization, notwithstanding the rate of poverty and unemployment, is alarmingly high. In addition to the

---

of the day would know to find their way to the ICH! The predominance of the elderly (40+ years) seems to keep the youth out of the ICH; for many of the younger generation male can be seen enjoying similar food and coffee at the roadside South Indian stalls in front of the ICH.

[126] Asrar Gandhi, Sanjay Saksena and DS Bhandari, Allahabad, interview, 24 October 2012; also Akshatlal Srivastava, Vaidurya Narayan Sahi, and Vaibhab Maini, e-mail.

[127] Ramesh Grover, interview, op. cit. Amal Bhattacharya, who began visiting the place as a college student in 1961, still visits the ICH once a week from his home in Ichapore in the suburbia. He too thinks that the Coffee House has not changed; interview, 4 February 2011; Mohammad Anas, 'Indian Kaffee Haus: Jahan Hoti Hai Ddesh ke Har Mudde par Bahas' (ICH: where all concerns of the country are debated), http://www.iamin.in/hi/allahabad/news/indian-coffee-house-where-conversations-start-40806.

problems of underemployment/disguised unemployment, there are increasing discrepancies between different sectors of the economy, between small formal and large informal sectors, and between urban and rural sectors that need urgent attention. Although the services sector has undergone an increase, the large agricultural sector has been hard hit and commodity production is low.[128] Consequently, while the upper and middle classes have benefitted from the growth, workers in the primary sector have to toil under circumstances that can be best described as medieval or pre-modern where: [129]

> the lack of health care, tolerably good schools and other basic facilities important for human well-being and elementary freedoms, keeps a majority of Indians shackled to their deprived lives in a way quite rarely seen in other self-respecting countries that are trying to move ahead in the world.

Recent economic globalization has resulted in the creation of special economic zones under the forces of global capitalism that has changed the face of the earth and the life of the people living in those special zones. While this development has been embraced by a considerable section of the middle class, old and new, and other sections of the population where the light of the 'Shining India' does not reach. As evident from the analysis of the cooperatives in Chapter Three, it is precisely from this section that the workers of the the Indian Coffee Workers' Cooperatives are recruited. An ongoing research on the opportunities available to the new middle class male youth in the age of the liberalized economy highlights the satisfaction of this group about the situation that enables them to find their space in the cities. With a starting salary for a barista at Starbucks in Mumbai, Delhi and Bangalore around Rs 12,000

[128] Jan Breman's works argue e.g. that not only that enonomic liberalization has not benefitted the poor, it has created a new class of footloose labour in rural India. To mention one of his works in this connection, *The Poverty Regime in Village India: Half a Century of Work and Life at the Bottom of the Rural Economy in South Gujarat*, Delhi: OUP, 2007.

[129] Jean Drèze and Amartya Sen, *An Uncertain Glory: India and its Contradictions*, Princeton, NJ: University Press, 2013, ch. 10.

($200) a month, this group considers the job as a springboard for better opportunities.[130] Ironically, a young Samir Das (25) in ICH Calcutta expressed similar satisfaction regarding his job as a member of the cooperative. As his father died when he was a child, Samir succeeded his grandfather Bhuvanchandra Das (part of the cooperative movement in 1958), and joined the Calcutta Society as a kitchen boy in 2003 at the age of fifteen (on paper he was eighteen, the minimum age for becoming a co-operator). 'If you think of the job market outside, the ICH is comparatively a much better space to work.'[131] I have shown that coming from poor rural families with an unstable income from agriculture, male members of the family begin working in one of the outlets of the ICH at a very early age, and are very often the sole wage earners in the family. Mantu Das of the Calcutta Society is from Mohanpur area in Medinipur district. He attended primary school for some time and is barely literate. Poverty and hunger at home took him to Calcutta where he began working at Putiram's when he was 12 or 13. He was familiar with a few workers of the ICH, including Keshto Nayek, a worker from Kendrapara, Orissa. When Mantu was 18, he was introduced to the ICWCSL in the early 1980s. 'I shall never be able to repay my debt to Keshto-da', is how Mantu remembered the favour. His son, an Arts graduate, would begin his career with the ICWCSL if he failed to obtain any other employment.[132] With little or no formal education, persons like Mantu and Samir in Calcutta, Peter John in Bangalore and those serving in the coffee house of Ambarnath Gupta would have no place in the new cafés, or the new shopping malls. The Coffee Workers Cooperatives in different regions of India have been sustaining generations of rural poor, and in the case of Samir, from grandfather to grandchild spanning about six decades. By the same token, that

[130] Michiel Baas, personal communication, 12 February 2014.

[131] Interview, 12 February 2014. Samir had appeared for the secondary examination but was not able to clear all subjects. See Chapter Three for similar position by his colleagues; cf. if they (the workers) lose the Coffee House, they will have no work', Gautam Shenoy, in connection with ICH Bangalore.

[132] Mantu, interview, 23 August 2013.

the career option has not changed sheds as much light on dark corners of the changing India as the findings about the new middle class allude to.

Seen from this point of view, it appears narcissistic on behalf of the cultural elite to reminisce about the past *adda* alone in their reference to the ICH. Since its inception, the ICH has been a part of the urban experience of many who are now established in their respective fields. Naturally, the outlets have been a site where, in spite of the conflicting social relations of the agents, both customers and workers have jointly protested against any intervention detrimental to their interest. In the mid-1950s, when the workers were threatened with the loss of employment, protest on behalf of the employees of the Coffee Board found support in the customers' understanding of the gravity of the cause, a process described in Chapter Three. Again in 1964, as seen in Chapter Five, protest from the site of the ICH ensured the opening of a new outlet in CP. The same chapter also noted what happened when the freedom to express opinion was severly curtailed during the Emergency, when the Tent ICH was demolished. As a cooperative, the ICH in the cities covered in this work has so far been able to accept the challenge posed by the new mall culture and the new cafés run by multinationals.[133] It is a counter-challenge, a resistance these poor, mostly semi-literate workers put up against a highly corporatized coffee sector, and the tension is often hard to conceal.[134] At places where the dividend

[133] See Asad Zaidi's remarks on the necessity of resistance the burden of which is often borne by the poorest of the poorin 'Doomed Democracy', *Frontline*, 14 June 2013; http://www.frontline.in/arts-and-culture/doomed-democracy/article4735863.ece#test. I am grateful to Nitin Varma for drawing my attention to this article; also, Colin Todhunter, 'The Indian Coffee House Chain: Simply Coffee', http://www.hackwriters.com/mycoffeehouse.htm.

[134] In the course of the field research for this study, I have been approached by management experts and multinationals asking to be a mediator in the process of improving the condition of the Coffee Houses or creating an alternative in the lucrative space they occupy in the heart of the cities that match with the needs of the current times better. In ICH Bangalore, the old-time patrons are hesitant to spend more than an hour or so over a cup of coffee because they feel that in order to survive the

is low, there have been occasions when members of the individual cooperatives have felt tempted to take recourse to steps revealing their lack of faith in cooperation. In 2009 the ICH in CP was on the verge of closure when the New Delhi Municipal Corporation (NDMC) took the ICH to court due to the non-payment of rent. The consumers claimed that since it was difficult to close this popular public space, the management and property dealers had colluded to hatch a conspiracy back in 2000 when the cooperative stopped paying the rent on grounds that the NDMC had left reparation work begun in 1995 incomplete. Although they resumed paying the rent in 2004, it was stopped again in 2006, and according to the NDMC in 2009 the ICH owed them Rs 48 lakhs. Soon it was found out that the then secretary had been lured to accept a formidable amount of money in order to hand over the property to an estate agent who had made a deal with McDonald's for an outlet at the site. Underlining the importance and legacy of the institution, the Consumers' Forum there vehemently demanded that the unique social space—the only one of its kind in central Delhi—be saved. In the opinion of Ram Shastri, the secretary of the Forum, the media campaign, like the one in 1964, publicized the cause of the Coffee House.[135] In Calcutta, a Coffee House Consumers' Forum was set up in 1993–94 when the end of the property lease threatened the existence of the ICH. There was an intervention on behalf of the influential (ex) patrons who took up the matter with the state government that had acquired the building. It is due to the intervention on behalf of the customers that the attempts made by the private enterprise Bengal Shelter to take over the ICH on College Street could be averted. Even in Bangalore and Trivandrum, where the resistance against the regeneration of space in the wake of economic liberalization was not strong enough, the coffee workers' cooperatives were resilient enough to re-incarnate in an alternative space.

cooperative has to make profit. So they leave the space for others who may come for breakfast, lunch etc.

[135] Pankaj Bisht, 'Muft Bazaar', and 'Kaffee Haus: Punascha' (P.S. Coffee House), *Samayantar*, August 2009, 34–35; Ram Shastri, interview.

At one time the Coffee Board decided to close down our coffee house [on College Street] and remain happy with the 5CA outlet. The fear of losing our shelter made us restless. We created a committee consisting of the leaders of different adda groups. We took the resolution that we would never allow the ICH to be closed....By then, there were new faces in the ICH like Gaurishankar Bhattacharya, Gour Kishore Ghosh, Samaresh Basu, Manishankar, Bimal Mitra, Bhavani Mukhopadhyay, Sunil Gangopadhyay and others from many new literary groups. Gaurishankar proposed to write an informative piece on the coffee house and publish it from Mitralay, his own publishing house. That would carry a sketch drawn by me. This would help ordinary people to understand the significance of the coffee house and partcipate in our movement'. Debabrata Mukhopadhyay, *Coffee-r Cup*

To revel in the romance of nostalgic past and cultural ethos is to fail the social space created and nurtured by earlier generations. The responsibility of further developing the ideology of cooperatives created by the nationalist elite rests both upon the cultural elite and the workers. Beginning with N.S. Pillai in the 1940s to Samir Das in the new millennium, workers still join the workforce long before they are adults. It is upon the state to ensure that a minor in his early teens does not have to leave the village in order to support his family. Some of the cooperators interviewed indeed pointed out that some training in connection with their duty and obligation towards the goal of the cooperative would be helpful. Left to their own, the workers are not in a position to implement such programmes. Regular interactions with consumers' forum may be made mandatory. However, since a considerable section of the patrons move away from the place for a variety of reasons, the nature of their relationship with the place remains fleeting.[136]

[136] Individual interviews with Sarasija Basu, Shyamal Basu and Bodhisattva Kar convinced me that in Calcutta the Coffee House Consumers' Forum exists only in name. In Delhi, however, the Coffee House Consumers' Forum is composed predominantly of regular visitors who negotiate with the workers and the government of Delhi on a more regular basis.

Those who use the social space are not able to successfully engage with the workers seriously as to the performance of the cooperative societies, the ideology, the potential it represents, let alone the rights of the consumers. Anxiously copying the practices of their patrons, ICWCSL Calcutta has joined the race of commodifying the Coffee House culture.[137] The reproduction of the personal, fictitious familial bond serves the interest of the middle class visitor who may occasionally negotiate the everyday life of an individual worker enjoying a satisfaction for the favour received from the patrons.[138] But the patrons have not been able to engage in a day-to-day dialogue with the workers regarding their demand/right as a consumer or to widen the vision of the workers in the larger, longterm interest of the cooperative, and the cooperative has now fallen prey to divisive electoral politics. When it no longer suits them, the middle class are able to distance themselves from the ICH.

The myth of the middle class discourse that the ambience of space that belongs to them is contested due the undercurrents created by the presence of the workers and the working class people around the Coffee House. The vivacity of the latter with all the comings and goings, the cacophony produced by hasty placing of plates and cutlery on the table, pulling and pushing of chairs, calling out a friend, futile attempts to draw the attention of the worker in charge often successfully submerge the normative aspect that needs to be discovered through familiarity and patience. These aspects of the Indian Coffee House make it an institution, only one of its kind, far more public than any other.

CONCLUSION

The space of the ICH provides a unique window to the complex public-private boundaries in India since Independence. It is the ICH where the normative public sphere, the networks of sociability of the

[137] This effort sees a part of the space reserved for a part of a specific day for the shooting of a period film.

[138] By helping him to get his child admitted to a school or an occasional treatment by a specialist medical practitioner.

middle class and the practical public sphere of the everyday messy life of the working class came face to face. By giving a foothold to ideologies like PWA, radical humanism and secularism in the pre-Independence days and continuing this trend in its support of the workers, female consumers, radical students and various civil societies that emerged in post-colonial India, the India(n) Coffee House represented a new institution where members of all all these sections of the society felt at home. Up until now many civil society institutions like APDR, PUDR and LSM, meet at ICH for the production and circulation of discourses critical of the state.

The Coffee House, however, does not create a genius or bring about a change. It is a mirror of society in that the social practices of the agents here are embedded in the social relations at large. The opportunities available to the different segments of the middle class, the quality of the education accessible to them, the social capital they have accumulated through familial and social networks determine their practices in the space that facilitates unending informal meetings, nurtures and brings potentials to fruition through unlimited discussions, especially in the field of vernacular literature.

The India Coffee House was created by the coffee industry with the direct intervention of the state. Since the early 1950s when the movement of the workers of the Coffee Board saw the Coffee House transformed into cooperatives, the institution has struggled repeatedly in order to suvive the aggression of the market. The survival of the ICH points to two fundamental contradictions that economic liberalization has not been able to resolve. Whether it is in the ICH in Calcutta or the private coffee house of Ambarnath Gupta in DSE, there is no dearth of fresh workers recruited from the rural areas at a tender age, taking up a menial job with a low salary, and often a miserable living condition in the city. Consequently, just as new generations of the middle class from the greater metropolitan area and migrants to the city are discovering the social space as the only one of its kind where they can be their own, there is a counter-movement to capital on behalf of the surplus labour in the rural areas it cannot absorb that is finding its way to the Indian Coffee

Workers' Cooperatives and similar enterprises.[139] Thanks to these contradictions, resulting in a consensus between the workers and the customers, that the institution survives despite continuous attempts to convert it into something else. The logic of the production of space as Lefebvre outlined, demands that it makes the old space redundant and creates a new one.[140] None of the globalized café chains are in a position to address these contradictions which have to be resolved before the phoenix of some such differential space rises from the ashes of the India(n) Coffee House.

[139] Side by side with the success stories of malls and multiplexes, there are examples of such projects not taking off. In Patparganj, New Delhi, a multiplex set up 2006 was deserted in 2007. Of the 1200 malls in the metropolitan cities in the country in December 2012, an average of 45–55 percent of mall-space was vacant, ASSOCHAM 'Over half of the malls in Delhi-NCR are vacant'. The CPI (M) led government in West Bengal had announced in 2007 that the famous College Street Municipal Market was to be handed over to a private partner called Bengal Shelter Limited, 'for development into a composite modern market focused on books and cultural events, alongside large conference and exhibition spaces, a multiplex, parking for a large number of cars and so on. It was to be a public private partnership (PPP) project. This project came to a nought due to the defaulting private partner, Pradeep Gooptu, 'Varnaparichay: A Key Education Project Derailed', in *Post Mortem,* 15 November 2013, http://educationaffairs.in/varnaparichay-key-education-project-derailed/.

[140] Lefebvre, *The Production*, 26.

Glossary

adda	agendaless, informal conversation
addebaaj	connoisseur of *adda*
addebaji	to take part in an *adda*
antlami	Bengali for intello
aphim ke laddu	a sweet prepared with opium
bhabhi	(elder) brother's wife
bhaavmoorti	image
bhang	cannabis
brun maska	hard-crusted bun with butter
cha, *chai*	tea
chaat	popular roadside savoury snacks
chacha	paternal uncle
chaprasee	bearer
chaupal	public place in the village
Congress-I	the section of the Congress Party named after Indira Gandhi
chukku kaapi	coffee blended with spices and herbs
daab	tender coconut
dada	elder brother in Bengali and grandfather in Hindi
dahi	yoghurt
Darshini	popular self-service restaurant in South India
Dussehra	the festival to commemorate the victory of god Rama over the demon king Ravana
Diwali	*festival of lights*
dastango	public story-telling
dhaba	popular Punjabee eating house

dhikr	*community worship among various Sufi orders*
dosa	South Indian savoury crêpe prepared with a mixture of raw, fermented rice and lentils
Emergency	refers to the near-absolute rule in India during 25 June 1975–21 March 1977 under article 352 (1) of the Indian Constitution proclaimed by the then Prime Minister Indira Gandhi.
falooda	fine vermicelli used with syrup in preparing cold desserts
Ganga-Jamuni Tehzeeb	composite culture cherished especially in the tract between the two rivers
ghazal	North Indian light classical music
ghee	clarified butter
guppbaji	to participate in an *adda*
halwai	sweet maker
idli	steamed South Indian snack prepared with a fermented mixture of rice and lentils
jalebi	crisp, swirl-shaped, deep-fried, syrup-coated sweets
kaapi	coffee
kabiraji	cutlet batter-coated, deep fried minced meat dumplings
kachori	spicy, fried (stuffed) puff pastry
kameez	loose upper garment
kef	café
kulfi	traditional Indian ice-cream
kuwan	well
lassi	yoghurt drink
lathi	stick
majlis	similar to *adda*, but usually organized
mamlet	omlette
masala	spices
masala chai	tea blended with spices and herbs
masalchi	kitchen boy

maska pau	butter on bread-roll
matka	cotton-silk mixed textile
mehfil	programme of music
mushaira	writers' and poets' gatherings
namkeen	salted snacks
paan	betel leaf
pajama	loose-fitting comfortable trousers
pakora	batter-coated, deep fried pieces of vegetables or fish, meat etc.
panjabee	tunic like comfortable upper garment for men
parampara	tradition
parantha	a flat, layered pan-fried bread
patloon	loose, comfortable pair of trousers made of thin material
phut phut	a four-wheeler, so named for the sound it made
puri	deep-fried flat thin bread
qahwa	coffee
qahwakhana	coffee house
qawwali	Sufi devotional music popular in Northwest India and Pakistan
romanchokar	adventurous
sambhar	a lentil-based stew with vegetables served with South Indian food
samosa	*a* stuffed, triangular deep fried, savoury snack
sarbavuk	omnivorous
sharbat	cold beverage, also spelt as *sarbat*
shehnai	*a* musical instrument descending from the Persian *surna*
shudra	the lowest in the Hindu caste hierarchy
Swadeshi	the anti-colonial movement propagating the use of indigenous products (among other things)

thali	South Indian meal of rice served with side dishes
thandai	a milk-based cold drink mixed with almond and spices
toash	toast
tonga	horse-drawn carriage
vada	deep fried (South) Indian snack
vamsha	lineage
vanaspati	vegetable (in the current context)

Indian Coffee House Through Photographs

Firpo's Restaurant in Calcutta. Entertaining the expatriate and Indian upper middle classes with a 3-course luncheon menu at Rs 2.75 in 1945, Firpo's was a class apart. (Courtesy: Enrico de Barbieri, http://www.enricodebarbieri.com/afirpo.html)

Favourite Cabin, Calcutta—The favourite gathering place of the literary group *Kallol*.

Luminaries at ICH, College Street, Calcutta—Shibnarayan Ray, Amlan Datta, Amitabh Sengupta, Jaya Ganguly. Shibnarayan Ray was the biographer of MN Roy, Amlan Datta, a famous economist, Jaya Ganguly—an artist. Amitabha Sengupta—photographer and artist.
(Courtesy: Amitabha Sengupta)

Indian Coffee House, Calcutta.
(Courtesy: Kanigas Feed)

Indian Coffee House, College Street, Calcutta.

Indian Coffee House, Jadavpur, Calcutta.

Darbari Building in Allahabad, the site of the Indian Coffee House.
(Courtesy: Dr RN Darbari Charitable Society)

Allahabad: Indian Coffee House in the winter sun.

K. Lalitha, widow of N.S. Pillai, is one of the very few women members of the coffee workers' cooperatives.

Nadakkal S. Parameswaran Pillai, one of the pioneers of the Indian Coffee Workers' Cooperative Societies Ltd, who left a memoir, the only document presenting the workers' point of view. (Courtesy: K. Lalitha)

The ICWCSL in Kerala opens and closes outlets as necessary. Opening ceremony, Peroorkada Trivandrum, Kerala.

Jawaharlal Nehru sipping coffee prepared by ICH, Delhi.

The Puri sisters-in-law running Karviska (1958–64), the successor to the India Coffee House on 66 Janpath; (L-R): Shukla, Vishnu, Krishna and Raj.
(Courtesy: Nita and Rajeev Puri)

Coffee fans, who arranged to get coffee at 25 paise per cup outside the Coffee House in New Delhi on Saturday, serve it among themselves. They have boycotted the Coffee House following the increase in its rates.

When the price of coffee increased by 10 paise in 1964, Coffee fans arranged to make and sell coffee at 25 paise on the pavement in front. *The Statesman*, 20 September 1964.

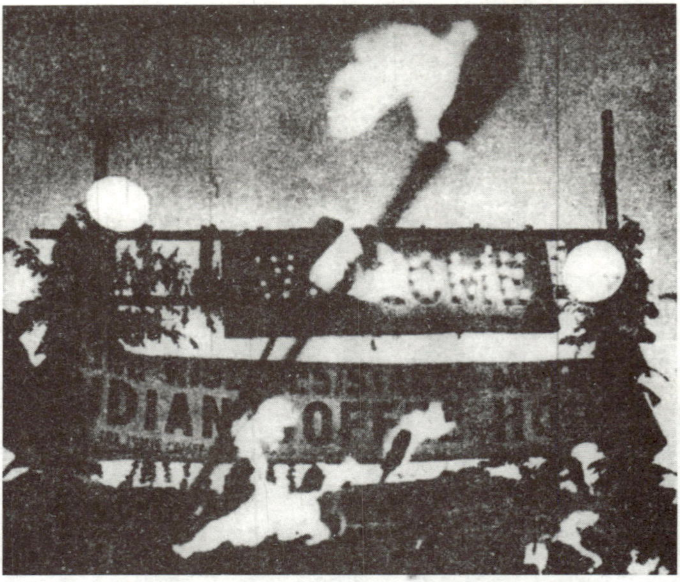

A torch-bearer of the Price Rise Resistance Movement arrives at Indian Coffee House with flame which was lit in the old pavement coffee house in Janpath and taken around in a procession through the corridors of Connaught Place on Monday, 16 November, 1964.

Indira Gandhi in front of the Tent Coffee House, Delhi.

Members of the underground resistance paper *Subterranean Sun* during the Emergency. Second from left Gautam Varma. (Courtesy: Pablo Bartholomew)

Chamouli and the late Bhura Singh (in white uniform), Indian Coffee House, Connaught Place in Delhi.

ICH is a place where prohibitive notices may be flouted at ease. A regular customer at Indian Coffee House, Connaught Place in Delhi.

Different kinds of public in the Indian Coffee House, Connaught Place in Delhi.

The literary sphere of Allahabad—Lokbharti writers' meet. (Courtesy: Dinesh Chandra Grover, Lokbharti)

APPENDIX XII (a)

Total Turnover From Propaganda Units Year-War 1939-40 (August to July)

Year	Number of prop. units functioning as on 31st July 1957	Sale of Liquid coffee in cups	Quantity of powder sold		Quantity of Raw Coffee sold		Total consumption of Raw Coffee		Sale proceeds of liquid and Dry Coffee	Catering Sales and other Receipts	Total Turnover
			in Lbs.	in Kgms.	in Lbs.	in Kgms.	in Lbs.	in Kgms.			
1	@ 2	3	4 (a)	4 (b)	5 (a)	5 (b)	6 (a)	6 (b)	7	8	9
1939-40	15	11,38,033	7,007	3,178	—	—	43,994	19,955	63,270	10,083	73,353*
1940-41	18	17,03,857	53,111	24,091	—	—	1,24,236	56,352	1,34,576	24,855	1,59,431*
1941-42	21	20,01,328	1,31,108	59,470	—	—	2,35,803	1,06,958	2,62,975	67,335	3,30,310*
1942-43	24	39,28,618	2,67,983	1,21,555	—	—	4,50,240	2,04,226	9,34,433	3,15,900	12,50,333
1943-44	31	69,59,595	4,37,200	1,98,311	—	—	7,50,943	3,40,622	13,56,674	7,42,201	26,98,875
1944-45	42	93,10,120	8,52,270	3,86,583	—	—	13,05,691	5,92,269	26,91,316	9,82,574	36,73,890
1945-46	46	92,79,388	15,85,819	7,19,319	—	—	20,95,183	9,50,361	37,05,256	9,68,947	46,74,203
1946-47	47	98,51,953	18,87,594	8,56,194	—	—	24,76,108	11,23,141	43,29,784	12,03,565	55,33,349
1947-48	49+1	88,61,088	26,89,197	12,19,801	—	—	35,41,582	16,51,798	64,87,152	12,81,700	77,68,852
1948-49	49+1	78,02,206	23,04,206	10,45,167	—	—	32,88,262	14,91,528	68,88,311	12,22,258	81,10,569
1949-50	48+3	72,63,598	19,65,570	8,91,567	—	—	27,46,729	12,45,892	69,65,569	11,16,068	80,81,637
1950-51	50+3	78,86,582	24,06,034	10,91,357	—	—	33,60,398	14,52,651	77,34,337	11,53,607	88,87,944
1951-52	50+3	82,22,803	18,78,453	8,52,054	—	—	27,91,987	12,66,421	71,36,113	10,53,836	81,89,949
1952-53	46+2	75,08,686	15,19,537	6,89,246	—	—	24,82,146	11,25,883	68,69,207	8,88,706	77,57,913
1953-54	45+3	79,81,790	12,52,832	5,68,274	5,88,994	2,67,162	23,30,605	10,57,144	59,87,797	8,68,715	68,56,512
1954-55	46+4	80,92,433	12,26,646	5,56,395	7,77,711	3,52,764	24,75,630	11,22,924	62,10,790	8,58,734	70,69,524
1955-56	55+4	89,32,532	14,14,620	6,41,666	7,32,128	3,32,088	26,84,966	12,17,881	67,54,401	9,11,904	76,66,305
1956-57	54+7	85,08,319	15,23,311	6,90,962	7,66,148	3,47,519	27,93,598	12,67,155	70,71,682	9,20,243	79,91,925
1957-58	47+2	45,20,129	11,66,163	5,28,963	9,95,615	4,51,602	24,67,039	11,19,033	59,75,934	6,27,452	66,03,386

Note: 1. * These figures are from July to June. 2. @ "Prop. Units include India Coffee Houses, Buffets, Depots, Vans & the Board's stalls at Exhibitions have been included as shown separately since 1947-48.

SOURCE: COFFEE BOARD ANNUAL REPORT, 1957-58, V. 1, p. 54.

Coffee House Table from original accounts ledger.

Sucheta Kripalani with members and patrons of the Coffee Workers' Cooperative in Delhi.

The Allahabad virtuosi: Vijaylakshmi Pandit (2nd from left), Amarnath Jha, Narendra Deva.
(Courtesy: Tejakar Jha, Maharajadhiraja Kameshwar Singh Kalyani Foundation, Darbhanga)

Indian Coffee House (Albert Hall Coffee House), Calcutta.